THE ELEMENTS OF FORESTRY

THE ELEMENTS OF FORESTRY

DESIGNED TO AFFORD INFORMATION CONCERNING THE PLANTING AND CARE OF FOREST TREES

FOR ORNAMENT OR PROFIT

AND GIVING SUGGESTIONS UPON

THE CREATION AND CARE OF WOODLANDS

WITH THE VIEW OF SECURING THE GREATEST BENEFIT FOR THE LONGEST TIME, PARTICULARLY ADAPTED TO THE WANTS AND CONDITIONS OF THE UNITED STATES

BY

FRANKLIN B. HOUGH, PH.D

Chief of Forestry Division, U. S. Department of Agriculture
Member of the American Philosophical Society, etc.

GYAN

Published by

Gyan Publishing House
5, Ansari Road
Daryaganj, New Delhi-110002
Phone: 011-47034999, 9811692060
E-mail: books@gyanbooks.com

Distribution Network
gyanbooks.com
India, USA, Canada, UK, Australia, France

ISBN : 978-81-212-6051-0 (PB)
First Published, 1882

2nd Impression 2022

Printed at: Gyan Press, Delhi.

THE ELEMENTS OF FORESTRY
Author: FRANKLIN B. HOUGH, PR.D

THE

ELEMENTS OF FORESTRY

DESIGNED TO AFFORD INFORMATION CONCERNING THE PLANTING AND CARE OF FOREST TREES

FOR ORNAMENT OR PROFIT

AND GIVING SUGGESTIONS UPON

THE CREATION AND CARE OF WOODLANDS

WITH THE VIEW OF SECURING THE GREATEST BENEFIT FOR THE LONGEST TIME, PARTICULARLY ADAPTED TO THE WANTS AND CONDITIONS OF THE UNITED STATES

BY

FRANKLIN B. HOUGH, PH.D

Chief of Forestry Division, U. S. Department of Agriculture
Member of the American Philosophical Society, etc.

1882

PREFACE.

In preparing this work, the author has endeavored to present, in a concise form, a general outline of the subject of Forestry in its most ample relations, without attempting to be exhaustive in any thing. Technical details have been avoided as far as was thought possible; but in mentioning the names of trees and other organic objects, the scientific as well as the common names have generally both been used, chiefly because the latter are often quite uncertain in their application, while the former can never be mistaken when rightly applied, and are alike in the scientific literature of all languages. In noticing the various subjects embraced, care has been taken to mention the economical uses and commercial values that pertain to them, and in describing different methods, a preference has been stated whenever it was thought to lead to best results.

The engravings in this work are chiefly derived from the following sources: Those occupying full pages, and showing details of structure of some of the principal species of Timber-trees, and the laws of development and growth, are from "Der Wald," by E. A. Rossmassler, an approved German author. The engravings showing details of wood structure, are chiefly from "Les Bois," by M. M. Dupont and Bouquet de la Grye, and some of the illustrations of botanical species are from the "Guide du Forestièr," by the latter. The figures of insects, and their ravages, are from "Les Ravageurs des Forêts," by H. de la Blanchère. Those of Charcoal Kilns, are from the "Journal of the U. S. Asso. Charcoal Iron Workers," and those of Charcoal Meilers, from the American edition of Svedelius' "Handbook for Charcoal Burners." A few of the smaller illustrations of Botanical species are from an English work, entitled "Woodland Gleanings," and those showing defects in timber, in part from Laslett's "Timber-Trees." Three or four are from Dupuis' "Arbres d' Ornement" and his "Conifères de Pleine Terre," and the sketches of western conifers and other species, are from Prof. J. S. Newberry's Report, embraced in Vol. VI, of the "Pacific Railroad Surveys." The remainder are from the author's first Report upon Forestry, presented in 1877, and published by order of Congress, except some small sketches drawn for the present work.

Wherever the language of an author has been quoted, the citations given will generally lead to more extended information, and in the absence of references, it is believed that the facts and principles here presented will generally be found such as are supported by approved experience and well established observation.

Although many special works upon planting, arboriculture, botanical descriptions, and other subjects relating to particular departments of Forestry have been issued, at various times, this is, so far as we know, the first attempt to present, in our language, and in one volume, the subject of Forestry in the comprehensive sense that we have defined it. It would have been much easier to do this in a larger volume, and it was often found a difficult task to condense into the space that could be allowed to the several divisions of the subject, all that it was desirable to present concerning it. We have endeavored to adapt this work to the want of students in Forestry, whether in the class-rooms of an institution, or engaged in practical labors; and it has been our special aim to present information that is applicable to our own country, and to those regions where tree-planting is most needed, and often most difficult. If it is found to meet this intention, our object will be attained.

WASHINGTON, *July* 1, 1882.

CONTENTS.

CHAPTER V.

OF THE VARIOUS MODES OF PROPAGATION OF FOREST TREES.

CHAPTER VI.

PLANTING CONTINUED.

CHAPTER VII.

OF THE STRUCTURE AND FUNCTIONS OF THE VARIOUS PARTS OF GROWING TREES.

CHAPTER VIII.

GENERAL VIEWS IN REGARD TO FORESTRY.

CHAPTER IX.

ACTS OF CONGRESS RELATING TO TIMBER-RIGHTS.

CHAPTER X.

EUROPEAN PLANS OF FOREST MANAGEMENT.

CHAPTER XI.

ORNAMENTAL PLANTING.

CHAPTER XII.

HEDGES, SCREENS AND SHELTER-BELTS.

CHAPTER XIII.

CUTTING AND SEASONING OF WOOD. DEFECTS IN TIMBER.

CHAPTER XIV.

FUEL. CHARCOAL. WOOD-GAS.

CHAPTER XV.

FOREST FIRES.

CHAPTER XVI.

PROTECTION FROM OTHER INJURIES THAN FIRES.

CHAPTER XVII.

INSECT RAVAGES IN WOODLANDS.

CHAPTER XVIII.

PROCESSES FOR INCREASING THE DURABILITY OF TIMBER, OR FOR IMPROVING ITS QUALITY.

CHAPTER XIX.

RESINOUS AND OTHER PRODUCTS OF CONIFERS.

CHAPTER XX.

USE OF WOOD IN THE MANUFACTURE OF PAPER.

CHAPTER XXI.

TANNING MATERIALS.

CHAPTER XXII.

DESCRIPTION OF PARTICULAR SPECIES.

CHAPTER XXIII.

THE CONIFERS.

CHAPTER XXIV.

TREE-PLANTING IN KANSAS AND NEBRASKA.

ELEMENTS OF FORESTRY.

CHAPTER I.

DEFINITIONS.

1. *Forestry*, in its most comprehensive sense, is that branch of knowledge that treats of woodlands—their formation, maintenance, and renewal, the influences that may affect their welfare; the methods employed in their management, the removal, preparation, and use of their products, and the economies that may be gained by skillful operation.

2. *Sylviculture*[1] is that part of Forestry which relates to the planting and cultivation of groves and collective bodies of forest trees.

3. *Arboriculture*[2] treats of the cultivation of trees. It is sometimes limited to the cultivation of fruit-trees, but the term may properly be extended to include the planting and care of trees generally, whether for fruit, ornament, or other use.

4. Forestry involves the application of many branches of science:

(*a.*) From natural history it derives the description and classification of trees, and of the animal and vegetable life that affect their welfare.

(*b.*) From geology and mineralogy, it learns the origin and composition of soils and sub-soils, and of the rock formations from which they are derived, their constituent parts, their permeability, and their fitness for the successful growth of particular kinds of trees.

(*c.*) By the aid of chemistry it determines the elements of the soil, the composition and changes that take place in the growth and decay of wood, the methods that may be used for increasing its durability or improving its quality, and the various operations concerned in the production and use of its chemical products.

(*d.*) From mathematics it derives aid in all processes of measure-

(1) From *sylva*, "a grove." (2) From *arbor*, "a tree."

ment and calculation concerned in forest lands, materials, management, working, or revenues.

(*e.*) From mechanics, it applies the various agencies employed in cutting, transporting, and manufacture of wood and timber in every form.

(*f.*) From physics and meteorology, it determines the various questions of atmospheric influence and of climate that may arise, whether as cause or effect, and seeks to learn how these may be improved to best advantage, and, in some cases, controlled.

(*g.*) From political economy, it applies the principles that determine questions of supply and demand, of public policy, and of financial profits, the interests that are involved, and their mutual dependence, the laws of trade, as they concern forest products or properties, and whatever principles may relate to their creation, production, or management.

5. An intelligent system of Forestry aims to impart knowledge as to the conditions best adapted to cultivation, the best methods of securing a growth of trees by seeding or planting, the use of measures that shall secure their thrifty growths, protection from injuries, natural renewal at period of full maturity or time for use, and a constant tendency toward improvement of the products.

6. A *Tree*, is a plant having a woody root, trunk, and branches. We generally apply the term *shrub* to trees that are less than fifteen feet in height at maturity, and the term *bush* to those that grow to six feet in height or less. These terms are however arbitrary, in their use, and can not be with certainty applied to any species.

7. Trees may increase from within, as in the case of palms, or by the deposit of wood in annual layers under the bark. The former have no bark proper, and are called *Endogenous*, a term signifying "growing from within." They are represented in the Southern States by the palmetto (*Sabal palmetto*), and a few other species, but on account of their slight relative importance as forest trees, they will be no further noticed in this work. The latter are termed *Exogenous*, a term signifying "growing from without," and increase by the deposit of new layers of wood on the outside, under the bark. This great division includes, with the above exception, all of the native and naturalized trees of the United States.

8. A *Species*, when used in Forestry, is understood to mean a group of trees or other plants, resembling in the details of their structure,

and producing the like forms of growth from their seeds. They are subject to many variations, due to differences of soil, climate, and other causes, and occasionally produce unusual forms in their leaves, size and color of flowers, quality of fruit, or habits of growth, which are called "sports." In other cases, hybrids will form by cross fertilization, the result being a tree that partakes of some of the characteristics of both species. This is occasionally seen in the oaks and the willows, but as a rule the species remain distinct. These deviations from the normal type may be perpetuated by budding, grafting, or layers, but when they bear fertile seeds, they do not produce plants having like peculiarities, and tend to return to their original forms.

9. A *Genus*, is usually a group of species having common resemblances in the structure of the flowers and fruit, and generally, in their leaves and in the habit of growth, such as the pines, maples, birches, etc. In some cases, however, a genus may include but one species. They are sometimes divided into groups or sub-genera, having some common resemblance, and occasionally these may be further arranged into other groups, having common forms or properties. Where there are several species in a genus, they may be generally grafted upon one another, but in other cases this can only be done successfully within the group or sub-genus to which the species belong.

10. A *Natural Order*, in botany, is a class of trees or plants that usually embraces several genera, having a common resemblance in the structure of the seed and fruit and in manner of growth, differing from all others and constant within itself. These are again sometimes divided into sub-orders, families, or groups, depending upon a common resemblance, and instances occur in which a natural order includes but a single genus.

11. We have examples of natural orders in the *Coniferæ*, embracing the pines, firs, spruces, cedars, junipers, etc., and in the *Leguminosæ*, or bean-like fruited plants, which include, among trees, the locusts, honey-locusts, acacias, Kentucky coffee-tree, and many others.

12. The description and classification of orders, genera, and species among trees form a part of the province of botany, and will not be attempted in this work. In mentioning the common names

of trees, we shall generally give with them their scientific or botanical names, as a means for more exact designation.

13. The common names are very uncertain, and may in one region be applied to species very unlike those where they are used in another. But the scientific names, rightly applied, are exactly understood in every language in which the sciences are taught, and can not be mistaken for any others. They are very generally derived from Greek or Latin words, expressing some quality or character in the genus or species to which they are applied. The generic name is more commonly derived from the Greek, and the specific name from the Latin. The former always begins with a capital letter—the latter only when it is derived from a proper noun. Where a number of species are mentioned in succession, the initial letter only of the genus will be used after the first one, as *Pinus strobus*, *P. mitis*, *P. rigida*, etc.

CHAPTER II.

OF SOILS AND THEIR PREPARATION—EFFECTS OF SLOPE AND ASPECT.

14. The soil or loose material that generally covers the surface of the earth to a greater or less depth, partakes in a large degree of the chemical character of the rock formations from which it has been derived. These may be the subjacent rocks, or the material may have been transported by former geological agencies, as in "drift," or deposited by those now in action, as in alluvial mud, or littoral sands.

15. Besides these mineral components, the soil generally contains more or less organic material, derived from vegetation, or, to slight extent, from animal life. In the native forests, this "vegetable soil" has been mostly created by the trees and herbage, from materials taken up in solution by the roots from the soil, and absorbed by the leaves from the air, and has gradually accumulated from the decay of the leaves, or of the trees and plants themselves.

16. This organic material is called *humus*, and its quality and amount depends upon the kind and quantity that has been allowed to decompose. It is sometimes known as "vegetable mold," and has no definite chemical composition, but contains Humic acid ($C_{20}H_{12}O_6$), and various other organic compounds. When vegetation decays in moist places, as in swamps, it forms *muck*, and

in some situations *peat.* These vary considerably in composition, and the latter contains so large an amount of carbon that it is used profitably as a fuel. The former, when mixed with animal manures, and the latter, when its acidity has been neutralized by lime or alkalies, become valuable as fertilizers. Both humus and peat absorb water with avidity, and retain it with tenacity. It is partly on this account that vegetable mold, when mixed with other soils, tends to impart fertility by retaining moisture within the reach of vegetation.

17. The term *Loam* is attached to a class of soils composed of different earthy materials of dissimilar particles, not easily ductile, readily diffused when thrown into water, and easily penetrated by the roots of trees and other plants. A mixture of humus renders it porous and fertile, and in a forest, this fertility tends constantly to increase, and hence the growth of trees is one of the best means for restoring exhausted soils.

18. The soil has an influence upon the growth of trees in two ways: it gives them *support,* and it furnishes them with *nourishment.* In order to give support, the soil should be permeable by the roots, without being too tenacious to resist their extension, nor too light to hold them. In nursery plantations, the proper qualities may be secured by artificial mixture of materials, but except in a very small degree, we can not modify them, and must seek to improve by the choice of species, the conditions as we find them.

19. As the roots of trees penetrate much deeper into the soil than those of agricultural plants, the welfare of woodlands often depends much upon the depth and character of the sub-soil, as is observed in the "Landes" of south-western France, where a vigorous and profitable growth of trees is obtained upon lands that are almost utterly barren for cultivation in farm crops. In other cases, as in flat limestone districts, the surface soil may be too thin for cultivation, while in the fissures there is sufficient soil for supplying the roots of trees. These roots, when they decay, besides leaving the organic material of which they were composed, also leave open passages penetrating deeply into the soil, and affording opportunities for drainage. These may become filled in with mold from the surface, and thus they in some degree assist in rendering the soil fertile to a greater depth than would be possible from the simple deposit of organic materials upon the surface.

20. The state of division of the soil, as to whether coarse or fine, has also an important influence, especially with reference to its permeability by water, its drainage, and the like. Upon these properties, and the organic materials, in connection with the local climate, the fertility of a given soil may be said to depend.

21. It matters not what the chemical or physical properties of the soil may be, it will remain unproductive unless there be seasonable and sufficient rains, or their equivalent supplied by irrigation, and unless the conditions of temperature be consistent with vegetable growth.

22. Although soils present infinite variety in their constituent parts, they may be classed under four principal divisions, viz.: *siliceous*, *calcareous*, *argillaceous*, and *alkaline*.

23. In *siliceous* soils, the principal constituent is gravel or sand, composed of silex or quartz, more or less finely divided, and nearly or quite destitute of the power of absorbing of retaining water, unless underlaid by a retentive sub-soil, or unless it is but moderately above the level of a standing water, from which, by capillary attraction, its moisture may be drawn.

24. In *calcareous* soils, the carbonate of lime is found, either from the decomposition of limestones, or from marls of more recent organic origin. Such soils have the property of absorbing and retaining moisture in a high degree, but, although saturated they do not become impenetrable to the air, and when turned up and exposed to its action they fall to dust, and this the more readily when assisted by frost. They will effervesce when thrown into acids, and this affords a convenient, but not absolute test.

25. In *argillaceous* soils, the silicate of alumina, in the form of clay, forms the principal ingredient. These soils have a strong affinity for water, and hold it with great tenacity; yet, when exposed to solar heat, they crack into deep fissures in times of drouth. The water that falls upon clay soils does not penetrate, and they often afford much resistance to the roots of plants.

26. In *alkaline* soils, the soluble salts of soda are in excess. Where these soils occur, there is a noted deficiency in the rain fall, and a marked sterility from this cause, for the excess of alkali appears principally due to the want of moisture for dissolving it out and carrying it away. When such soils are irrigated, they become fertile, and improve as the excess of alkali is reduced. A lime-like deposit

is found in hollow places where this soil prevails, and the sage-bush (*Artemisia tridentata*) and grease-wood (*Sarcobatus vermiculatus*) form the principal vegetation.

27. Although none of these soils can alone be called fertile, their proper mixture, and especially of the first three, with humus, affords conditions highly favorable to success.

28. Besides the qualities resulting from their chemical composition, and their relations to moisture, soils differ greatly in their capacity for absorbing, retaining, and radiating heat. A soil covered with siliceous pebbles retains the heat better than fine sand, and hence it is one of the circumstances that favor the growth of the vine. In the wine districts of France, differences in the time of maturing the fruit have been traced directly to this cause. A sandy soil radiates heat very readily in clear summer nights, and frosts injurious to vegetation are more apt to occur upon these soils, where exposed.

29. The color of a soil has much effect in determining absorption of solar heat. If dark colored, it becomes warm sooner and to a greater depth and degree than if light.

30. The character of the underlying rock itself has also its influence upon the growth of plants and trees. If siliceous and solid, their roots get no nourishment and no hold. If friable and composed of mineral elements that may be taken up in solution by the roots, their fibers will insinuate themselves into the fissures and assist the disintegration, especially where moisture is present, and where the frost can act. This operation takes place more readily where the rock is stratified in thin layers that are highly inclined.

31. It is a fact familiar to geologists that certain forms of vegetation, and especially of trees, are characteristic of the rock formation that underlies them. We have examples of this in shales rich with potash, that are congenial to the elms. A limestone soil is favorable to the maples but not to the pines, while the latter flourish best on siliceous soils, if suitably mixed with other ingredients. A line of outcrop of some rock formation upon a hillside may be made known in some cases conspicuously by the color of the foliage of the trees that grow upon it, especially when they are colored in autumn or remain green in winter.

32. The soil upon a sloping surface is generally deeper, more humid, and richer near the foot, and tends gradually to become thin,

dry, and sterile toward the top. These differences become greater as the inclination is more steep. Upon such slopes, it becomes highly important that the surface should be covered with vegetation and consolidated by its roots. There is no growth so favorable for this purpose as that of trees, and elsewhere we will notice the disastrous results that have followed from their clearing off upon steep mountain sides. In some cases, the damage is beyond remedy, while in others it may be arrested and utility restored.

Of the preparation of the Soil for sowing or planting Forest Trees.

33. In preparing land for a grove or woodland, the soil should be thoroughly mellowed by previous working or cultivation. Upon new prairie land there is but little chance of success in starting a successful growth of trees until the sod has been turned over and thoroughly rotted. This can best be done by cultivating at least one or two years previously with some farm crop.

34. The first breaking up of the sod can only be done to advantage in the season when vegetation is most active, and it varies somewhat in different years and in different localities. It may be generally said to last through the month of June, and it sometimes may continue longer. Toward the latter part of summer and in autumn, the soil is too dry and hard for breaking up, and the herbage does not so readily decompose. The first furrows must be broad and thin. The subsequent plowing should be deeper, and the soil should be rendered perfectly mellow by harrowing.

35. For windbreaks and hedges, this preliminary work may be in the line of proposed planting, and at least four feet wider than the intended borders.

36. In the planting of trees for avenues, the soil near the surface, which is generally more fertile, should be placed by itself, and this should be the first that is used in covering the roots. In hard clay soils, there is an advantage in preparing the holes in autumn, and leaving them to the action of the air and the frost through the winter, in readiness for the next spring.

37. It is sometimes necessary, and often advantageous, to fertilize at the time of planting, and the best material that can be used is well-rotted leaf-mold from the woods. It may be first mixed with the soil that is spread next to the roots. Where stable manure is used, it should be placed near, but not in contact with the roots, or it

should be used as a top-dressing. In the common practice of forestry, and at present prices of labor and of timber, we can not usually do more than to sow or plant the species that appear to be best suited to the conditions, and we can only fertilize in nurseries and special plantations. It is not improbable that methods of fertilization upon an extensive scale may hereafter be employed in forest planting, and with profitable results.

Of the Slope and Aspect of Surface, and their Effect upon Tree Growth.

38. The slope of a surface is sometimes mentioned in degrees of the angle that it rises above the level. It may be called a *gentle slope*, if under 10°; *somewhat steep*, if from 10° to 20°; *steep*, if from 20° to 34°; and *very steep*, if from 35° to 45°.

39. The aspect or direction of a slope is found to have a perceptible, and often a notable influence upon tree growth, and this effect is greater in proportion to the extent of surface. Upon isolated swells of land and small hills, it might be scarcely noticed, but on the opposite sides of mountain ranges, or in mountain valleys, it may be very great.

40. A *northern aspect* receives no full sunlight, or its rays fall obliquely in the morning or toward evening, according to the angle of elevation. The winds are colder and dryer, but in the growing season generally not strong. The soil retains moisture, and the growth is often rapid. The trees retain their regular shape, and the wood is softer, not as strong, but generally well adapted to manufacture. As vegetation is a little delayed, the spring frosts are not so apt to do harm, but from the late and imperfect hardening of the new wood, the frosts of winter may do injury. As the snows lie longer on these slopes, the forests are benefited by their delaying the growth in the first uncertain warm days of spring, and by the moisture that they retain. The starting of forests by seeding is more easily secured on a north slope than any other, and it is only upon this slope that forest-tree seeds are sown upon the damp snows in starting mountain forests.

41. An *eastern aspect* receives the sun in the cool morning hours, when the temperature and light are moderate. The winds in our Atlantic States are often damp, especially in winter. The soil retains its moisture fairly. Timber grows well, and acquires medium qualities that adapt it to the greatest variety of uses.

42. A *southern aspect* receives both the heat and light with greatest intensity, and is more liable to winds and storms, and the soil to erosion from rains, than any other. The trees, on the whole, are of slower growth, owing to deficient moisture, and are less regular in form, but the wood is firm, heavy, and strong, well adapted to all uses where these qualities are required. Seeding can seldom be secured on a steep southern aspect in a warm, dry climate, and trees must be set from nurseries and attended with greater care. The south side of a mountain is much more likely to be bare than any other, every thing else being equal.

43. A *western aspect* receives the sun obliquely, but in the warmest part of the day, and in our Western States, vegetation is most exposed on these slopes to drying winds. The soil is apt to become dry, and timber is therefore of slower growth and less regular in form, but in the main good.

44. These differences from aspect are more noticeable in elevated regions than in low grounds, and they depend in degree more or less upon the nature of the soil, and local climatic influences that may determine the direction of the surface winds, or otherwise affect the location.

45. The degree of inclination has also a notable influence upon vegetation, and on the action of rains upon the surface. If less than one in six, the conditions are generally good. From this to one in three, agricultural cultivation becomes difficult, and the surface is liable to wash; still, the roots of trees can find a hold; and, if they can get deep into the soil, forests will prosper. At still greater angles, cultivation becomes difficult without terracing, and the dangers from erosion become greater. Upon such extreme slopes, pasturage is apt to cause great injuries by destroying the herbage and allowing the soil to wash into the valleys. The true policy should be to keep them covered with woodlands, if possible, and to clear by selection. never exposing the whole surface at once.

CHAPTER III.

OF CLIMATE AND METEOROLOGICAL INFLUENCES.

46. We understand by *climate*, the atmospheric conditions of a given region, resulting from its latitude, elevation, temperature,

humidity, amount and distribution of its rains, character and force of the winds, intensity of light, and other general or local causes.

The Atmosphere and its Elements.

47. The atmosphere from which the trees, through their foliage, derive a part of their aliment, and to which they return certain gaseous elements in the process of growth, consists of about one part of oxygen to four parts of nitrogen by volume. It always contains, besides these, a nearly constant proportion of carbonic acid gas, and a variable amount of aqueous vapor.

48. *Oxygen.* This gas is necessary to the existence of all animal and vegetable life, and to combustion, respiration, fermentation, and many other processes of nature. It has a wide range of affinities, and forms a part of all organic and most mineral compounds. It is absorbed or disengaged in various operations of tree-growth, and, under certain conditions, it hastens decay.

49. *Nitrogen.* This gas has a comparatively small range of affinities, and in the air appears to dilute and moderate the action of oxygen. Of itself, it does not sustain life. It forms a part of some vegetables and of all animals, and, combined with hydrogen in the proportion of 1 to 3 (NH_3), it forms *ammonia*, which acts an important part in the vegetation of trees, as well as of the cultivated grains.

50. *Carbonic Acid Gas.* This is a compound made up of 2 atoms of oxygen to 1 of carbon (CO_2, or 72.73 of oxygen to 27.27 of carbon by weight). It has been estimated that this gas forms one thousandth part of the atmosphere, but recent experiments show that the proportion is less, ranging from two and a half to four ten-thousandths, or even less. It is very uniform, yet is slightly varied by local influences, being increased by combustion, respiration, and other causes.

51. It is from carbonic acid gas, either in the air or in the water taken up by the roots, that trees obtain the carbon that makes their principal bulk. This gas was probably more abundant in former times, as in the carboniferous period, since mineral coals are largely made up of carbon. It also forms a part of all limestones and marls, and of many minerals and ores. There is no evidence that the proportion in the air has changed within the period of human history.

52. *Aqueous Vapor.* The proportion of watery vapor in the air has a most important influence upon tree growth, and where the amount is small, their cultivation becomes difficult or impossible.

53. Water, when exposed, will slowly evaporate, the rate being greater at a high temperature and in a dry air. It is still greater when there is a wind passing over the surface, carrying off the vapor and bringing dry air in its place.

54. Aqueous vapor is always present in the air, although it may be imperceptible to our senses. There is, however, a limit, above which the excess becomes visible as fog or cloud, and falls as dew or rain. If the temperature falls below the freezing point, the dew becomes *hoar frost*, and the rain becomes *snow*.

55. The degree of temperature at which condensation begins is called the *dew point*. It may be ascertained by cooling down water in a bright and thin metallic cup until dew begins to form on the outside.

56. The humidity of the atmosphere is usually ascertained by the *psychrometer*, which consists of two similar thermometers set a few inches apart, one of them having the bulb covered with white muslin cloth, which is wet before an observation is taken. The wet bulb is gently fanned till the temperature goes down to a stationary point, and then both thermometers are read. By the aid of tables that have been computed for this purpose, we may very easily obtain from the temperature of the dry bulb instrument, and the difference between that and the wet bulb, two separate statements concerning the moisture present in the air, viz.: the *absolute* and the *relative* humidity.

57. The *Absolute Humidity* is the *elastic force* or *tension* of the vapor, as would be shown in its raising a column of mercury in a guage, and is usually given in decimal parts of an English inch. With a given difference between wet and dry bulb thermometers, it increases with the temperature, being greatest when the weather is warmest, as shown by Diagram 1. We see, for example, that at 90° it is 1.3 inches, the difference between thermometers being 10°, while it is but 0.3 at 55°, and but a little over 0.1 at 40°. The rate gains rapidly at high temperatures, and above the boiling point it becomes the power of steam.

58. As observed in a very warm atmosphere, there may be an abundance of moisture present in the air and no rain. At a fixed

temperature, the amount is least when the difference between wet and dry bulbs is greatest, and it increases as these differences become less, as we see by Diagram 2, where the lines descend from left to right. The rate of descent is similar at different temperatures, as we see the descending lines are parallel, but they become nearer together as the temperature is less. In this diagram, the degrees on the oblique lines are those of temperature in the open air. If we measure the vertical distances between these oblique lines, we would have a series of numbers increasing at a gaining rate, which might be shown by a curve something like those of the preceding figure.

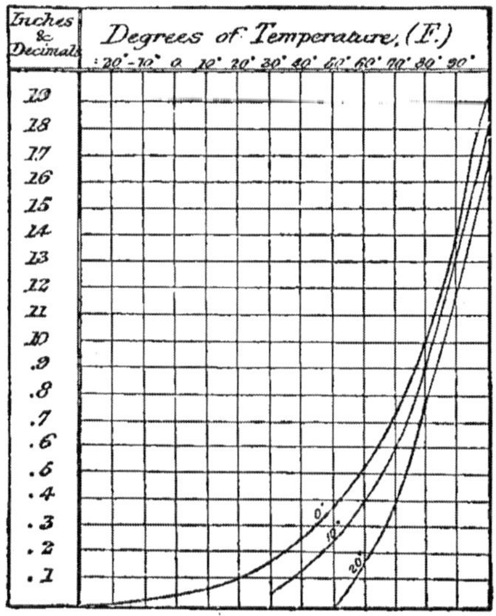

1. Absolute Humidity at different Temperatures, the Difference between wet and dry Bulbs being constant.

59. The *Relative Humidity*. This is the *percentage of saturation*, 100 being complete saturation, as in a fog (when the air can hold no more moisture in invisible form), and 0 being complete dryness. In our climate, we never find the air absolutely dry without artificial means. The degree of relative humidity also depends on the temperature, and with a given distance between wet and dry bulbs, it is greatest at high temper-

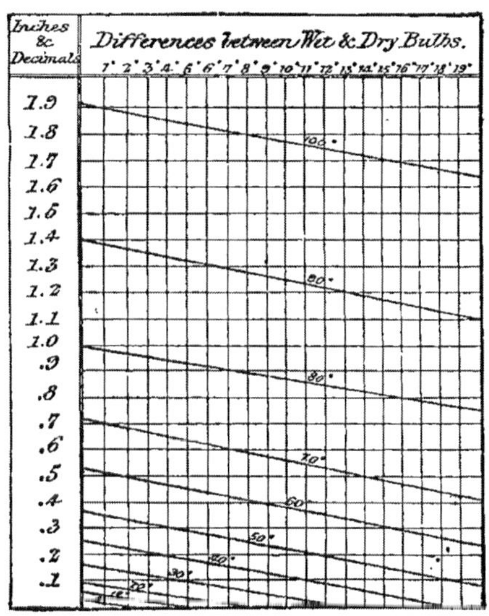

2. Absolute Humidity at fixed Temperatures, the Difference between wet and dry Bulbs being variable.

atures. The rate of increase forms a curve, as shown in the diagram annexed, but increasing in percentage more slowly as the temperature is high. These curves are higher when the wet and dry bulb thermometers are nearer alike, and grow smaller at a regularly decreasing rate as the differences between instruments increase.

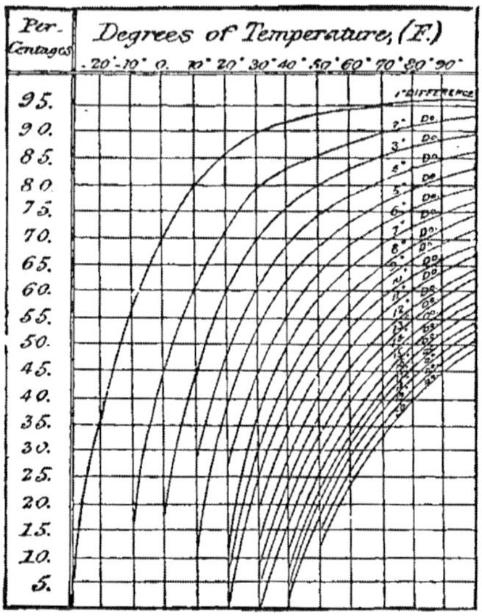

3. Relative Humidity at different Temperatures the difference between wet and dry Bulbs being constant.

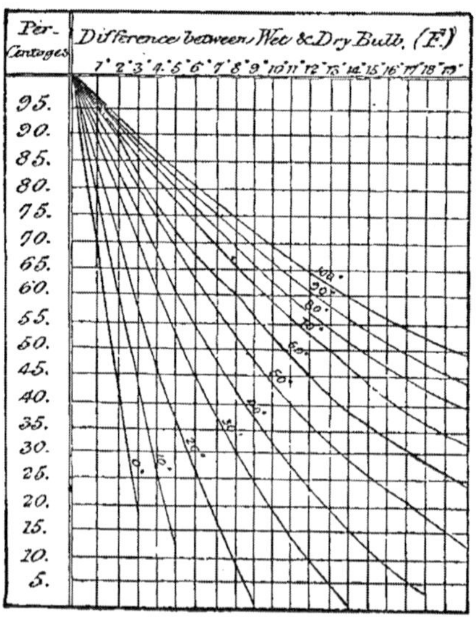

4. Relative Humidity at fixed Temperatures, the difference between wet and dry Bulbs being variable.

60. At all temperatures, the relative humidity diminishes in percentage as the difference between the instruments increases, as we see by the descending curves in Figure 4, but not at uniform rates, as we see that these lines are curves. The degrees marked on these curves from 0° to 100° are those of temperature in the open air.[1]

(1) The numerical statements from which this and the preceding figures are constructed will be found in a volume of meteorological tables prepared by Professor Guyot, and published by the Smithsonian Institution for the use of its observers, at the time when the former system of voluntary meteorological observation was in operation. The limits of this volume do not admit of their insertion in detail, nor of a statement of the principles upon which they are based.

61. The absolute humidity of the atmosphere is much greatest in summer, reaching its maximum in July or August (0.5 to 0.6 inches), and its minimum in December (0.1 or a little higher). The relative humidity follows a different law, and through a much less range. It ranges from 75 to 80 per cent in winter in the Atlantic States, descends to the lowest (about 65 per cent, on the general average) in May, rises to about 70 to 75 in the summer months, and a little higher in winter. These ranges of absolute and relative humidity, taken from the mean of many years' observation at the Magnetic and Meteorological Observatory at Toronto, in Canada, and at the State Agricultural Colleges at Orono, in Maine, and at Lansing, in Michigan, are shown by the accompanying engravings.

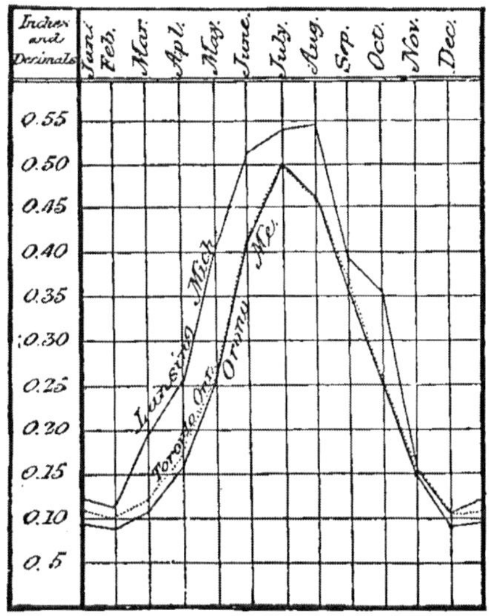

5. Absolute Humidity at three American Stations through the several Months, for a Series of Years.

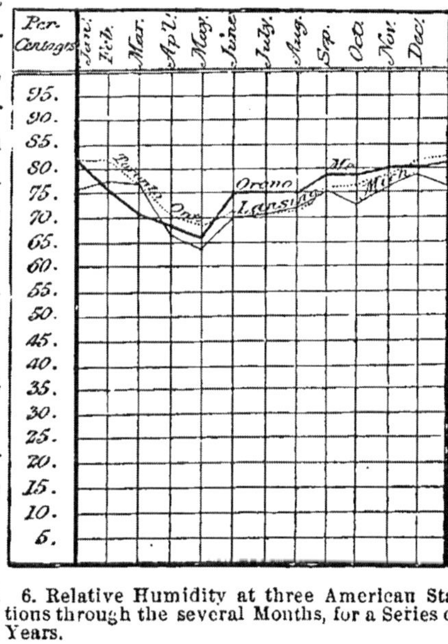

6. Relative Humidity at three American Stations through the several Months, for a Series of Years.

Effects of Heat and of Cold upon the Volume of Air.

62. It is a rule that heat tends to expand all bodies, whether solid, liquid, or gaseous, and that cooling tends to reduce their volume.

63. When any substance expands, it absorbs "latent heat," and becomes colder.

Condensation has the opposite effect, and the substance condensed becomes warm. It is by many astronomers believed that the sun's heat is caused by the condensation of gases going on upon or within its surface. Evaporation, or the passing of a liquid into gaseous form, is notably an expanding, and consequently a cooling process. The leaves of trees in the growing season evaporate abundantly, and hence the coolness of groves in summer. The condensation of vapors in the form of dew or rain, is always the effect of a cooling down of the atmosphere to below the *Dew Point* [§ 55], and is always attended with a diminution in the previous volume of the air from which it forms.

64. *Dew*, is the moisture deposited from the air when cooled at night by the radiation of heat from the earth's surface. It can only occur when the temperature is reduced to the "dew point," and is greatest in still clear nights. When covered with clouds, the radiations of heat are returned to the earth. The same effect is often seen immediately under a tree, which will remain dry, while all around it the dew on the grass may be heavy. This shows that the air under the tree has been a little warmer than in the open space around it, and that the general percentage of moisture in the air is relatively high.

65. On the contrary, we sometimes see the grass, boards, etc., under a tree wet with the dew, when the ground around it is dry. This occurs from the greater humidity of the air under the tree, in consequence of the evaporation of its foliage, and is seen only in a calm night, when the general humidity of the air is less. These effects are sometimes seen where a plank walk extends along under an avenue of large trees standing widely apart. The open portions may be white with hoar-frost (frozen dew), while the parts covered by the trees are bare, or the sheltered portions may be wet, as if rained upon, while the open spaces are dry.

66. *Fogs and Clouds*, are formed only when the air is at or below the dew point, showing that it can hold the moisture no longer, and the excess becomes visible, and may, in certain cases, descend as rain. They show a reduced temperature, and common summer clouds are often formed by the unequal heating of a portion of the earth's surface by the sun.

67. The air in contact with these heated portions expands, and, becoming lighter, rises—the air from surrounding spaces coming in

to supply its place. An upward current is thus formed, and the air rising and cooling finally comes to the dew point, and the moisture becomes visible as cloud. A column of smoke from a burning clearing will sometimes thus form a cloud, and may cause rain.

68. A country interspersed with groves of trees, presents contrasts in heating tendencies favorable to the formation of these upward currents of the air. Broad areas of cloud passing over a great extent of country, and usually accompanied by a low barometer, are due to more general causes, but always show a reduction of temperature in the region where they form.

69. *Rains*, are caused by a condensation of moisture from cooling below the dew point. The success of forest growth depends largely upon their amount and their seasonable distribution throughout the year, and especially their occurrence when vegetation is most active, and when the new layer of wood for the season is forming.

70. A rain guage on the ground will collect in a year more rain than one on the roof of a house, and the latter more than one on a high tower. Currents of air may tend to cause this difference in part, but it seems to show that the rain-drops gather in size as they descend.

71. On the contrary, in a dry time, we sometimes see filaments of rain descending from a cloud, which dry up and disappear in the warm air below without reaching the ground. When such clouds pass over large bodies of woodland, where the temperature is cooler and the air more moist, these filaments extend down and afford a shower of rain, but dry up again as they come to the warm air of the fields beyond. Applying these principles of humidity and temperature to Forestry, let us consider what effect a woodland can have upon them:

72. In the growing season, there is a vast amount of evaporation going on from the foliage of trees, the moisture being derived from the soil. This evaporation is a cooling process, and as it both increases the amount of moisture, while it reduces the temperature, it tends to bring the air to the dew point; in other words, to the condition favoring the formation of dews and rain. In the nicely balanced state of the atmosphere that we often find in summer, this change may sometimes be the turning point that decides between rain and drouth.

73. It has been found, many times, that where the trees and bushes are cleared away from large areas of rocky surface, the region begins to suffer from drouth. The rocks being heated by the sun, remain warm in the night, and the rain-clouds, which, in passing over the wooded surface, formerly condensed in gentle showers, now dry up, upon coming to the heated air, and perhaps yield a copious rainfall, over a better-wooded district beyond. These effects are more apparent where the clearings have been extended over considerable areas, and they could with certainty be overcome by allowing the rocks to be again clothed with a growth of trees.

74. *The effect of Woodlands upon the Rain that falls upon them* may next be considered. Admitting that the amount of rain that falls upon the woods is the same as that in adjacent fields, it is evident that a part would be intercepted by the foliage, and in transient showers be evaporated from it, without reaching the ground. But the air within the woods is always more humid in the growing season, and the surface is always shaded from the sun and sheltered from the winds. It is also generally covered with a layer of dead leaves and litter, so that the rain that does actually reach the earth, although it may be rather less in amount, is more in effect, because it is not readily evaporated. It sinks into the ground, instead of running off on the surface. It can not wear away the soil upon steep slopes, nor form sudden and destructive floods, as in a naked and treeless region. The streams rising in woodlands may swell after a rain, but more gradually, and they will subside again more slowly. If they rise in woodland swamps, they are scarcely liable to floods at any season, and tend to an even flow throughout the year.

75. Springs and wells in a wooded region have a much more uniform supply of water than in the same region when cleared. Instances have often been observed where these become dry upon clearing, and again well supplied with water as before when a forest growth was restored.

76. These principles become important when applied to the supply of water for cities and towns, and for the maintenance of water in canals, or for hydraulic power. The basins of supply should, if possible, be kept wooded, and the rivulets kept shaded, if we would avoid failure.

77. In Illinois, and some other prairie states, there has been ob-

served a noticeable increase in the dryness of the climate since settlement first began. This may in part be attributed to the clearing away of the belts of native timber along the streams. The roots of these trees formerly kept the channel at a higher level, and in some cases formed extensive swamps. The beds of these streams are now lower, and they drain off the water to a greater depth. The effect is shown in the failure of water in the wells, and in the more frequent occurrence of drouth, to the injury of agriculture.

78. There is nothing that would more effectually check this tendency to deepening of channels than the planting of willows along the sides, and it might eventually in some degree restore what has been lost by raising them to a higher level.

79. The rate of evaporation from the surface of water and from soils is found to be much more in the open fields than in woodlands, and the difference is greater in summer than in winter.

80. Instruments for measuring the evaporation are sometimes called "atmometers," and they are of various forms. We here present a section of one invented by Professor Lamont, of the Munich Observatory. It consists of a basin of water, *f*, *g*, with a narrow-opening at *A*, communicating with a reservoir in an adjacent cylinder. Into the latter a plunger may be pressed down or raised by the screw, *S*. It works through an air-tight collar, *a*, *d*, and by this means the water, by pressure or suction, may be adjusted in the open basin. When left for observation, the water is drawn down till it is just visible at *A*, and the scale, *s*, *s*, is adjusted to a zero point at *h*. It is then forced up till

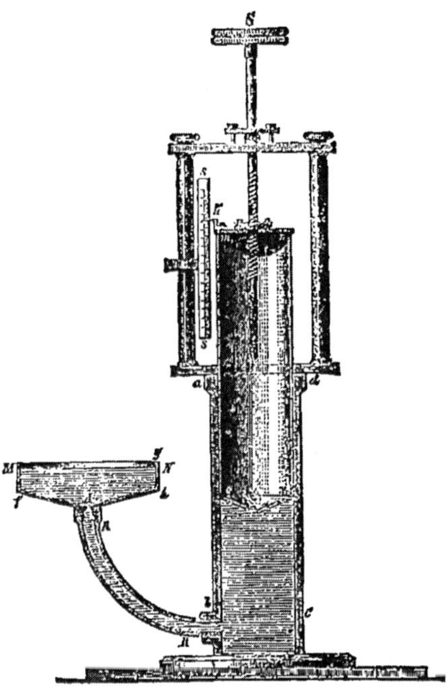

7. Lamont's Atmometer.

level with a line, *N*, *M*, and left. When next observed, the water is drawn down to *A*, and the scale will show how much has been wasted by evaporation. More water is added, and the scale is again set.

81. By a simpler plan, known as Piche's evaporator, a plain graduated glass tube, with its lower end open and ground flat, is filled with water. A disc of paper, first wet, is applied. It is then turned, with the closed end up, and the paper is found to adhere by atmospheric pressure. It continues wet, and by evaporation the water wastes away, the amount of loss being shown on the scale.

82. An open cylindrical dish of water may be used, the depth being measured at the beginning and end of the observation, and the loss supplied from time to time. The measurement may be made vertically by a scale, or by volume in a graduated measuring cup, or by weighing. It is necessary to cover with a wire screen, to prevent birds from bathing in it.

83. By an instrument shown in the annexed cut, the evaporation from soils, either naked or covered with grass, litter, or herbage, or by small growing trees, may be measured. The zinc-lined box, *A*, is connected with a reservoir of water, *C*, through a valve, *E*, so as to keep wet up to a certain level. The water may be drawn off from the faucet. The amount supplied from time to time shows the rate of evaporation.

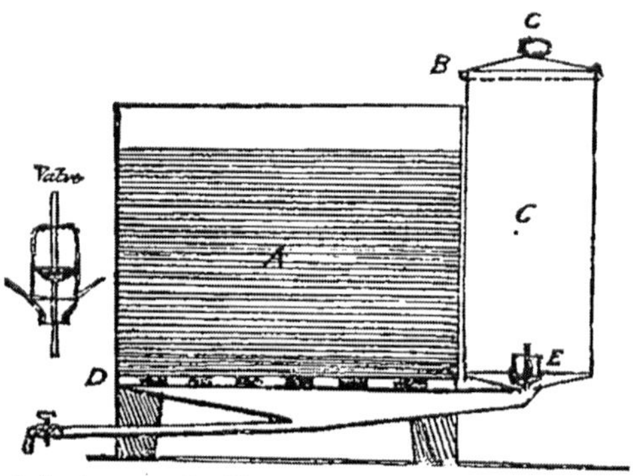

8. Instrument for Measuring the Evaporation from Soils.

84. The percolation of water through soils is measured by a *Lysimeter*. It consists of a vessel of known area at the surface, *A*, set in the ground, and the surface either clear or covered with litter, herbage, etc. The rains that fall on the surface filter down to the tube, *C*, and are measured in the receiver, *D*.

Relation between the Rainfall and the Native Forests.

85. As a general rule, we find our native forests more dense in proportion as the rainfall is greatest, as we see proved upon the Pacific Coast, and in the region south of Lake Superior. They become less as the rains diminish, and as we approach the great plains, the native timber is found only along the borders of the rivers and smaller streams, and finally it disappears altogether. As a rule, where the amount of rain is less than twenty inches in a year, and this chiefly in winter, the growth of trees becomes difficult, and with many species impossible.

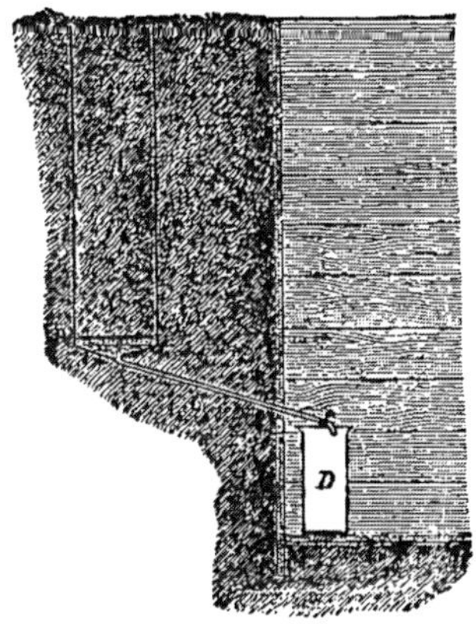

9. Lysimeter.

86. There is some reason to believe that the capacity for cultivation in a dry region may be increased by tree-planting, and gradually extended to a degree that would not be possible to secure at first.

Effect of Woodlands upon the Temperature of the Air and the Earth.

87. It is evident to the senses that the air in woodlands is cooler than in the open fields in summer and warmer in winter, although the actual difference in the latter is slight. When we measure the temperature of the soil, we find the effect of woodlands much greater, the difference between winter and summer being less in the woods than in the fields, and less at greater depths than at the surface. This difference is greatest in summer, when vegetation is most active. Various means are employed to measure this temperature. In one, a thermometer with a thick glass bulb (invented by Lamont, of Munich), is left to various depths, and when drawn up for observation it does not quickly change before reading. In other cases, long-stemmed instruments are permanently buried at different depths, with the scales above the surface.

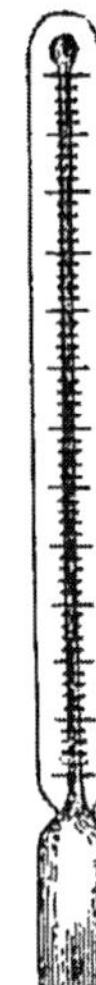

10. Lamont's Earth Thermometer.

88. *The Winds.* In considering atmospheric agencies, the drying effects of the winds should be noticed, as liable to be greatly increased by the clearing of lands, and to be lessened by planting. These plantations, in order to serve most effectually as wind-breaks, should extend across the direction from whence the prevailing winds blow. In the states west of the Mississippi, the dry and warm winds, most injurious to vegetation, come from the south-west, and it is against these that we should chiefly guard.

89. The winter storms of greatest violence, known in the North-western States as "blizzards," come from the north-west. There can be no doubt but that their local effects may be reduced, and to some extent their occurrence diminished by the plantations of groves of trees.

90. In some countries exposed to prevailing ocean winds, there will be ample rainfall under any condition, and woodlands can have but little effect; for, whether present or absent, the humid air from the ocean will precipitate its moisture when it comes over the land. In Norway, the amount of rain on the western coast is over 80 inches a year. In Great Britain and Ireland, and on the western coast of France, the rains will be abundant from these causes, as they will always be along our Pacific coast. But these ocean winds in passing over mountain ranges must necessarily be cooled down to a degree much below the dew point, and become dry by being thus depleted of their moisture as they pass inland.

The Agency of Water in Vegetation.

91. Whether in solid form, as snow or ice, or as a liquid, supplied by rains, dews, or irrigation, or as a vapor, water acts an essential part in vegetation, and is necessary for the existence of all vegetable life. For best effect it should be seasonable and sufficient, but not in excess.

92. As a general rule, seeds will not germinate under water, but in some trees the roots will bear submergence for a considerable time. The wood of trees thus exposed is often softer and more spongy than it would have been if grown on dryer ground. Generally, however, a sustained overflow of the surface causes the death of the trees whose roots are thus covered, and "beaver meadows" are thus caused.

93. The *Snow* is a slow conductor of radiant heat, while it allows

the sun's heat to pass through it with facility. The earth is thus covered and protected from the intense cold of winter, the snow allowing it to be warmed by the sun's heat, while at the same time it does not allow the warmth of the earth to escape. The melting of snows takes place largely from the under side, as we see evidence in the vacant spaces around every object in the snow as the spring approaches.

94. In forest shade the snow melts but slowly, and the water is thus allowed to sink into the earth, or run off gradually, instead of suddenly, as in the rains in an open country. By this delay in melting, the vegetation is kept back until warm weather is confirmed and injuries from spring frosts are less liable to happen.

95. In woodlands the snow does not drift, and this effect extends somewhat into the adjacent fields, which are thus kept from exposure to injurious frosts in winter.

96. In liquid form the water is taken up by the roots, and with it carbonic acid gas and various mineral substances in solution, the latter supplying the inorganic portions remaining as ashes when the plants are burned. In its chemical composition water consists of two atoms of hydrogen united to one of oxygen (H_2O), and it is produced when these elements are united by being burned together. The agency of water will be further noticed in connection with the functions of the leaves.

Of the Effects of Frost.

97. Many species of trees will not endure a freezing temperature; others are injured but not killed by it, and others appear fitted to endure the greatest rigors of winter without injury, yet in exceptional cases even these may suffer from intense and prolonged cold. The winters of 1683–4 and 1708–9 were memorable from the injuries they did in Europe to the forest trees, and in December, 1879, a severe frost in France did immense damage to young timber. It was found on this last occasion that the injury was greater where the sun struck the trees not protected by snow; the effect was greater in valleys than on high grounds, and varied much with the soil, the exposure, and the humidity of the air.

98. In these exceptional and fortunately rare cases, the condition of the wood as to maturity had doubtless much influence, as the winter appears to have found them unprepared for its rigors. It was afterwards found, that many trees, supposed to be dead, still put

forth new buds from the older wood, and thus were able to show hopeful signs of recovery.

99. The injury from frosts depends more on the season than on its intensity. A late spring frost will kill down the young shoots of conifers that would endure a severe winter.

100. Many trees, and especially oaks, pines, and firs, are found cracked into deep fissures from the unequal action of the frost upon their woody tissues. Such cracks do not heal up or grow over, but remain as a furrow always visible upon the outside, and greatly impairing its value for lumber.

101. A freezing rain may load down the branches of trees so as to break them. The roots of young seedling trees may be thrown out of the ground by frost, and the fruit-season may be checked by a frost that kills the buds or blossoms but that is not severe enough to injure the foliage; or its maturity may be prevented by an early autumnal frost.

102. Trees accustomed to alternately wet and dry seasons, such as conifers from the Pacific coast, become exceedingly liable to winter-kill, especially after a mild and damp autumn. A long-continued period of very cold weather in winter has been noticed as more likely to injure the growth of trees than more intense frost for a shorter period.

103. The effects of frost are always to be feared in high mountainous regions and in deep humid valleys, for the atmosphere is there always loaded with vapors that condense in fogs as soon as the sun is hid. Young trees bear these exposures with much peril until they get to a height of fifteen or twenty feet; that is to say, above the ground fogs, or at least above the level at which these injuries are most likely to happen.

Of the Injuries from Snows.

104. When damp snow falls upon the branches of forest trees, and especially the evergreens, it may break them down by its weight, especially when this is increased by rain, or, when frozen on, it is exposed to a strong wind. An instance occurred in Scotland, in the early part of 1879, when great damage was done to evergreen forests, and to less extent to the oak, birch, and larch trees, from the weight of snows.

105. In the Rocky Mountain region snow-slides often do great

injury to young timber, and these become more liable to occurrence as the wood near the summit is destroyed. The snow then drifts over and forms great overhanging masses on the leeward side, which are liable to become detached and to slide down into the valleys, carrying every thing before them.

106. Young seedlings when covered with the snow are sometimes broken down by its weight, as it settles from melting on the under side.

107. The *Timber-Line* is the upper limit of tree growth upon mountains. Its height is greatest within the tropics, and it descends as we go north or south, until it reaches the surface in the Arctic zone. It also decreases as we approach the sea-coast, and it is often, from local causes, higher on one side of a mountain than on the other. In the Himalayas, this line is about 11,800 feet high. On the Alps it averages 6,400 feet, and in the Rocky Mountains it varies from 9,000 to 12,000 feet.[1]

108. In ascending to the timber-line, no great difference in the size of the timber is observed until within a few hundred feet of the limit, when the trees begin to appear short and wide-spreading, and at last almost flat, and leaning from the prevailing winds. Above the line, no trees whatever are found, and but little vegetation of any kind, the mountain rising bleak and barren to its summit, or until it reaches the eternal snows. This snow-line varies with the seasons, and is in some years higher or lower than in others, according as the prevailing conditions of the weather may have varied.

Decline of Fruit Production and its Cause.

109. It is not unusual to hear old people recall the memories of their youth, when peaches and other fruits grew luxuriantly and without special care, in regions where they are now unknown, or are raised only in favorable seasons and with extraordinary care.

(1) Prof. C. C. Parry, in Prof. Hayden's Report of 1872, gives the height of the timber line in some twenty places, some of them being as follows:

	FEET.		FEET.
Mount Shasta, Cal	8,000	Gilbert' Peak, Uintas	11,100
Cascade Range, Or.	7,000	Audobon's Peak, Colo	11,325
Ward's Peak, Monta	8,784	Mt. Engelmann, Colo	11,518
Bridger's Peak	9,003	Gray's Peak, Colo	11,643
Near Henry's Lake, Idaho	9,366	Pike's Peak	12,040
Wind River Mts	10,160	Colorado generally	11,600 to 12,000
Long's Peak, Colo	10,800		

They will speak of winters of uniform but not extreme cold, and steady and long-continued seasons for making maple sugar, and other incidents of farm life, denoting a regularity in the return of seasons, and a similarity in their character that does not now exist.

110. In respect to loss of fertility, something may be ascribed to the exhaustion of the soil by careless cultivation, and something to the drainage of swamps and the deepening of water-courses. But the most conspicuous difference in the general condition of the country, and the most obvious cause of this decline, is to be found in the excessive clearing off of woodlands, and the loss of the equalizing tendencies which their presence occasioned.

The Ruin that is brought upon Countries by the Clearing off of Woodlands.

111. It is a familiar fact there are many regions in Asia and Southern Europe, once exceedingly fertile and densely populated, that are now utterly sterile and desolate. The country bordering upon the Euphrates, and portions of Turkey, Greece, Egypt, Italy, and Spain, are now incapable of cultivation from this cause. The Hon. Geo. P. Marsh, in a work entitled "Man and Nature," and a later edition entitled "The Earth as Modified by Human Action," has devoted a large space to the discussion of this question. A more recent illustration of these effects is published in the principal French Journal of Forestry,[1] and, for comparison, we place by its side a description of the same region only about fifty years before:

(*About* 1876.)

"The Khanate of Bucharia presents a striking example of the consequences brought upon a country by clearings. Within a period of thirty years, this was one of the most fertile regions of central Asia, a country which, when well wooded and watered, was a terrestrial paradise. But within the last twenty-five years, a mania of clearing has seized upon the inhabitants, and all the great forests have been cut away, and the little that remained was ravaged by

(*About* 1826.)

". . . The finest provinces of Tartary remain to be described, being generally known under the name of Great Bucharia. . . . The most noted and fertile of all the provinces is that of Sogd, so named from the river that flows through it. 'For eight days,' says Ibun Hankel, 'We may travel in the country of Sogd and not be out of one delicious garden. On every side, villages, rich corn-fields, fruitful orchards. Country houses, gardens, meadows inter-

(1) *Revue des Eaux et Forêts,* March, 1876, p. 93.

fire during a civil war. The consequences were not long in following, and has transformed this country into a kind of arid desert. The water-courses are dried up, and the irrigating canals empty. The moving sands of the desert, being no longer restrained by barriers of forests, are every day gaining upon the land, and will finish by transforming it into a desert as desolate as the solitudes that separate it from Khiva."

spersed by rivulets, reservoirs and canals, present a most lively picture of industry and happiness. The rich valley of Sogd produces so great an abundance of grapes, melons, pears, and apples, that they are exported to Persia, and even to Hindostan.'"

The same writer (Malte-Brun), again citing from the same author, says: "'I have often been at Kohendis, the ancient capital of Bucharia. I have cast my eyes all around, and never have I seen a verdure more fresh or abundant, or of wider extent. This green carpeting mingled in the horizon in the azure of the skies. The simple verdure served as a sort of ornamental offset to the towns contained in it. Numerous country seats decorated the simplicity of the fields. Hence I am not surprised that, of all the inhabitants of Korasan and Maweralnahr, none attain a more advanced age than those of Bucharia.'"—*Malte-Brun's Univ. Geography*, i, 470.

112. We need not go out of our own country to witness equal examples of irreparable injuries done by improvident clearings—perhaps on a smaller scale, but not less disastrous in result. In the older settled portions of New England, in the Middle States, and in the South, there are arid hills and worn-out fields, no longer worth any thing for cultivation or pasturage, and that offer, as the only chance of restoration to a useful purpose, the possibility of growing trees.

113. The abundance of cliff-dwellings and other ruins, in western Colorado and New Mexico, appears to show that that region was once capable of sustaining a larger population than would be now possible from existing means of cultivation. It is of course not known as to what has caused this difference, but the destruction of forests appears to afford the most probable reason.

114. Mr. B. H. Baden-Powell, in a report on the Administration of the Forest Department of India (1877, vol. i, p. 51), in speak-

ing of the central, high, arid lands of certain districts, says that in the worst of these there are found traces of ancient cultivation, river beds now dry, and remains of villages. In the parts outside of the arid region, the streams, once perennial and used for irrigation, are now without water, excepting when swollen to torrents in the rains. He adds: "This phenomenon, so commonly observed in all the Punjaub streams coming from the now denuded lower hills, points inevitably to the conclusion that forest denudation has deprived these rivers of their steady water-supply, and hence ruined the rainless countries that were dependent upon them."

115. We quote these facts in this connection, not because they are rare or unusual, for they are not. We present them as closely describing the condition of the now irrigated and fertile regions of Colorado, California, and the Territories, whose fertility is wholly dependent upon the streams that may be withdrawn from their natural beds and distributed over the surface in the growing season. As an inevitable consequence of denudation, these streams will swell to torrents in the winter rains and from the rapid melting of snows in spring, and become dry in summer, when most needed for irrigation. The mining interest, depending upon a uniform water supply, will share in this misfortune, which will also be felt in the loss of water-power, and in the failure of water for the supply of towns and cities.

CHAPTER IV.

REPRODUCTION FROM SEED.

The essential parts of the Blossom.

116. Flowers include the parts essential to germination, analogous in effect to sex. They consist of at least two distinct portions—*stamens* and *pistils*. The first of these bears an *anther*, containing at full maturity a yellow dust called *pollen*. The stamens, when few, are generally of some determinate number, and in perfect flowers are arranged around one or more pistils in the center. These have at their base the germ of the future seeds, enveloped in some covering, which is collectively termed the fruit. The anthers are generally supported or suspended by stalks or fibers called *filaments*. The pistil usually consists of the *stipe*, or supporting stem, and the *stigma* or terminal part that receives the pollen. The fertilization

of the blossom is secured whenever the pollen, at maturity, is conveyed to the stigma of the pistil.

117. The blossoms of trees are often unsymmetrical, and the parts essential to fertilization may be either in the same blossom, as shown on a subsequent page in the linden, or on different parts of the same tree, as shown in the hornbeam and the alder, in the accompanying engravings. In the latter, the germs for the early spring blossoms are formed the fall before. Such pendant blossoms in trees are called *aments*, or *catkins*. Their form and structure afford characters, upon which botanical classification in part depends.

11. Staminate. Flowers of the Oak enlarged.

118. Where both the staminate and pistillate blossoms grow upon the same plant, it is said to be *monœcious*, but when formed upon different trees or plants, as in case of the poplars and willows, it is said to be *diœcious*. In the latter case, the seeds can not be fertile, unless trees bearing both kinds of blossoms grow in the same neighborhood.

119. The winds have an important influence in disseminating the pollen from one tree to another, and the blossoms of such trees generally open in the windy season of the year, and before the leaves appear. The bees, in pursuit of honey, perform an important office in conveying pollen from one blossom to another, and there are many special arrangements in nature for securing fertilization.

12. Two Male Blossoms of the Hornbeam, and the Terminal Pistilate Blossom.

120. When the pollen of one species is conveyed to the pistillate flowers of another species, within the same genus, cross-fertilization sometimes occurs. This may occur naturally, or by artificial means,

and the hybrids thus obtained may, in the case of trees, be perpetuated by layers, cuttings or grafts.

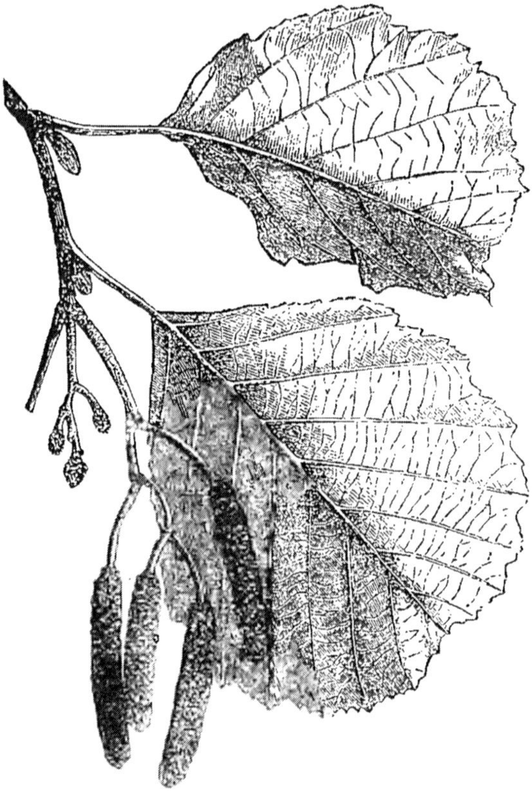

13. *Alnus glutinosa*—Alder.

121. When fertilization is secured, the staminate blossoms fall off or dry up, and the germs at the base of the pistils expand, and ripen into the fruit. This usually happens the same year that the blossoms appear, but in some of the oaks and the conifers, the ripening process is not completed till the autumn of the second year after fertilization takes place. Many trees have their fertile and their sterile years; indeed, but few trees bear steadily and alike from year to year. In the case of trees introduced into regions where they are not native, they may thrive and grow to large size, but without ever bearing fertile seeds, or even without blossoming. A dense shade is unfavorable for the formation of seeds, and trees, after being exposed to the air and light by the clearing away of trees around them, will usually bear fruit more abundantly in first or second year after.

Of the Natural Distribution of Forest Tree Seeds.

122. While the seeds of all trees may fall and take root under or near the parent tree, and there thrive, when properly supplied with

moisture and light, nature has provided many kinds with the means for being carried to a greater or less distance. This natural dispersion of the seed may occur in various ways:

123. *Dispersion by the Winds.* Most of the pines and firs have their seeds furnished with a thin membranous wing at one end, that enables them to be borne to a considerable distance by the winds. The elms have a thin disc entirely around the seed, and the maples have their seeds in pairs, each side being furnished with a membranous wing. In the ash the seeds have closely adherent leaves, which enable it to be carried by the winds, and in the hornbeam there is a leaf-like appendage, that aids in its dispersion. In the maples, the pairs of seeds, with symmetrical wings, takes a rotary, spinning motion as they fall. The poplars and willows have a downy tuft, which enables them to be carried by the winds, sometimes many miles from the tree where they grew.

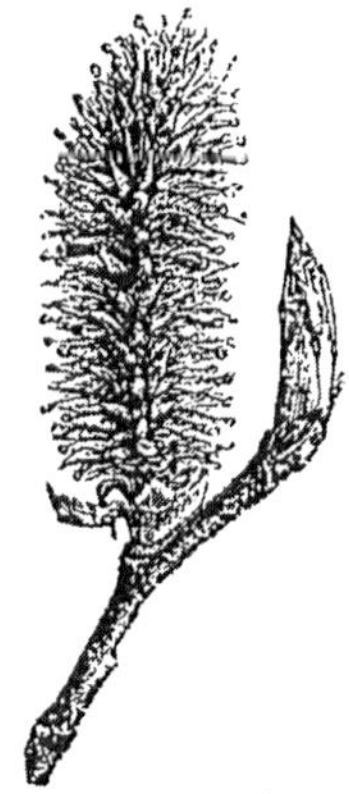

14. Pistillate Flowers of the Willow.

15. Pine Seeds.

124. The cottonwood, which belongs to the poplar family, derives its name from this downy appendage, which lies abundantly scattered over the ground at the season when it ripens. The basswood has a heavier seed, suspended on the under side of a leaf-like wing, which causes it to shoot off obliquely as it falls. In some instances, the seeds falling in winter upon a crust of snow, or upon the ice, may glide along before the wind a great distance, and in this way the pods of the locust, and other heavier seeds, in their capsules, or without them, may occasionally be scattered.

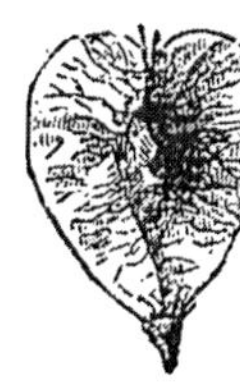

16. Seed of the Elm.

17. Seed of the Birch.

Of the Agency of Animals in the Planting of Tree Seeds.

125. We often find trees, especially such as bear edible nuts, or stone fruits surrounded by a pulp, growing in situations where the seeds have been dropped by birds or animals. In fact, the squirrels may be called the most industrious and successful

planters in the world, as during the nut season they are continually burying these seeds, just below the surface, under the leaves and in the rich soil, in conditions eminently favorable for vegetation. This is done at a season when the vitality of these seeds is greatest; and although some of them may be afterwards eaten, vast numbers germinate and grow to trees.

18. Seed of the European Hornbeam (*Carpinus betulus*).

126. This will sufficiently account for most instances in which the trees bearing heavy seeds, such as the oaks and the nut-trees, are found scattered through a forest of other kinds, where none were noticed before. Upon careful examination in a pine woodland, we may often find multitudes of young oaks, that spring up from the planting of squirrels, and that soon perish, unless the pines happen to be cut away, when they may take a vigorous growth, and thus become the principal kind. The seeds eaten by birds, and dropped undigested, may take root at greater distances from the parent tree.[1]

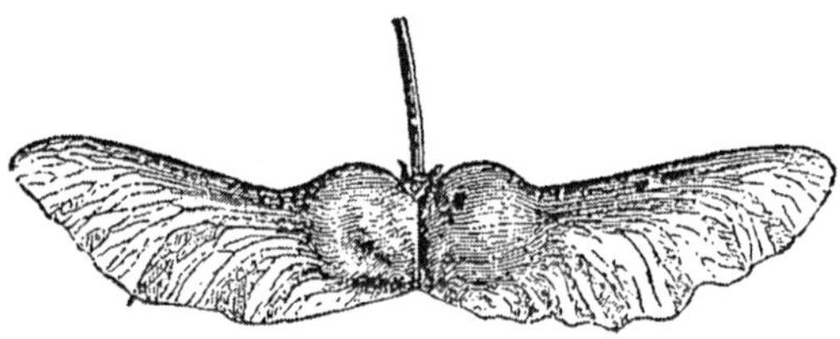

19. Seeds of the English Maple (*Acer campestre*).

Distribution of Seeds by Currents of Water.

127. Many seeds float readily upon the water while still in their capsules, and some of them without, and in this way they are carried long distances by rivers, and thrown up along the shores of lakes. It is thus that the sand-bars and shores of our western rivers are continually supplying an inexhaustible and ever-renewing supply of cottonwood and other seedling trees, that may be easily plowed up and planted at a small cost, upon the prairies of that region, and with much better chances of success than where cuttings

[1] A most interesting article upon this subject, by Henry D. Thoreau, will be found in the *Report of the Board of Agriculture of Massachusetts*, 1860, p. 11.

from these trees are set in the soil without roots. The success of cuttings depends much on the season; if very dry and hot, they may fail, and if moist and cool, they will grow. But a plant with sufficient root in the beginning has far better chances of getting well started, and when properly set, in a soil where it can get moisture, it is almost sure to succeed.

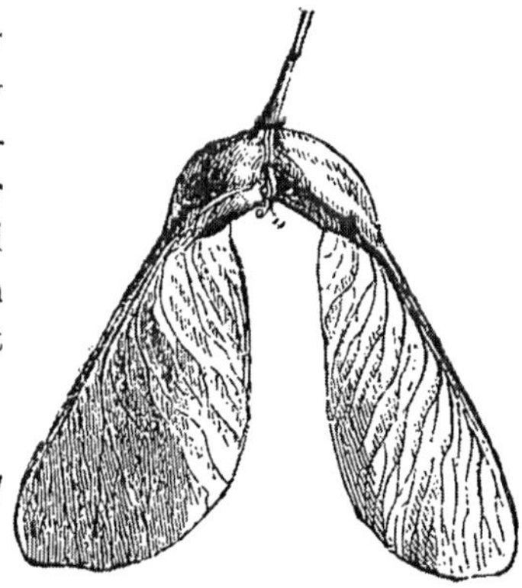

20. Seeds of the Sycamore Maple (*Acer pseudo-platanus*).

Seed that Ripen in Spring or Early Summer.

128. The elms, willows, poplars, and soft maples mature their seeds in the spring or early summer, and if not allowed to become too dry, may be carried to a considerable distance, but should be planted as soon as may be in the same season. They should be lightly covered, and the ground should be kept moist and partly shaded, until they take root and get well sprouted. Many of these seeds may be gathered from the surface of still water, as they have fallen from trees along the banks. When planted, they should be but thinly covered with soil, and shaded from the sun. They will generally get well rooted the first year, and ready for an early start in the next season.

21. Ripe Seeds of the Poplar before they fall.

The Gathering and Keeping of Seeds.

129. Tree seeds should generally be gathered as soon as they are ripe, and if not before, soon after they have fallen from the tree. They do not retain their vitality long; but if not planted the same fall, may generally be kept till the next spring. As a general rule, they loose their germinating power within a year. The mode of keeping them over is elsewhere described in different kinds of trees, and can not be generally stated, except that they

22. Seed and Tuft of the Cottonwood.

should not be allowed to heat, or mold, or become too dry, and in some cases they should not be allowed to freeze. Where large quantities of pine and other coniferous seeds are required for planting in Europe, drying-houses are constructed, using either solar or artificial heat for drying the cones, so that the seeds may be shaken out. Nuts and hard-shelled seeds may be kept fresh by packing in slightly damp sand, and keeping in a cool, but not too dry a place. Seeds having a pulpy covering should be washed out and dried in the shade before putting away. Small seeds may be kept in sacks or papers.

A Cheap Method of Keeping Nuts and Acorns for Planting.

130. As these may be spoiled by too much drying, or may heat and mold if in large heaps, or may sprout prematurely if too wet, the following method is sometimes practiced: A dry and sandy place is selected in a forest, where it is level, or a little sloping to the south, and where the shelter of large trees is low and abundant. The place must be fenced in, and should not be liable to standing water. A smali ditch may be dug around it for drainage. The acorus or nuts are spread on the ground as gathered, four or five inches deep, the leaves and litter being first removed. From the beginning they should be thoroughly raked daily, for the first month, and afterwards once in two or three days. By the end of December, the tendency to heat and mold will be over, and in very cold weather they should be lightly covered with straw or leaves; but this should be removed early, to prevent sprouting. In temperate climates no covering is needed, and in very rainy weather the raking should be repeated till time of planting.

131. Thin-shelled nuts, such as acorns and the chestnut, sooner loose their vitality in the sun and dry air, and are more liable to heat than those having a hard shell, like the black walnut, the butternut, and the hickories. They will not be injured by freezing, if protected by a thin covering of mulch—for nature provides such a cover in the herbage and fallen leaves. They will need protection from standing water, and from vermin and other animals. When kept under shelter, they should be spread evenly, and should be stirred from time to time, till the moisture has partly dried out, so that they will not mold.

Process of Germination of the Seed.

132. The seed contains the germs of the first growth of the future tree in an *embryo*, and the *cotyledons* or seed-leaves that will first appear. In the *conifers*, such as the pines, spruces, and cedars, there are several of these cotyledons, but in most other trees that we shall have occasion to notice there are two.

133. When living seeds are properly exposed to darkness, moisture, air, and warmth, they will sprout and grow. In this process, there comes out from the embryo a root, or *radicle*, which desceuds into the soil in whatever position the seed may chance to lie, while the cotyledons or germinal leaves seek the air and the light, forming the *plumule* or stem of the plant.

134. The time required for sprouting varies from a few hours to a few days, and in some cases it does not occur until the next season. The process may sometimes be hastened and assured by previously soaking the seeds, and in those having hard shells by scalding, as elsewhere more fully described.

135. The cotyledons of the acorn (*a*) are made up of a multitude of small cells, filled with a kind of starch, which performs an office quite analagous to the *albumen* of an egg, and is sometimes so called. It differs, however, from albumen as found in the egg, and in the serum of the blood, and is a form of *proteine*, not forming a part of the tissues, but contained in cells; as a thin jelly mingled with the juices. In other forms it is called *gluten*, and, with starch, it forms the principal bulk in grains and seeds.

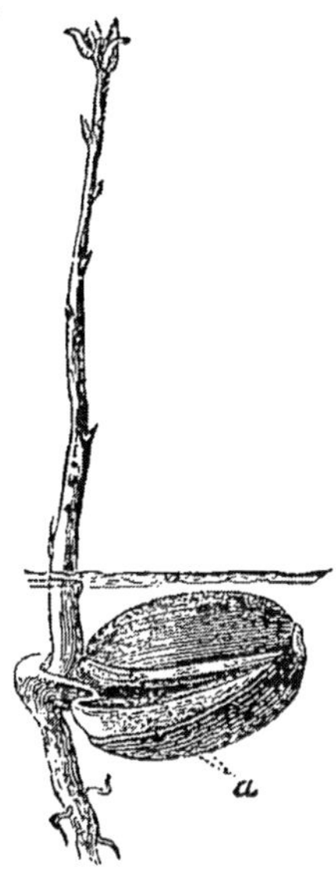

23. An Acorn giving out its Plumule and Radicle.

136. This, absorbing moisture from the soil, and having access to the air and carbonic acid gas in the soil, is changed into sugar, which is soluble in the juices of the young plant, and by the time that this supply is spent, the roots have got well started, and the young tree has all the elements of life that it requires for future growth.

137. There is often a little delay, after the germ has started, before the roots get a sufficient hold upon the soil to draw from it the nourishment necessary for a more rapid growth.

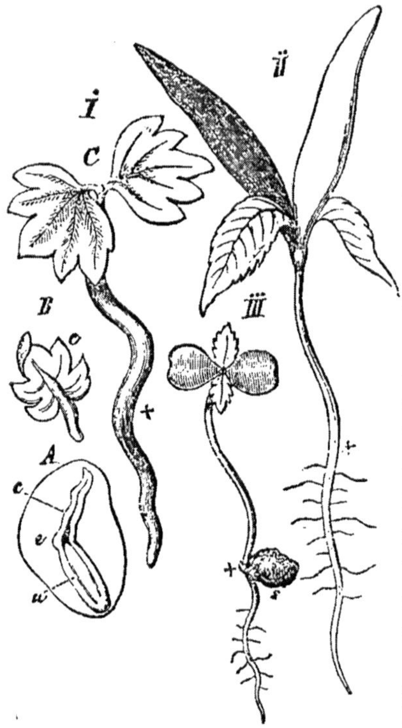

24. Modes of Germination of different kinds of Seeds.

i, *A*, the seed, with germ at *e*, and cotyledons, *a*, and *c*. *B*, a first leaf. *C*, the first pair. *ii*, first leaves of the ash. *iii*, leaves that come out, the external covering of the seed being left in the ground. The cross in each figure shows the place of the earth's surface.

138. In natural planting, the seed falls to the earth when ripe, and scarcely gets covered, excepting by the dead leaves. It sometimes will sprout the first season; but in other cases, as in nuts and stone-fruits, the germination takes place in the spring following, and after exposure to winter rains and in cold climates to the frost. It is a safe rule to follow this example, by planting or sowing the seeds while they are still fresh, and especially those that ripen early the same season.

139. As seeds of trees are liable to lose their vitality by keeping, they should be tested in doubtful cases. If dry and shriveled, they are probably dead. The best way to ascertain whether they are alive or not is to spread them upon flannel, cover them with another piece of flannel, and, after moistening them, place them in a dark and warm place. The proportion that sprout shows the relative quantity that are alive, and sometimes the price paid for tree seeds is governed by the results of this test.

CHAPTER V.

OF THE VARIOUS MODES OF PROPAGATION OF FOREST TREES.

140. In securing the growth of trees in a new grove or woodland, we may obtain plants by either of the following methods:

(1.) From the seeds sown broad-cast or planted where the trees are to grow.

(2.) From seeds first sown in seed-beds or nurseries, or that spring up from natural sowing, and that are transplanted for permanence.

(3.) From cuttings, layers, and other methods of propagation from parts of living trees, and that perpetuate the varieties peculiar to each. These may be separately considered:

1. *Seeds sown Broad-cast or Planted where the Trees are to Grow.*

141. In some species, this is done by nature in a general way, by self-seeding, as in case of the cottonwood, the chief requirement being in the way of preparation, a fresh mellow surface, in the season when the seeds are being scattered by the winds. Upon very steep surfaces, that would be liable to erosion from rains if broken up, the seed may be sown broad-cast, without previously disturbing the soil, and upon northerly slopes this is often done with advantage upon the snow.

142. In establishing a growth of trees upon loose sands, it is also necessary to sow the seeds broad-cast, usually with those of other plants that give them some protection when young; for, in this case, the first fibers of the roots strike deep into the soil, and they can not afterwards be removed without injury.

143. It is generally preferable to plant the seeds in rows, so as to admit of cultivation between the trees while they are small. This may be done by seed-planters, or by hand, as will be more particularly described concerning the several kinds of trees elsewhere described. In planting seeds directly, allowance should be made for loss from deep covering, depredations of birds and insects, and other waste, as well as from defective seeds, and from the various accidents to which the young plants may be exposed. In such cases they should be thinned out from time to time, and often the plants thus taken out may be used in filling up the blank spaces in the rows. In doing this, the hole should be first made, and the plant

with the soil around its roots should be taken up with a hoe or spade, and set in the new place. The "bore-spade," elsewhere described, may be used to advantage for this purpose. [§ 198.]

144. Seeds may be lightly covered with a hoe, or, better still, with an iron rake, which is made for this purpose. This is made

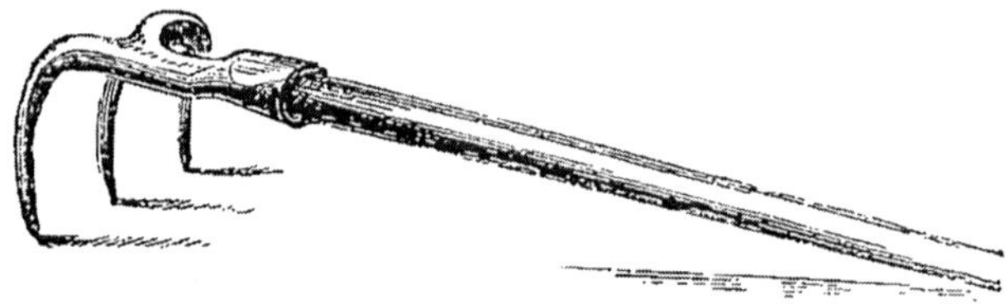

25. Strong Iron Rake for mellowing the Surface and covering Seeds.

of sufficient strength for working among the roots of trees, and is of great use in exposing a fresh surface when we would wish to sow seeds in vacant places in the woods, as well as for surface work generally, where we would wish to freshen the soil without moving it from its place. Another instrument is used to some extent by planters that may perhaps be understood without a figure. It consists of a heavy iron disc, some eight or ten inches across, with a long handle coming up from the center, and a series of long iron spikes on the under side. When this is struck into the ground, and turned around by the aid of a cross-bar in the handle, it mellows the soil on a circular spot as large as the disc, and as deep as the spikes are long. A dibble or pointed stick should never be used in planting seeds, or at least not unless it makes a hole much larger than the seeds and has a guard to regulate the depth. If small, and used carelessly, the seeds may be covered too deep, or they may lodge part way down the hole, leaving a void space under them.

The Planting of Walnut and other Nut-Trees.

145. In a dry climate, and in the fine prairie soil, it is difficult to transplant any of the oaks or nut-trees without great risk of losing them, and it will be generally found better to plant them where they are to remain. In doing so, it is an excellent plan, and sometimes very necessary, to give them in the first years some protection, by the aid of the fast-growing kinds, such as the white willow or the cottonwood, set in alternate places in the rows, and to provide a belt of the latter alone around the outside of the grove.

Soaking of Seeds before Planting.

146. Hard-shelled seeds, such as the common and honey locust, and the Kentucky coffee-tree, etc., will not grow until they have been soaked for some time, and sometimes not till the second or even third year after planting. Their germinating power is hastened by scalding for a short time, and by allowing them to macerate in warm water. The process may be repeated several times, the seeds that show signs of sprouting being first picked out, at each time, before exposing the rest to this treatment. They should be planted without delay; for, if allowed to dry after being once softened, their vitality is soon lost.

2. *Seeds Planted in Seed-Beds and Nurseries.*

147. In selecting grounds for a nursery, we should avoid those that are exceptionally rich, or that are too damp, because the young plants thus started will, when placed in less fertile and dryer grounds, either perish or lose their vigor, and be slow in recovering strength. A hard and barren soil is still more unfavorable, for the plants that start are feeble, and will not endure the hardship of transplanting. The grounds should be of good fertility, moderately compact, and well drained, sheltered from hot and from cold winds, and not exposed to drouth.

148. The soil should be prepared by deep cultivation, and be kept free from weeds. Sometimes this may be done by the cultivation of some hoed crop between the rows of young trees, when they are not liable to be shaded or injured by this practice. The presence of an adjacent woodland will often afford protection, and a stream of water near by will be found very convenient for watering the young plants or for irrigation in a dry time.

149. It is generally best to sow the seeds in beds, laid out in bands about four feet wide, and of indefinite length, with paths between. The seeds are sowed in rows, from six inches to a foot apart, and very close together in the rows. The covering should be light, and only just sufficient to prevent the seeds from being washed out by the rains. They may, with great advantage, be planted in and covered by a soil prepared from dead leaves and decomposed sod.[1]

[1] For preparing this soil, the following directions are given by *Lorentz and Parade:* "Select a shady place, not exposed to the south, but open to

150. The young seedlings of trees generally require shading a part of the time, and this is especially true of the conifers. This may be done by placing screens made of lath, with spaces between as wide as the pieces, and supported a few inches above the surface; or a kind of arbor may be made of poles, over the beds, high enough for a man to stand upright under them, and loosely covered with brush.

151. The object of these screens is to afford the same kind of shelter that the young plants receive under the parent trees in the forest, where the sunlight and shadow alternately passes over them, at different hours of the day.

152. In a dry time the seed-beds should be watered, and upon first sowing they may need the protection of a light covering of brush or grass to keep them from being disturbed by the birds.

153. In watering a seed-bed and nursery rows, in a dry time, the earth should be dampened to a considerable depth, and when begun in dry weather, it must be continued till the rains come; for, otherwise, a crust will form on the surface, which prevents access of the air to the roots. No other mode of watering is so good in a nursery as that of irrigation, especially in preparing young trees for transplanting in cities, and there we wish to secure an abundant mass of fibrous roots.

154. The seed-beds and rows should be kept free of weeds, the former by hand-weeding and the latter by hoeing; but in the part occupied by larger trees it is of less importance, but still necessary.

the sky, so that the air shall have free access; make one or more piles of dead leaves, ferns, and other succulent vegetation gathered before their seeds are ripe, and make other like piles of sods and the weeds pulled up in cleaning out the seed-rows and the alleys between them. These piles may be a yard or a yard and a half high. In spring and fall they should be turned, and in a dry time they should be watered. The sods will generally decay the first year, but it may require three or four years to decompose the leaves. A mixture of beech leaves with the leaves of conifers makes the best possible quality, and the process may be hastened by mixing in the foliage of the ash, maple, elm, willow, poplar, alder, locust, etc., that decay more rapidly. When the seed-beds have been prepared with a mixture of these soils, they will afterwards need but a thin covering every year to maintain the soil in the best state of fertility, and there will be no need of moving to a new place on account of the exhaustion of the soil."—*Culture des Bois*, 5th ed., p. 595.

In soils liable to heave with the frost, the young plants, when thrown out, should be carefully replaced in the spring, and the soil pressed down against the roots by hand.

155. The proper time of sowing in seed-beds is generally in the spring, but the seeds that ripen in the early part of summer, such as the elms and soft maples, should be sown the same season, and as soon as may be after ripening. We give elsewhere directions for the collection and preservation of seeds.

156. Experience has shown that this dense sowing in the seed-rows yields the best results, for the plants are not so liable to be crowded out by the weeds; and although the roots may interlock a little, they easily separate when taken out. The larger plants may be first taken out, leaving the feebler ones until they get stronger.

157. It is remarked by Carrière[1] that the seeds of some conifers very easily loose their germinating power,[2] so that it is desirable that they should be sown as soon as may be after they are ripe; but generally, as they ripen in the fall, they may be kept till spring. With such as have the seed imbedded in a fleshy or pulpy envelope,[3] it requires the greatest care to keep them alive till the next year. In all species the germinating power deteriorates more or less rapidly the longer the seeds are kept. There are great advantages in spring sowing, as is the common practice, and this may be done at any time from March to May. In damp mild seasons, success is certain; but in case of drouth, the young plants are sure to suffer, and in the large way it is impossible to water them. He therefore inquires in a way that half implies advice, as to whether it would not sometimes be best to sow late in autumn, there still being some chance of injury from the cold. This might in many cases still be prevented by a covering of leaves, or, perhaps still better, by sowing oats, barley, or some other grain with the coniferous seeds. These, springing up in the fall, would afford a covering to the young plants sufficient to protect them through the first winter. This sowing of

[1] *Traité général des Conifères*, p. 574.

[2] Such as those belonging to the genera *Abies*, *Araucaria*, *Arthrotaxis*, *Callitris*, *Cryptomeria*, *Cunninghamia*, *Frenela*, *Libocedrus*, *Sequoia*, *Taxodium*, *Thuja*, *Tsuga*, etc.

[3] Such as the *Cephalotaxis*, *Dacrydium*, *Gnetum*, *Podocarpus*, *Salisburia*, *Taxus*, *Torrega*, etc.

grain should be thin, so as not to smother the seedlings that they were intended to protect.

158. Other writers prefer the first heat of spring, for the sowing of conifers, excepting the silver-fir (*Abies pectinata*), which should not be kept over winter, as it quickly looses its life, and can hardly bear transportation for a great distance. In great operations they generally divide the sowing between the fall and spring, and take the chances for and against in each season.

159. In the fall of the same year, or in the spring following, the plants should be taken up carefully from the seed-beds and set in nursery rows. The roots should not be exposed to the air longer than is necessary, and those of conifers suffer much sooner than those of the deciduous kinds. They will always bear longer exposure in autumn than in spring, because the evaporation is then less, and the circulation is suspended. For this reason fall-setting is advised as preferable; but local climate and circumstances may determine one or the other time as the proper one, and in this, experience only can decide.

160. Young trees do best when they are transplanted once or twice in the nursery rows, or when they have been simply loosened and drawn up, to be at once replaced. This should be done only in damp weather.

161. Finally, when of convenient size, and from two to five years of age, the trees should be loosened with a spade-fork, drawn up, and carefully transplanted where they are to remain. If they are to be carried a considerable distance, they must be carefully packed so as to prevent the roots from drying up, yet not so as to entirely exclude the air.

162. It will be seen from the foregoing that the management of a nursery requires practical skill, and unless the proposed plantations are extensive, it will generally be found best to procure the young plants from nurserymen, rather than attempt to raise them from the seed. This is more particularly true of the conifers, that are as a rule more difficult to get started than the deciduous kinds. In extensive plantations, it is always preferable to establish nurseries near the grounds to be planted, as well to avoid the expense of transportation and exposure of roots by removal, as to secure conditions of soil that shall be as nearly as possible alike, so that the young

trees will suffer less from the change, and be in better condition to take a vigorous start.

163. Trees from nurseries should have their roots exposed as little as possible to the air, and they should be planted immediately after they are unpacked. It sometimes happens that lots intended for different persons are sent in one box, to one address. If the owners are not present to receive them, they may lie hours or days in the dry air, and when planted the chances are that none will be found alive. A little common sense and thoughtful care would prevent this disappointment. If the trees can not be at once planted, they should be at least "heeled in," by covering the roots with soil, and dampening it a little if dry. They may be sometimes thus kept through the winter, in cases where from overflow or mirey soil they can not be taken up from the soil where they have been started, in time for early planting.

164. The age at which trees should be set for permanence depends upon soil, exposure, and other circumstances that render it difficult to fix a general rule. For ordinary planting, however, one year in the seed-bed and two years in nursery rows, may be stated as the general rule. But for exposed hillsides, they do better oftentimes when the seedlings one year in the beds, and one year in the rows, or two years in the beds and one in the rows, are taken.

165. In the oak, it has been recommended to cut off the tap-roots with a sharp spade, when the plants are young, and before taking them from the seed-bed. They are allowed to stand the first winter, and when re-set the next spring, in nursery rows, the lateral roots appear abundantly. In time another tap-root will form, which is again cut off before final planting.

166. Another plan recommended by Duhamel consists in paving the seed-bed with flat stones, along the line of the rows, and at a proper depth below the surface, so as to stop the descent of the taproots, and compel the formation of laterals.

167. More recently a method has been proposed in France, for securing a dense growth of lateral roots in the seedling oaks, that has been found quite successful.[1] The acorns are thickly spread over a

[1] M. H. Levret, in a publication by the French Forest Administration, issued in 1878.

The same author suggests another method, which consists in pinching off the plumule within five or six days after it appears, by which the first im-

layer of broken stone, and are covered with as rich a soil as possible and watered. This arrangement secures free access by the air, and the plants send out an abundance of laterals, which extend up into the soil above them, and to but a limited extent downward. By covering a very hard stony surface with a very rich soil, nearly the same result is obtained.[1]

Spring or Fall Transplanting.

168. As to the time of transplanting no general rule may be given. In some countries, as in France, fall planting after the September rains, does best for the deciduous kinds, and spring, at the time when vegetation is just beginning to start, for the conifers, or resinous kinds.

169. When young plants are taken up in the dormant season of vegetation, their roots suffer less from exposure to the air than when the season of active growth is just beginning, and they will then doubtless bear transportation better. There are, in short, both advantages and disadvantages attending both fall and spring planting, and a safe rule would be to experiment upon both in new localities, before definitely adopting either to the exclusion of the other season. It would be unsafe to accept these results as final, until they had been tested for a series of years, because one winter might be unusually open, or a spring or summer exceptionally dry; or some other cause not of ordinary occurrence, may affect a result that would not occur again for many years.

3. *Propagation from Cuttings, Layers, and other Methods.*

Cuttings.

170. If we take healthy and vigorous shoots from the last year's growth, of many deciduous trees, and notably the cottonwood poplars and willows, and thrust them into the ground, they will under favorable conditions put forth roots from the lower end and the buds

pulse of growth is thrown with greater force into the root. He proposes to shade the seed-beds with thin cloth, which admit sufficient light, and all the rain, and prevent damages from frost. Upon the stone seed-beds he would place acorns at the rate of 1,000 to the square meter, or about 840 to a square yard.

[1] See preceding note.

that are covered, and become separate trees. They should only be taken when the leaves are off, and should be set early in spring. The lower end should be cut off smoothly and obliquely, and care should be taken not to injure the bark in setting.

171. If the shoots are cut late in fall and are put away in a damp cellar, or if they are buried below the reach of frost, a callus will form at the lower end, from which the roots will readily spring. In the finely divided soil of the prairies, they should be set deep, and in a dry climate but one or two buds above the surface will be sufficient. The soil should be pressed down firmly around the shoots, at the time of setting, and they should be kept free from weeds till they shade the ground. Cuttings may be set in the fall, if covered with a mulch in winter. This is done with gooseberries, currents, and the grape, but is not so certain as in early spring.

Layers.

172. This method, in common use among nurserymen, is sometimes employed to get an independent root to a branch before separating it from the parent tree. The branch is bent down into a hollow place made in the soil, confined by a peg or a stone and the end turned up, so that the leaves are exposed to the air. It is generally well to partly cut off the branch at the lowest part, leaving the upper half entire. The ground should be kept clear of weeds, and should be watered in a dry time, while the new roots are forming. After they have become well rooted, such plants may be carefully cut apart from the stock, and transplanted like seedling sprouts. This is a very sure and convenient way to perpetuate varieties of fruit and ornamental trees, and is usually done in autumn. It does not apply to coniferous kinds.

Grafting.

173. This is one of the most common and certain ways of perpetuating varieties in fruit and ornamental trees. It is done chiefly in spring, and before the leaves appear, and is most likely to succeed in mild moist weather. The stock should generally be a little more advanced than the scion, and to secure this the latter should be cut in winter, or even in autumn, and kept in a cool moist place, as in a cellar, with the ends set in damp moss or fine soil. They should be taken from thrifty shoots of the last year's growth. If cut from

lower branches, they will fruit sooner, but do not grow to so handsome a shape as those from the center or top of the tree. They are often taken from young trees in nursery rows.

174. There are various modes of grafting, which need not here be described in detail. They agree in bringing the newly cut surfaces of the scion and the stock together, so that the fresh bark and young wood of each are in close contact, the wound covered from the air by some plastic substance, and the parts held together till they unite. This is done by splicing, inserting in a clef, by binding two branches or trunks together, after cutting away the bark and wood of each so that they may be closely united, and in various other ways. Where two living trees are thus united, the connection is cut away from one of them, after the union is complete.

175. *Budding*, is the insertion of the bud of one tree under the bark of another, and covering and securing it till a union forms. It is done in midsummer and early autumn, from the 1st of July till the middle of September, and only when the bark of the stock will separate from the wood. Annular budding consists in taking a ring of bark from one tree, containing a bud, and placing it around a branch of the same size, from which a similar piece of bark has been taken in another tree. Sometimes a piece less than the entire size is inserted. By this means the injuries to bark by mice, etc., may sometimes be repaired.

176. By the aid of cuttings, grafts, and layers, we are able to secure the growth of some kinds of trees that never bear seed in the climate where they may be grown by transplanting, and especially we may perpetuate varieties to indefinite extent by these methods.

177. As examples of this, we find the Lombardy poplar, the weeping willow, and cut-leaved varieties of the birch, alder, beech, maple, etc., under cultivation, that would be lost in a single generation of tree-life, if they depended upon growth from the seeds. The sumac, so successfully grown in Southern Europe, does not ripen its seeds, even in Sicily, where it grows to the greatest perfection; and the English elm (*Ulmus campestris*) is almost always grown from layers, or suckers, taken from old trees, or by grafting upon other stocks. It may even be grown in moist rich soils, by burying the chips having bark with buds upon them, if these are cut in early spring, and planted at once before drying.

CHAPTER VI.

PLANTING.—(*Continued.*)

The Interval between Trees in Planting.

178. Upon a rocky and broken surface, no attention need be given to the regularity of spaces, the most convenient spots being taken wherever found, and often different species, as places best suited for their growth occur. But in a level, or moderately uneven country, there are great advantages to be gained from planting at fixed intervals. We will notice some of the methods that may be followed:

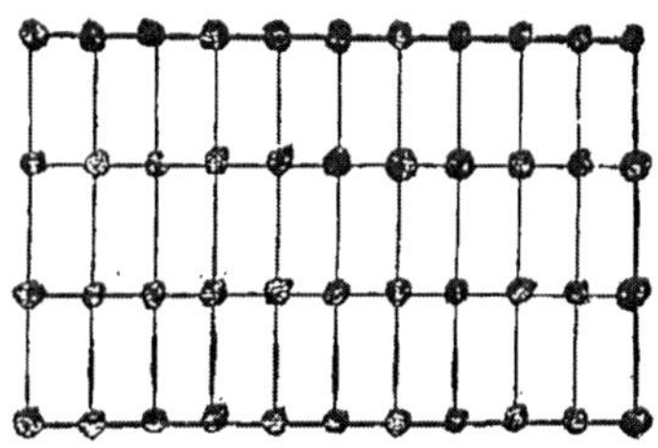

26. Mode of Marking for Trees Planted in Rows.

Planting in Rows.

179. In this, the intervals may be wider apart in one direction than in the other. The rows may be from 4 to 8 feet or more apart at first, and the trees in the rows from 3 to 6 feet. The advantages of this are, that the spaces between can be cultivated more easily for the first years, and by taking out alternate rows, as the trees become crowded, we can pass in between the trees in removing the products.

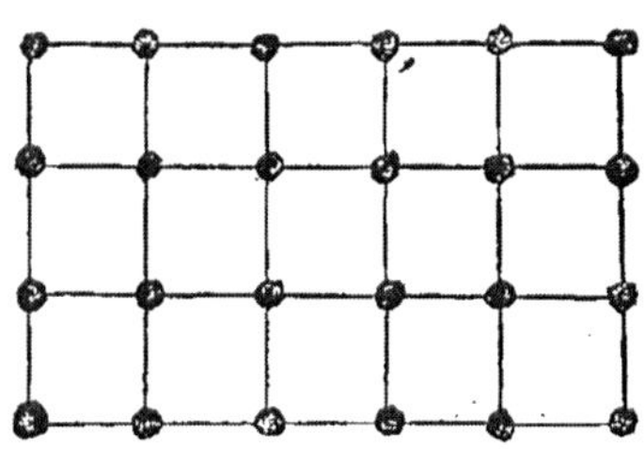

27. Mode of Marking for Trees Planted in Squares.

Planting in Squares.

180. In this, the spaces are at equal distances in both directions; and in this, as in the preceding, regularity may be secured by marking the ground after it is prepared, and by planting at all the intersections of the right-angled lines, omitting none.

Quincunx Order.

181. Here the trees are set at the corners of squares and in the central point within. The trees range in rows horizontally, vertically, and diagonally, and if the trees in the former are 10 meas-

ures apart, the diagonals will be slightly more than 14. This regularity is best secured by marking the ground off into small squares, and planting in alternate points of intersection each way, as shown in the margin. (Fig. 29.)

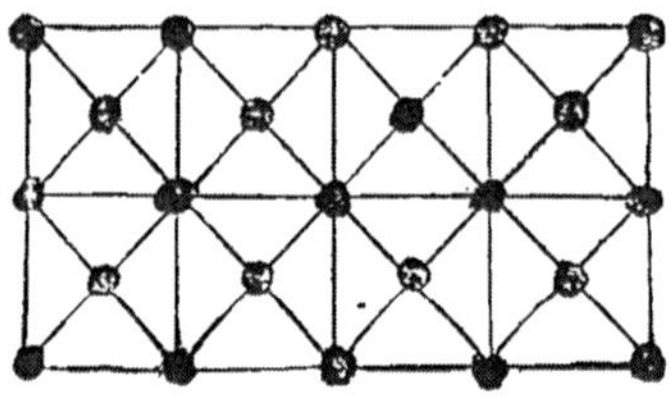

28. Mode of Planting in Quincunx Order.

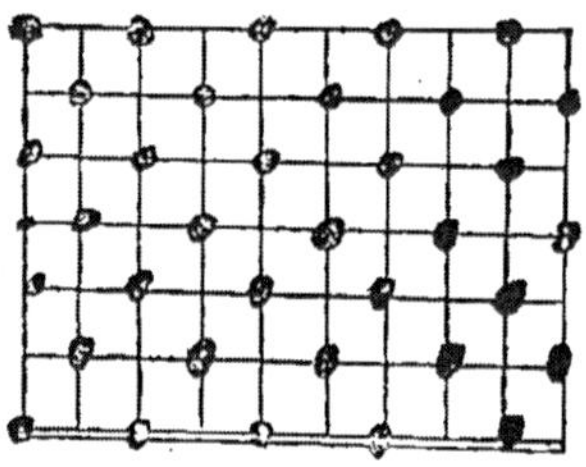

29. Mode of Marking for Quincunx Planting.

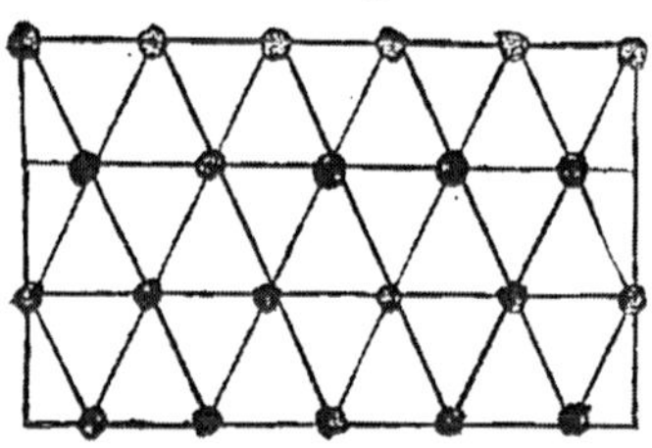

30. Triangular Order of Planting.

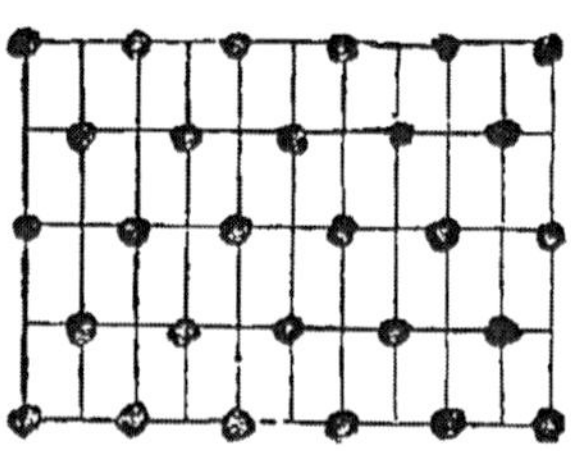

31. Mode of Parallel Marking to secure the Triangular Order.

The Triangular Order.

182. In this, the rows run in three directions, the trees being at equal distances in each at the corners of equilateral triangles; or, combining six of these triangles, we find that each tree is the center of a hexagon, with six trees at equal distances around it. We get the same arrangement by drawing a series of circles having equal radii, and so that the circumference of each passes through the centers of all of those around it. We nearly secure this in a practical way, by marking off a field by parallel lines, crossing at right angles, and at twice the distance apart in one direction more than in the other. If we plant at the alternate points of intersection, we shall have the triangular order. By plowing in the three directions between the rows, such plantations may be cultivated in the same way as squares, but the rows must be wider apart in order to do this to advantage.

183. *Number of Trees that may be set upon a Piece of Land* 100 *Yards Square on a side, in Right-angled Rows of equal and unequal Distances apart.*

Yards between Trees in the Rows. . . .	Yards between Rows.									
	1.0	1.5	2.0	2.5	3.0	3.5	4.0	4.5	5.0	5.5
0.5	20,000	13,333	10,000	8.000	6,667	5,714	5,000	4.444	4,000	3,636
1.0	10,000	6,667	5.000	4.000	3,333	2.857	2.500	2,222	2;000	1,818
1.5	6.667	4,444	3,333	2,667	2.222	1,905	1,667	1,481	1.333	1,212
2.0	5,000	3.333	2,500	2,000	1,667	1,429	1,250	1,111	1,000	909
2.5	4,000	2.667	2,000	1,600	1,333	1,143	1,000	889	800	727
3.0	3,333	2,222	1,667	1,333	1,111	952	833	741	667	606
3.5	2,857	1,905	1,429	1,143	952	816	714	635	571	519
4.0	2,500	1,667	1,250	1,000	833	714	625	556	500	455
4.5	2,222	1,481	1,111	889	741	635	556	494	444	404
5.0	2,000	1,333	1,000	800	667	571	500	444	400	364
5.5	1,818	1,212	909	727	606	519	455	404	364	333
6.0	1,667	1,111	833	667	556	476	417	370	333	303
6.5	1,538	1,026	769	615	513	440	385	342	308	280
7.0	1,429	952	714	571	476	408	357	317	286	260
7.5	1,333	889	667	533	444	381	333	296	267	242
8.0	1.250	833	625	500	417	357	313	278	250	227
8.5	1,176	784	588	471	392	336	294	261	235	219
9.0	1,111	741	556	494	370	317	278	247	222	202
10.0	1,000	667	500	400	333	286	250	222	200	100

In this table we may substitute any other denomination of linear measure in place of *yards.*

184. *Comparison between the Numbers set in Squares and in Quincunx Order.*

Yards * between Trees.........	In Squares or Rows at Right Angles	In Triangular or Quincunx Order	Yards between Trees.........	In Squares or Rows at Right Angles	In Triangular or Quincunx Order	Yards between Trees.........	In Squares or Rows at Right Angles........	In Triangular or Quincunx Order ....
0.5	4,0000	46,188	3.5	816	943	6.5	237	273
1.0	1,0000	11,547	4.0	625	722	7.0	204	236
1.5	4.444	5,132	4.5	494	570	7.5	178	205
2.0	2,500	2,887	5.0	400	462	8.0	156	180
2.5	1,600	1,848	5.5	333	382	9.0	123	143
3.0	1,111	1,283	6.0	278	321	10.0	100	115

*We may substitute any other unit of linear measure, as in preceding table. It will be seen that a little over 15 per cent is gained in number by the quincunx arrangement.

185. *Number of Trees required to Plant an Acre of Land in Squares, or in Rows at Right Angles, and at equal Distances apart both ways.*

Feet between Rows.	Number of Trees.	Feet between Rows.	Number of Trees.	Feet between Rows.	Number of Trees.	Feet between Rows.	Number of Trees.
1.0	43,560	7.0	889	13.0	257	19.0	120
1.5	19,360	7.5	779	13.5	239	19.5	114
2.0	10,890	8.0	680	14.0	222	20.0	108
2.5	6,970	8.5	603	14.5	207	22.0	90
3.0	4,840	9.0	537	15.0	193	24.0	75
3.5	3,556	9.5	482	15.5	181	26.0	64
4.0	2,722	10.0	435	16.0	170	28.0	55
4.5	2,151	10.5	395	16.5	164	30.0	48
5.0	1,742	11.0	360	17.0	150	40.0	27
5.5	1,440	11.5	339	17.5	142	50.0	17
6.0	1,210	12.0	302	18.0	134	....	....
6.5	1,031	12.5	270	18.5	127	....	....

The Necessity of Close Planting.

186. As a general rule, all trees growing in an open space have a tendency to spread out laterally, and not to grow as high as where they are surrounded by other trees. This tendency to branch from near the ground is greater in a dry climate and in places exposed to strong winds. It is therefore a common practice among skilled foresters to plant the trees much nearer together than they could stand when mature, and thin them out as they become larger.

187. We see this thinning-out process going on naturally in the native woods, where the stronger shade out and kill off the feebler, so that but a few of the many that started as seedlings come to maturity. It is best to do this at proper times, without waiting for this dying, and, as a general rule, it should be done at stated times and throughout a given piece of woodland at about the same time. If delayed too long, the stems of the trees will be slender and feeble. If done too soon, the effect of shade in carrying up the tree is lost. No fixed rules can be given for thinning, and the judgment of the forester with the conditions before him should be the principal guide. As a general fact, the conifers require less space than deciduous trees.

188. It is an excellent practice in the planting of valuable kinds, that we wish to have grow straight and high, to place them in alternate rows, and in alternate places in the rows, with other trees of more rapid growth, but it may be of less value. The latter may be taken out when their shelter and protection are no longer needed,

and when the kinds we wish to preserve have grown so as to soon shade the whole of the ground.

189. The oak is found to thrive exceedingly well while young when thus surrounded by pines. The willow and the cottonwood are excellent nurses for other trees, such as the walnut and the ash. In alternate rows of willows and walnuts, the latter were found at four years' growth at Lincoln, Nebraska, to be from three to five feet high and very thrifty, while in a full exposure to the sun they were but eighteen inches high and very scrubby.

The Planting of Young Trees from the Forest.

190. In transplanting native seedlings from the woods, we should select those that are somewhat separate from the rest, and best exposed to the air and light. If taken from a dense shade into the full light of day, the change may be too severe, even where the utmost care is taken to prevent exposure of the roots to the air—a precaution in which we can not be too careful.

191. The roots should be at once dipped in a puddle of rich soil, and packed in a box, standing upright, but not too close, and only one course in a box. They should not be too closely covered from the air, and should be set with as little delay as possible in nursery rows, or for permanence, the place being previously well prepared. Wild conifers should be cultivated two or three years before final setting. The process of taking them from their native place is much more likely to succeed when the air is humid, as in foggy and lowering weather, and is greatly jeopardized by a cold dry wind.

192. The trees taken small, and with an abundance of fibrous roots, are much more likely to succeed than those of a large size. They will get a better start, and in a few years equal and surpass those that were transplanted at a more advanced age. In most kinds, it is necessary to shorten the branches so that they may bear some proportion to the root. It is a good plan to cover the wounds with coal-tar or paint, but quite often the buds start out and branches form at some distance from the ends, which dry up and finally break off. It is a very common thing to see maple and other trees set from the woods with a dead stick coming out among the lower branches, it being the top of the original tree. These should be broken or cut off close to the trunk, so as to allow the wood on the side to grow over them. If too large, and left too long, they

may cause a rotten cavity to form, tending to make the tree hollow and short-lived.

193. In transplanting the oaks and some other hard woods, where the growth is languishing and the shoot is small, it is an excellent plan to cut off the stem near the ground, after the root has got started. This is best done when the leaves are off, in fall or winter. The shoot that comes up in such cases from the root will grow vigorously and much more rapidly than if left as before.

194. In "*grub-prairies*," in the Northwestern States, the soil is full of the roots of trees and bushes, often of the jack-oak, hazel, etc., that have been killed back to the roots by annual fires. They will sprout and grow if protected from cattle and from fires, and gradually other kinds will come in, displacing the first inferior kinds and forming a forest of more valuable trees. The change thus produced in twenty years in Wisconsin and Minnesota, where these grub-prairies are chiefly found, is sometimes remarkable.

Planting on the Sod.

195. In loose and very damp soils, it is sometimes found advantageous to plant wholly upon the surface, by simply spreading out the roots and turning the surrounding soil over them, so as to form a little conical mound. The soil thus heaped up around the trees is then covered, if convenient, with mosses or other non-conducting substances, and on the outside some inverted sod.

196. The trees thus set should have no tap root. An abundance of fine fibrous roots may be secured to help the first growth by sifting well-rotted leaf-mold over the roots as they are placed. From careful observation it is found that these mounds retain the heat of the day and cool slower in the night—that the evaporation from them is less than from flat surfaces, and that there is a perceptible disengagement of carbonic acid gas in the interior from the decomposition going on in the grass and other herbage that is covered. This method enables us to plant in places with less drainage, by raising the roots a little higher.

The Transplanting of young Trees without Disturbing the Fibers of the Roots.

197. The exposure of the roots of seedlings to the air, and especially to the sun and to dry winds, is generally to be avoided as

much as possible, and conifers are particularly sensitive in this respect. If the fibers of their roots are once dry, they are generally injured beyond remedy. In handling young evergreen seedlings, if there is an interruption of the work but for a short time, the roots should be covered with earth, or some other protection should be given them for retaining their moisture and preventing evaporation.

198. This sensitiveness of roots to the air has led to various devices for removing young trees and small seedlings without disturbing the roots. A "bore-spade" was invented many years ago by Dr. Heyer, of Giessen, for the purpose of transplanting young pines, and is often used in Europe for this purpose. It consists simply of a spade, with the blade bent almost into a cylindrical form, and from four to six inches across on the inside. The side opposite the handle is open, so as pass it around the young tree. It is then pressed down with the foot and turned around, loosening and including the roots and all the soil around them, which may then be set in its new place, if not distant, without the least disturbance of the soil within. Several thousand plants may be set from a seed-bed to nursery rows in a day with this simple instrument.

199. The patent office records in Washington contain various other devices for this object, in some of which two concave blades are connected, so as to act as pincers, to embrace a cylindrical ball of earth around the roots, and compress it as it is raised.

200. A simple contrivance consisting of four spades is sometimes used, in which the blades are pressed down inside of a frame serving as a fulcrum, and the handles are spread apart and fastened by pins in cross-pieces passing through their handles, as shown in the engraving in the margin. All of these methods are limited in their application to young trees, and to those that are to be carried but short distances. In the one last described, two sides of the frame that form the fulcrum are extended out into handles, so that the whole may be carried by two men, like a burden on a hand-barrow. In light and dry sandy soil, none of them would prevent the

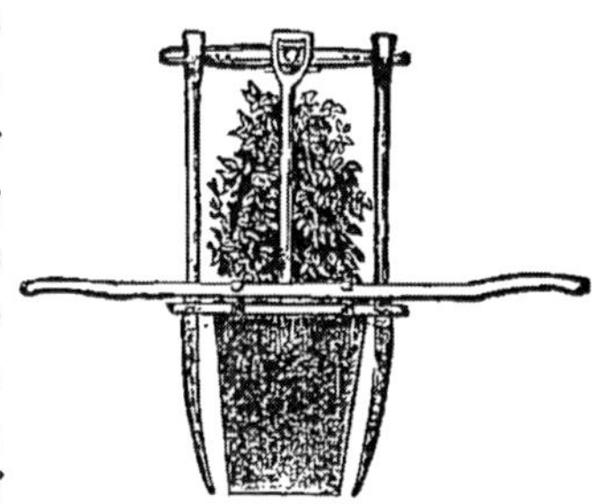

32. Four Spades in a portable Frame for removing the Soil with the Roots in transplanting small Trees.

sand from escaping, and only the methods described in §§ 202 or 203 could be employed.

201. For larger trees, an excavation may be made, leaving a mass of earth, nearly cylindrical, but rather smaller below, still in place and undisturbed around the roots, and this may be bound with hoops, or with coarse cloths, so as to keep the soil in place until the removal is finished. We notice, in §§ 205 and 206, other methods in speaking of the removal of large trees.

202. For young seedlings of cinchonas and other trees difficult to transplant, it is the custom in India to start the seeds in pieces of bamboo filled with rich soil, and at first set as close together as they can stand, for better management in sprouting. In this way they may be watered, shaded, and otherwise attended, as found necessary, and until they have grown to a size that will enable them to stand open exposure in the free air. They are then taken up, with the bamboo shell still upon them, and set for permanence, the roots soon finding their way through, as the shell decays. These shells are three or four inches in diameter, and prove amply sufficient when cut in lengths of five or six inches. The coffee-trees in Brazil are started in earthern jars, so constructed that they can be carried to the place of planting in the field, and the contents then transferred entire to the ground where the trees are to grow.

203. Slightly-made baskets of strong paper, reeds, bark, rushes, or thick wood-shavings, would answer the same purpose, if made of perishable material, sufficiently strong to last till the removal. By this means, with careful packing and handling, seedling plants can be transported safely to considerable distances. The expense would, however, limit its application to experimental plantations in the way of acclimatization, or to the propagation of trees for ornamental or special purposes.

204. Seeds started in wooden boxes, large enough to hold a dozen or two of seedlings, may be kept together for watering and attendance, occupying no more space than so many plants in a seed-bed, and then may be carried to the place where the plants are to be set. With proper care, they may be taken out with a curved trowel, and set without disturbing the soil. Slight shaving or pasteboard partitions, dividing the box into compartments, would facilitate the separation, and prevent the fibers from interlocking. This method is employed in planting the eucalyptus trees in the unhealthy district

near the city of Rome. By any of these methods of carrying the plants with the soil still around the roots, the operation of planting may be carried on all summer, and where the climate permits, at all seasons of the year.

The Transplanting of Large Trees.

205. This is always an expensive and uncertain operation, particularly with the evergreens. It is sometimes done with much success, where the tree is well supplied with fibrous roots near the trunk, by digging a trench around the tree at some distance, in the fall, and allowing the soil to freeze into a solid mass, which may be moved without separating it from the roots. In such cases, it is sometimes practiced to take off the surface soil, if not already rich, and to spread in its place other soil of great fertility, and to dig and fill the trench, as above described, with rich soil, a year or two before the time of removal. An abundance of fine fibrous roots will form in such cases in the fertile soil, which will tend to render the removal more certain of success.

206. In removing large evergreens, it is best done just as the vegetation is starting, by carefully following out and taking up the roots as far as possible, and wrapping them up in wet moss or hay as fast as they are taken out. When they have been thus taken from the soil, and protected from the air, the tree may be drawn to its new place, set upright, and well stayed; the covering should then be removed from the roots, which should be carefully spread out and immediately covered with fine rich damp soil. The whole should be well watered as soon as the planting is finished, and from time to time in dry weather, until the roots have got well started.

207. It is generally a good rule, and in light prairie soil absolutely necessary, to press down the earth firmly, not only in the hole before the tree is placed, but also upon the roots after planting; but in heavy clay soils this would do more harm than good. As a rule, the tree should be set deeper than before. The roots should not be cramped or doubled back, but as wide a space should be allowed as they may need, and they should be carefully spread before being covered.

208. In bracing trees, strong wire is better than cords, which are apt to shrink when wet, and blocks of wood should be placed where they are fastened to the tree, to prevent them from galling the bark.

Heavy stones placed over the roots will sometimes serve to keep them steady, as well as to keep the soil from drying. A mulching of straw or litter from the woods is always useful, and sometimes necessary, to keep the ground moist, and to screen it from the sun. Decaying wood-chips afford a most excellent top-dressing around trees of every kind.

209. Trees should be kept free from weeds and grass. A firm sod prevents the air and rains from penetrating the soil. A thin covering of stable manure over the roots of trees in winter will have an excellent effect upon the next year's growth. Various mineral salts, such as the nitrate of soda, and the phosphate of lime, as well as guano and other fertilizers, may sometimes be used to great advantage in nurseries and orchards, and in ornamental plantations generally, but are usually too expensive for profitable forest-culture.

The Disadvantages of Planting Cottonwood, and other Trees, from Cuttings of too great Size.

210. In the Western States, in Colorado and elsewhere, it has been the custom to set out poles of cottonwood, and of some of the other poplars and the willows, of considerable size, and without root or branch. In some cases, telegraph poles of cottonwood have thus taken root and become trees, where the soil was damp and all the conditions of growth were favorable.

211. But it has been found that such trees generally become hollow in a few years, and are short lived. The reason is obvious. The end in the ground readily absorbs moisture and decays, for it can never grow over like the wound formed on the trunk, after the amputation of a branch, and will remain exposed to all the agencies that cause decay, however vigorous the new growth may be around it. The top of such a pole will become dry, and the buds that start from the sides will come out at some distance below the end. This dead part finally become quite rotten, leaving a cavity that gradually extends down the trunk till it meets the one that is coming up from below. The success that such trees promise for the first few years is generally illusory, and it would be much more satisfactory to take smaller cuttings, which would, when well supplied with moisture, make a very rapid growth, and remain sound throughout. They might even overtake and surpass those that were planted of

large size, and they will certainly outlive them in almost every instance.

Planting of Rocky Surfaces.

212. It is one of the peculiar merits of Forest-culture, that it may be practiced upon broken and rocky surfaces that could not be plowed, or scarcely pastured, provided always that there is depth and quantity of soil among the stones, and in the crevices, to give a hold to the roots of the trees, and moisture enough in the soil to afford them adequate support.

213. No general rule can be given for the starting of woodlands upon such surfaces, where so much depends upon the circumstances. In doing this, it is well to study the indications afforded by nature, in the casual growth of trees in the region around, or the experience gained by artificial planting. The yield in growth of wood upon such stony surfaces may sometimes be equal to that upon smooth level land, and return a fair profit, where nothing else could be raised.

214. In planting upon a hill-side of moderate declivity, it is generally preferable to plow the land and to set the rows of trees in lines parallel with the base, or at right angles with the slope. The reason of this is, that the soil becomes less exposed to the wash of the rains, when so cultivated. The water from rains and melting snows is held in place, and tends to sink into the earth, instead of running off on the surface.

215. Upon very steep declivities of friable and decomposing rock, it is sometimes practicable to secure sufficient soil for the roots of trees, by digging horizontal terraces or notches at convenient intervals, securing their outer edge with brush held in place with pegs. In a year or two these notches will have probably become filled up by the crumbling away of the rock above, and in the soil thus formed trees may be planted with a prospect of success.

216. This form of planting becomes necessary in restoring a wooded covering to eroded mountain sides. Besides its use in reboisement, as described on a subsequent page, it might sometimes be used with advantage to secure the soil upon crumbling banks that overhang highways and railroads, and in other situations where danger may be expected from the sliding or washing of the soil.

Mulching.

217. In transplanting trees in a dry season, and especially in a dry climate, it is often necessary to place on the surface a covering of straw, litter, or other porous material, to protect the ground from the heating and drying influences of the sun and the winds. It also has an effect in preventing the growth of grass and other herbage, and to retain the moisture of rains. In a very dry climate, it may be found the only means by which trees may be made to survive the trial of the first one or two seasons, and it may need to be continued until the ground is well shaded.

It was found on the college farm at Lincoln, Nebraska, that the soft maple grew in much more regular shape, and more thriftily, when planted singly and for shade trees, where the ground around them was well covered with mulching, and the stems protected by wild grass or other substances tied around them to keep off the sun. When not so treated, the tops grew one-sided, and the trees soon died. Examples might be multiplied indefinitely to prove the benefits to be derived from this practice, both in regard to fruit and forest trees. Of course, when this becomes an absolute requirement of the climate, the cultivation of forests for profit is wholly unprofitable, and it must be limited to orchards and ornamental planting.

Of Thinning.

218. As elsewhere repeatedly stated, trees should be made to form a straight and tall body while young, by being somewhat closely planted, but should not be allowed to crowd too closely. A part must be taken out from time to time, to give the remainder a chance at the air and light. It should begin when we see it is needed, and is best done at one time for a given piece of woodland, rather than irregularly. The intervals of time must be regulated by circumstances, and should be greater as the trees become large. The only general rule to be followed is, that the trees should not be allowed to interlock their branches, and that the ground should be at all times well shaded. The effect is realized within a year or two in the vigorous growth of the branches that hasten to fill up the void spaces thus formed, and in the increased volume of the wood that is formed.

Trimming and Pruning.

219. Where forests are cultivated on a large scale, and for profit, nothing can be done in the way of pruning. This must be left to natural agencies, and if a proper density of growth is maintained, it will take care of itself. But in small groves, and especially in avenues of trees by the roadside, or plantations around dwellings, or in village streets and city parks, the growth and appearance of the trees may be greatly improved by judicious attention.

220. It is preferable to cut off a branch close to the tree, rather than to leave a stub. The incision should be left as smooth as possible, and it is of great advantage to cover the wound with coal tar. If left to rot off, the branch may form a wound like the one shown on the left-hand side of the annexed cut; but if smoothly cut off, it may close up completely in a few years. These cavities may extend down to the root, and they not only shorten the life of a tree, but tend to render its timber worthless. Where large cavities are thus formed in a favorite tree, the injury may be somewhat delayed by covering the opening with heavily painted canvas or other material that will conceal somewhat the deformity, and keep out the rain.

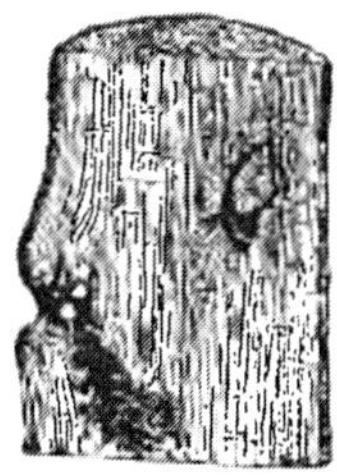

33. A Wound well healed and one badly healed in Timber.

221. In cutting off large branches, it is necessary to first make an incision on the under side, so as to prevent it from tearing down the side of the tree as it falls. The annexed cut, at *A* and *B*, shows the way this can be done. After the branch is off, the stump can be smoothed off, so as to leave a clean incision. It is found very advantageous to apply coal tar to such wounds.

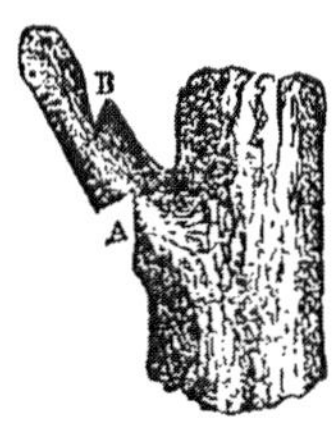

34. Proper Mode of cutting off Large Branches.

222. The season of the year has much to do with the success of pruning. It should generally be done after the growth of the season has been formed, and close to the trunk. If left in pegs, they will disfigure the tree, and heal over with difficulty. The unsightly growth shown in the

35. Tree that has been pruned late in Summer.

annexed engraving is very common in the button-wood, when carelessly pruned, or otherwise injured.

36. A Tree that has been Pruned some distance from the Trunk.

223. As for dead branches, such as we often see on the lower part of the trunks of coniferous trees, they may be cut at all seasons, and the sooner the better, if we would improve the quality of their wood. It becomes, however, in extensive woodlands an expensive process, and practically it must be left to nature, excepting in a favorite grove, or in avenues or upon lawns.

224. In all forest operations, it is needless to remark, that the use of climbing spurs, like those employed in repairing telegraphs, must be wholly forbidden, as they do irreparable injuries to the bark and the wood, and the laws should protect owners from their unauthorized use by any one, upon any occasion.

225. The tools most used in pruning are the saw, with a wide set, hand-shears, pruning-shears, pruning-chisels, attached to long handles, with an edge that cuts in drawing as well as in pushing, the common ax, and various other implements. A tool much used in France is the *serpe*, which consists of a heavy blade, with both edges sharp, and attached to a short handle. It is carried in a leather case, slung over the shoulder, and is used very skillfully. For small branches, they cut by an upward stroke.

37. Hand-Shears, for Pruning.

38. Pruning-Shears, for attaching to a long Handle.

39. The Serpe.

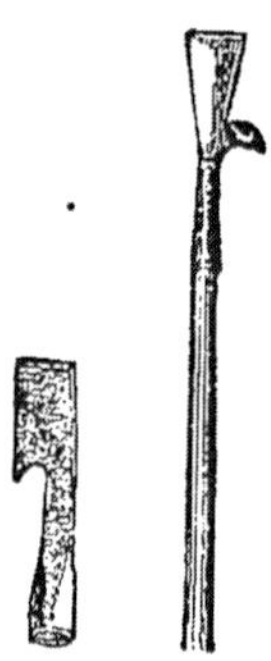

40. Pruning Chisels.

226. In trimming poplars and willows, the whole top of the tree is sometimes cut off. Such trees are called "*Pollards.*" They should be cut off just above where the lower branches separate, and not as shown in the middle figure by the line at *A*. Such trees will restore themselves without showing the effect of the injury, as shown in the right-hand figure, if properly cut. The practice tends to render

trees hollow and unsightly objects, but in some cases it is not without advantages. Along the Rio Grande Valley, in New Mexico, it

41. Improper Mode of Cutting Pollards.

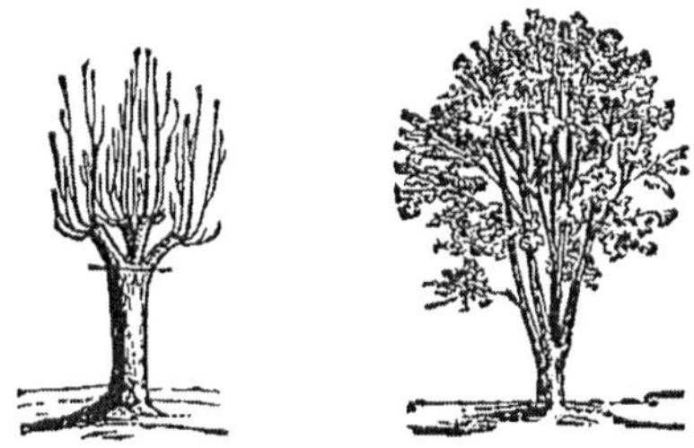

42, 43. Proper Modes of Cutting Pollards.

has long been the practice to thus cut back the tops of cottonwoods in order to obtain fuel.

227. A great advantage is gained in some cases by fore-shortening the branches by trimming off their ends, so as to give the top a more symmetrical form, and a denser growth. This practice has been very fully described, and its advantages shown by the Count Des Cars, in France, and previously by the Viscount de Courval. When applied to the oak, it has sometimes led to remarkable success in growth, and in ornamental planting it may be sometimes applied to great advantage.[1]

228. In Italy the olive is thus cut back to secure a more vigorous growth of the young wood, and the trunk often becomes hollow, but it will survive the injuries for a long time. The marbled and gnarled appearance of the grain of this wood, as often seen in ornamental work, is chiefly from this cause. The knotted heads of pollard poplar trunks are sometimes cut into thin plates for fancy work, and produce a beautiful effect.

229. An upright growth may be secured by lopping off the side branches, and bending the more promising ones upright, securing by a pole lashed to the tree, or driven into the ground, and sometimes by binding one branch around another, as shown in the adjacent cuts.

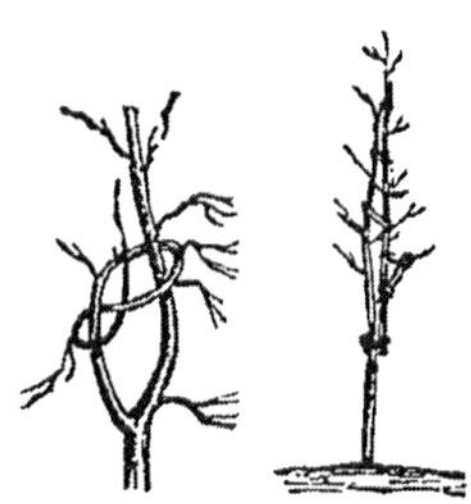

44. Modes of securing an Upright Growth.

[1] Full accounts of this method and its results may be found in our first Report upon Forestry (1877), pp. 92, 93, 98.

Stimulation of the Growth of Trees by removal of outer Bark.

230. Sometimes the peeling off of the outer bark of fruit trees will stimulate their growth. The operation should be performed just as the cambium layer is forming, which is generally in the latter part of June, in the Northern States. The cork tree is found in Southern Europe to thrive under peeling, and where elms in Paris and elsewhere have been shaved down to the live bark, in the Robert process, for destroying the larvæ of insects, they have taken a new start afterwards.

Arbor Days.

231. A pleasant custom was introduced in Nebraska, about 1874, at the instance of the State Horticultural Society, of devoting one day in spring to the planting of trees. The 2d Wednesday of April was designated, and it is claimed that 12 millions of trees were set on that day in that state. In Minnesota, the State Forestry Association designated the 18th Tuesday of May for this purpose, and 1876, 1,342,886 trees were reported as planted on that day. In the Year following, the number was 442,558. The Governor of Michigan, by proclamation dated February 22, 1876, recommended that the 15th of April be devoted to planting trees, but we have no data as to the result. The Governor of Ohio appointed an Arbor Day to be observed on the 27th of April, 1882.

231½. The custom is admirable as far as it goes, but it is liable to interruption from stormy weather, or seasons unusually early or backward, and in the granting of premiums for greatest number, or best success, it would be much better to have them apply to the *whole season*, leaving the day to be fixed by the planter as suited his convenience, and as weather favored.

CHAPTER VII.

OF THE STRUCTURE AND FUNCTIONS OF THE VARIOUS PARTS OF GROWING TREES.

The Formation and Functions of the Buds.

232. In common deciduous trees, there begins to form, in midsummer, in the axils of the leaves, a little cellular mass, communicating with a medullary ray, partly covered by the bark, and usually protected by imbricating scales. From these buds or germs, the leaves and blossoms of the next season are to grow. The leaf-buds are usually more sharp and slender than the flower-buds, a circumstance quite noticeable upon the elm, and upon many fruit trees.

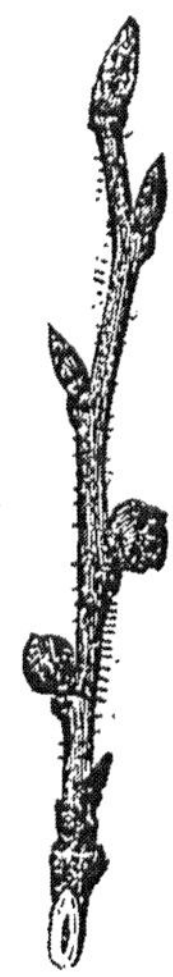

45. Buds of the Elm.

233. The end of a twig is *always* terminated by a bud, which advances as the twig extends in length, by the formation of new cells within. Trees and their branches increase in length and height by the formation of these new cells under the terminal bud; and elongate only during the season of active vegetation, in spring and early summer. The annexed engravings, from Rossmassler, represent sections of four kinds of buds. The first is a double one of leaf and flower, and the fourth is a flower-bud only. It will be seen that the rudiments of the future

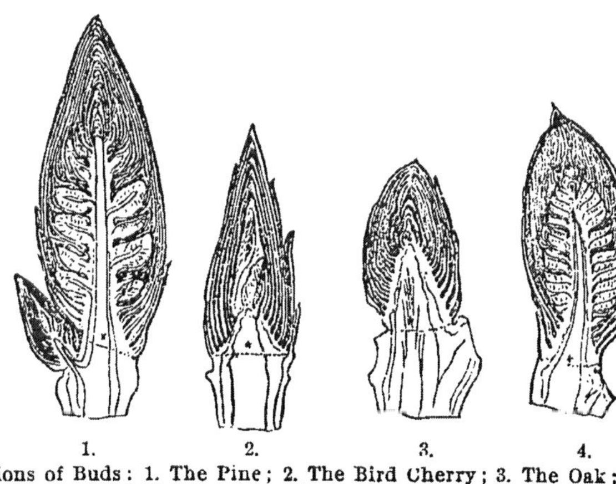

1. 2. 3. 4.

46. Sections of Buds: 1. The Pine; 2. The Bird Cherry; 3. The Oak; and, 4. The Aspen.

growth are obscurely foreshadowed in these embryo forms, to be displayed in full maturity, when the conditions favor—usually in spring, but exceptionally in autumn. The latter cases are rare, and occur only when a very dry summer is followed by a very mild, humid autumn.

Structure and Function of the Leaves.

234. Leaves are the respiratory organs of plants. The juices are there brought in contact with the air, when certain chemical changes occur that fit them for the processes of assimilation that transform them into every part of the growing tree or plant.

235. Trees present an infinite variety of forms in their leaves, but may be divided into two great classes: the linear, or acicular form (sometimes shortened into imbricating scales), that distinguish the coniferous order, and, with a few exceptions, remain green during the winter; and the broad-leaved form, supported by a network of ribs, and, in temperate and cold climates, generally falling from the trees upon the approach of winter. The latter are termed *deciduous*, when they fall from the trees in autumn, but this term also applies to a small number of the linear-leaved class, such as the larch and the bald cypress. A leaf-stem is called a *petiole*, and when there is no stem the leaf is said to be *sessile*.

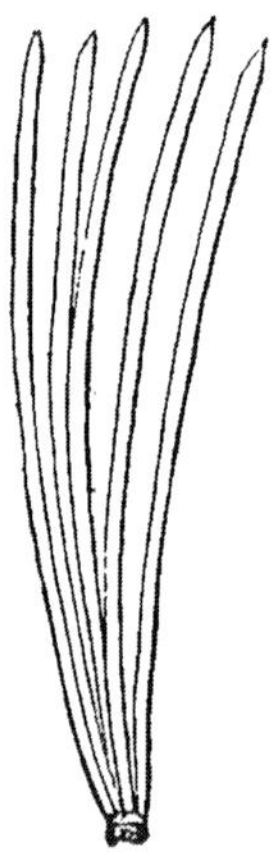

47. Leaves of the Pine.

48. Leaf of the Mulberry.

236. The framework of a leaf is filled in with a cellular structure, and these cells are filled with a green matter, in the form of small grains, called *chlorophyll*, and which, appearing through the transparent walls of the cells, give the leaves their green color. In most leaves, the upper side is more charged with chlorophyll than the lower, and is therefore of a deeper green. The form of these cells in the beech leaf are shown in the annexed engraving,[1] in which *oo* is the upper side, and *uu* the under side; *o*, the principal

[1] From Rossmassler.

cells of chlorophyll; *l* are air spaces; *u*, minute masses of chlorophyll, thus brought in near contact; and *sp*, "*stomata*," or breathing pores, through which the air enters. These pores are chiefly

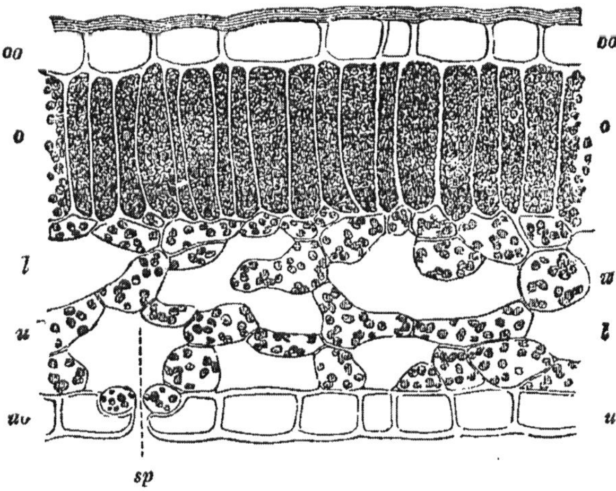

49. Vertical Section of a Beech Leaf, very greatly enlarged.

on the under side of the leaf, and vary in number from 1,000 to 170,000 to a square inch. In coniferous leaves there is no network of ribs, but a longitudinal and sometimes a diverging system of fibers. A cross-section shows a symmetrical arrangement of cells, some filled with grains of chlorophyll, others with air, and others with resinous matter. The arrangement of these cells is constant within genera, and to some extent in species, affording characteristics upon which classifications have been formed. The stomata upon coniferous leaves are more abundant upon the under and lighter colored side of the leaves, but in some cases where both sides are colored alike, they are found equally on both sides. The ginkgo (*Salisbaria adiantifolia*)), one of the Japanese species that is found to thrive in the Middle and Southern States, is a conifer with very exceptional form of leaf. It spreads out flat like a fan, and is deciduous.

237. The moisture of the soil, is brought up in the form of sap from the roots to the leaves, bearing in solution certain mineral and organic materials. These are then exposed to the air, and to the carbonic acid in the air, and under the action of the light the latter is decomposed. Its carbon is retained and oxygen given out. A vast amount of evaporation also takes place from the leaves, so that

as the sap descends under the bark it is much less watery, and is charged with the materials that by assimilation may form the new layer of wood, and every growing part of the whole structure.

238. The materials thus won from the earth and the air, are added to the tree, as it gains in size, or dropped to the earth with the falling leaves and the fruit—the leaves to add fertility to the soil, and the seeds of the fruit to furnish germs for new creations of the parent type.

239. The form and size of leaves may vary at different ages of the tree and upon different parts of the same tree at the same time. Upon thrifty young sprouts they are generally larger than upon the old branches. As a rule they become smaller at great elevations. In the eucalyptus, the young trees bear heart-shaped and horizontal leaves, and the old trees sickle-formed leaves that stand in a vertical plane, exposing both sides to the light, and shading the ground but little. The upper leaves upon the holly are less notched and less spiny, when the tree becomes old. In certain of the cedars, cypresses, and other conifers with imbricating leaves, the scales may at certain stages of growth elongate into linear leaves, very different from the more usual form. The same tree may present both forms at the same time, but the linear leaves are more common upon young trees than upon old ones. In certain forms of disease, the linear form is sometimes assumed by these imbricating leaves.

Structure of the Wood and Bark.

240. The trunk of an exogenous tree shows three distinct kinds of structure. In the twig of oak of one year's growth, we find the inner part is filled with the *pith*, *m*, an extremely light cellular body which appears essential to new growth, and is always present in a twig covered with leaves; but in the trunk of the tree it becomes nearly or quite obliterated, and in fact may perish altogether without apparently affecting the growth of the tree. The pith or medulla is surrounded by a sheath of hard cellular tissue, and outside of this

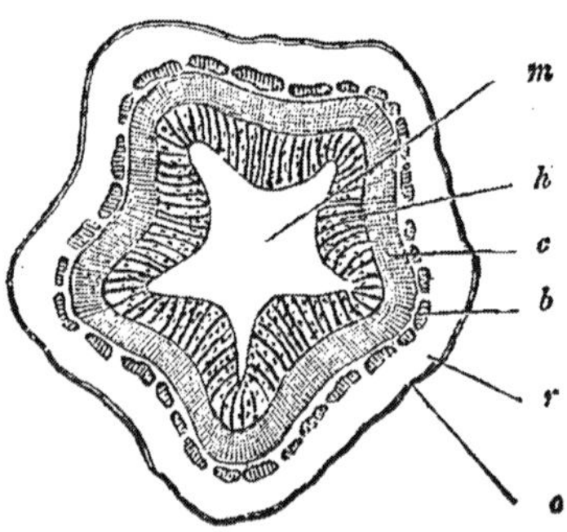

50. Cross-section of an Oak Twig of one Year's Growth.[1]

[1] This and the two following figures are from Rossmassler's work—"*Der Wald*," pp. 85, 88.

is a layer of wood, *h*, which from the first shows a radiating structure—the beginning of the "medullary rays." Outside of the wood, there is formed the cambium layer, *c*, which is to become a new layer of wood. Next a "*bast*" layer, or inner bark, *b*, beyond which is the bark, *r*, of coarse cellular structure, and over all an epidermis, *o*, covering every part.

241. When the wood has made two years of growth, the cross-section shows the structure represented in the annexed engraving, in which *m* (upper side) includes the pith—*m'*, the spongy portion, and *m* (lower side) the "medullary sheath." The wood, *h*, is the growth of two years, and is separated by the line, *jj*. The cambium layer is shown at *c*, and outside of this is the bark. Figures 1 to 7 show the *medullary rays*, which are continued outward through the wood and into the bark. The cross-section, *Q*, the radial section, *Sp*, and tangential section, *Sc*, show the relation which these rays (called by carpenters the "silver grain") bear to the other parts. In the oak these rays are very conspicuous. They are also very apparent but of much smaller size in the beech, plane tree, maple, etc., while in other trees they are scarcely to be seen.

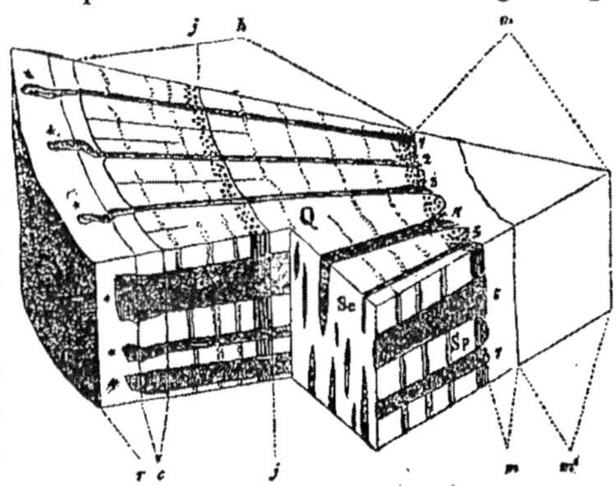

51. Structure of Oak at two Years of Age.

242. The medullary sheath and rays are composed of condensed cellular tissue, and although generally the latter extend through in a radial line from the sheath to the bark, and into it, there are many secondary rays that form in the wood, and have no connection with the pith, or with the other rays. In the conifers, these rays become reduced to lines in parallel bands, too minute to be seen without a microscope of high magnifying powers.

243. As wood is seen under the microscope, it is made up of elongated cells overlapping each other, and adhering by their sides. They present a great variety of forms, which are often peculiar to the families or orders to which they belong. Among these fibers, there are numerous ducts and passages. Some contain only air, others

in their season sap, and others the resinous or other secretions of the tree. Upon the length and adherence of these various vessels, the solidity and strength of wood depends. The accompanying figure represents a longitudinal section of beech, magnified 200 diameters. In this *g* represents dotted vessels; *p*, short cells with very abrupt ends; *pr*, elongated cells with oblique ends; *m*, sections through the medullary rays, and *q*, examples of the long annulated cells appearing in the sections like rows of spots.

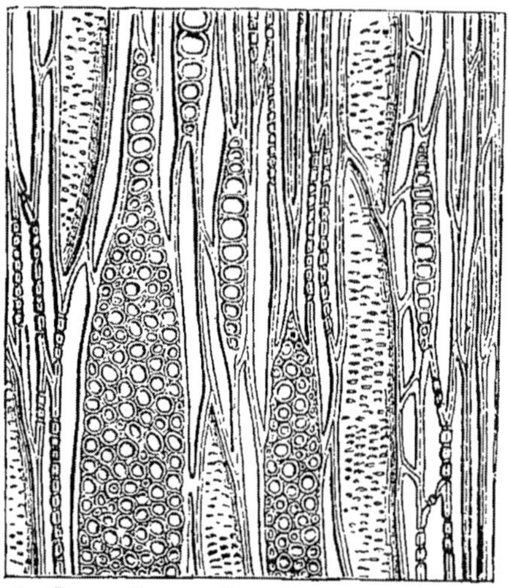

52. Vertical Section of Beech Wood, in a Plane tangent to Rings of Annual Growth.

244. Different kinds of wood exhibit the radiating structures due to the medullary rays in different degrees. In some, it is very conspicuous in the cross-section, while, in others, it can scarcely be traced by the eye, except in thin cross-sections, although always to be seen under the microscope.

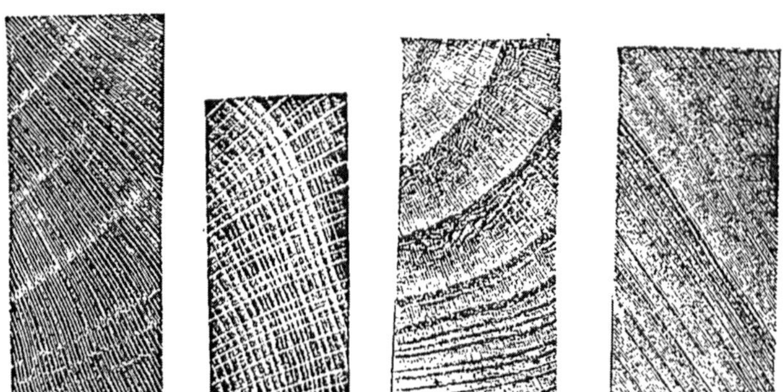

53. Different appearances of the Medullary Rays.

245. In many kinds of the "hard-woods," and especially in the oak, ash, elm, etc., each annual layer is more spongy and porous on the inner side, and harder on the outer side. The former is sometimes called the *spring* and the latter the *autumnal* growth. This autumnal growth is, however, formed in the summer, and its density and relative thickness appears to depend upon the character of the season that follows after it has been deposited. If it remains humid and cold, it will be less dense than if it be dry and warm. The amount of growth for the year is usually determined by the weather in the spring and early summer.

246. In exceptional cases, such as an early and protracted drouth, followed by heavy rains and a warm autumn, a second growth may start; the buds may expand into leaves, and blossoms may appear. In such cases, it is possible for a double ring of growth to form, but it will not be entirely distinct in every part. Such an autumn, if it is followed by a cold winter, is very apt to prove fatal to trees, or at least to check their growth for a time, if it does not destroy them.

247. In tropical woods, the annual layers are obscure, and the age of a tree can not be ascertained from them.

54. Section of Mahogany, showing indistinct Layers of Growth in a Tropical Wood.

248. In the soft-woods, there is scarcely any difference between the layers, and the separation between the growth of different years is sometimes difficult to find.

249. Deciduous trees, when stripped of their leaves, as sometimes occurs from insect ravages, will put forth a new crop, from the buds intended for the next season. The formation of wood is thereby greatly checked, and the foliation of the next season weakened. The chance of blossoms for the coming year may also be ruined.

250. In cross-sections made years afterwards, the record of the seasons for a long period may be determined, at least in effect, by the width of the rings of annual growth. We sometimes find, at recurring intervals, a narrow ring, perhaps in every third year, that may have been caused by the loss

55. Effect of Different Seasons upon the Growth of Wood.

of leaves from worms that appear at that interval, and that have thus left their record when every other proof of their presence has perished. We have seen sections of trees in the museums of Schools of Forestry, in which these proofs were recorded through a century or more of time, and the years could be definitely fixed by counting inward from the year when the tree was felled.

251. As a rule, the most favorable seasons for the growth of wood are those that are warm, cloudy, and humid in the early part of summer, followed by very warm and dry weather. The maturing process in the newly-formed wood appears to be due to the excess of evaporation from the leaves, as compared with the absorption from the roots, resulting in a hardening of the tissues, and an improvement in the quality of the new wood. Where the season continues wet, this hardening does not take place, and when followed by a severely cold winter, the growth may be checked for the season following, or the trees may be killed altogether, or at least the branches of younger growth.

In fact, so many causes affect the amount of growth in different years that there may be as much difference as is shown in the following engravings:

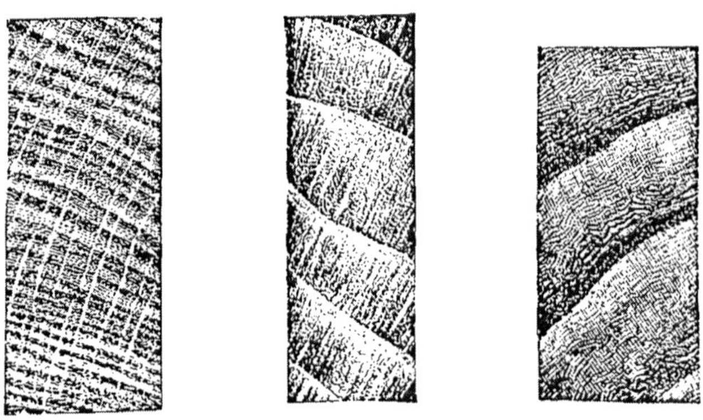

56. Differences in the Amount of Annual Growth of Wood.

Upon irrigated land, in Colorado, the cottonwood has been known to grow to a diameter of fourteen inches in eight years. If grown in rich, humid soil, but in a confined location, the growth may be rapid, but the texture light and spongy, and the wood of poor quality, although of ample volume. Even the teak, one of the strongest of woods, and presenting in its best conditions the texture shown in the annexed engraving, becomes brittle and soft, when rapidly grown, and does not harden into heavy, strong, and durable wood, until it has ripened with age.

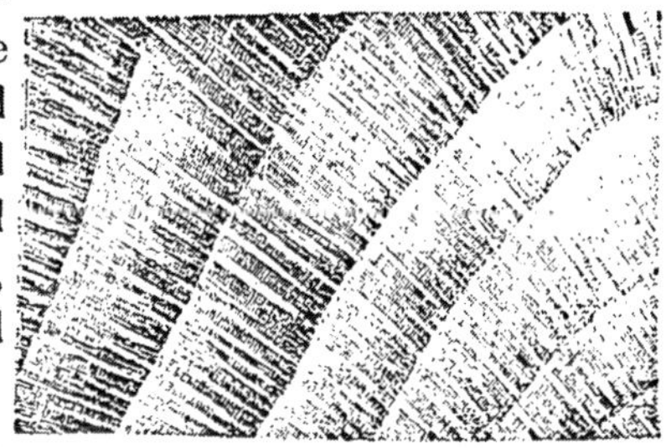

57. Wood of Rapid Growth, but Spongy Texture.

253. Trees grown as reserves, in a coppice, and exposed alternately to the open air and to the shade of other trees at different periods of their growth, have a harder wood than those grown in masses, but it is apt to be knotty from lateral branches—and such trees being more exposed to the winds and to other accidents, do not have so straight and regular a body, nor do they grow as high as when many are grown together. Such wood does not readily split into staves. A difference in the width of wood layers may be caused by the greater or less shade in which it has grown, so that the character of the seasons can never be learned definitely in the cross section of a tree, unless it has grown in an isolated position. Still, from the comparison of a great number of facts it might perhaps be possible to determine with some certainty the general character of the climate by this method.

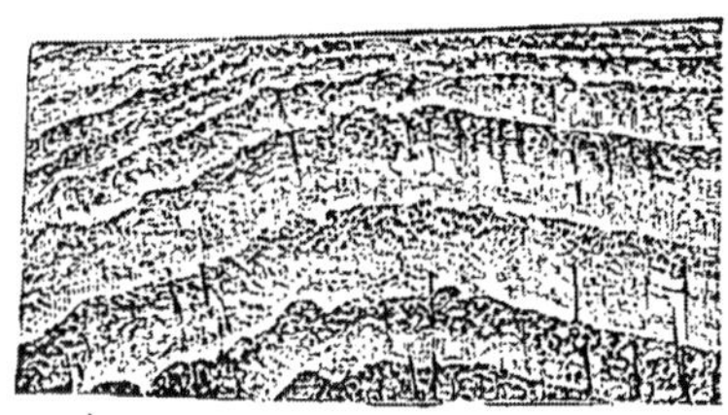

58. Teak Wood.

254. The wood of conifers, *as a rule*, is heavier, more elastic, and more durable, according as its growth has been slower, and the annual rings are narrower. We see this shown in the timber from the Baltic, and in the Siberian larch. These qualities are found greatest in the timber grown in cold climates, and differences may sometimes be detected in the north and south sides of the same tree. As a general rule, trees growing in swampy land have a more open and spongy texture than the same species grown on dryer land.

255. *Cellulose*, which constitutes the principal body of wood-fiber, is alike in all kinds of wood, when separated from other substances,

and consists of about 44.4 per cent of carbon, 6.2 per cent of hydrogen, and 49.3 per cent of oxygen.

256. However plants may differ in form and structure, they are all the result of cell-growth. These cells form in the interior of pre-existing cells by subdivision, and, by pressing upon one another, they elongate into fibrous forms, as already shown on page 68. When macerated, these fibers may be separated, and sometimes they afford differences that enable us to determine the class or group to which the woods belong. In the coniferæ, there are thin places along the sides of the cells, which can be readily seen under the microscope, and can be found even in the fibers of paper made from wood.

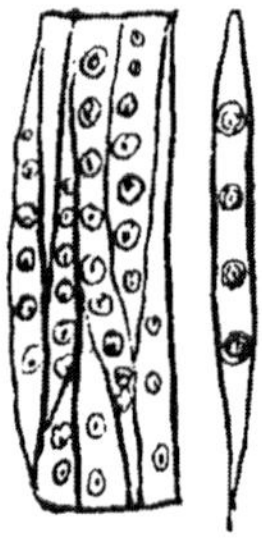

59. Structure of Coniferous Woods.

257. In some woods, as, for example, the oak, ash, walnut, etc., the cells grow to a larger size, so as to be visible to the naked eye. These form ducts, which are not continuous for great length, but are intermingled in various forms, presenting in cross-sections the appearance of pores. They usually contain air, and at certain seasons sap. In ascending among these fibers, the sap passes up between and among the fibers, and through their partitions. In some of the larger ducts, they have a spiral coil of fiber, or the sides are made up of rings, and they are sometimes marked with dots.

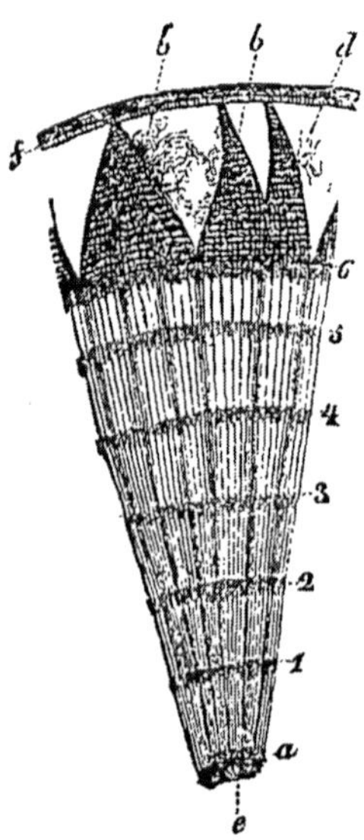

60. Section of a Linden Tree of Six Years' Growth.

258. In resinous woods, the turpentine is contained in larger cavities, surrounded by smaller cells. The abundance of this product depends in a great degree upon the vigor of growth, and exposure to the air and light.

259. The annexed cut shows a section of the linden six years old, enlarged about five diameters, in which the concentric layers are distinguished by a somewhat denser and slightly colored line along their outer margin, and their relation to the bark is shown. In this figure, *a* is the medullary sheath, *b* the liber or inner bark, *d* the cellular tissues of the bark, *e* the pith, and *f* the epidermis or outer bark.

260. In the bark itself, an annular layer of growth is also formed next to the wood, and in some cases we may count the distinct layers of growth of recent years; but in other cases they become a homogeneous mass, as seen by the naked eye, and the outer layers are gradually cast off. In some trees, like the birch and the cherry, the outer layers consist of strong fibers, running horizontally around the trunk and branches. These may exfoliate in loose shreds. This tendency to exfoliation is shown in the plane tree, where the outer bark falls off in hard masses, leaving a fresh surface, at first white, but becoming greenish, and in the Scotch pine (*Pinus sylvestris*), in which the outer bark peels off in thin flakes from the upper part of

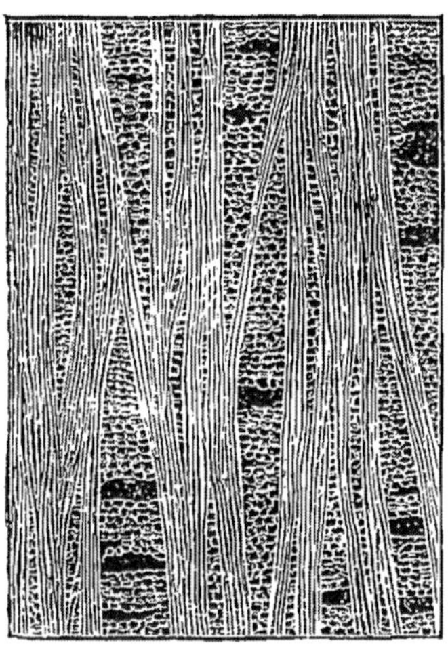

61. Longitudinal Section of the Bark of the Linden: showing the minute interlocking fibers of the bast-bundles, crossing the longitudinal fibers.(1)

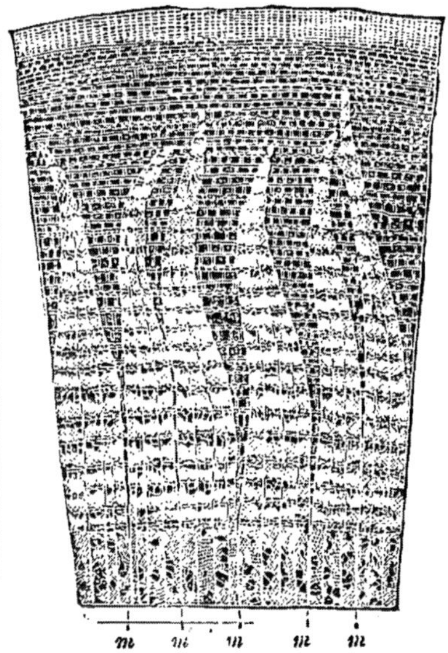

62. Transverse Section of the Bark of the Linden: showing the outer bark, *h*; the green cellular layer, *g*; the bast-layer, *b*; and the edge of contact with the wood, *gr*; with the medullary rays of the bark, *m*, *m*, *m*, *m*, *m*, extending into the green cellular layer.(1)

the trunk, and from the branches, leaving a smooth and fresh green surface.

261. When the bark and wood of a tree are cut or wounded by accident, as by the marking-hammer of the forester, or the ax of a

[1] From Rossmassler.

surveyor, the growth from the side will gradually close over the injury, and fill in the inequalities, so that, when afterwards split off, it will often show in relief any depressions or cuts on the original trunk. Many Forest Academies in Europe have in their museums specimens of timber-marks thus cut or stamped into wood, with the cast taken by nature from the mold. The land-marks of surveyors have thus been found more than a hundred years afterwards. Some scar, or, in coniferous trees, perhaps a gum-spot, would be noticed upon the outside, and by cutting down through as many rings of growth as there had been years since the former survey, the marks of the ax would be found.

1.

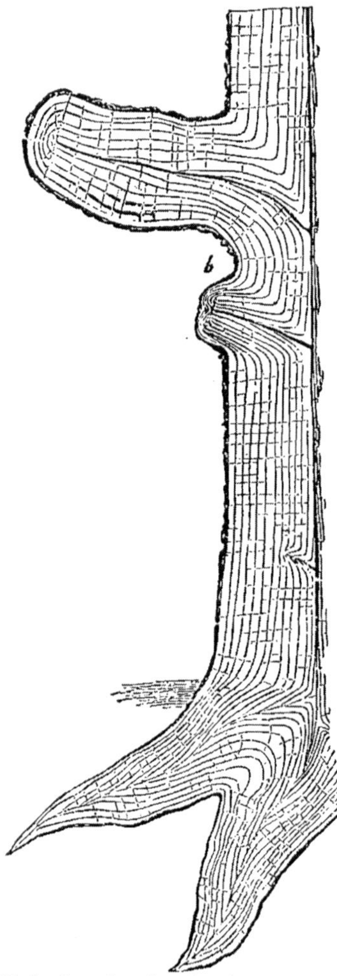

63. Section showing the Growth of the Trunk and Branches.(1)

Growth of the Trunk and Branches.

262. The successive layers of wood in the trunk and branches extend over their whole surface, more or less uniformly, as is shown in the accompanying sketch. The inequalities in thickness, often seen, are caused by differences of nutrition from particular roots and branches. They will fill up the slight irregularities of early years, so that a sapling may be somewhat crooked, and yet form a tree that is perfectly straight and symmetrical.

263. The actual size and form of the tree, at every stage of its former life (excepting as modified by the loss of branches), is preserved within, and might be shown by

[1] From Rossmassler's work—"*Der Wald.*"

removing the layers of growth that have formed since any given period.

264. A leaning tree has the center of growth on the upper side, and the same is generally observed in branches near the place where

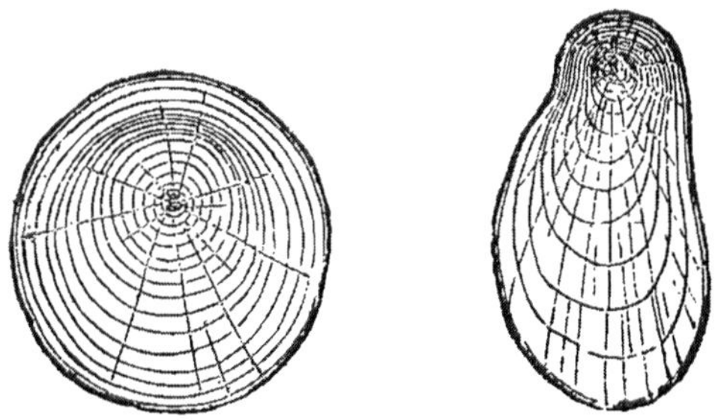

64. Excentric Forms of Growth.

they come out of the tree. This excentric growth is very common in tropical woods, and in some species there are secondary centers of growth within the principal ones.

265. In some of the conifers, especially in the firs and spruces, there is a remarkable symmetry in the branches, several (often five) springing from a single point, and dividing the angular space equally between them. The vertical distance between these branches generally represents a year's growth in length, and a cross-section above a set of branches has, of course, one less number of rings than would be found below them.

266. The rate of growth in wood differs very greatly, according to the soil, elevation, aspect, climate, humidity, temperature, prevailing winds, and other causes. It has been estimated that, on a general average, a forest will, if not specially cared for, grow about a cord of wood on an acre per year. It may often be much less than this, or much more, and may be largely increased by clearing out the undergrowth, and thinning out the trees that crowd too closely. It may be stimulated by fertilizers, applied as a top dressing, and may be retarded by taking away the litter that accumulates from the fall of leaves.

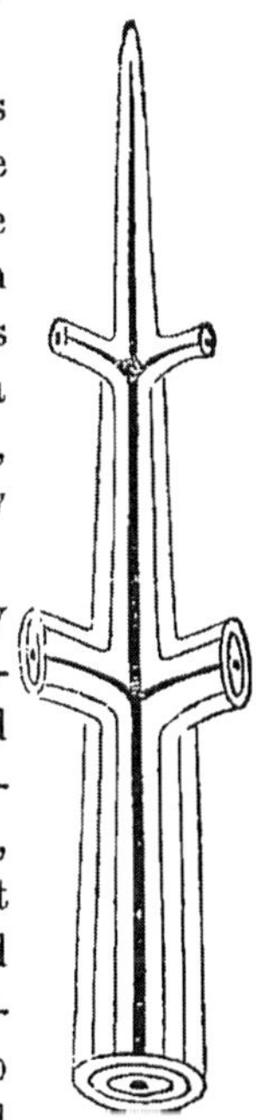

65. Section of a Spruce, showing Symmetry of Branches.

Form, Functions, and Manner of Growth of the Roots.

267. Roots may be divided into two classes: *Tap-roots*, which descend deeply into the soil, and derive their nourishment from the sub-soil; or *Tracing-roots*, that extend laterally and nearer the surface. The latter will sometimes run to a great distance.

268. It is sometimes found that a mixture of different species of timber trees makes a better growth upon the whole, in a woodland, than one kind alone. In these cases one has often a tap-root, and the other a tracing-root, thus drawing their support from different depths of the soil. The oak and the beech are examples of this kind, and we shall have further occasion to speak of this subject.

269. The roots of our common trees are made up of concentric layers, and grow by external addition under the bark, in the same manner as the trunk and branches. Their bark is generally thin, and they often grow one into another, and in a much more irregular form than the branches. There is often no apparent difference in texture, corresponding to sap and heart wood. The stumps and roots of trees are in European countries often used for fuel, and in making charcoal, and in the resinous kinds they, in some instances, abound in turpentine, and are used in making tar and pitch.

270. The fiber of root-wood is sometimes very strong and flexible, as in the young spruce. The stump and roots in some trees have a twisted and contorted grain that gives them great value for ornamental cabinet-work. The "Thuja," of the Atlas Mountains (*Callitris quadrivalvis*), one of the most highly prized of fine woods, is an example. The black walnut often furnishes in its stump and large roots, a beautiful grain in the wood.

271. The roots of trees will insinuate themselves into the thinnest crevices where they can find moisture and soil, and by their expansion hasten disintegration, and sometimes raise and displace heavy masses of rock. For this reason, trees should not be planted near the lines of covered aqueducts, or other important works of masonry that might be injured by displacement.

272. The roots of poplars and willows will fill water-pipes, and even wells, if they can reach them. This tendency to penetrate damp soil, renders these kinds, including the cottonwoods, very useful in consolidating the banks of ditches, especially those used for irrigation in arid regions. They doubtless evaporate a part of

the water in such cases through their leaves, but they give it out to the air where it most needs it, if there be crops under cultivation, and besides strengthening the banks, they shade the surface from the sun and winds. The roots of willows afford the best prevention against erosion of banks, in light soils, and these and other trees and plants most effectually hold in place embankments, and sands liable to drift by the winds.

273. The smaller roots of trees are covered, especially near their extremities, by radicles or fibers, through which the water in the soil, and various mineral elements in solution, are taken up and conveyed in the form of sap to the leaves, by passing up among the pores of the wood. The vigor of growth in a tree is generally proportioned to the abundance of its radicles, and success in planting depends upon their preservation to as great an extent as possible without drying.

274. Roots will often form buds and produce leaves, when exposed to the air, and in many species buds will form roots when buried as layers while still attached to the tree. In the mistletoe and other parasites, the roots will penetrate the wood of living trees upon which their viscid seeds get attached, thus weakening the vitality of the trees to which they fasten, by absorbing their juices.

275. In some cases the roots, and especially their bark, possess medicinal properties, often due to an essential oil, as in the sassafras. These qualities are generally more abundant in trees grown in hot climates, and become less in the same species where they will bear transplanting to cooler latitudes.

276. In rare cases, the roots of different trees of the same species will grow together under ground, so that when one is cut down its stump will continue to live, and even to increase slightly in size, from the nourishment it derives from the other tree. But where from close proximity trees of different species have their roots so closely interlocked that are apparently united as one, it will be found upon a cross-section that there is a line of bark or distinct separation between them.

277. In some cases, a fungus growth will attach to the root, and spreading from one tree to another, cause their destruction, the infection extending from a center in a circular form. This is most effectually arrested by digging trenches deeper than the roots reach,

and by digging up and burning the infected portions. A dying off of the chestnut trees in Italy, France, and Spain has been attributed to fungous growths upon the roots. A similar cause of decay is noticed in some species of the pine.

278. The truffle, a fungus that forms over the roots of the oak, in some countries, is a highly esteemed article of food, and becomes at times a product of much profit in the forests where it is produced. This fungus is formed chiefly in calcareous soils, and appears to require certain conditions of climate. In the neighborhood of Avignon, in France, the revenue from this source alone, in a single commune, sometimes exceeds $5,000 a year.

On the Pressure of Sap, and its Changes.

279. The moisture of the soil is absorbed by the roots, and passing through these to the trunk, branches, and leaves, descends again, more or less changed, to supply nutriment to every part. The action of liquids in passing through membranes and cellular tissues, amounting sometimes to a pressure of several atmosphere, is called *endosmose*, and is shown in a striking manner, when measured by gauges.

280. About 1720, the Rev. Stephen Hales, an English observer, began a series of experiments upon the pressure of sap, and the absorption of water by plants, carefully noting the changes observed, and publishing the results. These experiments form the basis of much that has since been determined in this line of research.

281. In the spring of 1873, a series of experiments was begun at the Amherst Agricultural College, Mass., by its president (Mr. W. S. Clark) and associates, which led to very interesting results. Several mercurial gauges were provided, and attached to trees that had been tapped, by screwing in a hollow plug of metal, to which the gauge was connected. The changes in pressure were read upon a scale. It was found that at some hours the pressure was *inwards*, and at others *outwards*. In the latter case only would the sap flow from the spouts in the usual way. These gauges, when attached to the birch, showed a much greater range of pressure than on the maple, and this even when connected with an isolated root in the ground.

282. The extreme range in the sugar maple was from + 46 to

— 23 inches of mercury, a difference of 69 inches.[1] In the poplar-leaved white birch, it was from + 35 to — 17, in the body of the tree, and from + 33.6 to — 20.2 in the root. In the yellow birch (*Betula excelsa*), it ranged from + 65.5 to — 18.5; in the canoe birch, from + 59 to — 7; and in the grape-vine, from + 74 to 12.7 inches. Where one gauge was placed near the root of a tree, and another near the top, they indicated a difference due to the hydrostatic pressure of a column of water equal in length to the distance between the two levels. Trials were made upon the butternut, ironwood, apple tree, etc., with corresponding results, but less in degree. These experiments were made before the leaves had opened, and the force of suction could not therefore be ascribed to evaporation from their surfaces.

Autumnal Colors.

283. The coloring of autumnal leaves appears to be due to the formation of organic acids from the absorption of oxygen, and caused by a ripening process, similar to that which colors ripening fruits. It is not the effect of frost, as many people believe, but may be hastened by the cool nights alternating with warm days, that often occur in autumn. The autumnal coloring of European forests is sometimes bright, but never as brilliant as in our Northern States and in Canada. Its prevailing colors are yellow, shading off into tints of pale orange and reddish brown, while in our northern forests it is often the brightest scarlet and orange, a rich golden yellow, or an intense purple, but all passing gradually into a nearly uniform shade of brown.

CHAPTER VIII.

GENERAL VIEWS IN REGARD TO FORESTRY.

Of the Investment of Labor and Capital in Forest-tree Planting—Questions of Profit.

284. As a general rule, the most profitable lands for planting, at present prices, are not those that would yield the best farm crops, although the best lands will always produce the best growth of forest trees. Upon such lands, forest trees would be sure to thrive, but the profits

[1] In these statements, the sign (+) is used to denote the *outward*, and (—) the *inward* pressure.

might be relatively less. In a region of hills and valleys, there are always some portions of the land that yield a much smaller return under equal care than others. They may be valleys and ravines, or steep declivities, or rocky and broken surfaces, and upon these a grove of trees may often prove the best investment.

285. In other cases, the soil may have been reduced to barrenness by improvident tillage, and then there is no better way to restore its fertility than by the growth of trees, and the accumulation of a new supply of vegetable soil from the decay of the leaves. In some sections of the country, where old fields have been abandoned for cultivation, a crop of pines, oaks, or some other kinds of trees, will come in and occupy the land, forming, in the course of a few years, quite a dense growth, but generally not of the most profitable kinds. The latter may gradually become introduced. It has been noticed that where we find a woodland principally composed of but one kind of timber, it is of comparatively recent origin, and that a great diversity of species indicates that the woodland has been growing for a long period.

286. In the midst of a well-settled country, with no prospect of increase in value from external causes, the probable revenues of land under common forms of farm cultivation are less than in many other kinds of property. The investment becomes especially desirable from the security that it affords, and a reasonable prospect that this value may be increased by improvements and the general advance in values as the country becomes older. There are many pleasing associations connected with the solid and enduring possession of a landed estate, and the comfortable independence that it secures. The value of farming land varies with the general wealth and capital of a country, and increases or declines, not only as affected by the prosperity of places near it, but also by those which may be more distant, but still large consumers of its products.

287. Except in the suburbs of cities and villages, there is little that is speculative in the possession of land, after the lines of transportation, and business points of a country have been fully established. Should a time come when forests are managed by great corporations, there is not the least probability that their capital stock would be liable to great and sudden changes, in the ordinary course of dealing. The returns would be slow in coming, but sure

under careful management, and very considerable at the end of the appointed periods.

288. To illustrate the rates of this increase, we will suppose that the annual rings of growth in a tree are of equal width. As a matter of fact, they are much wider in some years than in others, but, for illustration, we will consider them as uniform in thickness. Counting from the center outward, we would have the numbers 1, 2, 3, 4, 5, etc., showing the years of growth. The areas of these circles (each including those within it) are as the *squares* of these numbers, viz., 1, 4, 9, 16, 25, etc. By subtracting each of these from the preceding, we have the series, 3, 5, 7, 9, etc., that represents *the gain of each year upon the year preceding.*

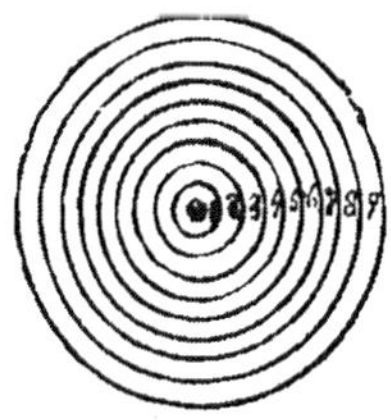

66. Concentric Rings of Tree Growth.

289. These relative rates may be shown by a simple diagram, in which the gain in diameter is represented by the lower diagonal, and the gain in area by the upper one. The numbers along the bottom in this figure represent the years, and those on the margin units of quantity. The rates thus shown are actually maintained for many years, while young, but become less as the trees approach maturity. They show the waste from cutting thrifty young timber at the period of most profitable growth, and should lead us to spare it, when possible, till it has gained its full value.

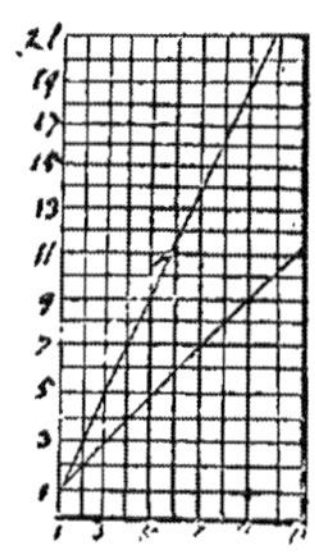

67. Gaining Rates of Diameters and of Sectional Areas.

290. But these gaining rates are only those of sectional area; the trees are at the same time gaining in height, and the timber is gaining in quality and value *per cubic foot,* as it grows older, for it can then be applied to more important uses, when it has grown to large size, besides being of intrinsically greater value, when fully mature.

291. The planting of forests, and their management afterwards, till grown to full maturity, can not be followed from fixed rules as to time and manner, but the business must be conducted with an intelligent understanding of the conditions that exist, and the circumstances that may influence their growth. Under equal circumstances, as in all other forms of business, the man who pays the closest attention to his affairs, and neglects nothing, will, at the end

of a given period, have the most to show for his labor. The care of woodlands is not generally as laborious as that of cultivated fields, and, if they are both united upon a farm, the alternation of care from one to the other, as the seasons and the occasion may require, serves to break the monotony of life, and contribute to its enjoyment.

292. There are incidental advantages to be derived from the planting of trees for embellishment and shade, that can not be separately estimated. That they increase the general value of an estate, can not be doubted, and perhaps this might best be understood by asking, *how much less would the property be worth without them.* As prices of timber may hereafter advance, the income from stated cuttings will doubtless form a comfortable source of revenue, and there is a point beyond which this may be greater than from any other form of cultivation.

293. In the planting of avenues and parks, in or near towns and cities, questions of public utility, of personal comfort, and of health become paramount to all others, and are altogether above pecuniary appraisal. There are other incidental advantages to be gained by the planting of village streets and parks in the neighborhood of cities that will be elsewhere more fully noticed.

On the Due Proportion of Woodlands to Cultivated Fields.

294. In considering only the wants of a country, we must admit that wood is absolutely indispensable for our use—that it can only be obtained by natural or artificial growth, and that therefore a certain proportion of land must be devoted to its production. Where from commercial facilities, or colonial possessions, this growth may be obtained by importation, and the land required for its production may be distant, still the proportion must be maintained, or a great future interest must be sacrificed to meet a present want. The actual and relative amount of forests in Europe will enable us to form some idea as to how this question stands at the present time in these countries.

295. *Forest Area of various Countries of Europe, from late Official Statistics.*

Countries.	Acres of Forests.	Per c't of total Area.	Countries.	Acres of Forests.	Per c't of total Area.
Russia	476,710,000	40.0	Switzerland	1,788,786	18.0
Finland	27,170,000		France	22,687,716	17.3
Sweden	43,395,430	34.1	Greece	1,721,029	14.3
Norway	18,920,509		Spain	7,833,647	7.3
Austria	45,309,411	29.4	Belgium	501,402	7.0
Germany	34,969,791	26.1	Holland	569,160	7.0
Turkey	20,503,280	22.2	Portugal	1,165,420	5.1
Roumania	4,940,000		Great Britain	3,106,824*	4.1
Italy	14,228,978	22.0	Denmark	464,360	3.4
			Total	725,985,743	29.5

296. It will be seen from this table, that the general average throughout Europe is between a fourth and a third; that the least proportion is in those countries where the facilities for foreign importation are greatest, or where the demand is least, and that the countries from whence for a century vast supplies have been drawn, are by no means so well wooded as to promise indefinite continuance or inexhaustible supply. The relative abundance in Russia is found only in the northern part, and nowhere can a contrast between plenty and want be more strongly shown. Moreover, it should be remembered that in case of need, the government might easily interrupt the exportation, if it became necessary to protect its own interest, or to make other countries feel their dependence upon it for supplies.

297. It is obvious that foreign demands must greatly influence the prices of a commodity in countries from whence it is supplied, without reference to causes that might operate within them; and since our country has furnished for a long period a large and constantly increasing amount of timber and lumber to foreign countries, these questions become with us matters of direct practical interest. It is proper, therefore, that we should take a general glance at the distribution and extent of the native timber resources of the

*This appears to be an over-statement. From statistics published in 1880, it is shown that there were then 1,435,434 acres of woodland in England, 162,135 in Ireland, and 811,703 in Scotland. The percentages of total area were 4.4.—3.4—and 1.6 respectively.

United States; but before doing this, we will notice some points of resemblance and contrast, due to great geographical and climatic causes, which we must recognize in all attempts at the naturalization of species, and which may afford a useful guide in their cultivation.

Resemblances and Contrasts in the native Timber-growth of different Regions of the United States.

298. There has been noticed a wide difference between the forests of the eastern and the western coasts of North America, and a strong resemblance between the woodlands of the Atlantic States and Canada and the eastern coast of Asia and the islands of Japan. These resemblances apply to identical or representative species of the genera that include the magnolias, lindens, sumacs, buckeyes, box-elder, yellow-wood, honey-locust, pear, shadbush, dog-woods, rhododendrons, holly, persimmon, catalpa, sassafras, osage-orange, planera, walnut, butternut, hazelnut, birch, alder, yellow and white pine, hemlock, arbor-vitæ, bald cypress, and yews.

299. None of these, excepting some representatives of the sumac, box-elder, pear, shadbush, and dog-wood, appear on the Pacific coast. The Himalaya region, Northern China, and Mantchuria contain many native species that may be cultivated successfully in ornamental plantations in our Atlantic States, and are already obtainable from our great nurseries. It is already ascertained that they have better prospects of success than most of the species that thrive so remarkably in their native localities upon the Pacific coast, but under a climate and in conditions that we can not provide for them in the Atlantic States. They are accustomed to heavy winter rains and long dry summers, and must have them.

300. The same difficulty occurs when we attempt to cultivate on the Pacific coast, many of the species that thrive in the Atlantic States. The hemlock, spruce, Norway spruce, and Austrian pine, among the conifers, and the sugar maple and the hickory among deciduous kinds, grow but slowly there. The pecan and the beech do better, but the locust tree is not at all reliable. Reasoning from this analogy, we would expect trees from the west of Europe to succeed in cases where they fail in the Atlantic States. It would well be worth trial as to whether the maritime pine, for example, that grows so luxuriantly in the rainy region of Southwestern

France, would not be found suited to similar conditions upon our western coast, and prove a profitable tree for forest-culture.

301. In determining the kinds of trees best adapted to a given region, it is well to observe what kinds have grown up, or that still remain of the native growth, along the borders of streams, or in places where they have been sheltered and protected.

302. It may generally be presumed that these kinds would succeed with much certainty, if planted again, although from exhaustion of the soil by cultivation, or its injury from fires, it may have been impoverished to an extent that would make it difficult to plant. Before much expense was risked, experimental planting might be tried upon a small scale, and in this it should be the duty of the government to assist, where the conditions are quite new and the probabilities are unknown.

General Glance at the Native Forest Resources of the United States and Canada.

303. It is estimated by Professor Brewer, of Yale College, that there may be eight hundred species of woody plants growing native in the United States, of which about three hundred attain a height of thirty feet, and about two hundred and fifty are tolerably abundant somewhere. Excluding semi-tropical species on the extreme southern border, and some others that are rare, there would still remain about one hundred and twenty species, of which about twenty grow to one hundred feet, twelve to two hundred, and five or six to three hundred feet or over. Of these one hundred and twenty, about fifty are conifers.

304. East of the treeless plains, which extend from north to south across the country, in a belt some hundreds of miles wide, east of the Rocky Mountains, the native forests were largely of deciduous kinds, and in great variety of species. West of this belt they are almost entirely conifers. One species, the aspen (*Populus tremuloides*), extends entirely across the continent. There may be a few others that are found in rare cases.

The New England States.

305. In generalizing by regions, Professor Brewer remarks, that in the New England States, once entirely wooded, there are eighty to eighty-five native species, of which about sixty grow more than

fifty feet high. The greater number of these are hard-woods, and the conifers are chiefly of the pine, cedar, and spruce families. As shade-trees, the elm and the sugar maple there perhaps attain their finest development.

The Middle States.

306. In the Middle States, from one hundred to oue hundred and five species occur, of which sixty-five to sixty-seven grow fifty feet or more in height. These states were once heavily wooded—the conifers in greater or less abundance being mingled among the deciduous kinds. Some of the oaks, the chestnut, beech, and some kinds of the ash, and the white-pine, there grow to great perfection in their favorite localities.

Southern States.

307. From Virginia to Florida, about one hundred and thirty species occur, of which about seventy-five grow to fifty feet or more, and perhaps a dozen to one hundred feet. The coast of this region produces the bald cypress, and towards the south the live-oak, the palmetto and other kinds.

308. A broad belt of long-leaved pine (*Pinus australis*) extends further inland, in irregular form, around through the middle of the Gulf States to beyond the Mississippi river. Still further iuland, and at higher level, the oaks and other hard-woods become more common, and on the mountains the northern conifers are found. The pine forests of this region generally present an open appearance, probably from their being overrun by frequent fires.

309. The coast region and the swamps bear a tree-growth that is dense and tangled, and although there may be timber of large size, it is difficult of access, as the swamps never freeze so as to facilitate lumbering as in the Northern States. In these swamps there is often a deep deposit of vegetable soil, and in some places buried cedar may be found still in excellent preservation.

310. At a short distance west of Trinity river, in Texas, the forests begin to disappear, and there are immense regions in that state, extending from the Gulf to the northern and western borders, that are wholly destitute of trees.

The Western States.

311. West of the Alleghenies, we find a country originally cov-

ered with heavy timber, excepting in "oak openings" and "barrens," where the trees had been destroyed by frequent fires, and the "prairies," where from this or other causes no timber was found, except along the borders of streams.

312. These open spaces of every description, when drained and protected, are found to produce trees readily under cultivation, there being scarcely any part that presents an inherent difficulty in the soil, and none in the climate.

313. According to the writer above cited, the country north-west of the Ohio river, contains from one hundred and five to one hundred and ten native species, of which sixty-eight to seventy grew to a height of fifty feet. In Southern Ohio and Indiana, oaks and various hard-woods grow to a very large size, and the walnuts, basswood, and tulip-tree attain their finest development.

314. The white-pine region begins in North-western Ohio, and extends into the states further north and west. In the interior of Michigan, around Saginaw Bay, and along both lakes, there were vast bodies of white pine, but much of this has been worked out, and according to careful estimates the supply can not last many years.

315. In the upper Peninsula of Michigan, in Northern Wisconsin, and in Eastern and North-eastern Minnesota, there were also large bodies of timber, generally a mixture of conifers and hardwoods. The forests south of Lake Superior were originally second only to those of the Pacific coast for their density, and the size of their growth.

316. In Illinois and Southern Wisconsin, and from the Mississippi river westward, the prairies begin to predominate, and the native forests are limited to belts along the rivers and streams. In some parts, these spread out into broad areas many miles in extent, and in others they are mere fringes, that gradually disappeared altogether further west.

The Rocky Mountain Region.

317. The sides and valleys of these mountains were in favorable situations covered with coniferous forest trees, sometimes occupying broad areas, and elsewhere of more limited extent. The number of species in this region is not over twenty-eight or thirty, of which the conifers form two-thirds the number in species, and by far the greatest proportion in quantity. The box-elder (*Negundo aceroides*) and the quaking aspen, are the more important deciduous trees.

318. The "divides" between river systems are generally wooded, but in scattered patches and irregular masses, that give a park-like appearance to the country, but do not afford for many years a supply, where mining or other settlements are made in their vicinity. The waste and improvidence with which this timber is being destroyed should lead to prompt and adequate measures for its protection. In some places, it can scarcely be made to grow again, when once cut off, and in others the rate of growth is so slow that five hundred years would scarcely replace the thoughtless waste of an hour.

319. The decaying remains of coniferous and other trees are not unfrequently found in this region and westward, extending farther out towards the plains than any of the kind are now found growing, or at least young and in thriving condition. This has been thought to indicate that at no distant period in the past, these trees flourished over a larger area than at present, and in places where, from changed conditions of the climate, they could now scarcely be made to grow by the most careful cultivation.

320. This recession will, in all probability, be hastened by the improvident waste that is now going on, and changes are already perceptible, although the time since settlements began is but brief. The nutritious bunch-grasses of the plains extend up into the borders of the timber belt, and in open valleys are found to nearly 11,000 feet above tide.

The Pacific Coast.

321. The forests of this region are for the most part restricted to the sea-coast, the borders of rivers, and the mountain sides, and are distinguished on account of the relatively large preponderance of the coniferous as compared with the deciduous kinds.

322. In speaking of the contrasts between this region and the Atlantic States, Dr. Asa Gray remarks:

"California has no magnolia nor tulip-trees, nor star-anise tree; no so-called pawpaw; no barberry of the common single-leaved sort; . . . no prickly-ash nor sumac; no loblolly-bay nor stuartia; no basswood nor linden trees; neither locust, honey-locust, coffee-trees, nor yellow-wood; nothing answering to hydrangea or witch-hazel, to gum-trees, viburnum, or diervilla; no huckle-berries, and hardly any blue-berries; no epigæa—charm of our earliest spring—tempering the April wind with a delicious wild fragrance; no kalmia, nor clethra, nor holly, nor persimmon; no catalpa tree;

. . . nothing answering to sassafras, nor to benzoin tree, nor to hickory; neither mulberry nor elm; no beech, true chestnut, hornbeam, nor ironwood, nor a proper birch tree; and the enumeration might be continued very much further by naming herbaceous plants and others familiar to botanists."

323. The enormous sizes to which some of the conifers of this region grow, has been the wonder of all travelers; but these immense growths do not cover large areas, and nowhere can such strong contrasts between abundance and scarcity be elsewhere seen. The heavy forests do not extend much beyond the coast region, the borders of rivers or the mountain sides and valleys, and these usually present remarkable peculiarities in the prevailing growth.

324. The consumption and waste that have been going on since settlement began, have already made serious inroads upon these apparently "inexhaustible" supplies, and probably already more than half, in all the accessible portions, is now gone. There is a most urgent need of conservative measures, and the time is not distant when the inhabitants of that region, and those depending upon these supplies, will be admonished by enhanced prices of the importance of economy and the value of a growing tree.

325. In *Canada*, there are found sixty-five native species of trees, in Ontario, Quebec, and the Maritime Provinces; of which about a dozen range as far north as James Bay. The birches, poplars, and tamarac are found in the more northerly region, and south of these the pines and the beech, the latter chiefly south of a line drawn from the outlet of Lake Superior to Quebec. West of Niagara river is a zone where the walnut, butternut, tulip-tree, sassafras, and chestnut occur, with an increasing abundance of oaks. The absence of trees and of mosses is a notable feature of the prairies of Manitoba and westward.[1] The principal pine forests of Canada have receded to the upper waters of the great rivers flowing into the St. Lawrence and the lakes, and from the investigations that have been undertaken by the government in recent years, it appears evident that the time of principal exhaustion is not many years distant.

Great Britain.

326. Of the native trees of Great Britain, there are only about a dozen genera and thirty species, that grow to thirty feet or more

[1] Drummond's *Canadian Timber Trees*, p. 5.

in height, and only two of these are conifers. By importation from other countries, the number now under cultivation is largely increased, and very many have been found entirely suited to the soil and climate. Among these, the larch may be mentioned as the one that has come into favor more than any other species, as a forest tree, especially in Scotland. The conifers of our Pacific coast, and especially the Douglas fir, appear in many cases to thrive well when cultivated as timber trees.

Alternations of Forest Growth.

327. It has been often observed that when a forest has been destroyed, and more especially if it has been killed off by fire, the growth that succeeds, when left to itself, is very often of a different kind. If the former growth was pine, the succeeding one may be cherry or poplar, and in some regions oak. In the Southern States, oak and hickory may be followed by pine. The white oak cut off at Valley Forge by the American army in 1777–8 was followed by black oak, hickory and chestnut. In Florida, the black-jack (*Quercus nigra*) often follows the long-leaved pine (*Pinus australis*).

328. These facts have by some been regarded as favoring a theory of rotation of crops in timber, by natural causes, as we practice with advantage in agriculture; but, according to the best received opinions, this alternation is not a law of nature, but rather the result of external circumstances, which will generally be found sufficient to account for all the facts we meet with. Either the deciduous or the resinous species can be introduced and maintained by the aid of judicious cultivation, in places where the conditions for their welfare exist in the soil or climate.

329. But as different trees do not draw equally from the soil, we should study the natural adaptation of the conditions of the locality, and seek to accommodate the species to them, to the best advantage. In another part of this work, we notice some of the agencies through which this natural seeding may occur.[1]

330. In seeking to continue the production of the same species upon a soil where it has formerly prospered, we must never allow the soil to become impoverished by the removal of the dead leaves

[1] See pages 30–33.

and rubbish. If this is done, the fertility is diminished, in a manner comparable to that of agricultural lands that will gradually become exhausted, unless manures are applied. In no form of forest-culture is there a tendency to general exhaustion of the soil by long continued use, as we observe in agricultural cultivation; still there may be an exhaustion of the local supply for the roots of trees in particular places, and when this occurs the trees may languish and die, or their growth may be checked. This sometimes happens in ornamental planting, where very fertile soil is used for filling in the holes, and where these holes are dug in a very poor soil.

CHAPTER IX.

ACTS OF CONGRESS RELATING TO TIMBER RIGHTS.

Entry of Land under the Timber-culture Acts.

331. By an act of Congress approved March 3, 1873, and amended March 13, 1874, and again June 14, 1878, any person who is the head of a family, or who has arrived at the age of twenty-one, and is a citizen of the United States, or who has filed his declaration of intention to become such, may apply at the office of the Register of a Land District, for the entry of any vacant land in such district as a *timber claim*, upon the following conditions:

332. The amount may not be more than a quarter section (160 acres) to one person, nor more than this amount can be taken up by any person in one section. The applicant must make oath that the land is composed wholly of prairie lands, or other lands devoid of timber; that the entry is made for the cultivation of timber, and for his own exclusive use and benefit, and in good faith, and not for the purpose of speculation, or directly or indirectly for the use or benefit of any other person; and that he intends to hold and cultivate the land, and fully to comply with the provisions of the law. He must also swear that he has not previously entered any lands under the present act, or the acts of which it is amendatory.

333. Upon the payment of a fee of $10, and the further sum of $4, for commissions, if for more than eighty acres, or of $5 and $4 if eighty acres or less, he receives a certificate of entry, and may occupy at once, upon the following conditions:

334. If the entry is for 160 acres, he must break or plow five acres the first year and another five acres the second year. The land

plowed the first year, must be cultivated by crop or otherwise in the second year. In the third year he must cultivate the five acres broken in the second year, and plant in timber trees, tree-seeds, or cuttings, the five acres first broken or plowed, and cultivate the remainder that has been broken. In the fourth year, he must plant in timber trees, tree-seeds, or cuttings, the second five acres.

335. If the entry is for eighty acres, the amount to be broken and planted must be one-half, or if for forty acres, one-fourth of the above amount. If the trees, seeds, or cuttings are destroyed by grass-hoppers, or by extreme or unusual drouth, for any year or term of years, the time for planting is increased one year for every such year when they have been destroyed. In applying for an extension of time, an affidavit by the applicant, corroborated by two witnesses, must be filed, setting forth the destruction of the trees.

336. At the end of eight years from the date of entry, or within five years thereafter, the person who made it, or if he or she be dead his or her heirs or legal representatives must prove, by two credible witnesses, that the amount of land has been plowed, cultivated, planted, and protected as above required, and a statement of the quantity and character of trees thus planted; that not less than 2,700 trees were planted on each acre;[1] and that at least 675 are living and thrifty, upon each acre, at the time of making such proof. This will then entitle him to a patent for the quarter-section, or less amount of land that was entered.

337. The claim is forfeited at any time before the eight years, upon neglect of any of the conditions, and may be entered by another person, either as a homestead or as a timber claim, the original claimant being notified as prescribed by rules, and his rights determined by evidence, as in other contested cases.

338. Timber-claims are not liable to the satisfaction of debts contracted before date of final certificate. The penalties prescribed with respect to oaths and affirmations falsely made in other cases apply to this, and the Commissioner of the General Land Office is required to issue rules and regulations for the execution of the act.

339. Entries made under the acts of 1873 or 1874 may be completed under the act of 1878, upon complying with its conditions, and in this case it is not necessary to prove that the manner of

[1] Equivalent to rows four feet apart each way.

planting begun under former acts were complied with. It may have been done under the manner prescribed by either of these acts.

340. With respect to the kinds of trees that might be regarded as timber trees, within the meaning of the law, the following were specified, viz.: "Ash, alder, beech, birch, black-walnut, basswood, black-locust, cedar, chestnut, cottonwood, elm, fir, including spruce, hickory, honey-locust, larch, maple, including box-elder, oak, pine, plane-tree, otherwise called cotton-tree, buttonwood or sycamore, service-tree, otherwise called mountain-ash, white-walnut, otherwise called butternut, white-willow, and whitewood, otherwise called tulip-tree."

341. The above list was only intended as a general guide, and will not be construed to exclude any trees falling within the description of trees recognized in the neighborhood as of value for timber, or for commercial purposes, or for firewood and domestic use.[1]

342. The preparation of the land and the planting of trees being acts of cultivation, the time so employed is to be counted as a part of the eight years of cultivation required by law. Final proof must be made in person, with his witnesses, and in the Land District where the land is located. The testimony must be given before a Judge or Clerk of a court of record in that Land District, and the identity and credibility of the party making the affidavit must be certified by the officer administering the oath.

343. The sum of $4, in addition to the amount paid upon entry, must be paid when the final proof is made. No additional fees are required or allowed.

344. By official rulings entries by subdivisions of quarter-sections may be made, if in the same section, and in a compact body, not exceeding 160 acres in all. Where an entry is made upon a claim that has been abandoned after breaking or planting, the second party is not entitled to any allowances for the work done. After entry of 160 acres, if from sickness the party can not complete the

[1] This general permission was granted by a decision of February 10, 1882. The omissions in the list previously enumerated had given rise to severe criticisms. Either of the following might in some localities be found worth cultivating as timber trees, and several of them may be classed among the more valuable kinds, viz: Ailanthus, blue-beech, cherry (especially the black cherry,) gum-trees, hackberry, iron-wood, osage-orange, peach, pear, apple, plum, etc.

planting, if the amount broken be as much as the law requires for a less amount, he may relinquish 80 acres, retaining the part on which work is begun. A claim once entered can not be exchanged for another.

945. A strict compliance with the terms of the law has been held as necessary. Should less than five acres be broken, for example, in one year, the difference could not be made up by an excess of plowing the second year. The word "cultivation" does not necessarily imply the raising of a crop. It may be done by plowing, harrowing, or otherwise.

346. Every timber-culture entry is made subject to a right of contest, by any person who can show non-compliance as a ground of forfeiture. He who faithfully complies with the law has little to apprehend, for contestants must pay the costs if not successful.

347. Where a scattered growth of trees exists on the margin of a stream or a section of land, and there are none growing elsewhere on the section, it has been held that the tract is "naturally devoid of timber" if there are less than 50 trees to the section. The quality of the trees, rather than their number, has determined questions arising upon this point. Because a tract was covered by a prior timber-culture entry, this is not evidence that the land is properly subject to the timber-culture law. The person who makes affidavit should assure himself of the fact.

Planting under the Homestead-Entry Act.

348. Under an act relating to homestead entries, in force from March 13, 1874, to June 14, 1878, a person entitled under the homestead act, who at any time after the third year of his or her residence thereon, had, in addition to the settlement and improvements required by law, brought under cultivation for two years one acre of timber, not more than twelve feet apart each way, and had kept it in good thrifty condition, for each sixteen acres of his homestead, he was entitled to receive a patent for the same, upon proof of the fact. The rights acquired while this act was in force, will remain valid, until the limitation of that act has expired.

Use of Timber by Railroad Companies.

349. By an act approved March 3, 1878, entitled "an act granting to railroads the right of way through the public lands of the United States," these companies are allowed the right of 100 feet on each

side of the central line of their road, and the right to take from the public lands adjacent to the line of said road the timber and other materials necessary for construction, and a tract not to exceed twenty acres in a place, once in ten miles, for a station.

Privileges granted to the Citizens of Colorado, Nevada, and the Territories.

350. By "An Act authorizing the citizens of Colorado, Nevada, and the Territories, to remove Timber on the Public Domain for Mining and Domestic Purposes," approved June 3, 1878, the *bona fide* residents of the above states, and the territories of New Mexico, Arizona, Utah, Wyoming, Dakota, Idaho and Montana, and all other mineral districts of the United States, were permitted to take any timber or other trees growing on the public lands, said lands being mineral, and not subject to entry, as they might need for building, agricutural, mining, or domestic purposes, subject to such regulations as the Secretary of the Interior might prescribe.

Sale of Timber Lands in California, Oregon, and Nevada, and in Washington Territory.

351. By an act of June 3, 1878, providing for the survey of public lands in the above states and territories which are chiefly valuable for timber but unfit for cultivation, and which had not been offered for sale, it is provided that such lands may be sold in quantities not exceeding 160 acres to one person, at a minimum price of $2.50 per acre. During the year ending June 30, 1881, there were entered the following amounts:

In California,	179 entries=19,829.66	acres.
In Washington Ter.,	134 entries=16,436	acres.
In Oregon,	49 entries= 5,044.55	acres.
In Nevada,	1 entry = 160	acres.

352. An applicant must make affidavit that he is a citizen, or has filed a declaration of intention to become such; that the land is unfit for cultivation, and chiefly valuable for timber (or stone); that it is uninhabited; that it has not gold, silver, cinnabar, copper, or coal; that he has made no previous application; does not buy on speculation; and has not made any agreement by which the benefit shall accrue to any other person. This allegation must be supported by that of two other persons who have no interest in the

transaction. After advertisement for sixty days, if no adverse claim is filed, the land may be conveyed. This act does not reserve land covered by timber and fit for cultivation from the operation of the homestead or pre-emption laws. A person resident on a timber claim has been allowed to change it to a homestead entry, upon relinquishing the former, under section 3, Act of May 14, 1880. Applicants are not allowed to remove the timber from the land embraced in their application prior to making proof and payment.

CHAPTER X.

EUROPEAN PLANS OF FOREST MANAGEMENT.

359. In countries where Forestry has been studied with most care, several different systems of management have been devised, in each of which certain advantages may be gained when properly employed. The preference that should be given to one or another, must in all cases be determined by the circumstances and conditions. They are as follows:

(1.) *Method of Selection.*[1]

360. In this method, the trees are cut out here and there, leaving others not yet mature to grow to their full size. It is the same plan that we see in common use, in the tracts of woodland reserved upon farms, in the older parts of the United States, where the timber is cut out here and there, as it is wanted for particular uses, or as it begins to decay.

361. It is also employed to some extent in the cutting of trees for lumber, chiefly in pine, cedar, or spruce forests, where all the trees above a certain diameter are cut out, and those of smaller size are left, until the tract can again be cut over in like manner.

362. It results from this management, that the forest always presents a great diversity of growth of young trees among the old, and the actual amount of wood upon such a tract is generally much less than where a great uniformity in size and age has been maintained. As too often practiced upon farms, if cattle and sheep are allowed to pasture in such woods, the seedlings and young sprouts

[1] Called by the French "*Jardinage,*" literally "gardening;" or sometimes "*fuertage,*" that is, "stealing" here and there from the forest, as described in the text.

are eaten off, or are broken down, and the tendency to ruin is hastened.

363. In such woodlands, where trees are felled every year, the young timber is very liable to injury,—bare places are very apt to form, and the general tendency is to a continual narrowing in of the boundary and final clearing off. In such irregular forests, the winds are apt to do more injury than where the growth is uniform, and the timber itself is generally not so valuable, on account of the injuries and accidents to which it is exposed when young, and the unequal growth that it forms. Nevertheless, in certain cases, it is the only form of management that is admissible, as, for example, upon a mountain side liable to erosion from torrents, if all cleared at once, or in places difficult of access, where large timber could not be got out, or upon loose sands that might be liable to drift, if fully exposed to the winds.

364. In the case of pine or spruce woodlands, and in cedar swamps, where an interval of several years occurs between the cuttings, and due protection is given, the practice of selection is a good one, because in such cases a chance for seeding is afforded at each partial clearing, and the younger growth has the benefit of air and light, most favorable to its welfare.

365. In all cases, where the young growth becomes too dense, so that the branches interlock, it is advisable to thin out a part, in order to favor the growth of the remainder. In some localities, the young trees thus taken out may be profitably used for stakes and poles, affording a small revenue to the owner.

(2.) *Method of Coppice-growth.*

366. The term "coppice" is applied to a woodland that is cut off completely when the timber has grown to a size for the uses to which it is intended, and a new growth is allowed to spring up from the roots and stumps.

367. We have scarcely an instance among the resinous species in which this can be done with advantage. But very few[1] will sprout

[1] The redwood of California (*Sequoia sempervirens*) is a notable exception to this rule, as it sprouts freely from the stump, and even from the fallen timber, if cut at the proper season. The pitch-pine of New England (*Pinus rigida*) shows some tendency to sprout, but the sprouts seldom attain much growth.

from the stump at all, and of these the after-growth does not produce a new crop of much value.

368. Although most deciduous trees will sprout when cut, some of them, especially the beech and the maple, will scarcely grow to advantage. In other kinds, as the chestnut, oaks, ashes, poplars, willows, linden, etc., the second growth under favorable conditions is very good. As a rule, the growth is best when the cutting is nearly or quite level with the ground, for then the sprouts are able to get independent roots.

370. If, however, a second growth had already been obtained, it would be better to cut a little higher, and in the new wood, where the growth would be more likely to succeed than under the hardened bark of the old wood.

371. To insure success by this method, the timber must be cut a little before the season when growth begins. In a climate so varied as we find in the United States, it would be quite impossible to fix this time by a general rule, and even in a given locality it might vary in different years. In the Northern States, the latter part of winter would be best; but in intensely cold and dry weather the frost might so injure and loosen the bark that it would separate from the wood, and the vitality of the stump would be weakened or detroyed.

372. In some species, the flow of sap will tend to injury if the cutting is done too near the time when it begins to start. It is desirable to have the full effect of the first impulse of growth, and if the cutting be delayed until after this has advanced the sprouts become weak.

373. In mild climates, where we have no fear of heavy winter frosts, the cutting may be done at any time after the fall of the leaves, or in the broad-leaved evergreens, as soon as the movement of the second sap has ceased.

374. If cut in midsummer or early autumn, after the growth of wood for the year has formed, no sprouts will form, or they will be feeble and transient.

375. It is further to be observed, that as the sprouts from a stump start from along the line of junction between the wood and the bark, care should be taken not to wound or tear off the bark when cut. It is an excellent plan to go over the stumps with a sharp adze, and carefully trim the edges, always cutting towards the center, so

as to leave the edges smooth and the stump convex. This will enable it to shed off the rains which might otherwise settle in hollow places and hasten decay.

376. As only a few of the sprouts that come up from the stump are wanted as trees, a part of them should be cut off. If some of them are bent down, secured in place by pegs, and partly covered with soil, they will take root and become independent trees, when separated from the parent stock. In putting down these layers, the part that is buried should be partly cut off, and the tip end be left exposed.

377. In some species, as in the locust, and in many of the poplars, we find a strong tendency to spread by sending up sprouts from the roots, often at a great distance from the parent tree. These sprouts will readily form thrifty trees, and where these tracing roots are broken, and the ends brought to the surface, they grow readily from these ends.

378. Where it is desirable to hasten the growth of trees from sprouts and the ground is full of small roots, we may break these and bring their ends to the air and thus hasten a new growth. This can be done where poplars have been cut off, and a new crop is desired.

379. It is needless to remark that a coppice growth scarcely admits of any kind of pasturage at any time during its growth, and that to insure success it should always be kept inclosed. In some countries, the leaves are gathered while still green, and dried for winter fodder.

380. The period at which a coppice may be cut depends upon the uses to which the wood is to be applied, and the conditions of soil, climate, and exposure under which it has grown. It should never extend beyond forty, and it may be reduced to fifteen, or even to ten years. It will be very liable to be governed by the wants of the owner and the market prices of timber. Generally, from twenty to thirty years is ample time for firewood, charcoal, railroad ties, etc. For hoop poles and other small wood it may be cut in five or six years.

381. As a general rule, the result is best where the period is uniform, but this can not be determined in a given locality until all the circumstances of growth and the opportunities for market are known. The wood should be taken out before the sprouts get up

so as to be liable to injury, and the brush should be burned as soon as may be—if possible in the spring of the same year.

382. Roads are of first importance for facilitating the removal of products, and when kept free from dry litter, they afford lines of defense in case of forest fires.

383. Sometimes one or two agricultural crops are taken off at the time of cutting of a coppice. The benefit in exceptional cases may be considerable, but as a rule it will do more harm than good.

384. One of the most important applications of the method of coppice growth, in Europe, is for the production of oak bark, to be used in tanning, as will be elsewhere more fully noticed.

385. As the trees in a coppice do not come to maturity, they seldom tend to seed themselves, or if this occurs it is apt to result that inferior species of easy and rapid growth may get an undue start, and tend to supplant the more valuable kinds. It is always advisable to notice the void places in a coppice woodland, and plant or sow them at the proper season. In this, attention should be given to favor the more valuable kinds. A proper mixture of species will sometimes yield a greater quantity of material and more profit, in a given time, than when it is all alike.

386. As coppice woods must be cut in the season when the sap is about to start, the durability of the wood is not so great as when cut in the dormant season. For some uses this is not important, but in others, as in the case of railroad ties, posts, and the like, it becomes a question for consideration as to whether the season of cutting should not be that which tends to greater durability, at the risk of failure of reproduction by coppice-growth.

387. It is to be remarked that the best success in reproduction after cutting, occurs in rich and humid soil, and in a damp climate, and that as we pass to those that are dryer the chances become less, until we approach those of the arid type, when they disappear altogether. From the greater dryness of our climate, as compared with that of Europe, we can not so uniformly depend upon this method as there.

388. In a given species it is observed that the tendency to send up vigorous sprouts diminishes with age, and that finally it ceases almost entirely. We should not therefore depend upon the stumps of trees of large size for the growth of coppice wood. In cases where it is desirable to hasten their decay, to get room for others,

they may be cut concave, so that the rain-water will settle upon them instead of running off.

389. In skilled forestry there is a constant effort to increase the production of a given area, and to improve the quality of the wood grown. Since coppice woods are generally cut before maturity, their timber has not the size or excellence that allow it to be used where pieces of large dimensions and great strength are needed, and it has been customary at every cutting to reserve some of the finest and thriftiest trees and allow them to grow to a second, third, fourth, or fifth period, thereby attaining their greatest size and value.[1]

390. These reserved trees affect the young growth around them, either by their covert or their shade.

(*a.*) The *covert* of a tree is the action that a tree may have upon the space that is covered by the top and branches, and it is generally injurious, by intercepting a part of the rain and much of the light, and by preventing the formation of dew.

(*b.*) The *shade* is the shadow which a tree casts at different times in the day, and where it does not rest too long, and alternates with sunshine, it is almost always salutary to the young growth. It tends to prevent evaporation, while it does not hinder the free access of the air.

391. As a rule, the reserves should not cover more than from the twentieth to the sixteenth part of the surface, and they should be distributed as uniformly as possible. At every cutting some should be taken out, so that the number of each class becomes less.

392. The oak, when thus left under an unusual exposure of the sun and air, is especially liable to put out large lateral branches of vigorous growth. These "gormand" branches should not be allowed to become large, and can best be trimmed off close to the trunk, and late in summer. They will then be less liable to sprout the next spring, and may sooner heal over with new wood. It is a good practice to paint over these wounds with coal-tar.

[1] The trees thus left, received certain names according to the periods they are left over. In French forestry these names, with their English equivalents, as nearly as can be rendered, are as follows:

1st period. *Baliveau*—"young reserves."
2d period. *Modernes*—"moderns."
3d period. *Anciens, 2d class*—"old, of 2d class.
4th period, *Anciens 1st class*—old, of 1st class.
5th period. *Vieilles écorces*—"old-bark."

393. In the case of timber used for ship building, the knees and other curved or angular parts are generally taken from trees that have the desired shapes. These are oftener found along the borders of a woodland than in the interior, and the reserves affording these forms being more desirable, more of them may be left in proportion to their number than of others that are more upright. It has been practiced to some extent, to bend and confine young trees, to secure these curves and forms that give them special value for certain uses. This may be done by fastening one branch to another of the same tree, or by binding it to the ground, or fastening it to a plank molded to the proper curve, until it will stay in place.

(3.) *The Growing of Woodlands to full Maturity.*[1]

394. For the production of large timber, of great strength, and fit for the most important uses in civil and naval constructions, a special course of management is required, which we will briefly describe, although it has not hitherto been much followed, except upon lands belonging to governments, and in a large degree for the supply of their own wants.

395. In this form of cultivation, the trees are generally all started at the same period, and at all stages of growth they are of the same age and size, but progressively become less in number, by thinning out from time to time, in order to allow the remainder a better chance to grow.

396. The period of "revolution" with the same kinds varies with the richness of the soil, the climate, and the exposure, and it is longer in some kinds than with others.

397. The deciduous kinds most prized for this are the English oak,[2] beech, elm, ash, sycamore, maple, hornbeam, birch, and locust, often more or less mixed, and sometimes with spruces, firs, and pines. The conifers can be cultivated only in this way or by "jardinage." [§ 360.]

398. The beginning is secured either by sowing or planting (upon

[1] We have no single word in the English language to express the idea which the French convey in the word *futaie*, and the Germans in *hochwald*, meaning a forest grown to full age, in a period ranging from 60 or 70 years, to 150 or 200.

[2] *Quercus pedunculata*, and *Q. sessiliflora*, by some botanists regarded as varieties of the same species, which they name *Quercus robur*.

ground previously prepared) over its whole surface, or in squares or pockets, so as to be near enough together to shade the whole ground in two or three years, and thus take an upward growth to reach the air and light. They should be thinned out when too dense, but no rule can be given as to the time when, and the extent to which this thinning should be done, where so much depends upon circumstances, and the judgment of the forester in charge.

399. In Germany, upon a good soil, and a uniform growth, the number of trees at different clearings, after the trees get to be of a considerable size, is about as follows:

1st clearing,	at 30 to 40 years,	1,300 to 1,600	trees left to an acre.
2d "	" 50 to 60 "	500 to 600	" "
3d "	" 70 to 80 "	300 to 400	" "
4th "	" 90 to 100 "	200 to 250	" "

400. In the evergreen or coniferous kinds the number left may be greater, because, with a given size of body, the foliage is less. Upon poor soils and in rude climates it may be greater, because the trees will be smaller, and upon mountain sides the same, because the trees do not then shade one another so much, and are better exposed to the light.

401. Much importance is attached to these thinnings, for they secure a great gain in value of the final product, besides that derived from the trees taken out, and that would have perished from shading out if left to themselves. From the first of these thinnings they have a value, which increased at every time, from poles to timber of useful size; and at all stages they furnish wood for fuel and charcoal.

402. While these accessory products afford in advanced stages a revenue, much above the whole cost of supervision and labor, their removal stimulates the growth of the remainder in a notable degree, and they gain much faster in size, as their branches and roots find more room to spread. By letting in the sun and the air, they contribute to give qualities of solidity and elasticity, that they could not acquire in a dense shade.

403. In a well kept woodland, dead and dying trees should be taken out whenever found, as their presence favors the breeding of beetles, that might injure the remaining trees. It is a poor policy to allow the dead leaves and the litter to be taken out; but when the

trees become large, the fattening of swine upon the nuts and acorns is usually allowed.

404. In such a forest, in best condition, the trees are much nearer together than as we commonly find them in a wild-wood :[1] the ground is so shaded that no grass will grow, and the seeds that fall soon perish for want of air and light. In fact the trees themselves do not bear seeds as freely as when they have more space.

405. At the time of these thinnings, the soft woods of more rapid growth, such as the poplars, birches, alders, etc., should be taken out where they are not wanted; but a mixture of kinds, such as the oak and beech, or the beech and Scotch pine is often encouraged, as they agree well together, and make a more profitable product than either would alone. As the oak yields a more valuable timber, they generally prefer to give it a greater chance.

406. Care should be taken to clear out the brambles and shrubs, good for nothing but faggots, and which are bound in bundles and sold. The branches of trees cut in thinning are also used as faggots.

407. Finally, as the time for general cutting draws near, and it becomes necessary to provide for a new forest-growth, the seeding of the plants that are to form the future forest is secured without cost, and with great success, by a simple course of management that deserves careful notice :

408. At first, they take out some of the trees uniformly over the whole surface, so as to let in the air and light, and thus favor the remaining trees in bearing fruit. The seeds that form fall under or near the parent trees, and become lightly covered by the leaves of the same season. Being on the surface of a rich soil, which has been forming for a long period, from the decay of foliage, and now exposed to the sun's light and warmth, they spring up as young

[1] Nothing can be more impressive to one accustomed only to the irregularity of an American forest, than the sight of a well kept European plantation in full growth. As he looks into the gloomy recesses, the trees stand in rows like organ pipes, greatly exceeding in number those ever found from spontaneous growth, and with a symmetry in size and height that is remarkable. When seen at a distance, such forests appear level at the top, and we often see different levels, indicating differences in age. The best cultivated forests of Germany are worth from three to five times as much as native woods.

plants, and in a year or two the whole surface of the woodland is carpeted with the fresh green foliage of young seedling trees.

409. These tender plants would soon wither and perish in the full light of day in an open field. They need just the kind of shelter that the parent-trees afford. The sunlight comes down sprinkled here and there, and the shadows pass over them, so that with this alternation of light and shelter the plants receive just the proportion that is needed for their most thrifty growth.

410. As they gain in size, they need more light, and will bear more exposure; and finally, when they need shelter no longer, the remaining trees are carefully taken out, and the young forest starts off on a new period, to supply timber for the use of generations unborn.

411. This period in the larch and the birch ranges from 50 to 60 years, or with the former in cold regions it may extend to 120 or 140 years. With the locust and the maritime, Aleppo and Corsican pines, it is from 60 to 70 years; with the Scotch pine, it is from 80 to 90 years; with the beech, from 80 to 140 years; with the ash, from 90 to 100 years; with the chestnut, from 90 to 120 years; with the spruce, from 90 to 140 years; with the fir, from 100 to 140, the average being about 120 years; with the elm, 100 to 120 years; and with the oak, 120 to 200 years.

412. The profits of a full-grown forest, as compared with a coppice, are very great. It is shown by Hartig, a noted German author, that a high forest cut at 120 years bears to a coppice cut once in 30 years, through the same time, the proportion of 7 to 4, all receipts and expenses being taken into the account.

413. Whenever the time shall come that our only supplies of timber are furnished by cultivation, great corporations will doubtless be formed, for managing great forest properties, under skilled agents, and with a capital that can afford to wait a long time, so long as it is earning a good rate, and promises a sure profit. By such means, forests can be grown to great advantage, but best upon an extensive scale.

European Forest Administrations.

414. In every country upon the continent of Europe, considerable tracts of woodland belong to the government. The local municipalities (communes, cities, etc.) own other tracts, generally near or

within their limits, and often subject to rights of common usage, such as the supply of wood for fuel or building purposes, pasturage, feeding of swine upon acorns, and the like. Many public establishments, such as churches, monasteries, charities, etc., also own forest estates, as a part of their endowment.

415. Over all of these the government has supervision, and there has grown up an organized branch of the public service, known as the *Forest Administration*, with regular grades of promotion, and generally pensions to those who have spent their strength in the service until their working days are over.

416. In the German States, and in the Scandinavian kingdoms, the Forest Administration is generally a branch of the Ministry of Finances; in Russia, in that of the Imperial Domains, and in Austria, France, Italy, and Spain, it is associated with the Ministry of Agriculture, or of Agriculture and Commerce, with some differences due to the organization of the several governments.

417. They agree in having a central administrative office, from whence all important business is ordered, and to which reports are made. They generally have in the superior grades of service a number of inspectors, who make periodical visits to the different forests, to observe their condition, and detect any fault or neglect that may have crept into their management. It is in some countries the custom to transfer the local superintendents from time to time to new fields of duty, as tending to a more faithful discharge of their trusts.

418. There is also a system of forest-guards, sometimes organized upon a military basis, for the protection of timber and game, and to see that the work of cutting and removal of products is done in accordance with regulations. These guards, when on duty, always wear a uniform, and are commonly armed with a carbine. They may make summary arrests, and are held accountable for any damage or trespass done within their districts which are not promptly reported by them for investigation and punishment.

419. For every grade of service a uniform is prescribed, to be worn when on duty, and on certain public occasions, as in our army and navy. Green, among Foresters, is a favorite color, and an oak-leaf-and-acorn is a common symbol of the profession. A marking-hammer is also a symbol of the Forester, as is the anchor with the sailor, or the pick with the miner.

Forest Societies: Periodical Literature.

420. Forest societies of various kinds are organized in most countries. These generally meet quarterly or annually for the discussion of subjects of professional interest, and their proceedings are usually published. These annual meetings usually last several days, and excursions are commonly made to places of interest. Besides these associations, composed of proprietors and professional foresters, there are various other associations, some for mutual relief of members, and some for special objects, such as the maintenance of schools of Forestry, the prosecution of experimental researches, the interests concerned in the lumber and timber trade, etc.

421. There are also a great number of periodicals, issued at regular intervals, and wholly or partly devoted to the interests of Forestry. If we include quarterlies and annuals with those issued monthly or oftener, the number would amount to nearly fifty. Many of these are conducted with great ability, and afford substantial aid to the interest to which they are devoted.

Schools of Forestry.

422. Nearly every government upon the continent in Europe has established one or more Schools of Forestry, for preparing young men for service as officers of the forest and administration. None can enter this service until they have passed through the studies and practical exercises at these schools. The course generally lasts two to three years, and the students must first finish their studies in the public schools. They are taught mathematics, natural sciences (especially botany and entomology), chemistry, meteorology, physics, sylviculture, drawing, surveying, forest and hunting laws, forest management, etc., and make regular excursions with the professors, for observation and practice.

423. The following are the principal schools of Forestry in Europe. Those preceded by a star are connected with some university or other institution :

Austria: *Vienna, Eulenburg, Weisswasser, Lemburg, Aggsbach, Bergenz, *Schemnitz, and *Gratz, and of lower grade in other places.

Denmark: *Copenhagen.

Finland: Evois.

France: Nancy, Barres, and *Paris. (Institut Agronomique.)

GERMANY: *Baden,* *Carlsruhe; *Bavaria,* Aschaffenburg, and *Munich; *Hesse-Darmstadt,* *Giessen; *Prussia,* Eberswalde and Münden; *Saxe-Weimar,* Eisnach; *Saxony,* Tharand; *Wurtemburg,* *Tübingen.

Italy: Vallombrosa.

Norway: At two or three places small elementary schools.

Portugal: *Lisbon.

Russia: St. Petersburg, *Moscow, Lisino, and *Nova Alexandria (Poland), besides a short course at six farm schools.

Spain: Escorial.

Sweden: Stockholm, and small schools at seven other places.

Switzerland: *Zurich.

Turkey: Constantinople.

424. These schools generally have forest gardens, laboratories, collections in natural history, and especially in Forestry, and special libraries connected with them. In Austria, several of them are supported by Forest Associations, composed of land proprietors and others interested in Forestry. In many universities and polytechnic institutions, Forestry is incidentally taught as a part of their general course.

Planting of Dunes.

425. On certain coasts the sands thrown up by the waves are drifted by the winds into hills, sometimes two hundred feet or more in height and miles in width, which are constantly changing in form, and gradually advancing inland. These drifting sands, by closing the mouths of streams, generally cause a series of ponds to be formed behind them, which may render the country sickly, as well as the soil worthless from overflow. In various places on the northern and western coast of France, villages and hamlets have been buried by drifting sands, and considerable tracts of fertile land have been thus overwhelmed.[1] The planting of these "dunes," and their control, may be reckoned among the proudest achievements of Forestry.

426. In these exposed places, the plants need shelter in getting started, and the first thing to be done is to compel the winds to build a high and regular embankment for their protection. To se-

[1] We have an example of these disasters at Grand Haven, Michigan, where a railroad station has been buried by drifting sands.

cure this, a line of obstructions is placed along the shore, three or four hundred feet from the water's edge, consisting of bundles of faggots set in diagonal rows near together, or planks three or four feet high, with a space of an inch between. A part of the sand as it glides along will lodge in front of these obstructions, and a part will pass through and settle behind.

427. As they get buried, a new series of bundles of faggots is set, or the planks are drawn up, from time to time, and a huge mound of sand is finally formed, with a gentle slope towards the sea (7° to 12°) and one more abrupt (about 22°) on the land side. These slopes are then sown with beach-grass and other maritime plants, in squares like a chess-board, so that they will spread and cover the whole surface, and behind they sow the seeds of trees.

428. On the southwestern coast of France, the most ample success has followed from planting the maritime pine (*Pinus pinaster*), the seeds being sown with those of beach-grass, and covered with brush. This work was begun by Brémontier, an engineer under the auspices of the government, in 1787, and is now practically finished and the whole coast covered with a profitable growth of timber.[1]

429. In other regions, where this pine will not thrive, various grasses, with tracing roots, Scotch pine, poplars, willows, tamarisk, and other plants are set, as the opportunities present.

430. Upon the coast of Cape Cod, in Massachusetts, the pitch pine (*P. rigida*) and the beach-grass (*Calamagrostis arenaria*) are planted on the dunes with great success. Upon the Florida coast, and further north, the Bermuda grass (*Cynodon dactylon*) has been used with success, and the maritime pine may succeed there, although it has failed upon the Massachusetts coast.

431. There are occasionally places in the interior where the sands exposed to the winds will thus drift, and the surest way to prevent this is by planting. In this we should begin on the side of the prevailing winds, and if the soil is somewhat damp, willow cuttings

[1] In October, 1881, we rode some twenty miles on horseback among these dunes, in the neighborhood of Arcachon and La Teste. The pines are largely used for the production of turpentine, and are cut out from time to time, as they become large, to make room for a younger growth, but never in bodies together, or so as to expose the sand. Many years ago the government placed a monument in the midst of the pines that Brémontier planted, to commemorate his great achievement.

may provide the best defense. If seeds are sown, it may be necessary to cover them with brush, that is fastened down with stakes. Under this cover, the plants may get well rooted; and if this is secured, the success of the work is certain.

Reboisement.

432. By "reboisement," we mean the planting of woodlands where they have been destroyed, and especially where their destruction has caused great injury from torrents by the eroding of mountain sides, and covering the valleys below with stone and gravel. The desolation and sterility thus occasioned is increased by pasturage, especially by sheep and goats, so that regions once highly fertile and densely populated have often become utterly desolate and solitary.

433. In recent years, most European governments have taken measures to stop these ruinous practices, and have with much success, but at vast expense, secured a gradual return of fertility, and an effectual prevention of future injuries. These measures may be described under two heads:

(*a.*) *Barriers for checking the Torrents.*

434. These are made of stone, in the bottoms of the ravines, and convex up-stream, the top being lowest in the middle. They are sometimes made of bundles of willow securely fastened down. They will then often spout and grow, thus by their roots preventing further erosion.

(*b.*) *Reboisement of the denuded Slopes.*

435. This is by far the most important, and often the more difficult work to be done, as it tends to prevent the formation of the torrents. The rains that fall upon a wooded, or even a sodded slope, have their force broken, and they quietly filter into the soil, or flow down with so many obstructions that they do no injury. But on a bare surface, they begin to wear little channels, which presently enlarge in width and depth, till they become enormous chasms.

436. To secure a wooded or sheltered surface, the soil should be

disturbed as little as possible in sowing or planting, and on a north slope the seed may sometimes be best sown on the snow.

437. Steep banks that will probably slide or crumble down, should be rendered more sloping before trees are planted. They are dug away at the top, and the soil slid into the ravine below, or sometimes thrown down by blasting. A drain may be secured by first filling in the bottom with trees and brush.

438. To obtain a chance for the roots of trees, the steep naked slopes are dug into horizontal notches or terraces, beginning at the top, and the edges of these are planted with almost any thing that can be made to grow, or at least are secured by fascines and strong stakes. These bands are nearer together where the slope is steeper, and the brush by slow decay helps to fertilize the soil. These terraces tend to get filled up in a year or two, and thus afford a soil deep enough to hold the trees, and then lines of young trees from nurseries are set along these belts of deep soil. If they get fairly rooted, they will secure the object intended, and will prevent the recurrence of further damages.

439. Paths are made along the banks, to give access to the work, and for future use in the removal of products, but in these situations no tree will ever be taken, unless others are coming on to replace it. By these costly but necessary methods, about one-fourth part of the work to be done in France in the way of restoration by reboisement, which was begun in 1860, had been accomplished in 16 years, and 63,168 acres had been replanted with trees, at an enormous cost; but this expense was less than the damages which a single flood might produce, and which wooded slopes on the hills and mountains would have prevented.

440. In many parts of our own country, and especially in the mountainous regions of the interior and upon the Pacific coast, the greatest injury is being done from the clearing and burning off of mountain sides, and we already notice a marked effect upon the climate, aside from the local damages to the surface from this cause.[1] The same, in less degree, may be seen in every part of the country, wherever there are steep slopes exposed to heavy rains; and private interests should lead to watchful care, in every case where these effects are in operation, or are liable to occur.

[1] See Forestry Report, 1877, p. 334, for a statement of these effects.

On the Management of Forest Plantations in Scotland.

441. A Forester of great experience[1] has given the following summary of the course usually pursued in the management of woodlands in Scotland: "For ordinary planting, the size of plants preferred are one year as seedling and two years transplanted; but for bare heathery hills, that are much exposed, fir plants one year as seedling and one year transplanted, or two years' seedling are considered best. These are planted by notching.

442. "The most approved mode of planting coniferous trees here is as follows: If the soil and situation are considered likely to produce larch (*Larix Europea*) to maturity as sound timber, it is generally planted as a pure crop, with a very slight intermixture of silver fir (*Abies pectinata*) and Scot's fir (*Pinus sylvestris*) among the larches. If there is any doubt of the larch being overtaken by disease, then we plant larch and Scot's fir in equal numbers, at four feet apart, regularly intermixing them.

443. "In training them, the plantation may be trained up as a mixed one, or if the larches prove healthy, it may be converted wholly into a pure larch, or if otherwise, into a pure Scot's fir plantation. Hence we plant a larger area under Scot's fir, with a considerable mixture of larch, and often on soft moorland a considerable number of spruce and silver fir; but the ground, where requiring it, is thoroughly drained first. The trees are put in by slitting.

444. "Oak and all other hard-wood trees are planted at from 12 to 15 feet apart, and the intermediate spaces are filled up generally with larch to four feet apart. A slight intermixture of other coniferous trees is often introduced, so as to augment the ornamental character of the plantations. The larches and other firs are gradually thinned out as the plantation advances, leaving a few intermixed for the ultimate crop. Oak and other hard-wood trees are planted by pitting.

445. "The thinning of fir plantations commences when they have stood about ten years, and is repeated at intervals of 4 to 6 years,

[1] Mr. Wm. McCorquodale, who for 45 years has held the office of wood-manager to the Earl of Mansfield. Mr. C. has also, during this period, surveyed and reported upon the future management of over 160 other forest estates in Scotland.

till the plantation arrives at about 40 to 45 years of age. At each thinning, the trees are left standing about clear of each other. At certain stages of growth, the trees might be thinned out to stand at one-third of their height apart, as, for example, trees of 21 feet might stand 7 feet apart.

446. "We have generally, for the permanent crop, about 200 to 250 trees per acre. After the last course of thinning, the trees are not interfered with again until they arrive at maturity. When the crop comes to the age of 60 to 80 years, it is sold in sections, in the growing state, and the ground is again replanted as soon as it is cleared off and properly prepared.

447. "Hard-wood plantations are treated as follows: As soon as the nurses are interfering with the hard-wood trees, their thinning begins, and it is gradually carried on till they are all removed, by the time they arrive at thirty years of age, with the exception of such as are left for ornament, to grow to maturity."

448. An idea of the relative profit of trees of different kinds in Scotland, we give the following list of prices of timber per cubic foot, in 1882:

Larch	1*s.* to 1*s.* 2*d.*	Oak (standing)	2*s.* to 3*s.*
Scot's fir	6*d.* to 9*d.*	Ash	1*s.* 3*d.* to 1*s.* 6*d.*
Spruce	4*d.* to 6*d.*	Beech	10*d.* to 1*s.*
Silver fir	6*d.* to 10*d.*	Elm	1*s.* 3*d.* to 1*s.* 6*d.*

In 1876, fifteen acres of Scotch fir timber, 80 years old, near Perth, Scotland, sold for £132 per acre. A handsome revenue had been previously got from the thinnings.

CHAPTER XI.

ORNAMENTAL PLANTING.

449. Although the leading object of this book is to convey utilitarian ideas upon the subject of tree-planting, and to indicate the methods and opportunities for doing this with most profit and surest success, it should be borne in mind that these objeots are not in the least degree inconsistent with a due appreciation of the beauties of woodland scenery, whether presented in the somber shadows of a dense forest, the cheerful shade of a grove, or in the grandeur or grace of an isolated tree.

450. In fact, there is nothing that will so effectually promote a taste for sylviculture, and a familiarity with the methods of Forestry, as the adornment of homesteads and villages by ornamental planting. The pleasures to be derived from this employment have been described by Addison, in the simplicity and elegance that characterize his style, in one of the numbers[1] of the *Spectator:*

451. "There is, indeed, something truly magnificent in this kind of amusement. It gives a nobler air to several parts of nature; it fills the earth with a variety of beautiful scenes, and has something in it like creation. For this reason, the pleasure of one who plants is something like that of a poet, who, as Aristotle observes, is more delighted with his productions than any other writer or artist whatsoever. Plantations have one advantage in them which is not to be found in most other works, as they give a pleasure of a more lasting date, and continually improve in the eye of the planter. When you have finished a building, or any other undertaking of the like nature, it immediately begins to decay on your hands; you see it brought to its utmost point of perfection, and from that time hastening to its ruin. On the contrary, when you have finished your plantations, they are still arriving at greater degrees of perfection, as long as you live, and appear more delightful in each succeeding year than they did in the foregoing."

452. To realize how much the imagery of the poets and of beauty in landscape painting depends upon sylvan scenery and rural associations, we need but imagine how blank and dreary would poetry and painting be without them. Whatever tends to cultivate and extend this appreciation of the beautiful in nature is in direct advancement of Forestry. In this the taste and good sense of one, may become an example for another, as in every phase of life, and in every pursuit of business or of pleasure. Mankind are largely influenced by the example of others, and can often assign no better reason for this imitation than that it is the practice of neighbors.

453. It has sometimes been a custom to plant a tree to commemorate an event—the birth of a child; the visit of an illustrious guest; the graduation of a college class, and other occasions, which give a lasting interest to the act. It occasionally happens that some historical incident becomes associated with a tree, as the Royal Oak

[1] No. 583.

that once sheltered Charles the Second; the Charter Oak at Hartford, and the Treaty Tree at Philadelphia, which were monuments while they lasted, and were cherished as relics when they fell.

454. It is a pleasant thing on any commemorative occasion, as the centennial of a town, the dedication of a church, or the foundation of an institution, to plant a tree as a living witness of the occasion. It should be of some long-living and large-growing kind, to the end that it may for a long period bear in remembrance the occasion that gave it a place, and that claims for it a protection.

455. In considering the subject of ornamental planting, it may be presented under the three following divisions, viz.:

(1.) Home-adornment, and the planting of private grounds.

(2.) Village-improvement, and the planting of the wayside.

(3.) City parks, and the plantation of grounds in rural cemeteries, and around public institutions.

(1.) *Home-adornment, and the Planting of Private Grounds.*

456. In respect to this class of ornament, the author will venture to quote from a paper read by him before the Department of Superintendence of the National Educational Association, at its meeting held in New York city, in the spring of 1881, as presenting thoughts concerning the motives and their effect, that may be deemed of interest in this connection:

457. "The man who has cleared a farm out of the forest seldom or never plants a tree. He has come, from long custom, to look upon trees as an incumbrance to be removed; and whenever his home presents a noticeable amount of sylvan shade, it is more likely to be the work of a younger generation, who have no sympathy with his aversion, and a better idea of the comforts of home-life. Americans have been reproached for having but slight attachment to the homes of their childhood; and this willingness to sell to a stranger the land that a parent has cleared and cultivated, and on which their own early years have been spent, has been ascribed to a certain instability of character, and an uneasy desire for change. There is doubtless a strong affinity between a love of home and of country, and it is true that an attachment to a homestead because of ancestral possessions and family associations, would greatly tend to increase our national prosperity and happiness. It would lead to substantial investments for permanence and future enjoyment, that the

transient and speculative owner would never make, and it would tend to the more solid foundation of our public institutions generally. The man who settles temporarily for business, and expects to depart when he becomes rich, spends no money upon public libraries, and cares nothing for the charitable and educational establishments of the place, provided they do not burden him while he remains. His influence will generally be adverse, if these objects require expenses that bring no return during his stay, and he will prefer temporary expedients to permanent investments, if they but serve to bridge over the time of his sojourn. The solid and substantial foundation of our institutions is laid by those having a permanent interest in the prosperity of the places where they are located. It is this class alone that erects monuments, and that leaves evidence that its members have lived for the welfare of those who are to come after them. It is a point worthy of inquiry, as to whether much of this indifference to the home of childhood and to the possessions of ancestors with which Americans have been charged, is not due to their bleak and cheerless surroundings. We can not doubt that the influence of a pleasant rural homestead and the choice memories of refined associations in early youth, are as capable of making as strong an impression upon our native population as in any country whatever, and although in the absence of laws of entail, and under the impulse of adventure, or motives of interest, or the force of circumstances, a change of ownership may often happen, and the choice and cherished homestead become the property of a stranger, still the chances become less as the attractions are greater, and a motive worthy of earnest and honorable effort is presented, in favor of maintenance in the family line."

458. In the choice of a site for farm buildings, while there is an obvious convenience in having them near a highway, there are advantages to be considered in placing them more or less in the interior, where a spring of water or perennial stream may offer conveniences that money could not carry to a roadside residence, and a gentle swell of land a site for building that a prince might envy. The saving of labor and team-work, in cultivating such a centralized farm, should not be overlooked.

459. A neatly painted gateway should distinguish the main entrance from others opening upon the highway, and if the farm be of size to warrant the steady employment of a laborer with his

family, English taste would place his cottage by the gate. A mass of shrubbery upon each side of the entrance gives a pleasing effect.

460. A good road, bordered by an avenue of trees, should lead by gentle curves, as the surface required, to the premises of the owner. There may be a fence or not, as there is occasion, but a well kept hedge is better. One advantage of the trees would be to afford a guide by night, as well as shade by day. They should be set at measured intervals, and all of one kind. Such an avenue, when fully grown, gives a stately effect, and an air of stability and opulence far surpassing that of an irregular one, as if from trees reserved in a clearing; and it may be had at no considerable cost. If an intervening grove hides the dwelling until near approach, and then presents it in full view, the effect is increased.

461. Large trees in the back-ground, and those of smaller size and of less common kinds, in the foreground, produce the finest effect. It is there that the species most ornamental from their blossoms, their fruit, or their bright-colored ornamental foliage, may be used with greatest advantage. There should be a studied effort to imitate nature in the groupings of trees and shrubbery, and this can not be done by placing them in rows or in symmetrical order, but in clumps, with openings here and there, and with a studied avoidance of the formal in their arrangement.

462. With such approaches and surroundings, which do not require a large investment, a dwelling of itself not large or expensive, may display an air of comfort, and even of opulence, which a more costly mansion by the roadside, unadorned by trees and shrubbery, could never be made to present. It gives to the observer the impression that its owner has not only means but taste, and is a strong indication of domestic happiness within.

463. The opportunities of a brook for supplying a fountain, or feeding a fish-pond, may often occur, and the observing owner may secure these ornaments at a moderate expense. His fountain will not need costly castings or masonry—the jets may issue from piles of rustic rock-work, and his ponds may be bordered with a line of rude stones, half concealed by ferns and wild flowers, and the bottom covered with clean white sand.

464. But in case the buildings are already near the highway, and there be no desire to change them, there are still opportunities for rural adornment, to ample extent. The roadside may be bordered

with lines of trees as we approach from either way; screens of evergreen may be planted on the cold side or the warm side, as there may be need of shelter from the cold, or heat, or to conceal objects not pleasing to the eye, and groups of shrubbery may be planted in clumps, or in masses, as may be found most pleasing and natural. There should, upon large grounds, be a suitable variety, but if the space be small, it is not wise to attempt too much. A single phase of beauty, of whatever type the circumstances most favor, is sure to be pleasing; where, if too many objects be to closely crowded the effect is confused and lost.

465. Large and dense evergreens in the foreground would be very likely to produce a gloomy and somber impression; they will be found to show to best advantage, rising in the back-ground, behind and among the deciduous kinds.

466. Trees should not be planted too near a dwelling. Their shade and humidity are unfavorable to health, if in excess, and they tend to cause damp, moldy walls. They hinder ventilation and the access of air and light, so conducive to health, and sometimes breed insects that prove a nuisance. Their roots will find their way into the walls; and trees planted near a building become one-sided and deformed, from their unequal exposure to the light.

467. There is always something to conceal. An old stump, or broken and dead tree, may possibly be still made beautiful with the Virginia creeper or the ivy. Barns and out-buildings may be partly hidden, or entirely screened from notice by trees, and a barn-yard may be made comfortable for stock, both in winter and summer, by dense shelter-belts. A useless pile of bowlders, or a rock, may be covered with ferns and myrtle, by giving their roots a hold in the soil. A brook, a marshy spot, or a pond, may be made ornamental, by drooping willows, or clumps of alders, and by a variety of aquatic shrubs and plants.

468. It is in good taste to separate the kitchen garden by a hedge, from the lawn plantations, and it is generally profitable to surround the orchard with a shelter belt, or an evergreen screen. Clumps of thrifty evergreens, here and there in an orchard, are of great advantage.

469. The Lombardy poplar forms an admirable wind-break; but in ornamental planting it shows to best advantage when it rises from behind, or among trees with rounded tops—not at measured

intervals, but here and there. The same may be said of the evergreens having a pyramidal growth, unless they are purposely intended as a screen or wind-break. The eye will tolerate a symmetry of arrangement where there is an obvious object, while symmetry without a motive may fail to please.

470. In planting poplars and willows, we should remember that their roots have a great liking for drains and wells, and will sometimes fill them if too near. They may cause leaks in aqueducts of masonry, and the roots of these and other trees may heave foundations and displace stone walls, if planted close by them, in a deep mellow soil. These qualities become of the greatest value in consolidating the soil of eroding streams, and upon embankments, the borders of irrigating ditches, and upon sands, where moisture can be reached by the roots. They should be used in ornamental planting, where they can be placed to best advantage, but should generally have a secondary place.

471. In the immense range of opportunity which our country presents, there is an infinite variety of conditions, and in the vast number of our native species, and of exotic kinds that prove suitable for cultivation, no general rules could be followed in homestead planting. If the general idea of studying the pleasing effects in natural grouping be observed, and proper judgment is used in the selection of kinds suited to the soil and exposure, the result will be satisfactory.

472. It may be added that such a homestead *is worth more money* than one wholly unadorned. This is indeed a low motive, as compared with the more refined and honorable aims of life; but if we can secure the enjoyment that these improvements afford, and at the same time enhauce the value of the estate, let us by no means miss the opportunity.

(2.) *Village-improvement, and the Planting of Way-sides.*

473. Nothing gives a more inviting appearance to a village street, or a country road, than well kept avenues of trees. To secure the best effect, attention should be paid to the following rules:

(*a.*) In a village or city, the planting and care should be under one direction, although the expense may be chargeable to the property adjacent. This may be some officer designated by law, or a committee of citizens whose authority is recognized by general consent.

(*b.*) Upon a given street, the trees should be all of one kind. The different streets may be planted with different kinds, and a pleasing diversity thus secured.

(*c.*) The lines of trees should not be less than six feet, and in wide streets not less than eight or ten feet from the outer line. In *very* wide and quiet streets, not thoroughfares, a charming effect is secured, by having a line of trees in the middle, with carriage-ways on each side, and at proper crossings.

(*d.*) The trees should be protected by proper guards while young, and generally by a railing on the side towards the middle of the road when they have grown to a large size.

(*e.*) They should be protected by well-enforced ordinances, and by public sentiment, from being used as hitching-posts for horses. To prevent the necessity, such posts should be provided, far enough away to be free from danger to the trees; it may still be within their shade.

(*f.*) For immediate effect, as well as ultimate advantage to the plantation, the trees first set may be at half the distance apart that is intended for the full-grown trees; and the alternate ones may be of some quickly growing kind, that should be taken out as they crowd the more valuable kinds which are to remain. These temporary trees will tend to render the growth of those between them higher, and will leave less trimming necessary afterwards. The cottonwoods, soft-maples, poplars, and willows afford convenient trees for such uses.

(*g.*) Care should be taken that the soil be kept mellow around the roots, and that they be watered while young in times of great drouth.

474. In streets much traveled, a grating placed in the pavement, and extending a yard or so on every side, would be useful. In Europe, iron gratings of ornamental design are placed around the trees, but not in contact with them. They are on a level with the pavement, and so placed as not to obstruct travel. Through these gratings the air circulates freely, and the roots are fully exposed to the rains. They may be watered and fertilized in case of need, and the soil mellowed by spading from time to time. We here present the sketch of a grating suitable for such a purpose. It may be made

highly ornamental, and a monogram, a trade-mark, a sign, or any other device may be introduced, that fancy might suggest. In front of premises owned by a city or a state, the crest of the official arms would be very proper. The part with radiating bars, in this sketch, might be of several sizes, to be changed as the tree became large, and the grating might be supported by wrought-iron bars, as represented by dotted lines. The inner disc should be cast in two sections, and the outer one in two or more. In our figure we have shown three divisions. They should be securely fastened down, and would be very durable. They might be circular, oval, or in any other form, and being flush with the pavements, they would not in the least interfere with their use. The edge nearest the tree should have a flange turned up, so as to prevent injury to the bark by sliding objects.

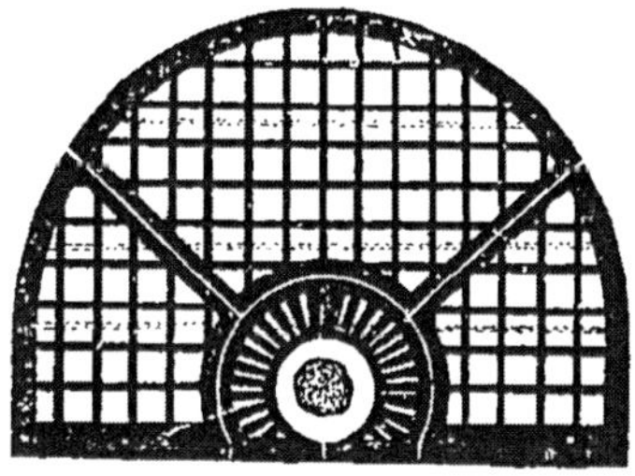

68. Screen for placing over Roots of Trees in Pavements.

475. With respect to the kinds of trees most suitable for streets and roadsides, it is impossible to give a rule. There are some, like the horse chestnut, the catalpas, and the conifers generally, that appear to better advantage alone or in groups, upon a lawn or in a park, while others, like the elms, box-elder, maples, locusts, poplars, lindens, and many of the oaks show to fine advantage in avenues.

476. In Germany, we see many miles of continuous lines of apple trees by the roadside, and in the absence of fences marking their direction for great distances across the country. In France, it is common to find the Lombardy poplar thus planted; and in Italy, the mulberry and the olive, often supporting festoons of grapevines, and in their season loaded with fruit.

477. In planting the roadsides in a prairie, a rod or so of land should be thoroughly broken up and cultivated along the line, before the trees are set, and some hoed crop may be cultivated to advantage between and around them till they get well set.

478. In planting screens of evergreen to prevent snowdrifts in exposed places, the trees should be set in several oblique rows, as in the quincunx order [§ 181], and should be protected, if need be, by a fence, until able to protect themselves.

479. In planting avenues of trees, it is best to have the holes all dug before the young trees are brought upon the ground. The holes should be deeper than the tree is to set, and wide enough to allow the roots to be well spread. Some fresh soft, mellow, and fertile soil should be thrown upon the bottom, before the trees are placed, so as to bring up the tree nearly to the level at which it formerly stood.

480. Observations have been made to ascertain whether a tree does better when set in the same position with respect to points of compass that it stood in before planting, the conclusion being that there was no perceptible difference.

481. After spreading the roots, sprinkle over them first the richer soil from the surface, so that it shall settle closely in among them, leaving no void places. Then fill in the holes, putting the soil from the deepest part on top. In prairie planting, and especially in dry regions, there is no danger in pressing down the soil firmly over the roots. In a strong clay soil, this practice would be injurious.

482. The young fibers of the roots require moisture at once. In a moderately damp soil, they can find it, but in a dry soil they should be well wet as soon as planted, and in a dry season afterwards until the plants are well rooted.

483. The most effectual security against injury from drouth is in mulching; and for this, decayed chips, hay, grass, straw, or dead leaves may be used. This practice will sometimes double the growth in a single year, and save the life of a young tree in dry seasons.

484. Before leaving the subject of planting in villages, we should not omit to notice the advantages to be derived from *Village Improvement Associations*, in the cultivation of a taste for rural ornament, and the development of town pride and public spirit. In many villages in New England and elsewhere, such associations have been formed, and from the concert of action and unity of purpose that they secure, they have done much to adorn and beautify their localities, thus rendering them more agreeable to their citizens and more inviting to the transient visitor, and to those who may be seeking a pleasant rural residence.

485. To give these associations permanence and regularity, they should have the form of a regular Society, with a Constitution, By-laws, and rules of membership, and their object may extend beyond

the simple ornamenting of streets by planting and paving, to their grading and drainage, the maintenance of grass plats and flower-beds upon public squares, the providing of fountains and drinking troughs, the clearing off of snows in winter, lighting of streets at night, and other subjects of like character.

486. Extending beyond the material, they may wisely include the intellectual welfare of their localities, by the formation and maintenance of a public library and reading-room, courses of public lectures, local museums, and, in short, whatever tends to elevate and refine the taste, or to promote the enjoyment of the citizens by uniting them in common interests, wherein each one contributes his share, and from which he derives pleasure.

487. An attractive plantation of streets and squares in one village, becomes an object for imitation in another, and by friendly emulation, each may tend to stimulate the efforts of the other in securing a beautiful effect.

488. Where the children in the public schools, and students in academies can be interested in these improvements, the impressions formed may be permanent, and will find application in after life in diffusing a correct taste for rural adornment in places far remote, while the memory will travel back to these scenes of quiet beauty, and rest with satisfaction upon the incidents that they recall.[1]

(3.) *City Parks, and the Plantation of grounds in Rural Cemeteries, and around Public Institutions.*

489. It is only in recent years that the advantages of providing places of public resort, under official management, in the neighborhood of our cities and large towns have been recognized, or the op-

[1]The form of a charter of a "Village Improvement Association," by George E. Waring, Jr., is given in Scribner's monthly for May, 1877, and the subject is further noticed in our Forestry Report for 1877, page 217. The Hon. B. G. Northrup, Mr. N. H. Egleston and others, have done much to promote these objects, and their writings may be consulted with great advantage.

The city of Tuscaloosa, Alabama, is sometimes called the "*Druid City*," from the oaks planted some forty-five years ago, at the instance of Mr. Thomas Maxwell. The city of Cleveland is called the "*Forest City*," through the plantations induced by the late Leonard Case, and other property owners. New Haven is called the "*City of Elms*," and well deserves its name.

portunities afforded by wild and rocky suburb, or of waste and vacant grounds for rural adornment, have been improved. In other cases there are still barren wastes, river banks, shores, islands and points of land, within or near a city, and sometimes belonging to the corporation, that have not yet been noticed, where, at a moderate expense, there might be secured a little paradise of beauty, and an inviting place of resort.

490. In laying out city parks, the leading idea should be to make them easily accessible, and as widely useful as possible.

491. They need not, therefore, embrace *wide* areas, unless there be convenient bodies of land available, but they should be as *long* as may be. They may sometimes consist of separate pieces connected by broad, well-planted boulevards or avenues. It is an excellent plan, where the space is ample, to lay out the boundary-street, at one or two hundred feet distance, within the actual line of ownership, at the beginning, and to sell or lease this strip of land outside, upon condition that dwellings shall be built and maintained upon plans prescribed or approved by the commissioner in charge, and that their future use for purposes injurious to the general objects of the park be forbidden in their title deeds or leases.

492. In some instances, vacant grounds near cities have been highly improved with plantations, fountains, lakes, and other objects of rural interest, upon private account; and the adjacent and intervening lands sold upon conditions tending to maintenance and to great profit upon the investment. Where persons of congenial tastes, and united by a common sympathy in social, educational, religious, or other matters, can establish suburban colonies of this kind near our large cities, they may multiply the enjoyments of life indefinitely, and by carefully arranging a plan of organization in the beginning, they may secure the maintenance of their object, by the exclusion of any thing that might interfere with its operation. Even as a simple speculation, such enterprises have an admirable effect, and in some instances present an inviting field for investment.

493. The traveler in Europe will often find the line of fortifications of a former period now converted, or in process of transformation, into a line of gardens and pleasure-grounds, the moat affording ready-made a meandering lake, and the slopes and ramparts still left presenting that diversity of surface most desirable for ornamental plantation. Upon certain of these points admirable sites are found

for the erection of statues and monuments where they will appear to best advantage. The cities of Copenhagen and of Leipzig may be mentioned as examples, while the "Ring-Bahn" of Vienna, one of the finest streets of Europe, owes its beauty to the line of public and private buildings which have been built upon the line of its former defenses.

494. It occasionally happens that certain points in these meandering gardens have a local history of thrilling interest, as being places of successful attack, or of heroic defense, or as the point where the fate of a battle was decided, or the fortunes of a commander made or lost.

495. In a city park, a native woodland can often be improved to great advantage, and artificial plantations are most successful where they truly represent the features of a native forest. In the planting of trees in parks, with the exception of avenues of approach or connection, there should be a studied diversity in location, and a great variety in the species.

496. There should also be—what is not often seen—at least some portion specially planted as an *arboretum*, embracing in groups, by natural families, as great a number of species of each genius as can be made to grow, *each being labeled with its scientific and common name.*

497. In planting small parks upon college grounds, or in the midst of great thoroughfares, we must remember that persons upon business always hasten to their object in *direct lines.* They are impatient at curves and winding ways, and will strike straight across a plat of ground or a corner, unless absolutely prevented by a barrier.

498. It is therefore unwise to contend against this fact, in the arrangement of walks in such places, and it is better to lay out a few straight paths in the lines of most travel, at the sacrifice of what might be thought a principle in taste, or a rule in landscape gardening. Such walks may still be made attractive by flowers and shrubbery along their borders, and comfortable by the shade of trees.

499. If the space allows, there should generally be provided in these small parks such winding paths as the surface and the circumstances favor. They will be used only in moments of leisure, and by persons seeking quiet and rest.

500. If there be summer-houses, grottoes, fountains, monuments,

or objects of historical interest, that attract attention, or invite to repose, they should be placed near these winding and less frequented paths, rather than along the great thoroughfares of a park, and along these chiefly should seats be placed.

501. It is the custom, however, in Europe, to place monuments or other structures intended to inspire patriotic sentiment, or remind the passer-by of a religious duty, in the most conspicuous parts of public grounds, and often in the midst of the most frequented thoroughfares. The little areas formed by intersecting city avenues present the best opportunities for costly monuments and fountains, as they may be seen to a distance from several directions. If possible they should be inclosed, with a grass-plat or beds of flowers around them, but no shrubbery or trees that would conceal any part.

502. In squares reserved for military parade, the area must necessarily be left open, and planting can be done only around the borders. There may often be laid out an avenue for promenade, shaded by a single or double row of trees, and at the entrance there should be beds of flowers or colored-leaved plants, as the opportunities offer.

503. Upon the grounds belonging to universities, colleges, and academies, we insist upon the labeling of trees, as above mentioned, as one of the most important features of education, by familiarizing the student and the visitor with these names, aud of enabling them to form true ideas concerning the resemblances and differences in the form, foliage, and other characteristics of forest trees.

504. The best labels are tablets of porcelain, or of white earthenware, with the names in black enameled lettering. The cheapest are strips or plates of zinc, with the writing in a corrosive ink, that leaves indelible black lines. Neither of these will suffer from the weather, and both will last for an almost indefinite time.

505. In rural cemeteries, there is great opportunity for effect in the plantation of avenues of approach, and of masses of shrubbery and flowers around the entrance, and in the circles and plats formed by intersecting avenues. There should be, if possible, a belt of woodland, or its equivalent in a screen, that shall isolate it as far as convenient from the busy world, and impart that aspect of separation and quiet, consistent with the general object of the place.

506. Custom has given to the "funerèal cypress," and to other evergreens, a prominence in cemeteries, and there is a certain fitness

in their use; but they should not exclude the proper introduction of the deciduous kinds. In this we should, above all, avoid the planting of those that have tracing roots, as they are continually liable to send up shoots, and, if neglected, to overrun the premises, or at best occasion constant care in their suppression.

507. The planting and removal of trees in a cemetery should be wholly under the control of a superintendent or a board, and by this means alone can harmony of arrangement and an agreeable effect be secured.

508. Upon the grounds of public institutions generally, and in all forms of ornamental planting, there is an additional interest secured by the use of exotic and unusual species, provided always that they prove hardy and reliable. In this, the forest flora of Eastern Asia and Japan, from its general resemblance, yet specific differences, and the forests of the Himalaya region, have furnished many species that deserve to be widely planted, and more generally known. It is not improbable that by this wider diffusion, some species will be noticed that show an unexpected vigor and success in growth that may entitle them to notice for planting as timber trees.

509. The English elm (*Ulmus campestris*) appears to be a better tree for cities and smoky villages than our native elms. It will grow on dryer ground and endure a greater degree of drouth.

CHAPTER XII.

HEDGES, SCREENS, AND SHELTER-BELTS.

Hedges and Screens.

510. A hedge is a living fence, generally planted with some thorny tree or shrub, and strong enough to prevent the passing of domestic animals. A screen is more frequently a closely planted wall of verdure, generally of some evergreen tree, intended to conceal some unsightly object, or to afford shelter from the winds and protection to gardens, nurseries, orchards, stock-yards, or buildings. They may both be classed among ornamental plantations, and either of them may perform the offices of both.

511. In no line of planting will there be found so great a variety of opinions with regard to the kinds that should be planted, and as

to the time and manner of planting, and after-treatment, as we find with respect to hedges. Perhaps every one of those that have been confidently recommended might be entitled to preference in some particular localities, and it is certain that none have a general adaptation to all parts of the country.

512. It is therefore necessary to well consider the conditions of a given locality, as to its soil and climate, before making considerable investments in any one kind, until its fitness has been proved. In doubtful cases, and in a new-settled region, it would be well to experiment in a small way with several kinds, and if they fail, the loss will not be much; while if they succeed, the result may lead to a wide-spread benefit.

513. We will first present a list of the species that have been successfully used for hedges and screens, and afterwards state some of the principles that apply in their planting and management:

Coniferous evergreens: Chiefly the spruces, cedars, and junipers, viz.:

Norway spruce (*Picea excelsa*).
Black and white spruces (*P. nigra* and *P. alba*).
Hemlock (*Tsuga Canadensis*).
White cedar (*Thuja occidentalis*).
Chinese cedar (*Thuja orientalis*).
California white cedar (*Libocedrus decurrens*).
Red cedar (*Juniperus Virginiana*).
Common juniper (*Juniperus communis*).

514. These are chiefly useful for screens, and should all of them be started in nurseries. They should be set in spring, upon ground previously well prepared, and with the slightest possible exposure of the roots to the air, and they should be well watered. In a dry climate, they should have some protection on the south side, and it might be well to provide a shelter by planting some quick-growing trees parallel with the line of the proposed screen, two or three years previous, to be taken away when no longer needed.

515. An evergreen screen can be best made to thicken up by pinching or clipping off the ends of the branches. The terminal shoots should be allowed to grow to the height of the proposed screen without disturbance, and then it may be checked. For an effectual screen there should be two parallel rows of trees, in which case most of the branches will strike out, on each side, towards the light.

They may be set from one to three feet apart in the rows, and those in one row opposite the spaces in the other, as follows:

* * * * * * * *

* * * * * * * *

516. In a cool, humid climate, the hemlock makes a beautiful hedge. It can often be transplanted from the woods, and it should be set in double rows, to produce the finest effect.

517. For the dryer climate of Iowa and the region west of the Missouri, the native red cedar is preferable to all others, and about the only kind of evergreen that can be grown for a hedge with much certainty.

518. For the Southern States, some species not coniferous, such as the tamarisk (*Tamarix*), the Spanish bayonet (*Yucca aloeifolia*), the Cherokee rose (*Rosa lævigata*), various species of the cactus, and other plants may be employed to great advantage. The native thorny and ornamental shrubbery of that region affords many evergreens not conifers that would be available for this use, and it would be advisable to select such as are best known to be suitable for the soil and conditions, and that are proved to be hardy.

519. For the Northern and Middle States, the following (chiefly deciduous) have been found successful in various localities:

Buckthorn (*Rhamnus cathacticus*).

Crab-apple (*Pyrus coronaria*).

English Hawthorn (*Cratægus oxycanthus*).

Native thorny trees (*Cratægus*, various species).

Privet (*Ligustrum vulgare*).

Honey-locust (*Gleditschia tricanthos.*)

Holly (*Ilex opaca*).

Osage orange (*Maclura aurantiaca*).

520. For the more northerly parts of the North-western States, the white or gray willow has been used with great success. For the more arid regions further west, the mesquit (*Algorobis glandulosa*), the buffalo berry (*Shepherdia eleagnoides*), and the *Caragana* may be tried with advantage.

521. Of all these, where the climate will permit, the osage orange, a native of Arkansas, Louisiana, Texas, and the Indian Territory, has the most decided preference, and the methods of its planting and management are as follows:

522. The seeds should be procured fresh from their native locali-

ties, where their preparation for market now forms a regular business. The fruit is collected and rotted, and the seeds washed out and dried. They should not be dark-colored, nor moldy, but bright, and will weigh about 35 pounds to the bushel. They are best if grown the year previous, and should not be more than two years old.

523. It is usually better to obtain the plants from those who make a business of raising them for the market. They are started from the seed by first pouring on very warm, and almost scalding hot water, draining off the surplus, covering, and allowing them to lie (being frequently stirred) till they are swollen and ready to sprout. They are then at once planted by hand, or by machine, in rows about 18 to 24 inches apart, and cultivated to keep down the weeds. Late in the fall they should be mowed down, and the roots, after being loosened up by plowing, should be picked out, assorted, tied into bunches, and buried in dry trenches or kept in a cellar till spring.

524. Having previously prepared the ground along the line of the hedge, by thorough plowing and cultivation, mark the lines with a cord, and set the plants with a spade, dibble, or trowel, about two inches deeper than they grew before, and in rows from 8 to 12 or 15 inches apart, the richer soil requiring a wider distance between.

525. For a strong hedge, it is sometimes well to set two rows, as already described. These rows may be from 6 to 9 inches apart.

526. To secure an effectual hedge, two methods are employed. The first and best one is to obtain a broad and dense base, by cutting back, but allowing the plants to stand upright; in the other, they are allowed to grow high at first, but are then bent down, interwoven and confined in a sloping or horizontal position.

527. It is not usual to prepare a bank and ditch, as is prescribed in many English books upon hedge-making, but across wet grounds, it would be advisable to do so.

528. The care required the first year, is to keep the ground mellow and free of weeds, and in very dry times it may be advisable to protect the plants by mulching. If the object be to secure a dense upright growth, the plants should be mowed off close, in the spring of the second year, vacant places should be filled up, and the cultivation continued. In mid-summer, the upright stems should be cut back to within four or five inches of the ground, leaving those that spread out laterally. If the growth is still vigorous

they may be again cut back at the top, but not so low as before. In the third year, the cutting back at the top is renewed, but higher up, and under favorable conditions the hedge is now broad and very dense near the ground. The subsequent care consists in keeping the hedge trimmed to a convex curve on each side, and if the roots appear to spread too far, they may be kept back by cutting them off with a sharp coulter attached to the beam of a plow, and drawn along on each side, as near as a team can be driven.

529. There are quite a number of patents issued for bending down, interweaving with wires, confining by hooks and by stakes, and the like, which can not be easily described without a greater space than the limits of this article allow. In some of these, the stems are partly cut off, and then bent down and confined. In some, the branches are interwoven in lattice form. The most convenient tool for handling the plants (which are covered with cruel thorns), has a strong iron head, consisting of two prongs, like the tines of a fork, one of which is straight, and the other recurved, and firmly fixed in a long handle. This instrument can be used both for pushing and pulling, and by its aid, two men, one upon each side, can bring the stems into place without difficulty.

530. All hedges have the disadvantage of impoverishing the soil adjacent, to a perceptable degree; and the honey locust, the poplars, and the willows, have a tendency to send out tracing roots into the adjacent plowed lands, and there sprout where they are not wanted. The osage orange does not generally show this tendency, and this fact has been mentioned as a motive in its favor. It has, however, a somewhat tender habit, and when planted beyond its proper limits, it is very liable to be killed back or killed altogether by a cold winter.

531. Its northern limit can not be described with certainty. Being a native of a mild climate, it is not readily grown in a cold one, and perhaps it would be safer not to depend upon it in Iowa, or further west in the same latitude. As the young shoots do not ripen well, they are apt to be killed every year by the frost, and they can hardly long survive these repeated injuries.

532. Among the enemies that a young hedge of osage orange is exposed to, in the more Western States, is the gopher, a burrowing rodent, that will follow a line of hedge many rods, and destroy the roots. They may be killed off by poisoning. A fire, if allowed to

get in among the dry materials that lodge in a hedge, will be sure to kill it, and the strictest care should be taken to prevent this accident.

533. In very poor soil, a trench may be dug along the line of an intended hedge, and filled in with the more fertile soil of the adjacent surface, or elsewhere. It should be heaped above the former level, to allow for settling.

Shelter-Belts.

534. As their name implies, these are belts of woodland, primarily intended to protect the fields or places adjacent to them from the winds, and to equalize to some extent the temperature and humidity of a country, by mitigating the extremes of heat and cold, and by lessening the effects of drouth. They are of special benefit to fruit culture, and when planted around an orchard, in a dry climate, they tend to maintain a uniform and increased yield, the effect of which is often made apparent by comparisons with the barrenness and failure of orchards not thus protected.

535. Their effect in diminishing the damages that occasionally happen from grasshoppers, and other insects, is well proved; and by favoring the breeding of insectivorous birds, they further promote the destruction of the enemies of our fruit and field crops.

536. Their direct influence upon pasturage and meadows is seen in the fresh green color of the herbage, and its perceptibly larger growth. They have been known to double the yield of grain in fields surrounded by them, by preventing injuries to which open and naked fields are exposed.

537. In snowy countries, an important effect is secured in their preventing the drifting of snows, which cover the surface longer and melt away more slowly. The water will settle into the ground, and the soil remain moist for a longer period than in broad open fields. Their immediate shelter to gardens, buildings, and stock yards, and the cheerful and pleasant aspect that they impart to a country, are obvious.

538. A shelter-belt should be planted more closely than would be advantageous in a forest, and as the outside gets more air and light, the trees along the borders will be more thrifty than those in the interior. It should be not less than four rods in width, but ten rods would be better. For full benefit, they should not be more than a quarter of a mile apart.

539. As our public lands were all surveyed in lines running north and south, and at right angles to this course, these directions form the natural ones for the subdivisions of farms. The act for encouragement of tree-planting in Nebraska affords certain premiums for trees, if planted in belts running east and west, which implies that they are there thought to afford most protection against winds from the north or south. In summer, we have most to dread from the latter, and in winter from the former. In a region where such belts are on every farm, the one that shelters from the north affords a southern protection to the lands adjacent, and both farms are benefited.

540. In an east and west belt, the south side being most exposed to the sun, should be planted by kinds that suffer least from heat and drouth, and that in a dry region afford the most shade. The north side of such a belt will be the most favorable for a double belt of evergreens, which will thrive in such a place, if they can be made to grow anywhere, and which by their close evergreen foliage will give the belt more decided effect as a *shelter* against the hot and dry winds of summer, and the sweeping storms from the north in winter.

541. There are some careful observers who express decided preference for a shelter-belt running north and south. In this direction, both sides are exposed an equal number of hours to the sun, but the west side receives more heat, as being in the sunshine in the hottest part of the day. In such a belt, a line of evergreens would do best in the *middle*, or a little nearer the east side, if not overshaded by other trees.

542. It is our decided opinion that belts would prove of greatest benefit to agriculture, if planted in *both directions*, and if this custom were generally adopted in a prairie country, farms would protect one another against injurious winds from any direction, and if in sufficient proportion, the humidity of the climate would be perceptibly increased, and the tendency to drouth lessened.

543. The planting of a shelter-belt does not materially differ from that elsewhere described for groves. The soil should be cultivated a year or two before, to thoroughly decompose the sod, and the seeds, cuttings, or young plants should be set in quincunx rows, and be kept clear of grass and weeds till they shade the ground. They must be protected from stock of all kinds until beyond their

reach or power of injury, when they may be used for their shelter in winter.

544. The inside rows may be planted with black walnut, oak, catalpa, ash, or other kinds of most value for timber; and when a belt becomes old and thin, it would be better to cut it off, after starting a new one under its shelter. The ground fertilized by the decay of leaves for many years might be broken up and cultivated for a time with great advantage. In older countries, the rules of rotation in the culture of timber and of farm crops have been settled by long practice, and the advantages from this are well understood; but in our country they are as yet unappreciated, and to a great degree unknown.

545. For a narrow, but effectual wind-break, a double row of Scotch or white pine, in rows eight or ten feet apart, and at about the same distance between the trees in the rows, will form, in six or eight years, in a climate where they can be grown, a close and effectual screen.

Protection of Railroad Cuts from Drifting Snows by Tree-Planting.

546. In no form of planting do shelter-belts show greater benefits than along the deep cuts of railroads, in an open country liable to deep snows. They should be planted, in these cases, upon both sides of the road, but wider on that exposed to the most wind, which will generally be the north or west sides.

547. In preparing the soil for this planting upon new prairies, it should be broken up in June, in strips a rod and a half to two rods wide, parallel with the line of road and about seventy-five or eighty feet from the center. The ground should be back-set by plowing deeper in September or October, and again as deep as practicable as early in the spring following as may be. Immediately after plowing, the ground should be harrowed, and set with cuttings, or planted with seedlings, in lines from four to six feet apart, and about a foot apart in the rows. In general, there should be four to six rows on the side most exposed, and not less than three (but better more) on the other side.

548. In places particularly exposed to oblique winds along the valleys, the plantation might widen out to advantage, forming a grove of some extent. The kinds most certain in northern and snowy region are the cottonwoods and willows. Where the soil and

climate favor, the evergreens, and especially the white and red cedars, the Scotch pine and the Norway or black spruce are most effectual. They should be started in nurseries *in all cases*, as evergreens require more care at first.

549. When planted or set, the rows must be thoroughly cultivated by stirring the ground with a cultivator or by hand-hoeing until the trees appear to need it no longer. For the first and second years a double cultivator may be used, if care is taken to protect the row between with cloths under the forward part. If bent down, the trees will straighten up, and if not broken, or the bark torn, they will not be injured. Plantations thus set will need thinning as they become well started, and will require protection against cattle and against fires.

550. For the prevention of injury from prairie fires, lines of fresh earth should be formed outside near the trees, and at a distance of one or two hundred feet parallel with them, by plowing two or three furrows, and burning off the space between in a still time, and as early in the fall as fire can be made to spread. The grass between the belts, along the track, should in this manner be also cleared off every fall, and by these precautions the chances of accident from fire would be almost wholly removed.

551. In the North-western States, the planting time lasts about a month, and ends about the middle or twentieth of May. It begins again in October, from the tenth to the fifteenth, and lasts till freezing weather. Farther south, the spring planting begins earlier, and the fall planting later, and both will vary in different years.

552. Much success has attended the planting of trees along the sides of railroad cuts, to prevent the drifting of snows in the winter in lines crossing the steppes of Russia. The first of these experiments was begun in the spring of 1876, near Nikitooka, on the Kursk-Kharkoff-Azov Railroad, about 1,000 feet above the sea, in a region that was treeless, and utterly unpromising. It was in fact selected with the view of securing a strong argument in favor of the measure, in case the trees could be made a success. Towards the end of March, a strip of land was broken up, and afterwards sub-soiled and harrowed. On the 10th of April, the season being well advanced, over 100,000 trees and shrubs were set from nurseries, in 7 rows, about 6 feet apart, and 6 feet between trees in each row, the nearest one being 84 feet from the track. The kinds set

were the hawthorn (*Cratægus oxycantha*) furtherest from the track; next the elms (*Ulmus effusa* and *U. suberosa*), the maple (*Ascer tartaricum*), locust (*Robinia pseudacacia*), the *Caragana arborescens*, and last, towards the track, another row of hawthorn. There was no heaping up of the earth around the roots, but the soil was beaten down level and smooth. The hawthorn lost its leaves, but it budded again, and came on in good healthy condition, and proved a great success. The loss was not over one per cent, chiefly the locust, which had been planted too deep. The *Ulmus suberosa* was found the most hardy. The plantation was cultivated by hand-hoeing and with horse-cultivators.

553. In August, when the dry season came, and almost all the vegetation of the steppe was dried up, and the ground completely covered with cracks, the soil in this plantation remained moist, and could be rolled into balls. At the end of the season some of the trees were taken out, and it was found that the roots had grown from two to four feet, and were well provided with fibers.

554. In establishing a nursery for supplying the trees used for this work, the ground was surrounded by rows of trees (maples, elms, and caragana), and the seed when sown were well watered, and the ground covered with straw until the plants began to appear. This litter was then gradually removed, and laid in the paths between the seed-beds, in order to keep the moisture as much as possible in the soil. It was still found necessary to water the plants in the beds, until they had got well started. By the end of summer the locusts had made a growth of from 6 to 18 inches, and the others averaged 10 inches. The so-called autumnal sowings began in August, and was continued up to the middle of December, and all of them were covered carefully with straw.

555. It is found on the steppes that successful planting depends upon thorough cultivation and deep sub-soil plowing. The example of the railroads is being followed by many of the farmers who have witnessed the result, and who had been strongly prejudiced against any attempts at planting, believing that it could not succeed.

556. Upon other lines of railroad extensive plantations have been commenced, the usual number of rows being seven, and the series adopted upon one of them being as follows, counting outward from the track, viz.: *Caragana arborescens*, *Robinia pseudacacia*, *Ulmus suberosa*, *Acer tartaricum*, *Robinia pseudacacia*, *Acer tartaricum*, *Ulmus*

suberosa mixed with the locust, and the last two rows the *Caragana* alone. In one case plants were taken too old, and the drouth and cattle caused the destruction of 25 per cent. In another case it was 21 per cent, and in another some of the pines were planted, but with poor success. The general results are, however, deemed satisfactory, and in many cases the loss did not exceed eight per cent. In all of these plantations, the seeds were sown in local nurseries along the lines of the roads, and the transplanting is done before the trees become of much size. The preparation of the soil is deep and thorough, and its subsequent cultivation carefully kept up.

CHAPTER XIII.

CUTTING AND SEASONING OF WOOD; DEFECTS IN TIMBER.

The proper Time for Cutting Timber.

557. As a general rule, timber cut in the season when vegetation is suspended, or in deciduous species, when the leaves are off and the growth of the year is ended, lasts longer and seasons more readily than when cut in the season of active growth, and when the tree is full of sap. In the winter season it is found that there are stored up in the interior cells, the elements that are to serve for the first growth of the next season, such as starch, etc. This is proved by applying chemical tests, such as solutions of iodine, which will color the medullary rays of winter-cut wood, in thin sections, with a deeper violet-tinge than in wood cut in spring or early summer. In cases where the wood is to be peeled, the timber can only be cut in early summer. Hoop-poles should never be cut when the bark will peel, as their utility and value are lessened.

558. Summer has, from time immemorial, been the favorite season for cutting coniferous timber in the Vosges of Eastern France. Perhaps one great advantage in this, results from the fact that it can be peeled at that season, and thus saved from the injuries that are very likely to occur from the attack of bark-boring insects. All timber that is to be peeled, must be cut in the early part of summer. It will then season more readily than it could if the bark had been left on. Coniferous woods will generally remain white, and the lumber will be lighter in weight. There are, indeed, certain advantages to be gained by summer cutting, which have led an ap-

proved French writer[1] to remark as follows: "The result of this experience has a tendency to contradict the received opinion relative to the time of cutting the deciduous woods, and seems also to afford an argument in favor of cutting these trees in summer, after the movements of the sap has ceased—if not with respect to their calorific properties, at least in favor of their durability. But it would be imprudent to give a positive opinion upon this point until the facts have been accurately ascertained by numerous exact and comparable experiments, aud until this has been done, it would be safer to follow the old rules. It is, furthermore, probable that the difference is chiefly shown in the more or less complete maturity of the sap-wood, and that it is greater in that part." It appears, therefore, that the question as to the proper season for cutting can not be regarded as settled, until more carefully settled by observation.

559. It may be of some historical interest, but probably of not much practical importance, to notice the superstitions that have prevailed, and which are still observed, with respect to the effect of the moon's age at the time that trees are felled. It is traced in the writings of the ancients and is mentioned by Columella, Cato, Vitruvius, and Pliny. The first Napoleon directed that the time for felling naval timber should be "in the wane of the moon, from November 1st to March 15th." The wood-cutters in some countries act in accordance with this belief.

560. It is laid down as a precept by Behlen,[2] that "all building timber must be felled two or three days before or after the new moon, and in a dry time, and oak timber always at the new moon," and adds, that the timber cut at that time has greater durability. He gives nearly two pages of precepts, extending to particular days of the week in connection with the moon's age, and varying somewhat in different seasons of the year. We deem these rules as quite without reason, and can see no other effect from the moon's presence or absence than that due to a moderate amount of light without heat.

The Seasoning of Woods.

561. Wood when newly cut, contains from thirty-seven to forty-eight per cent of water, depending upon the kind, age, and the season

[1] H. Nanquette, late Director of the School of Forestry, at Nancy, France.

[2] *Real-und Verbal-Lexicon, der Frost und Jagdkunde.*—iv. 676.

of vegetation, the older wood being generally heavier than the young, and the weight greater in the active, rather than the dormant season.

562. This water is not chemically united, and a part of it is given out when exposed to the air. But at a certain point it ceases to become lighter, and after that it gains or looses in weight, as the temperature and moisture of the atmosphere vary. The following table shows the changes, in percentage of weight, that occur with some kinds of woods by seasoning:

Percentage in weight of Water in Woods, at different periods after Cutting.

Kinds of Wood.	Round Wood from Branches.				Round Wood from Young Trees.			
	6 mo.	1 year.	18 mo.	2 years.	6 mo.	1 year.	18 mo.	2 years.
Beech	33.48	24.00	19.80	20.32	30.44	23.46	18.60	19.95
Oak	31.20	26.90	24.55	21.09	32.71	26.74	23.55	20.28
Hornbeam	31.38	25.89	22.33	19.30	27.19	23.08	20.60	18.59
Birch	37.34	28.99	24.12	21.78	39.72	29.01	22.73	19.52
Poplar	35.69	26.01	21.85	19.44	40.45	26.22	17.77	17.92
Fir	28.29	17.14	15.09	18.66	33.78	16.87	15.21	18.09
Pine	35.30	17.59	15.72	17.39	41.49	18.67	15.63	17.42

563. It appears from this table, that there is generally nothing gained, but something lost in keeping woods any longer than eighteen months, as some of them, such as the beech, fir and pine, become damp rather than dry by longer keeping, and the others gain in dryness but feebly after that time. Mr. Marcus Bull, in his experiments upon the properties of woods, many years since, ascertained that wood, after being perfectly dried, when exposed in a room without fire for a year, absorbed on an average, of 46 kinds, 10 per cent of their weight, in common states of the weather, and 8 per cent in the dry. A coincidence was noticed in the weight of charcoal from these woods similarly exposed. The amount of moisture absorbed was not found to diminish with their increase of density, while green woods in drying lost uniformly less in weight, according as their density was greater. Hickory, from green to absolutely dry, lost 37½ per cent; white oak, 41; and maple, 48. Assuming the general average at 42 per cent, we have a striking illustration of the economy in freight, between the carrying of wood green or dry, and in burning wood before or after seasoning.

564. Wood that has been floated will season sooner and become lighter than that which has not. By long exposure in the water, with repeated drying, wood becomes extremely light, as we often see in flood-wood.

565. For seasoning to best advantage, wood should be piled in the open fields, rather than in the woods, and it is customary in many parts of Europe to lay some pieces lengthwise of the pile, well braced at the outer end, and meeting at an obtuse angle in the middle. These afford a kind of arch, open at the bottom for the air to circulate under the piles. Where fire-wood is piled in quantities for seasoning, there should be intervals between the piles, in order to give access to the air within.

566. Coniferous wood will season quicker if left with the branches on until the leaves fall off, as they seem to evaporate the moisture from the wood. Trees felled towards the north are more exposed to the sun, and season sooner than in other positions.

567. The seasoning of lumber is sometimes hastened by artificial heat, but in this case provision must be made for ventilation, or the vapor must be condensed by the circulation of cold water through upright pipes placed within the apartment.[1]

568. Oak timber is sometimes very effectually seasoned by being peeled while still standing, and left for several months before cutting. This was remarked by Vitruvius, a Roman architect. It was tried by Duhamel, in the preparation of ship-timber, and he explained the result by saying that although such trees may live for a time after peeling, they can not form new layers of wood, and that the growth due to a new deposit of wood was carried into the cellular tissues of the sap wood, and perhaps the heart wood, rendering it heavier and stronger, but more liable to crack. This method is expensive, and is now scarcely ever used.

569. The seasoning of wood is always hastened by taking off the bark, and in the case of willow, cottonwood, and some other kinds, it tends to harden the wood and increase its durability. As a general rule, all railroad ties, telegraph poles, and posts last longer when peeled, and no timber or lumber should be used in constructions of any kind before seasoning, unless in places where the air has full access.

[1] Geo. Wood's patent.

570. Seasoning tends to secure the durability of wood not exposed to the weather, or in contact with the earth, or with damp walls, if sufficient ventilation is allowed. The presence of moisture, and especially of the starch, sugar, and albumen of the sap in wood, tends to hasten fermentation and decay. If these are partly dissolved out by placing the freshly cut timber in running water, it drys more readily. Seasoning by smoking has the effect of increasing the durability of wood, by charging it with creosote, but this is corrosive to iron, and should not be used in contact with it.

571. In the process of seasoning, wood tends to shrink, from the contraction of the tissues as they become dry. As there is more moisture and less wood fiber in the outer layers, the contraction is greatest toward the outside, as shown in the annexed engraving. The process takes place more slowly, and with less cracking in winter. It is still further improved by delaying the drying, which may be done by placing in the shade, where the air circulates freely between the pieces, but it should not be exposed to the drying winds.

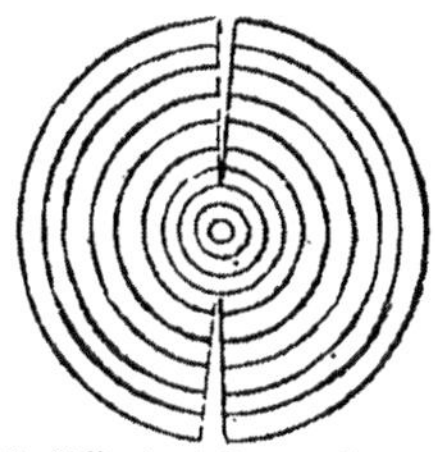

68. Effect of Seasoning of Round Timber, showing the Shrinkage greatest in the outer Wood.

572. It is desirable to prevent the cracking of timber at the ends, by which means a loss is suffered in the more valuable kinds. This may be prevented in a great degree, by pasting heavy paper over the end, or by painting or washing with diluted muriatic acid, neutralized with lime.

573. If there be nothing at hand better, the timbers may be lightly shaded from the sun by branches of trees or any other slight covering, where it is desirable to prevent deep crevices from being formed. Shrinkage tends to distort timber that is dressed green, as shown in the annexed cut, and unless the center of growth is in the center of the piece, it will need to be dressed over again to secure a true form. Boards and plank when cut green will warp from this cause, the contraction being strongest on the side furtherest from the center of growth, and least in the direction of the medullary rays.

69. Tendency to Distortion of Square Timber by Shrinkage.

70. Tendency to Warp by Contraction nearest the Outside of the Tree.

574. Wood cut in planes radiating from the center can not warp. When sawn into this form, there is a waste from a feather-edge on one side, and from extra thickness on the other, but the silver-grain is brought out with great beauty in some species by this mode of cutting, and for some uses it may be preferable. When wood is to be used as the foundation for veneering, it should be cut as near as may be in the direction of the medullary rays, and it must be thoroughly seasoned.

575. English shipwrights generally consider that three years are required to season large timbers. They are usually cut to shape a year before they are framed, and then left another year in the skeleton before being planked.[1] All wood used in carving requires the most careful and thorough seasoning.

576. Hard-woods season more slowly than those of light open grain. They may often be cut to nearly the shapes required for use before being put away to dry, and should be piled open with spaces for the air to circulate between the pieces. It may be desirable to pile them over again, from time to time, so as to expose the parts at first in contact.

The Strength of Timber, with respect to its Form, and to the Lines of Growth.

577. The strength of the timber when used in horizontal pieces depends upon its form, and upon the manner in which it is cut, with reference to the layers of annual growth. If laid flatwise,

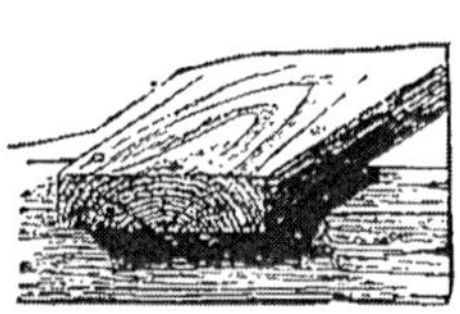

71. Proper Mode of placing a Plank to secure Durability and Strength.

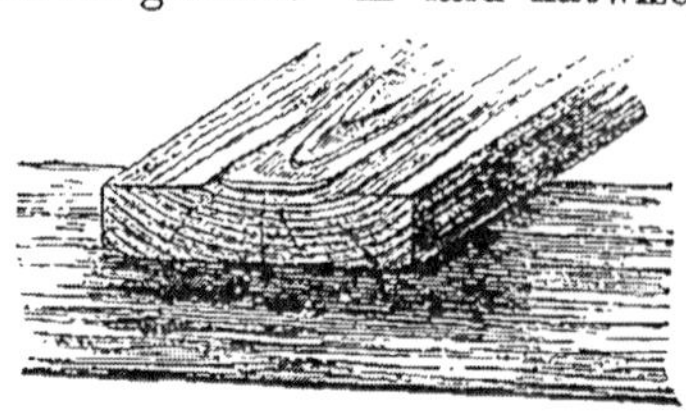

72. Improper Mode of placing a Plank to secure Durability and Strength.

with the layers convex on the upper side, they act as an arch, and tend to give it strength. If the same piece were laid edgewise, like a joist, it would be much stronger than if the lines of growth were transverse, and when such pieces break from over-loading, the crack is more apt to be between, than across, these layers of growth.

[1]*Britton on the Dry Rot*, p. 68.

If, on the contrary, a plank be laid flatwise, with the hollow of the grain up, the pressure of whatever weight is applied, will be on the inside of the arch, and if exposed to moisture, the water will tend to settle between the layers of growth, and thus hasten its decay. These principles find application in the laying of planks in sidewalks, bridges, platforms, the floors of warehouses, and the like.

Defects of Timber from Various Causes.

578. Timber is liable to acquire certain defects from old age, shrinkage in seasoning, or other causes, that more or less injure its quality for strength, and its value for use, when sawn into lumber. One of these is the "heart-shake," perhaps most frequently seen in old timber, and caused by the contraction of the inner portions of the tree, as the first symptom of decay.

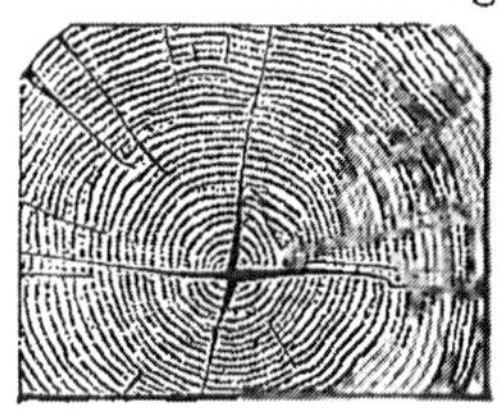

73. Heart-Shake.

579. The "star-shake" consists of a similar contraction, but often wider towards the outside, as seen in young timber when exposed to rapid drying after being cut green. It, however, is often seen in the tree before cutting, and sometimes a bulge on the outside of the tree shows where these cracks come to the surface.

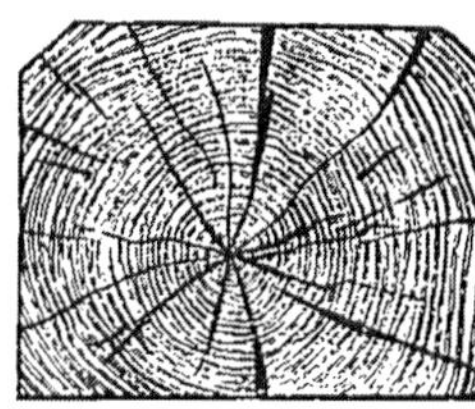

74. Star-Shake.

580. The "cup-shake" is a separation between the rings of growth, more frequently found near the roots of the tree. It may be caused by a sudden change of temperature, frosts, storms, or other causes, and in some cases it extends through the whole length of the tree, especially if the ring of separation is complete at the base. If only a segment is separate, it does not usually extend far up. Again, there are various combinations of these defects that may impair the value of timber, against which there is

75. Cup-Shake.

76. Combined Star and Cup-Shake.

no known prevention, and in many cases there are no means of knowing their presence until the tree is cut. So far as caused or increased by rapid seasoning, they may be prevented by cutting only in the season when vegetation is dormant, and by drying slowly in the shade.

581. Wherever the bark becomes loose on a tree, to that extent the wood looses its vitality under it, and it can only be healed by the growing over of the wood from the side. These accidents may be caused by external injuries, scorching from fires, sun-scalds, or frost when the wood is full of sap. When the wood from opposite sides meets over such a place, it will in two or three years consolidate entirely, and form continuous layers over it, but the dead wood within, if not previously decayed, remains unchanged. These bare spots should be covered over with coal-tar or paint, if the tree is valuable, but if there are decayed places these should first be cleaned out, and the surface should be dry when the tar or paint is applied.

582. In some cases wood in the first stages of decay shows a change of color, before its strength or texture is impaired, as in some species of the pine. It will generally be stopped by drying, and may not affect its value. The tint of wood is in a great degree influenced by the nature of the soil upon which it has grown. The larch and the fir on a dry, level, and deep sandy soil, are often of a slightly reddish tinge, while in other situations they are nearly white. It is probably from some chemical differences in the soil that mahogany and other tropical woods of the same species are of deeper shades of color in some localities than in others.

CHAPTER XIV.

FUEL—CHARCOAL—WOOD-GAS.

The Qualities desirable in Wood for Fuel.

583. The best qualities of wood for fuel are found when it burns easily and uniformly—neither too fast nor too slow—and when, in a given volume, it gives the greatest amount of heat. These qualities are found in highest degree at full maturity, and before decline. In coppice-woods, grown from the sprouts, this quality is reached sooner than from seed, and in those from old stocks sooner than

from the younger ones, the period ranging from 25 to 40 years. If we wish wood for burning only, the coppice is more profitable than full-grown timber, although, in a given quantity of best fire-wood from each, a cord of the latter would be worth the most.

584. But, for charcoal, the point of greatest excellence is almost reached in middle age, when the difference is very small, between its excellence then and at full majority.[1]

585. In 1826, Marcus Bull, of Philadelphia, a gold-beater by profession, a member of the American Philosophical Society, and much interested in scientific studies, first published the results of experiments carefully made by him upon the heating and coaling qualities of many kinds, chiefly of native wood. They possess permanent value, and may be concisely stated as in table on the following page.

586. It should be remembered that woods differ according to the soil, aspect, elevation, and other conditions under which they have been grown, and that allowance must be made for these differences in applying the above or any other statements.

Charcoal.

587. When wood is heated to about 530° (Fahr.), or above, the volatile parts pass off in the form of watery vapor, acetic acid, tar, etc., with certain non-condensible gases, and there remains a fixed residue called *charcoal.*

588. This substance is black, porous, brittle, and when struck, sonorous. It breaks with a glossy conchodial fracture, and when prepared at a low degree of heat, it retains the form and structure of the wood, but in reduced bulk. It is among the most indestructible of substances when exposed to the open air, or in the ground, and for this reason billets of charcoal are buried in the soil, to mark the corners of sections and their subdivisions in our public land surveys.[2]

[1] *Karsten*, cited by *Lorentz & Parade*, 5 ed., p. 443. In the oak, the proportion was 25.45 to 25.60; in the beech, 25.50 to 25.75; and in the hornbeam, 24.90 to 26.10.

[2] In visiting the ruins of Herculaneum, in 1881, we noticed the woodwork of doors and windows that had been charred by a lava-stream nearly two thousand years ago, in which the kind of wood could be determined, and even the form into which it had been wrought.

Comparative Qualities and Values for Heating Purposes of different American Woods.

Number.	Common names.	Specific gravity of dry wood.	Weight of dry wood in a cord.	Product of charcoal from 100 parts of dry wood, by weight.	Specific gravity of dry charcoal.	Pounds of dry charcoal in one bushel.	Pounds of charcoal from one cord of dry wood.	Bushels of charcoal from a cord of dry wood.	Time that 10° (F.) of heat were maintained by combustion of one pound.	Percentage of value for fuel, Shell-bark Hickory being 100.
									h. m	
1	White Ash	0.772	3450	25.74	.547	28.78	888	31	6.40	77
2	Apple Tree	0.697	3115	25.00	.445	23.41	779	33	6.40	70
3	White Beech	0.724	3236	19.62	.518	27.26	635	23	6.	65
4	Black Birch	0.697	3115	19.40	.428	22.52	604	27	6.	63
5	White Birch	0.530	2369	19.00	.364	19.15	450	24	6.	48
6	Butternut	0.567	2534	20.79	.237	12.47	527	42	6.	51
7	Red Cedar	0.565	2525	24.72	.238	12.52	624	50	6.40	56
8	Chestnut	0.522	2333	25.29	.379	19.94	590	30	6.40	52
9	Wild Cherry	0.597	2668	21.70	.411	21.63	579	27	6.10	55
10	Dogwood	0.815	3643	21.00	.550	28.94	765	26	6.10	75
11	White Elm	0.580	2592	24.85	.357	18.79	644	34	6.40	58
12	Sour-Gum	0.703	3142	22.16	.400	21.05	696	33	6.20	67
13	Sweet-Gum	0.634	2834	19.69	.413	21.73	558	26	6.	57
14	Shell-bark Hickory	1.000	4469	26.29	.625	32.89	1172	36	6.40	100
15	Pig-nut Hickory	0.949	4241	25.22	.637	83.52	1070	32	6.40	95
16	Red-heart Hickory	0.829	3705	22.90	.509	26.78	848	32	6.30	81
17	Witch-Hazel	0.784	3505	21.40	.368	19.86	750	39	6.10	72
18	American Holly	0.602	2691	22.77	.374	19.68	613	31	6.20	57
19	Hornbeam	0.720	3218	19.00	.455	23.94	611	25	6	65
20	Mountain Laurel	0.663	2963	24.02	.457	24.05	712	30	6.40	66
21	Sugar Maple	0.644	2878	21.43	.431	22.68	617	27	6.10	60
22	Soft Maple	0.597	2668	20.64	.370	19.47	551	28	6.	54
23	Large Magnolia	0.605	2704	21.59	.406	21.36	584	27	6.10	56
24	Chestnut White-Oak	0.885	3655	22.76	.481	25.31	900	36	6.30	86
25	White Oak	0.855	3821	21.62	.401	21.10	826	39	6.20	81
26	Shell-bark White Oak	0.775	3464	21.50	.437	22.99	745	32	6.20	74
27	Barren Scrub Oak	0.747	3339	23.17	.392	20.63	774	38	6.30	73
28	Pin Oak	0.747	3339	22.22	.436	22.94	742	32	6.20	71
29	Scrub Black Oak	0.728	8254	23.80	.387	20.36	774	38	6.30	71
30	Red Oak	0.728	3254	22.43	.400	21.05	630	30	6.20	69
31	Barren Oak	0.694	3102	22.37	.447	23.52	694	29	6.20	66
32	Rock Chestnut Oak	0.678	3030	20.86	.436	22.94	632	28	6.	61
33	Yellow Oak	0.653	2919	21.60	.294	15.52	631	41	6.10	60
34	Spanish Oak	0.548	2449	22.95	.362	19.05	562	80	6.20	52
35	Persimmon	0.711	3178	23.44	.469	24.68	745	30	6.30	69
36	Yellow Pine	0.551	2463	23.75	.333	17.52	585	33	6.30	54
37	Jersey Pine	0.478	2137	24.88	.385	20.26	532	26	6.40	48
38	Pitch Pine	0.426	1904	26.76	.298	15.68	510	33	6.40	43
39	White pine	0.418	1868	24.35	.293	15.42	455	30	4.40	42
40	Yellow Poplar	0.563	2516	21.81	.383	21.15	549	27	6.10	52
41	Lombardy Poplar	0.397	1776	25.00	.245	12.89	444	34	6.40	40
42	Sassafras	0.618	2762	22.58	.427	22.47	627	28	6.20	59
43	Wild Service	0.887	3964	22.62	.594	31.26	897	29	6.20	84
44	Sycamore	0.535	2391	23.60	.374	19.68	564	29	6.30	52
45	Black Walnut	0.681	3044	22.56	.418	22.00	687	31	6.20	65
46	Whortleberry	0.752	3361	23.30	.505	26.57	783	29	6.30	73

Botanical Names of the foregoing kinds of Trees and Shrubs.

1. *Fraxinus Americana.*
2. *Pyrus malus.*
3. *Fagus sylvatica.*
4. *Betula lenta.*
5. *Belula alba*, var. *populifolia.*
6. *Juglans cinerea.*
7. *Juniperus Virginiana.*
8. *Caslanea vesca*, var. *Americana.*
9. *Cerasus Virginiana.*
10. *Cornus Florida.*
11. *Ulmus Americana.*
12. *Nyssa multiflora.*
13. *Liquidamber styraciflua.*
14. *Carya alba.*
15. *Carya porcina.*
16. *Carya* ——.
17. *Hamamelis virginica.*
18. *Ilex opaca.*
19. *Carpinus Americana.*
20. *Kalmia latifolia.*
21. *Acer saccharinum.*
22. *Acer rubrum.*
23. *Magnolia grandiflora.*
24. *Quercus prinus palustris.*
25. *Quercus alba.*
26. *Quercus obtusiloba.*
27. *Quercus Catesbaei.*
28. *Quercus palustris.*
29. *Quercus Banisterii.*
30. *Quercus rubra.*
31. *Quercus ferruginea.*
32. *Quercus prinus monticola.*
33. *Quercus prinos acuminata.*
34. *Quercus falcata.*
35. *Diospyros Virginiana.*
36. *Pinus mitis.*
37. *Pinus inops.*
38. *Pinus rigida.*
39. *Pinus strobus.*
40. *Liriodendron lulipifera.*
41. *Populus dilatata.*
42. *Sassafras officinale.*
43. *Amelanchier Canadensis.*
44. *Acer pseuda-plutanus.*
45. *Juglans nigra.*
46. *Vaccinium corymbosum.*

589. Charcoal is a slow conductor of heat and a non-conductor of electricity. When exposed to the most intense heat, without access of air, it remains unchanged, but it burns freely without flame or smoke in the open air, leaving as ashes a part of the mineral constituents of the wood from which it was made.

590. It absorbs and holds moisture with great readiness, and is an active absorbent of gases. It will take up many times its bulk, but this amount is much greater with some gases than others.[1] It is for this reason a most valuable disinfectant, and a material for filters.

591. The chief use, however, of charcoal is as a fuel in smelting ores, and in forges, furnaces, and other metallurgical operations, and for these uses immense quantities of wood are annually required.

592. The wood for charcoal should be cut only in winter, and it is generally piled for partial seasoning till the next autumn. It is found, as is shown elsewhere under the head of "seasoning," that wood acquires its greatest dryness in about eighteen months, but practically a single summer's drying is found sufficient.

593. There are several modes of charring wood in use, but by far the most common one is that in "*meilers*" or "coal-pits." For

[1] De Saussure found that boxwood charcoal would absorb 90 times its bulk of ammonia, 55 times of sulphuretted hydrogen, 35 times of carbonic acid gas, $9\frac{1}{4}$ times of oxygen, $7\frac{1}{2}$ times of nitrogen, and $1\frac{3}{4}$ times of hydrogen. The absorbing power is greatest when the wood has been charred at a low temperature in a damp atmosphere, and with a high barometric pressure of the air. The absorption of gases is attended with an increase of temperature.

these, a place should be selected where the ground is dry, and a little descending from the central part; the rubbish should be carefully cleared away, the soil beaten down hard, and the greatest precaution taken against the escape of fire. In Europe, the law generally requires that a trench should be dug around the coaling-ground, and that a sufficient supply of water shall be near. The place should be well sheltered from the winds, and the soil should be compact, and not so porous that air can enter through it from below.

594. Three stakes are first set in a triangular form, and around these the wood is piled as closely as possible, and generally as cut in lengths of 3 to 4 feet. It is either laid horizontally or vertically, as shown in the accompanying cut, taken from Karsten's Atlas. The

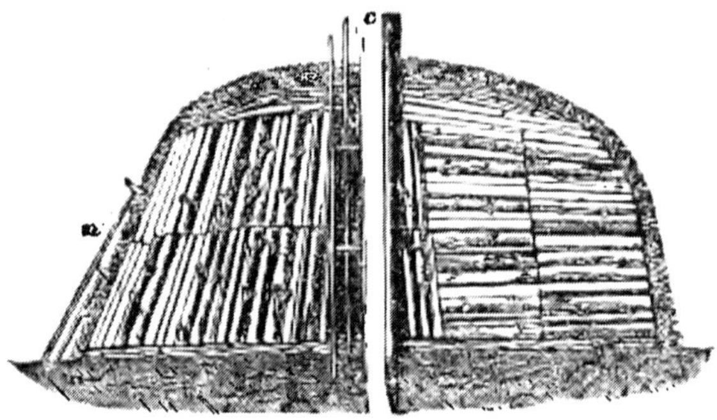

77. Vertical Section through the Centers of two Different Kinds of Meilers.

more common way is to set the wood endwise, sloping towards the center, and there is usually a second course, with the top filled out and made convex by wood piled flatwise.

595. The whole is then covered with straw, dead leaves, or sod, and over this with earth, and the fire is dropped in at the top. Around the bottom holes are left for the admission of air; or sometimes a passage is left on one side for introducing the fire. It is best to kindle early in the morning, and in fine weather, because it requires much attention at first to get the ignition begun. When this is fairly established, the top is closed with sod.

596. At first, a great deal of steam is generated, which condenses on the inner surface of the cover, and especially around the base, which is left open; and explosions may occur from the admission of air to the inflammable gases within, especially with dry resinous woods.

597. When the sweating stage is over, the openings around the base should be partly closed, but some vent-holes must be left for the escape of gases. If hollow places form, the cover must be removed, and their place hastily filled in with wood. The process must be watched day and night until it is completed, which is known by the color of the smoke. The time required for cooling is generally about three weeks. The meiler is then packed as closely as possible, to exclude the air, and when cool enough the coals are drawn out.

598. It is stated from experience that it is best not to wait until the fire is wholly extinguished, but to quench with water such sparks or burning places as are found.

599. Sometimes a meiler is made higher and narrower than in the preceding figures, and in every form it is convenient to have platforms around the sides, at one or two levels, so as to be able to reach conveniently every part. In the annexed figure, *a*, *b*, represents the central opening for applying the fire, *c*, *d*, a bank of earth, with a step at *e*. An upper step, *g*, is supported by braces on various sides, as at *f*, and near the top the cover is laid open until the whole part is well ignited, and the steam has principally passed off.

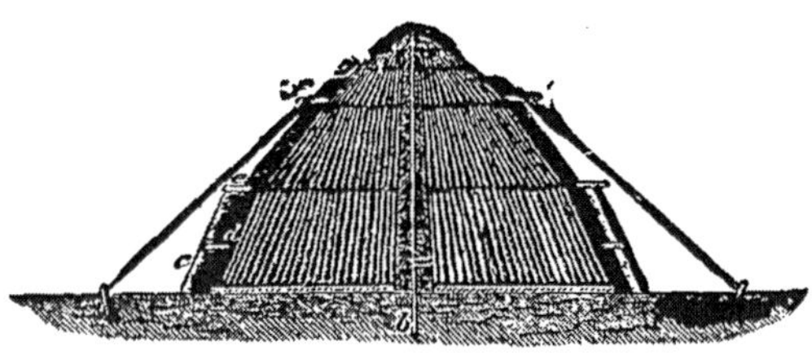

78. Section of a Meiler, or Coal-pit, prepared for Firing, as Practiced in Bavaria.

600. It is sometimes preferred to burn charcoal in kilns. They are generally made of brick, and the following sizes, among others, are in use:

	Length.	Width.	Height.	Capacity (Cords.)
Used in New England	50 feet.	12 feet.	12 feet.	55 feet.
	40 "	15 "	15 "	70 "
Type of those used in Mexico	40 "	19 "	18 "	75 "
A kind used in Michigan	48 "	17 "	18 "	90 "

It requires from 35 to 40 M. of brick for a kiln of 45 cords, and 60 to 65 M. for one of 90 cords. These rectangular kilns are arched at the top, and supported externally by a wooden framework, and iron tie rods. They have an iron door (*d*) capable of being made air-tight, and near the top a smaller door (*e*) for filing the upper part. Along the sides are air-holes (*a*, *b*, *c*,) that may be closed at will.

Fig. 1.

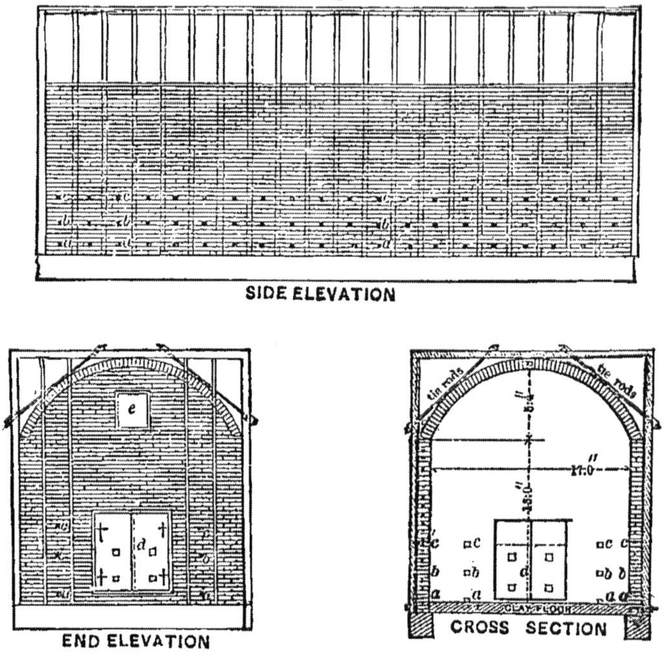

79. *Charcoal Kilns.*—Side elevation. with air-holes, *a*, *b*, *c*. End elevation, with air-holes, *a*, *b*, *c*, an iron door, *d*, for filling with wood and withdrawing coal, and small door, *e*. for completing the filling. Cross-section, with air-holes, doors, etc., as in end elevation. The figures on dotted lines are feet and inches.

601. Other kilns are cylindrical, with a low arch for a cover, but the principle of their operation does not essentially differ from that above represented. They all have openings for admitting air around the base, and for the escape of gases from above, all of which may be closed at will.

602. In another method, the kilns are of brick or stone made round and somewhat conical like a hay-stack, with openings on the side for filling and emptying, and air-holes for regulating the burning. They are of various capacities, but generally hold from 40 to 60 cords of wood. They are best built upon sloping ground, with doors on the upper side for filling, and at the bottom for removing the coal, and in both rectangular and conical kilns there is a further ad-

vantage from having several near together, that they may be watched and attended at less expense.

603. In kilns of every form it will be found that the acid vapors of the smoke tend to act upon the lime in the mortar, and to corrode the iron-work exposed to its action, requiring attention, in order to prevent failure or accident from this cause. It is this action of smoke upon the mortar in chimneys that sometimes renders them unsafe when they become old.

604. Charcoal made at low temperatures contains relatively more carbon and other gaseous elements than at a high degree of heat. The quantity also depends on the temperature, and the duration of the process. The weight and excellence is generally in proportion to the dry weight of the wood from which it is made, and it is more easily kindled, if made at a low heat.

605. The average yield in weight and volume varies, as will be seen by the following table:

Percentage of Charcoal made in Standing Meilers, as shown by European Experiments.[1]

Kinds of Wood.	In Kilns or "Standing Meilers."		In Temporary Meilers.	
	In Weight.	In Volume.	In Weight.	In Volume.
Birch body-wood	20–21	65–68	18	53
Beech and oak body-wood	23–27	52–54	19	47
Beech round-wood	18–20	56–62	......	......
Pine body-wood	24–28	60–70	19	58
Pine round-wood	20–24	42–50	18	53
Pine stump-wood	21–25	50–65	......	......
Spruce body-wood	22–25	60–64	20	52
Spruce round-wood	18	57	16	42
Larch body-wood	24	75	22	60
Larch round-wood	......	......	18	55
Silver fir body-wood	20–28	60–65	19	52
Silver fir round-wood	20	50	......	......
Alder body-wood	......	......	20	50
Alder round-wood	......	......	25	54
Alder branches	......	......	18	37

606. In laying-meilers, the average per cent of the coniferous woods is about 23 by weight, and 60 by volume—and for beech woods 22 per cent of weight, and 50 by volume.

[1] From *Fromme's Austrian Forest Calendar*, 1882, p. 255, upon various authorities there cited.

607. By the *Dromart Process* a kiln is constructed of cast-iron plates that form the floor and sides, and may be set up and taken down from time to time as it becomes desirable to change the site. Beneath the iron floor there are flues leading to equi-distant points in the bottom, and a fire is kindled externally for supplying in part the heat required by the process. There are air-holes around the side and a chimney at the top, all of which may be opened or closed at will. The wood is set up endwise, and fills the entire space. In this, as in all other kilns, the volatile products may be saved.

608. The *Moreau Process* proposes to secure carbonization in sheet-iron receivers of cylindrical or prismatic form, and capable of holding a cord or two each. They are filled at the top through an opening that may be closely sealed, and the air is admitted through perforated tubes from below. These receivers are so arranged that several may be attended by the same men simultaneously, some being filled or emptied while the others are at work. They have no bottom, and are speedily emptied by being turned over on their side. It is claimed that they afford 41 to 43 per cent in volume, and 30 in weight.

609. Charcoal is an ingredient in gunpowder, and the best is made from the alder buckthorn (*Rhamnus frangula*), although the common alder, willow, soft maple, hornbeam, basswood, and poplar are used. It is best prepared in iron retorts, in which the heat is applied externally, and the wood should be peeled, to avoid accidents from the ignition by sparks from sand in the bark in manufacture.

610. The percentage of ash in woods, as a rule, decreases as well in the bark as the wood, from below upwards, being more in the branches than in the trunk, and most in the twigs and leaves. In coniferous trees, the alkalies, magnesia, phosphoric acid, and sulphuric acid in various combinations, occur most in the needles, and lime, iron, and manganese in the bark, and small branches.

611. By far the most ashes are contained in the cambium and bark bundles, and more in the sap-wood generally than in the heart-wood. As the cellular system ceases to be active, it appears to give up its alkali and phosphoric acid to the use of the younger formations, and thus in the life-process the same atoms may be used over and again in the same tree.

612. It follows, from this, that the tree when young requires relatively more food than when old, and that nurseries exhaust the soil

more rapidly in proportion than a forest of large trees. The process of assimilation may be compared to that observed in animal life, where the structures are formed in early life.

Red Charcoal.

613. About 1836, a method was introduced in France for semi-carbonizing wood, by placing it in chambers at the mouths of furnaces, and exposing it to a heat by which the water and acetic acid are expelled, and the combustible gases left. This product, sometimes called "torrified wood," is used in melting pig-iron for casting and other purposes. It ignites freely, does not impair by keeping, and burns with a copious flame and intense heat. It is said for certain purposes to afford 30 per cent more of heat than fully-burned charcoal. The process being stopped just at the point where carbonization begins, the wood retains its texture and appearance; it may be split, cut, or sawed, but has lost its strength, and is of a reddish brown color.

Distilled Products of Wood.

614. In all forms of kilns the volatile products may be condensed and saved. The smoke is drawn from the kilns and condensed. The methylic alcohol or wood-spirit is first separated by distillation; the residue of dilute acetic acid is then neutralized with lime, and evaporated to dryness. About two gallons of the wood spirit are produced from the smoke of a cord of hard wood, and when purified it may be applied to all chemical uses for which common alcohol is employed, but chiefly in making paints and varnishes. After the spirits are distilled out, the residue, with lime added, yields about 200 pounds to the cord. It is chiefly used in making white lead.

615. Besides these, a large number of chemical products may be derived from the distillation of wood, having use in calico printing, and in other industries, and the value from a given quantity of wood from these sources, at present prices, amounts to more than twice that of the charcoal made at the same time. The gases remaining in this process have not much illuminating power, but are used in supplying a part of the heat required for the evaporation

Illuminating Gas from Wood.

616. It is found that wood exposed to cherry-red heat in close retorts, yields a gas which, when purified, has a much greater illuminating power than the best obtained from coal. In this way chips and other waste pieces of wood have been turned to profitable account. The heat in this process must be carried to a greater degree than in the making of charcoal, and hence the residual product is of inferior quality. The different kinds of wood are about alike as to value in furnishing gas for illumination, the quantity averaging, in eight of the common kinds, about 582.35 cubic feet to 100 pounds of wood.

617. The condition as to dryness, however, is of great importance, since the vapor of water coming in contact with the incandescent charcoal will form an oxyde of carbon and of hydrogen, that will reduce its illuminating power. The wood should therefore be dried as much as possible just before being placed in the retort, or else it will again absorb moisture from the air.

618. Where steam-power is used, the waste steam may be carried in pipes through the drying chamber, and a current of air may be driven or drawn through the wood, securing the requisite degree of dryness, without much expense. The retorts may be like those for coal gas, but larger, and as the process gives the best result when heated rapidly, the furnaces should have a larger amount of grate-surface. A charge is worked out in an hour and a half, and the charcoal formed is at the end drawn out into sheet-iron extinguishers and tightly closed for cooling. As the liquid products are corrosive to iron, copper pipes must be used, and the gas must be purified before being used.[1]

CHAPTER XV.

FOREST FIRES.

619. There is no subject in Forestry more important than the prevention and control of forest fires. They every year do a vast amount of injury, not only to standing timber and young trees, but

[1] Those wishing to look further into this subject, will find detailed information in the Forestry Report of 1877, published by the Department of Agriculture, p. 133, and in the authorities there cited.

to fences, bridges, buildings, farms and mill property, and to cord-wood, lumber and bark cut in readiness for market. Not only this, they sterilize the land by burning out the vegetable mold, so that trees can not be made to grow again, until in some degree this material is restored by the decayed herbage, and the fall of leaves from an undergrowth of bushes—a process which requires many years to accomplish.

620. Sometimes the fire runs from tree to tree in the tops, instead of spreading along the ground, as in the great Miramachi fire of New Brunswick, in 1825, and the Peshtigo fire of Wisconsin, in 1871. Upon each of these occasions, many hundred human lives were lost. The Michigan fires of 1871 and 1881 were memorable from the destruction of towns, villages, bridges, and farm property that they occasioned.

621. In the great fires above mentioned, the forests had been long exposed to intense solar heat and to drouth, and vegetable matter in every form would ignite from the least spark, and burn beyond control. The currents of air which the flames excited, became furious gales of wind, and swept every thing before them in a tornado of fire.

622. Without giving historical or statistical details, we will present the subjects under the three heads of *causes*, *prevention* and *control*.

(1.) *Causes of Forest Fires.*

623. These fires generally originate from the following causes, and somewhat in order of importance as here placed:

(*a.*) From fires that escape in the clearing of lands, and the burning off of brush and stubble in preparing the ground for cultivation.

(*b.*) From sparks and coals of locomotives along lines of railroad.

(*c.*) From fires purposely set to improve pasturage, upon mountains and in marshy grounds. This is a very common practice in the Southwestern and Southern States, the fires being often set by persons who do not own the land, to afford grazing to their few head of cattle, upon lands not their own.

(*d.*) From fires carelessly left by persons camping, hunting or fishing, and by tramps.

(*e.*) From the careless use of matches, that are thrown down and not extinguished, or from tobacco-pipes, cigars, or gun-wads.

(*f.*) From fires that escape from coal-pits and other operations carried on in the woods.

(*g.*) From malicious design.

(*h.*) From natural causes, such as lightning, friction between dry wood in high winds, and spontaneous combustion.

(2.) *Prevention of Forest Fires.*

624. A constant vigilance in the use of fire, and in extinguishing every spark, when left, and proper care in the clearing away of all combustible materials around the place where a fire is kindled in or near a woodland, would render every other prevention almost needless. The danger from fires should be thoroughly impressed upon every one, and especially upon children, at home and at school, so that they may grow up with careful habits in this respect.

625. A kind of safety-match is made in immense quantities in Sweden, and is used extensively throughout Europe. It can not be ignited except when rubbed upon a surface that is chemically prepared, and that is placed upon one side of the box in which they are sold. The use of matches prepared like these, and the habit of extinguishing them when lighted, would prevent accidents from this cause. Gun-wads are also made that will not burn, and that are entirely safe as to retaining fire.

626. The risk of fire from locomotives may be largely diminished by the use of spark-extinguishers and other arrangements, many of which have been patented. The law in most states renders railroad companies responsible for the damages that they may cause, and this law rigidly enforced would greatly tend to the exercise of more care in this respect. As a further precaution, the leaves and rubbish along railroads should be raked off and burned, at a time when the fires can be managed. Piles of old decaying ties should be removed. Belts of timber, less inflammable than pines, should be planted along railroads that run through pine forests, and railroads should be patrolled in a dry time, for the purpose of extinguishing the fires that may be set, before damages are done.

627. In regions where fires are exceedingly liable to occur, the burning off of belts of land in winter, when the fires do not spread beyond control, and need some help to burn at all, is a safe precaution; such fires, however, injure the young trees, and they should be allowed to extend no more than necessary.

628. Damages from prairie fires are best prevented by plowing a few furrows in parallel lines, fifty or a hundred feet apart, and burning off the grass between, soon after it is killed down by frost, and before it is very dry. This practice along the sides of railroads in a prairie region, is excellent.

629. In Europe, fire-guards are made through the woods, by clearing away all trees and all matter that can burn, in belts from fifty to one hundred feet wide. To be effectual, they must be cleaned out every year or two. If such belts were planted with deciduous trees, that do not take fire so readily as conifers, they would afford some protection, but not as much as the bare soil.

630. Common roads answer the same end, and in a region liable to fires, they should be wide and the sides well cleared. The French Ordinance of Waters and Forests (1669), prescribed that public roads through forests should be at least seventy-two feet wide, and that all thorns and bushes within sixty feet should be cleared off on each side.

631. Avenues through a forest present the unavoidable disadvantage of exposing the timber to the winds. This effect is greatest in heavy-topped hemlocks, etc., and least where the woodland has grown up with the space reserved, as the branches of the trees on the outside are then strong, and extend lower down, affording much resistance to the wind.

632. Where streams of water flow through nearly level woodlands, they may sometimes be raised by dams, so as to form a series of narrow ponds for long distances, that would check all ground-fires. Stone walls, mounds of earth, and cactus-hedges afford some protection.

633. Our state laws should provide for the designation of some existing officer, or the election of some special officer, who should have authority to call out help for extinguishing forest fires. Such men should be thoroughly familiar with their districts, and with all lines of defense that can be used to oppose an advancing fire. Persons when thus called upon, should be liable to a fine if they refuse to assist without reasonable excuse.

634. Laws rendering all persons responsible for the damages that may be done from fires that they set, whether carelessly or intentionally, should be enacted and enforced. In Pennsylvania they have a law rendering the counties responsible for the expenses in

hiring men to extinguish fires, and it should be adopted generally. If farmers found that they might have taxes to pay for damages done by this cause, they would be very careful in burning their fallows, and in seeking to prevent it from being done carelessly by others.

635. A ground-fire that runs through a young plantation of ash, oak, catalpa, and other deciduous trees, may kill down the tops, and apparently destroy them entirely. We should not give them up as ruined, for they will often sprout from the roots, and grow as vigorously as before. The most that can be done in such cases, is to cut off the old stems and all but the thriftiest of the new ones. As for the old one, it only does harm by preventing its place from healing over. Several small growing sprouts from one root are not so desirable as one strong one.

636. In humid climates, and in damp grounds, the undergrowth sometimes comes in so as to cover the surface, to the injury of the growth of the trees.[1] It is necessary, in order to secure the greatest benefit, to clear out the bushes and ground-herbage and burn it. For this purpose the material, after being pulled up, is best arranged in piles, at some distance from the trees, covering it with sod before setting it on fire. By avoiding a dry time, this can be done safely, as the fire will smolder away, with much smoke and little flame, until the whole is reduced to ashes. These are then spread over the ground, tending to renew its fertility. The larvæ of many kinds of insects that find shelter in the litter, are by this means destroyed.

(3.) *Control of Forest Fires.*

637. Among the means employed for stopping the progress of a forest fire when started, the following are the most important: Throwing water and wetting a line of ground; sand and soil thrown upon the edge of a line of fire will sometimes do almost as well; the fire may be whipped out with green bushes; the rubbish may be raked away toward the advancing fire and burned; and sometimes furrows may be plowed, to present a line of fresh earth.

638. *Back-firing*, consists in setting a fire commencing along some road, stream of water, wall, or other line where its spread in one

[1] In French Forestry this undergrowth is called "*bois mort*," literally "dead wood."

direction may be prevented, and allowing this fire to run till it meets the principal fire. Great fires sometimes cause an inward current of air that favors back-firing. As fires advance down hill more slowly than they ascend, the counter-fires may often be set to best advantage at the bottom of a valley. The crest of a ridge is, however, a much better line of defense.

639. After a fire has apparently been brought under control, it should be carefully watched until it is entirely extinguished. If neglected it will sometimes get under way with more energy than before, even some days or weeks afterwards. On a rocky surface, full of deep fissures, there is very great danger to be dreaded from these concealed fires, that may smolder unobserved for a long time.

640. It is always a safe precaution to have water, buckets, spades, axes, etc., in readiness for use in case of fires. In some regions in Europe, a system of signals is arranged, and persons are on watch from towers on high hills, for the special purpose of discovering fires, and making known their locality. A system of telegraphic signals, consisting of willow-baskets by day, and of lanterns by night, has been proposed in Spain for this use, and by a simple combination representing numbers, a correspondent may receive a great variety of messages in a brief space of time, by the aid of books in which these messages are referred to by corresponding numbers.

CHAPTER XVI.

PROTECTION FROM OTHER INJURIES THAN FIRES.

641. A young woodland needs protection even more than a grain-field, because the injuries done, may destroy the growth of several years instead of one. These damages may be done by wild or domestic animals, or by insects; or they may be caused by disease, by storms of wind, by the obstruction of water-courses that may overflow level lands, and in various other ways, many of which can be prevented or removed.

Pasturage of Woodlands.

642. In European governments, the rights of pasturage in the public woodlands are regulated by law, and sometimes they are sold, for one year at a time, at public auction. In many cases it is a common right, subject to regulation by the local government.

The practice is forbidden altogether in young woods, until the growth has reached a size that would prevent injury from being done.

643. As a general rule, sheep and goats do much more harm than horses and cattle, and in some countries they are altogether excluded at all times. The fattening of swine upon acorns and nuts is considered of no injury to large trees. The pasturage of steep mountain slopes is much more injurious than upon level land, and has tended to produce immense injuries by exposing the soil to erosions, as elsewhere more fully noticed.

644. It is an admirable practice to plant groves of trees in pasture grounds, to provide shade for stock, but such groves must be protected by fences until the foliage is above the reach of cattle, and the trunks of the trees are so large that they would not be liable to injury.

Injuries to Seeds, Seedlings, and Trees, by wild Animals.

645. In noticing the agencies for the distribution of seeds, we have elsewhere given credit to birds, and especially to squirrels, as planters [§ 125]. We must, however, guard against the latter, in keeping nuts in heaps for spring planting. The liability to injury by moles and mice in winter, is a principal reason for our delaying to plant nuts, acorns, and other seeds till spring, instead of planting in the fall, as is done in nature. [§ 130.]

646. These animals do injuries to nurseries and plantations in winter, especially when the snows are deep. Rabbits are very fond of gnawing the bark from young trees, and where these animals are kept, it is necessary to guard against their injuries by stone walls, laid from below the reach of their burrows, or by wire screens.

647. Fruit and shade trees may be protected by binding tarred paper around the trunks near the ground, and by treading down the snows around them in winter. Hedgehogs will feed upon the bark and twigs of the hemlock in winter, and certain birds may do injury to trees by biting off the buds.

648. The gopher (*Geomys bursarius*) is one of the most troublesome pests in the Western States, from its eating off the roots of young trees; and a single animal has been known to follow a line of newly set osage orange hedge, in the soil soft from recent planting, and destroy the roots for many rods. They may be poisoned

by placing strychnine or arsenic in a carrot, apple, or a potato near where their burrows come to the surface—but caution should be taken in the use of these dangerous poisons.

649. In parks and forests where game is protected, there is sometimes much sacrificed from their propensity to gnaw and rub. Deer are as destructive to the herbage of young trees as sheep or goats. In Europe, it is customary to feed hay and turnips to herbivorous game in winter.

650. In sowing pine seeds, it becomes necessary to guard against some of the gramnivorous birds, who seem to be attracted, as if by instinct, to the feast. The white-throated and white-crowned sparrows, appear to be particularly fond of these seeds, and after the young shoots have come up, they become dainty food for the common yellow-bird. The best remedy against these birds, is a thin covering of marsh-grass or of fine brush, care being taken that it does not smother the young plants. A better one would be an old seine, suspended upon poles a few inches above the seed-beds in the nursery.

CHAPTER XVII.

INSECT RAVAGES IN WOODLANDS.

651. Our limits do not permit more than a general notice of the damages done to trees from insects. They begin with the seed—are found in the young shoot, and in the bark or wood of the roots, trunk and branches, at every stage of growth—in the leaves, the blossoms, and the ripening fruit. They sometimes appear in small numbers, and every year alike, and at others they increase in immense number, and either progressively or simultaneously destroy every thing before them.

652. Among those most systematic in their movements is the processionary caterpillar, shown in the annexed engravings, copied from De la Blanchère.[1] The moth appears in August or September, and for some days remains motionless under the leaves and branches, flying only in the twilight. The female lays some two hundred eggs upon the bark, and from these the worms soon hatch out. They live together in a common net, often changing their abode till the third moult, when they set out in the evening

[1] *Les Ravageurs des Forêts, et des Arbres d'Alignement*, i. 170.

80. *Bombyx processionea.*—(The Processionary Caterpillar.)

81. Female Moth of the *Bombyx processionea*

82. *Calosoma*. a Carnivorous Beetle, destructive to the Processionary Caterpillar.

in an orderly march—first one, then two, three, and four abreast, and so widening by one at every rank, in solid triangular phalanx, and in immense legions. When there are no more oak leaves to destroy, they consume the undergrowth, and they do not fail to take harvests and gardens before them. The hirsute appendages with which they are covered cause irritating inflammations when in contact with the naked skin or a mucous surface, and neither man nor beast can remain in a forest when they are abroad.

653. Against enemies like these man is scarcely able to defend himself, but there are enemics that also appear abundantly when their food becomes plenty, that

tend to limit these injuries. One of these is a carnivorous beetle, that hatches out at about the same time. Although they have wings, they attack them on the ground, and mount upon the trees to seize their prey.

654. Usually beetles of the general form shown in the foregoing engraving, with long sharp jaws and very rapid movements, belong to the carnivorous class. Something may be done to prevent the injuries of the worms above described, by scraping off the eggs from the bark. They are always deposited on the outside trees of a forest, and never within it.

655. Of bark-boring insects the conifers have an unusually large share, there being, perhaps, no species that is entirely free from their ravages. They are sometimes very symmetrical in their work, the bark, externally, showing a row of holes at equal intervals, and, between the wood and bark, burrows running sometimes horizontally, at other times vertically or obliquely, with numerous branching burrows that seldom or never run into one another, however nearly they may approach.

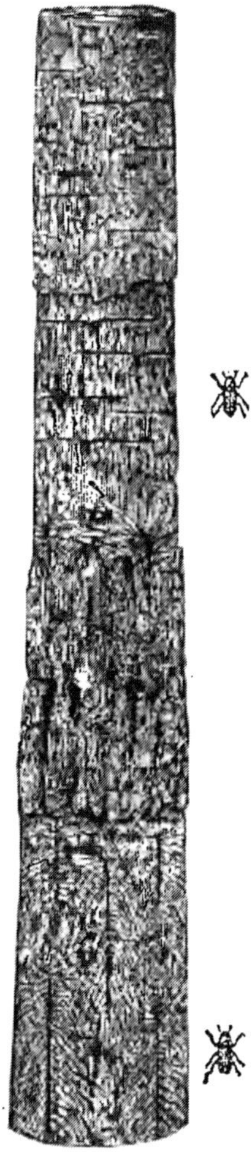

83. Insect Ravages under the Bark of Trees.

656. The main stem of these burrows is made by the parent-insect, who, as she advances, deposits her eggs on the sides. From these the larvæ hatch, and, because small, the passage which they make is at first narrow. It widens as they grow in size, and at the end may expand into a little chamber. When the worm has finished this stage of its growth, it becomes a pupa, and finally eats out into the open air, as a perfect insect. Its natural size is shown by the side of the above engraving.

657. The immense numbers in which these insects appear in some years, render their ravages very destructive, and as they often produce two broods in a year, a single insect may, in three or four seasons, when the increase is not checked, multiply in enormous quantities.

658. As a general rule, these bark-boring insects are most liable to attack fallen timber, and especially that which has been overthrown by storms in the season of active vegetation, or trees that have had their vitality weakened from being scorched by fire.

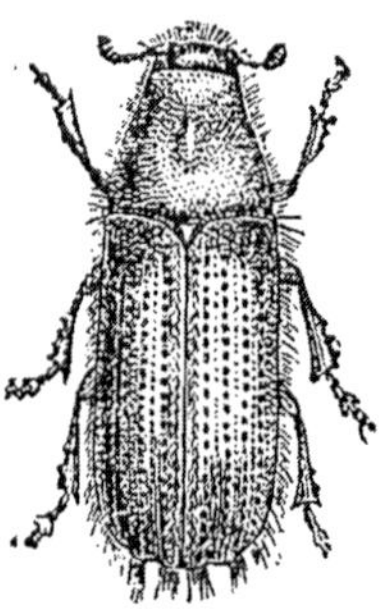

84. *Hylesinus piniperda* (greatly enlarged).

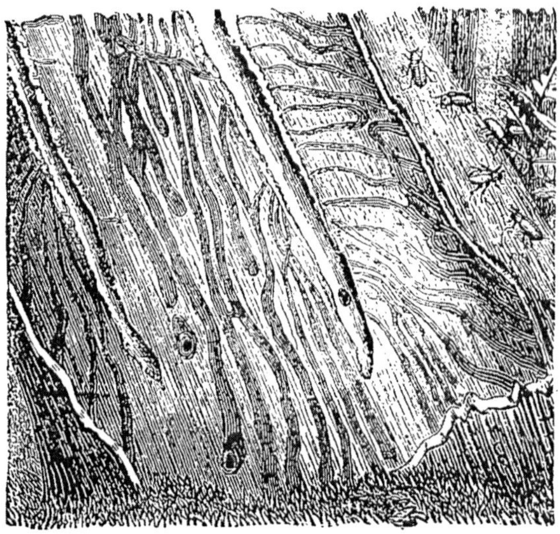

85. Burrows of the *Hylesinus piniperda* under the Bark of the Scotch Pine, with the Insects of natural size.

659. The damage done to logs cut for lumber may be lessened by taking off the bark as soon as the trees are felled. The above engravings represent an enlarged view of one of these bark-insects, with the form of its burrows, and the insect of its natural size.

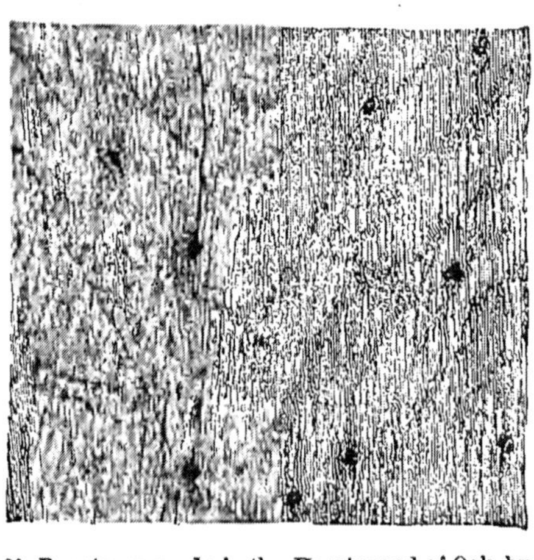

86. Punctures made in the Heart-wood of Oak, by a *Lymexyelon*, natural size.

660. With respect to wood-boring insects, the amount of injury done to the timber depends upon the uses to which it is to be applied. If slight, it

may still be good for carpentry, but improper for coopers' use; if the burrows are large, they tend to admit moisture, and to become great open cavities, and in certain other cases the wood is so eaten that it becomes nothing but a shell—perhaps sound and without the least appearance of injury externally, but wholly eaten out into caverns within.

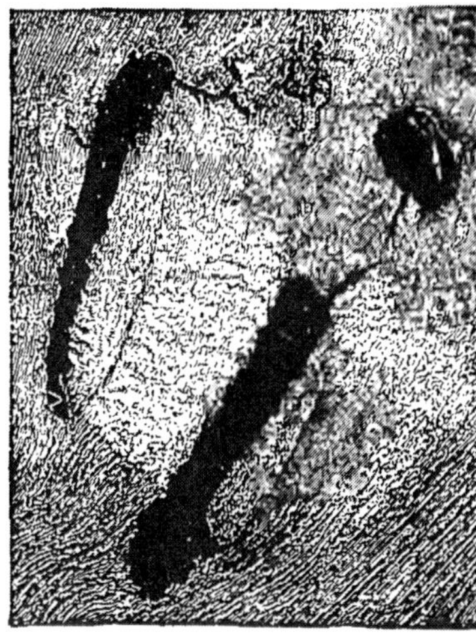

87. Cavities made in Fallen Timber by the Larvæ of Insects, tending to rapidly hasten its Decay.

661. These wood-eating insects are especially common in decaying wood, and where they are strictly limited to this, they can scarcely be considered as of great injury, and in some cases they may be even beneficial, in hastening its decay.

662. There are other classes of insects found upon wood and leaves, and even in burrows in the wood and bark, that are predatory in their habits, pursuing other insects and destroying them, either in the perfect state, or as larvæ, or by feeding upon their eggs.

88. Wood that has been thoroughly ruined by the Larvæ of the *Cerambyx heros.*

662½. These carnivorous insects are the surest agency for counteracting the inordinate increase of the injurious kinds, and when the latter multiply to undue extent, the abundance of food thus offered leads to their increase also, until the balance of nature is again restored. We here present a cut of the larva of the great capricorn beetle; that which sometimes proves destructive to the oak, and that causes the damages shown in the last preceding engraving.

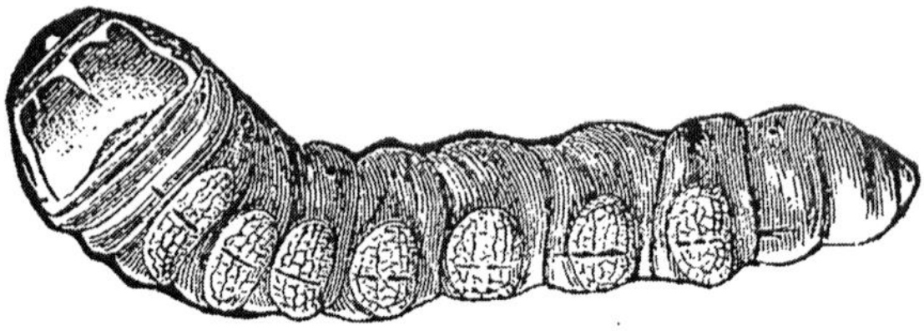

89. Larva of the *Cerambyx heros.*

These insects require three years for their transformations, and do not usually attack the timber until it has passed its stage of full maturity and has begun to decline, but while the wood is still hard and sound. The capricorn beetles to which this insect belongs, are among the most destructive of wood-borers; some inhabiting the trunks of trees, and some only the limbs. There are other insects that devour the pith or the roots, and some are found only in herbaceous plauts.

663. The insects that burrow under the bark, or that mine into the wood, are sometimes very systematic in their operations, and this symmetry may all be due to the work of one insect, that deposits her eggs at equal intervals along the burrow. These, upon hatching into larvæ, eat their way from the main burrow, sometimes to but a short distance, and without enlargement at the end, and at

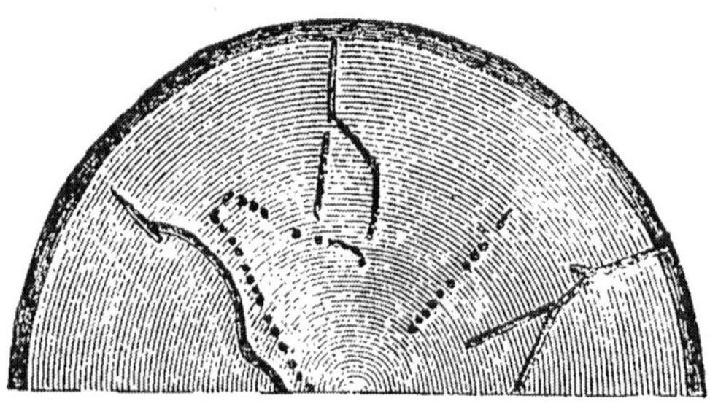

90. Cross-section showing the Burrows of the *Bostrichus lineatus.*

other times widening as they gain in size, till they reach their limit of growth, and then, after completing their transformations, they emerge through holes eaten in the bark, and come forth as perfect insects.

664. Climatic vicissitudes have great influence upon the multiplication or decrease in the number of insects. A very hot and dry season may favor an increase, or an unusually cold, wet, and backward one may destroy them.

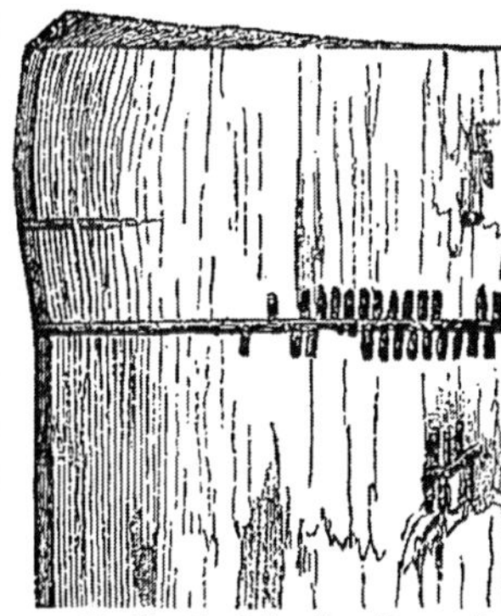

91. Vertical Section through the Burrows of the *Bostrichus lineatus*.

665. Insectivorous birds do much to keep injurious insects in check, and where there is an abundance of this food, they will sometimes appear in great numbers. The presence of these birds is therefore to be encouraged; and as groves and belts of timber are multiplied, the conditions favoring their coming and sojourn, to the benefit of our grain and fruits, are increased. For these reasons they should be strongly protected by efficient game laws, and by public sentiment, against their destruction, or the disturbance of their nests.

665½. In some countries, as in France, the importance of protecting birds is taught in the schools, and the children are shown how to distinguish the useful kinds of birds, small animals, reptiles, and insects from those that are injurious, and the best means for protecting the former, and of destroying the latter. Little "Protection Societies" are organized among the children, for preventing injuries to birds and their nests, and various means are devised to impress the young with correct ideas concerning the interests depending upon the allies of the field.

666. In nurseries, gardens, orchards, and parks, we may sometimes adopt measures for the destruction of insects, when they appear in unusual number, by some kind of poisons, such as Paris-green, London-purple, white-hellibore, etc., but where they invade a whole forest, and especially when they occur in regions remote from settlements, we can do nothing, and must await the operation of natural causes for restoring the balance, through the natural agencies of climate and the antagonism in insect life.

667. In some countries this can be done by costly methods, such as cutting down the infected trees, and burning the tops and the

bark. But these heroic remedies are practically much beyond our means for successful application in a large way. Fortunately these great invasions do not last many years in succession. They may leave a wide-spread ruin behind them, but some other species of timber tree with fewer insect enemies will come on to supply the place; and generally the timber killed may still be used for lumber or fuel, if cut within a year or two afterwards. In the case of timber bored into cavities, of course the value is greatly impaired for many uses, and its decay is generally hastened by these causes.

668. Where the tree survives the injury of an insect year, the effect is generally seen in the diminished growth of that season. We have seen in the Museum of a School of Forestry, a section of a tree some hundreds of years old, in which for long periods together every third ring of growth was narrow, as we see in one of the rings in the annexed engraving. This was caused by the eating off of the leaves every third year by a caterpillar.

92. Effect of Insect Injuries to the Leaves upon the unequal Growth of Wood.

669. If the leading shoot of a young conifer is eaten off by insects, or killed from any other cause, its growth is checked until another, and sometimes two shoots are formed in its place. This gives a defective form, and injures its value. In a lawn or nursery, this damage may be repaired by herbaceous grafting from the terminal shoot of another tree, as elsewhere described.

670. The damages done by insects to a forest are sometimes immense. In recent years the spruce timber in New Brunswick, Maine, and Northern New York has been thus destroyed to the extent of millions of dollars in value.

671. Kaltenbach, an approved European writer upon Forest Entomology, enumerates 537 species of insects injurious to the oaks, 107 to the elms, 264 to the poplars, 396 to the willows, 270 to the birches, 119 to the alder, 154 to the beech, 97 to the hazelnut, and 88 to the hornbeam. Of coniferous trees, the pines, spruces, larch, and firs are fed upon by 299 species, and the junipers by 33.

672. In the United States, while many observers have given their attention to this branch of natural history, much still remains to be known upon this subject, especially as relates to the geograph-

ical range of species, their migrations, the causes that favor or hinder their increase, and the means for diminishing their damages.

673. In a recent publication of the U. S. Entomological Commission, prepared by Prof. A. S. Packard, Jr., of Providence, R. I.,[1] there has been collected a summary of all that had been previously published concerning the forest-insects of the United States. We will present some of the more important facts of this Report, concerning the more injurious of these insects. As it will be necessary to refer to the orders under which insects are classed, they may be first concisely defined:

(1.) Coleoptera (*Beetles*).

674. These are insects with jaws, two thick wing-covers, in a straight line on the top of the back, with two filmy-wings, which are folded transversely. They pass through four stages of life—the egg, the larvæ or grubs (generally provided with six legs), the pupa, and the perfect insect. In most cases the greatest damage is done in the larva state. The coleoptera are divided into several great divisions, the principal of which are as follows:

675. (*a.*) The *Scarabæidæ*, embracing an immense number of species, known as ground or dung-beetles, tree-beetles, etc. Their larvæ do great damages to the roots of trees, and the perfect insects to the leaves and twigs. They fly in the evening, and may be destroyed to some extent by shaking them off from the trees in the morning, first spreading cloths before jarring the trees.

676. (*b.*) The *Lucanidæ*, or stag-beetles, which are distinguished by the great size and peculiar form of their upper jaws. The grubs of the larger kinds are said to remain six years before changing to a perfect insect. They live in the trunks and roots of trees, and bore into the solid wood.

677. (*c.*) The *Bupestridæ*, or saw-horned beetles, so called because the tips of the joints of their antennæ project more or less on the inside, somewhat like the teeth of a saw. They are often brightly colored, and have usually a hard shell and an oblong form, tapering behind. They keep concealed at night, and are abroad only by

[1] Bulletin No. 7. *Insects Injurious to Forest and Shade Trees*, 1881, p. 275. This Commission consists of Professors Charles V. Riley, of the Department of Agriculture at Washington, Dr. A. S. Packard, Jr., of Brown University, Providence, and Prof. Cyrus Thomas, of Carbondale, Ill.

day. The larvæ are wood-borers, and chiefly attack forest and fruit trees that are past their prime. The pine and hickory trees especially suffer from their ravages. Their larvæ are long, rather flat, yellowish white, and widened near the forward part. The head itself is small, and provided with teeth for boring. They in-

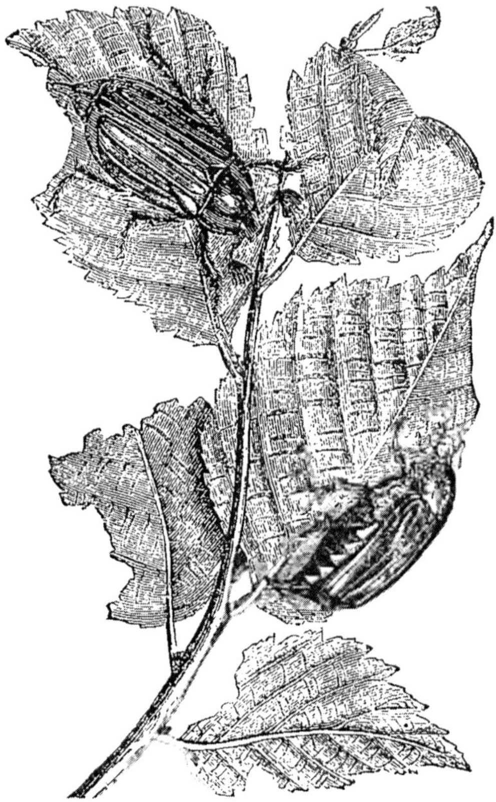

93. *Melolontha vulgaris* (Male and Female).

clude the flat-headed larvæ found under the bark and in the wood of our fruit trees, and may to some extent be kept out by surrounding the trunks with tarred paper, and by soaping, white-washing, and cutting out, or by seeking and destroying the perfect insects.

678. (*d.*) The *Elateridæ*, or spring-beetles, are most destructive to wood and roots in the larva state. They are sometimes called wire-worms, and some are wood-eaters, living under the bark; and in the

trunks of old trees. The timber-beetles, so destructive in ship-yards, belong to this division. The foregoing beetles, although differing greatly in form and habits, agree in one character, viz., their feet are five-jointed, while those that follow are four-jointed.

679. (*e.*) The *Rhynchophoridæ*, or weevils, mostly of very small size, so destructive to grains, and upon trees, boring into the bark, leaves, buds, fruit, and seeds, and feeding upon the juices and soft parts therein. They are day-insects, and love to come out in the sun-shine. Some fly well, but others have no wings, and generally they are slow and timid in their motions. The weevils are divided into several great families, and include an immense number of species.

680. (*f.*) The *Scolytidæ*, or cylindrical bark-beetles, mostly very small, but often doing the most serious injuries, especially in pine and spruce forests, by mining under the bark, and boring galleries in the new wood.

681. (*g.*) The *Bostrichidæ*—formerly classed with the preceding, but now separately. They are often of large size, and especially in tropical countries, they may prove very destructive. Their larvæ bore galleries in the solid wood of living trees.

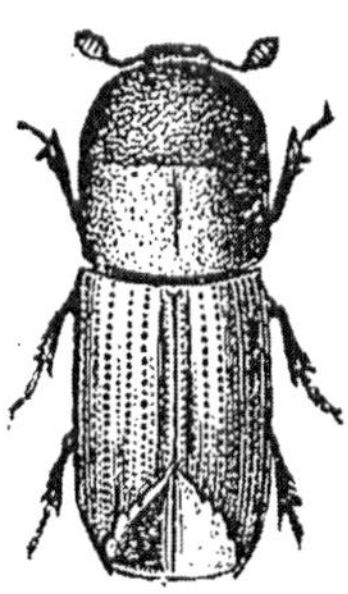

94. *Bostrichus typographicus* (greatly enlarged).

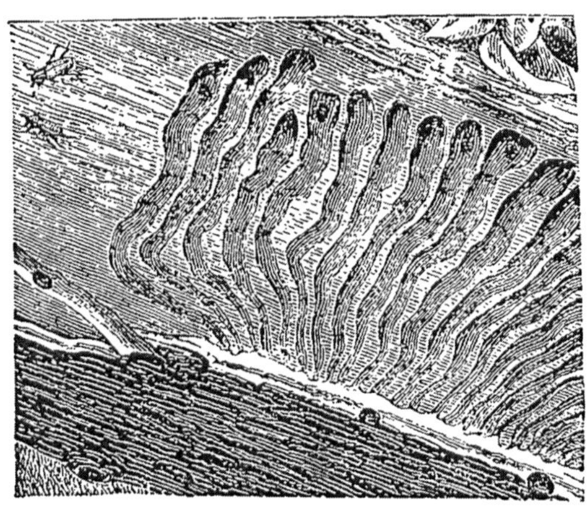

95. Burrows of the *Bostrichus typographicus* under the Bark of the Spruce, with the Insects of the Natural Size.

682. Two nearly allied species of the *Bostrychus* have proved very destructive to spruce forests in Europe. They are always found more or less under the bark of decaying trees, but when the condi-

ditions for their increase are multiplied, as in case of many trees being prostrated by a gale, they increase in enormous quantities, and destroy whole forests. In such cases, they appear to attack perfectly healthy trees. The first of these (*B. typographicus*) does the most harm, and is found chiefly in and under the bark of the trunk and large branches. The preceding engraving represents a set of burrows made by the larvæ hatched from the eggs of one insect, and an enlarged view of the insect itself.

683. The burrows of the *Bostrichus calcographus* are generally found at the same time, and upon the same trees as those of the preceding species, but only upon the smaller branches. The only

96. Burrows of the *Bostrichus chalcographus*, with the Insects of Natural Size.

effectual remedy known against these insects, is that of cutting down the trees, and peeling and burning the bark. In an invasion of these insects in the Jura region in South-eastern France, following as one of the consequences of a storm that happened in November, 1864, it became necessary from 1867 to 1873 to carefully examine every tree in a forest, and to cut down every spruce that showed signs of the insect, and to peel and burn the bark upon over

181,000 trees. By this energetic means, the ravages of these insects were arrested.

684. In the United States, at present prices of labor, and of timber, such a remedy would be wholly impracticable, but this statement serves to illustrate the great importance attached to this subject in Europe, and the sacrifices that are sometimes made to check these injuries.

685. (*h*). The *Cerambycideæ* — the long-horned or capricorn beetles, are destructive wood-borers. They generally rest by day upon the trees, and fly by night. Their larvæ are long whitish grubs, with the head smaller than the first ring, and provided with short but powerful jaws. These grubs, in some cases, live several years before coming to maturity. They are divided into three families and many groups, some species in the tropics measuring five or six inches in length and two inches in breadth.

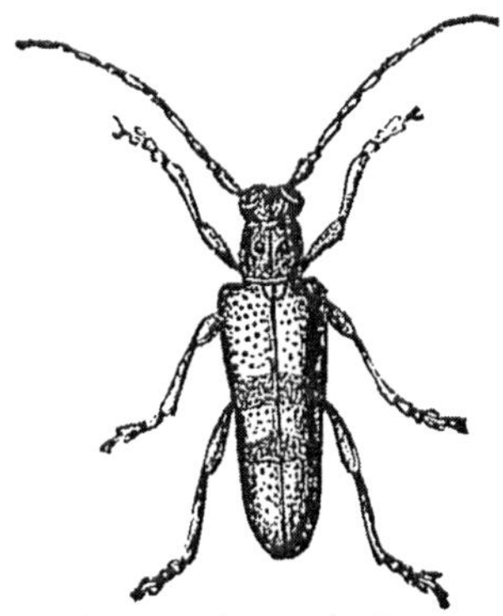

97. *Cerambyx carcharias.*

686. The remaining divisions of the beetles, some of which are injurious to trees, and especially to the leaves, can not be here described in detail. Some species are leaf-miners, eating out the soft parts and leaving the skeleton, and some doing injury in the larva form while others injure as perfect insects. Many of these appear to be governed by climatic influences, appearing in some years very abundantly, while at other times they disappear for a series of years altogether.

(2.) Orthoptera (*Cockroaches, Crickets, Grasshoppers, etc*).

687. These are insects with jaws, two rather thick and opaque upper wings, overlapping a little on the back, and two larger thin wings, which are folded in plaits. Transformation partial, larvæ and pupæ active, but wanting wings. All insects of this order—except the camel-crickets, which prey upon other insects—are injurious

98. Mole-Cricket.

to man. The mole-cricket is one of this class, and in Europe is very troublesome in nurseries and gardens, by eating the roots of trees and plants. A single brood will destroy a whole seed-bed. By breaking the crust of hardened earth in June, their nests are exposed to the air, and the eggs perish.

(3.) Hemiptera (*Bugs, Locusts, Plant-lice, etc.*).

688. These are insects with a horny beak for suction, four wings, of which the upper are generally thick at the base, with thinner extremities, and which lie flat and cross each other on the top of the back, or are of uniform thickness throughout, and slope at the sides like a roof. Transformation partial, larvae and pupae nearly like the adult insect, but wanting wings. Some, like the cochineal insect, are useful, but the damages done by plant-bugs, locusts, tree-hoppers, froth-insects, plant-lice, bark-lice, mealy-bugs, and the like, by sucking the juices of plants, is very great.

(4.) Neuroptera (*Dragon-flies, Lace-winged Flies, May-flies, Ant-lion, Day-fly, White Ants, etc.*).

689. These are insects with jaws, four netted wings, of which the hinder ones are the largest, and no sting. Transformation complete or partial, larva and pupa various. White ants, wood-lice and wood-ticks, are almost the only noxious insects of this order, and even these do not injure living plants. Many of them destroy other insects for their food.

(5.) Lepidoptera (*Butterflies, Sphinges, and Moths*).

690. These insects have a mouth with a spiral sucking tube; wings four, covered with branny scales. Transformation complete. The larvæ are caterpillars, and have six true legs, and from four to ten fleshy prop-legs. Pupa with the cases of the wings and of the legs indistinct, and soldered to the breast.

691. Of the butterflies proper, the forester has not much to complain. The perfect insects feed upon flowers, and the larvæ upon vegetable substances. They usually change their skins about four times before they come to full size. Their life in the final state is brief, and in the splendor of colors they rival sometimes all other forms of animal life.

692. The *Sphinges* or hawk-moths derive the name "Sphynx" from a fancied resemblance of their caterpillars, when at rest, to the Egyptian sphynx, supporting themselves upright by their fore-legs. They include a peach-tree borer, and some other species injurious to trees. We present in the margin an engraving of the perfect insect, the larvæ of which infest the wood of the elm, always boring at the base of the trunk, where it unites with the root, and appearing to divide the territory with the *Cossus*, that bores only in the trunk.

99. One of the Hawk-moths or Sphinges (*Sesia*), in Form of perfect Insect.

693. A night-moth nearly allied with the Bombyces, and by some naturalists classed with them, but by others made a separate family, named *Zeuzeradæ*, is very often found in Europe upon the horse-chestnut. The larvæ are white, soft and naked, or slightly downy, with brown horny heads, spots on the body, as shown in the engraving, and sixteen legs. They are wood-borers, and are also very destructive to the pear, apple, lilac, and occasionally to the young elms. In favorite trees it may be killed by a wire inserted into its burrow, the opening of which may be known by the dust that falls out, and a violet-colored tinge on its border. The genus to which this belongs is European, and, according to Davis, has not been found in this country. We have many others, however, of closely allied forms, and of very destructive nature.

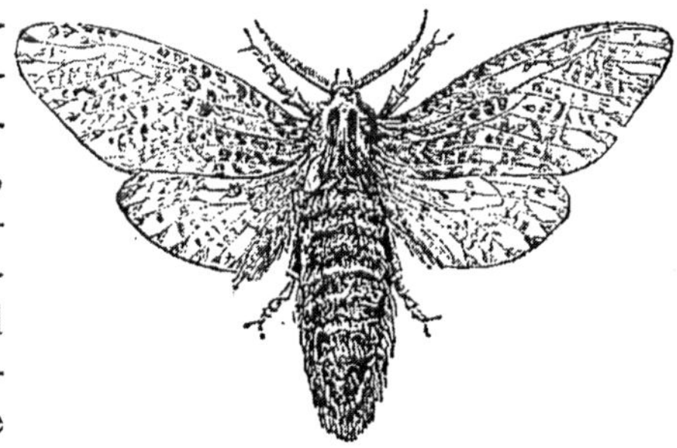

100. *Zeuzera æsculi.*

101. Larva of the *Zeuzera.*

694. Linnæus divided the *Moths* into eight groups, viz.: *Attici*, *Bombyces*, *Noctuæ*, *Geometræ*, *Tortrices*, *Pyralides*, *Tineæ* and *Alucitæ*.

The first of these has, by later naturalists, been merged with others, but, with this exception, these groups have been considered as well marked, and are generally retained. We present a few examples of some of these forms.

695. The *Bombyces*, or spinners, are thick-bodied moths, with feathered antennæ, at least in the males, tongue short or wanting, thorax woolly but not crested, and the larvæ generally spinners. The figures here given show one of numerous species of this group. They have sometimes proved exceedingly destructive, by eating off the leaves of trees, while in the larva state. We here present a view of the perfect insect, the larvæ of which prove very destructive to the Scotch pine. Whole forests

(*Male.*) (*Female.*)
102. *Bombyx neustria.* (Perfect Insect.)

103. Larva of the *Bombyx neustria.*

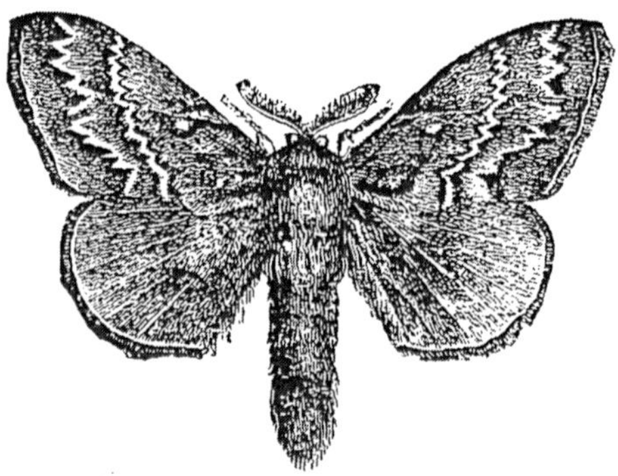

104. Bombyx of the Pine. (Female.)

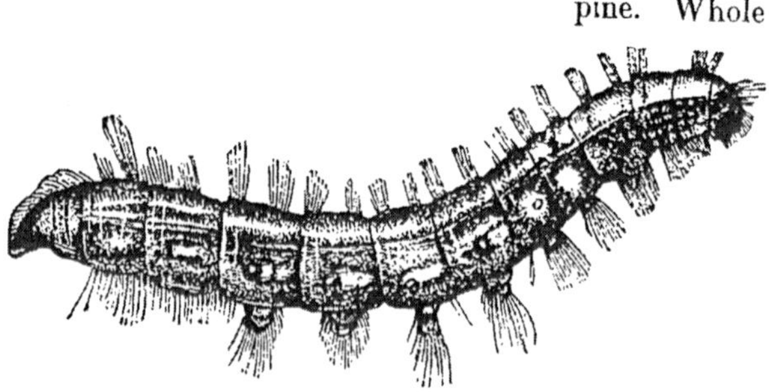

105. Larva of the *Bombyx pini.*

are sometimes laid waste by these devourers. They will even fill ditches that have been dug to arrest their progress, aud the only way to control them is to collect in winter and burn the mosses in which they are concealed.

696. The *Noctuæ*, or owlet moths, chiefly fly by night, and are thick-bodied, swift-flying moths, that do considerable damage to vegetation, and some of them live exposed on the leaves of trees and shrubs, but the greater part feed only by night.

697. The *Geometræ*, or spăn worms, live mostly in the larva state only on the leaves of trees, and undergo their transformation in the ground. Their larvæ derive their name from their manner of crawling, by drawing up the body into an arch, and then reaching forward for a new hold. When disturbed, they drop by a silken thread, till the danger is over, and then climb back again to their former place, with a tolerably rapid motion, by seizing the thread with their jaws and forelegs.

106 Male Moth of the *Geometra brumata*, one of the Span-worms.

698. The canker-worm female moths are nearly without wings, and are sluggish in their movements. They instinctively make their way from the ground where they have been hatched towards the nearest trees, and slowly creep up the trunks, pairing with their winged mates in their ascent. They are chiefly injurious to the apple and elm trees, but also attack the plum, cherry, and lime trees, and strip them of the pulpy part of the leaves, leaving the midribs and veins remaining.

107. Female Moth of the *Cheimobata brumata*.

699. The *Tortrices*, or leaf-rollers, are so called from the cylindrical rolls that they form around themselves at the close of their larva-life. Very few of them make cocoons, and most of them go through their transformations in their leaf-cases. The moths of this tribe are mostly small, and they fold their wings over their bodies when at rest, like a steep roof. Most of them when dis-

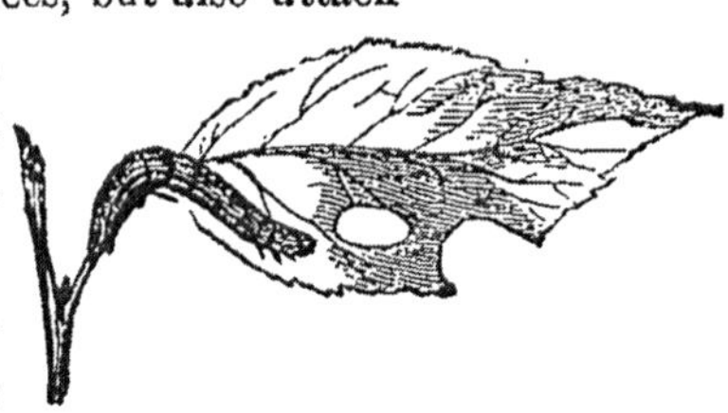

108. Larva of the Canker-worm, and the Effect of its Ravages.

turbed in the larva state will drop by a silk thread like the preceding kinds.

108. *Tortrix resinianæ.* (The Insect at Rest of the Natural Size; the Larva and Flying Insect Enlarged.)

700. The *Pyralides* are nearly akin to the geometers, and are sometimes called delta-moths, from the triangular manner of closing their wings. This tribe includes the meal-worms of old flour barrels, the grease-moths, the hop-vine caterpillar, etc., but they are not particularly injurious to trees.

701. The *Tineæ* are chiefly destructive to clothing and household stuff, but some of them burrow into leaves, and make winding passages in the pulpy substance of plants.

702. The *Alucitæ*, or feather-winged moths, is a small tribe of not much importance from the injuries done.

(6.) Hymenoptera (*Saw-Flies, Ants, Wasps, Bees, etc*).

703. These are insects with jaws, four veined wings in most species, the hinder pair being the smallest, and a piercer or sting at the end of the abdomen. Transformation complete. Larvæ mostly maggot or slug-like; of some, caterpillar-like. Pupæ with the legs and wings unconfined.

704. In the adult state, these chiefly live upon honey, the pollen of flowers, and the juices of fruits. As slugs or false caterpillars they sometimes injure plants. Some are wood-borers and wood-eaters, the pines and firs suffering most. Others cause galls and excrescences upon leaves and twigs, those upon the oak furnishing the nut-galls of commerce. On the whole, the injury they do is far more than counterbalanced by their benefits, especially in the ichneumon flies, which destroy enormous numbers of noxious insects, by puncturing their eggs or their larvæ, and depositing their own eggs within them.

705. Others lay their eggs in the provisioned nests of other insects, whose young are starved by the food being first eaten by the earlier-hatched intruders. The larvæ in which the ichneumon fly has laid its eggs do not at once die. They may even complete this stage, and form a cocoon, from which, in due time, an ichneumon fly will emerge in place of the original insect.

706. The wood-wasps, sand-wasps, etc., are predaceous, and feed upon other insects. Our honey-bee and the bumble-bee belong to this order, and serve a most useful purpose, by conveying the pullen from one blossom to another, and thus fertilizing them.

(7.) Diptera (*Musquitoes, Gnats, Flies, etc*).

706½. These are insects with a horny or fleshy proboscis, two wings only, and two knobbed threads, called balancers or poisers, behind the wings. Transformation complete. Their maggots have no feet. These are generally not injurious to trees. The *Cecidomydiadæ* includes the midges, or gall-gnats, whose effects are often seen on the leaves of trees, but generally not so as to materially injure their growth. The wheat-fly, Hessian-fly, and fruit-flies belong to this order.

707. Some writers have assigned the rank of a separate order to certain groups that present intermediate or anomalous characters, but for the present purpose the above may be sufficient, and in speaking of these orders, we will use the numbers above given, instead of their names.

708. *Insects that attack the Oaks.* Of these 223 are enumerated, of which about 38 belong to the 1st class, 9 to the 3d, 103 to the 5th, and 64 to the 6th. To the 1st class belong several destructive flat-headed and bark borers, the oak-pruner, a leaf-roller, and several species of borers that live in stumps and decaying timber.

709. The 3d class includes the seventeen-year locust (*Cicida septemdecem*), which spends the interval between its appearance as a perfect insect, in the ground, attached to the roots of trees or other plants, and when it comes out to breed does considerable damage to the twigs or trees by stinging them, for the purpose of depositing its eggs.

710. The 5th class includes the carpenter-moths, whose larvæ bore large holes in the wood, acorn-worms, the leaf-miners, tent-caterpillars, oak-worms, tussock caterpillar, American silk-worm (from which silk of good quality may be made), geometer moths, and leaf-rollers.

711. The 6th class includes the gall-flies, that sting the twigs and leaves, of which there are many species. Of these something can be done to destroy the flat-headed borers, by applying soap to the trunk, and by cutting in and extracting them. Where branches fall, from the work of oak-pruners, they may be gathered and burned, to destroy the eggs or insects that are in them.

712. *Insects injurious to the Elms.* Of these about 47 are known, of which 14 belong to the 1st class, 1 to the 2d, 4 to the 3d, 25 to the 5th, and 3 to the 6th. The 1st class includes the elm-tree borer (*Saperda tridentata*), bark-borers, and great elm-beetle. The 3d includes the gall-louse; the 5th, the canker-worms, span-worms, fall web-worms, and American silk-worm, of the same species found upon the oak (*Telea polyphemus*); and the 6th the saw-flies.

713. As a remedy against the canker-worm, printer's ink spread on tarred paper, or the use of troughs filled with oil, or cotton fastened around the tree, will prevent the females from ascending it.

Web-worm nests can be removed with mops dipped in carbolic acid solution or kerosene.

714. The elm is liable to suffer from a beetle which makes its attack upon the bark, in the interior and on the under side, and without showing much appearance externally. The tree will begin to languish, apparently while in the full vigor of growth, and, when cut down, the bark will in a little while loosen and fall off, disclosing a multitude of burrows.

110. Perfect Insect of the *Scolytus destructor*, of natural size above, and enlarged below: together with the Larva and Pupa, of natural size and enlarged; and the Burrows, under the Bark, made by the *Scolytus multistriatus*.

715. A remedy has been proposed by Dr. Eugene Robert, of Paris, which consists in shaving off the outer bark down to the liber or live bark, from the whole trunk, and on scarifying down to the wood the smaller branches, by drawing a sharp, three-bladed hooking instrument (with the middle blade somewhat shorter than the others) lengthwise along the surface. This is, of course, an expensive process, and only to be practiced in city parks, and other places where the elms are prized as shade trees. It should be done only after the summer growth is ended, and before the sap starts in spring. The disagreeable color which this process leaves, may be covered up with a paint composed of coal tar and yellow ochre, to imitate the natural shade of color of the bark. It is not found necessary to burn the bark that comes off, unless it contains the perfect insects, for the larvæ will die without further attention, and the eggs, if they should hatch, would find nothing to feed on.

716. *Insects injurious to the Hickories.* Of these 97 species are

enumerated, of which about 35 belong to the 1st class, 1 to the 2d, 33 to the 3d, 8 to the 7th, and the remainder to the 5th. The 1st class includes the hickory-borers, twig-girdler, and bark-borers; the 2d the walking-stick; the 3d various bark-lice, gall-lice, tree-hoppers, phylloxeras, etc; and the 5th the tussock-moth, leaf-rollers, etc.

717. The 1st class includes various hickory-borers, the most destructive of which is the *Scolytus tetraspinosa*, affecting the bitternut, shell-bark, pig-nut, and probably the pecan. It mines under the bark and into the wood of the trunk and branches. The *Cyllene picta*, a borer found in this tree, is the same that proves so destructive to the locust.

718. *Insects injurious to the Black Walnut.* About a dozen species are found on this tree, the most destructive being the borer so injurious to the locust and the hickory (*Cyllene picta*).

719. *Insects injurious to the Butternut.* About 20 species feed upon this tree, of which 2 are of the 1st class, 6 of the 3d, 1 of the 6th, and the rest of the 5th. It is comparatively free from injuries, the more important ones being bark-lice, hoppers, and scale insects, and occasionally the larvæ of moths upon the leaves.

720. *Insects injurious to the Chestnut.* Of these, 20 are mentioned, some being uncertain as to classification. They are chiefly borers, that pierce the bark, the wood and the fruit, or leaf-hoppers and phylloxeras, that feed upon the leaves. The white ant sometimes consumes the interior of chestnut fence-posts, etc., as it also mines in the elm, pine and other woods.

721. *Insects injurious to the Locust.* Twenty-two insects are mentioned as infesting this tree, of which by far the most important is the locust-borer (*Cyllene picta*), which has so effectually destroyed the plantations begun with much success in the early history of tree-planting in the prairie states. It is a beetle of velvet-black, with transverse bands of yellow, and is often found feeding on the blossoms of the golden-rod. It lays its eggs in the crevices of the bark near the roots, in September, and, after mining in the wood in the larva state, it comes out a perfect insect in the month of June following. It appears to have migrated westward, being first noticed about 1845 near Chicago, and, in 1863, at Rock Island. Two years after it was in Iowa, and it is now common in most parts of that state and westward.

722. In densely planted groves in the eastern states, it chiefly at-

tacks the outer trees only. Something may be done to save a valuable tree by soaping the trunk in August, or by whitewashing, or covering with grafting composition. This tree suffers from several leaf-miners (against which there is no remedy but hand-picking), and several gall-flies and midges.

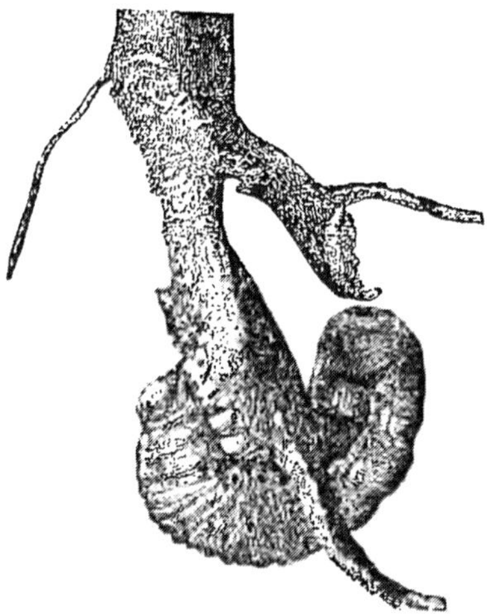

111. Larva of the *Melolontha*, upon the Root of an Acacia.

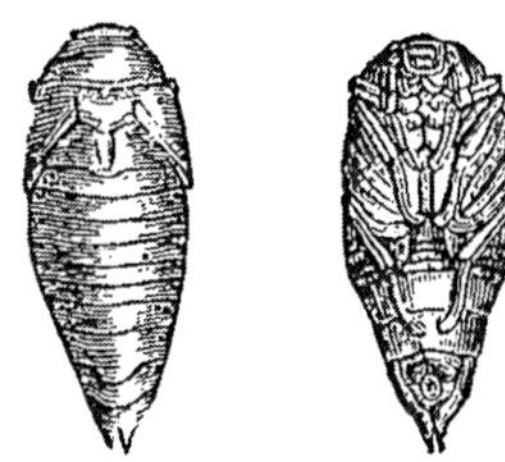

112. Pupa of the *Melolontha*, (upper and under sides).

723. The pods and seeds of the locust are at times inhabited by a weevil, and dead locust timber is liable to be consumed by borers differing from those that pierce the living trees.

724. *Insects injurious to the Maple.* Of these 38 are mentioned, including a borer that pierces the solid trunks of sound sugar-maple trees (*Glycobius speciosas*), the flat-headed borer that is also found on the apple tree (*Chrysobothris femorata*), and various worms—the larvæ of moths that strip the trees of their leaves. The American silk-worm (*Telea polyphemus*) sometimes attacks the maple, and does much damage.

725. *Insects injurious to the Cottonwood.* Of these 16 are named, chiefly beetles that bore the wood or consume the leaves. There are several saw-flies and gall-insects that affect the leaves and twigs.

726. *Insects injurious to the Poplars.* Of these 36 are named, including borers, span-worms, gall-lice, several leaf-rollers, and miners that eat out the soft parts of the leaves. The larvæ of the genus

Sciapteron, a moth much like that which injures the currant-bush by boring, has proved very destructive to the poplars in Nevada and in California. One species attacks also the locust, in the latter state. The accompanying engraving shows one of the insects that attacks the poplars in Europe, and the effect of its ravages.

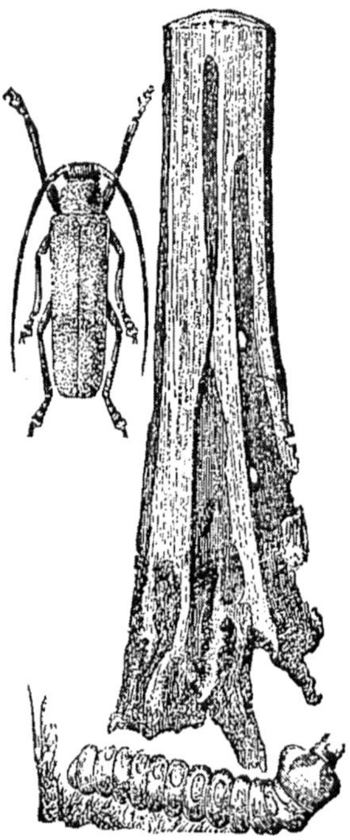

113. Ravages of the *Saperda carcharias* upon the Poplar. (Insect and Larva of Natural Size.)

114. The Poplar Twig Borer (*Saperda* ———).

727. *Insects that injure the Linden.* The basswood has 23 known enemies, including borers, inch-worms that consume the leaves, leaf-beetles, and leaf-miners. Some of these are the same that feed upon the poplars.

728. *Insects that injure the Birch.* Of these there are 19, including plant-lice, leaf-hoppers, etc., chiefly attacking the leaves. This tree is comparatively free from these injuries.

729. *Insects that injure the Beech.* Of these 15 are named, chiefly eating the leaves.

730. The *Willows* have 99 species of insects feeding upon their wood and leaves, a very large number being gall-insects, plant-lice, and leaf-rollers. Of the remaining deciduous species, there is no one but that has several insects upon its leaves, or other parts, and there is perhaps not one that wholly escapes alive when these are in excess.

731. We next come to consider the coniferous species, some of which suffer severely, especially when their leaves are attacked, because these do not put forth new leaves again, as do most of those enumerated, and when the leaves are stripped off, the tree must die. They can not sprout from the roots, and seldom put forth side branches to save life when severely injured. Taken as a whole, coniferous forests are much more liable to general ruin when attacked than others.

732. The *Pines* are liable to attack from about 110 species, of which about 62 belong to the 1st class, 16 to the 3d, 21 to the 5th, 8 to the 6th, and 2 to the 7th. Of the 1st class are many species of wood and bark-borers, that are generally more liable to attack old trees that have passed their prime.

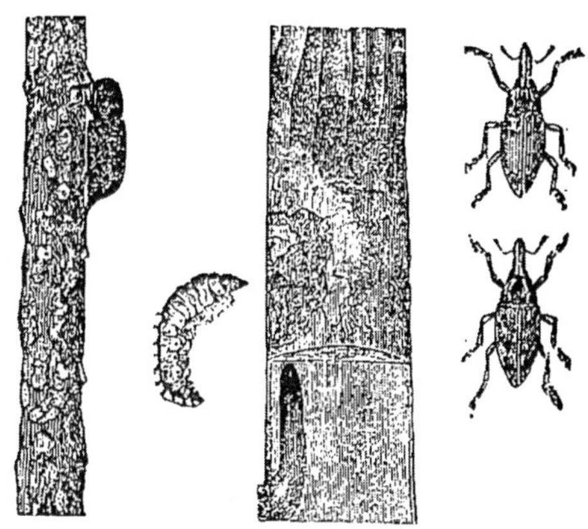

115. Pine Weevil (*Hylobus* ———).

733. The pine weevil is a very destructive insect, breeding under the bark, but doing the greatest injury after it has come to the perfect form. It then attacks the young trees, generally those of from three to six years of age, eating out the terminal shoot, the buds and the young stems. It is not much inclined to fly, and in very hot weather, as also in the cool of night, it conceals itself among the herbage and litter on the ground.

734. The white-pine weevil (*Pissodes strobi*), allied to the species here presented, does great damage to the young pines, by eating

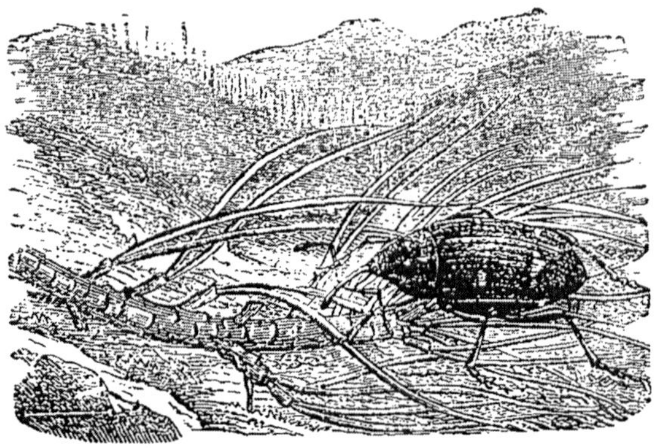

116. *Pissodes notatus.* (The Length of the Insect is indicated by the White Line in the lower left-hand Corner.)

into the leading shoot. A method is practiced in Europe of destroying these and other insects of the pine, which consists in sticking some newly cut branches of the pine-trees in the ground, in some open place, at about the season when the insects are laying their eggs. In a few hours the branches will be covered with beetles, which may be shaken into a cloth and burned. This is, however, altogether impracticable in a forest, and the best check upon their increase is provided by nature in the ichneumon flies that deposit their eggs in their bodies, and thus finally destroy them. The accompanying engraving shows the effect of these injuries upon the young twigs of the pine.

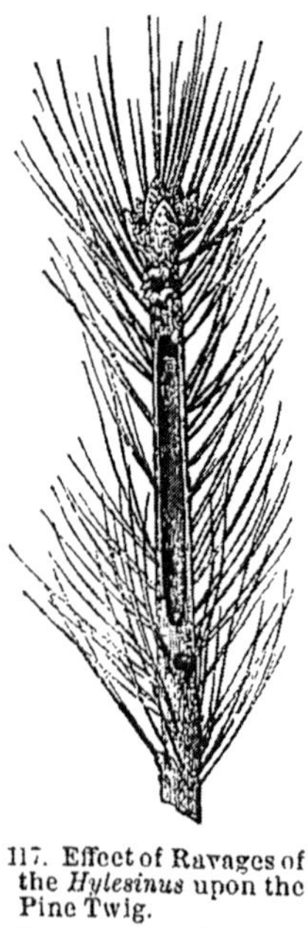

117. Effect of Ravages of the *Hylesinus* upon the Pine Twig.

735. The *Spruces* suffer very much in the same way as the pines, but the number of species noticed is only about a quarter as great. The most destructive are the bark and wood-boring beetles, which although generally attacking trees that are on the decline, appear at times nevertheless to bore into perfectly sound and healthy trees. The family of coleoptera known as *Scolytidæ*, which may be called

"cylindrical bark-beetles," appears to be the most destructive, especially the genera *Hylurgus*, *Tomicus*, *Scolytus*, *Xyloterus*, *Bostrichus*, *Xyloborus*, *Crypturgus*, etc., as variously described by authors.

736. They are very small, but occur in immense numbers, and by burrowing under the bark, and in the newly formed layer of sap-wood, effectually girdle the trees and destroy them. There are also various span-worms and larvæ of caterpillars, saw-flies, bud and leaf-lice, and other insects that feed upon the leaves and buds.

737. The *Balsam Fir* suffers from the same long-horned beetle that proves so destructive to the pines and spruces (*Monohammus confusor*), and from a saw-fly (class 6), and from the larvæ of various moths and butterflies.

738. The *Hemlock* suffers from borers in the wood, and inch-worms upon the leaves, but seldom to much extent. The same may be said of the red and white cedars, the junipers, the larch, and other conifers.

739. Very many of these destructive insects have their insect enemies, some of them being carnivorous beetles, others mites that fasten upon them, or ichneumon flies, that lay their eggs in their bodies. It has also been noticed that certain insectivorous birds, and especially woodpeckers, will appear in unusual abundance in spruce and pine woods infested with bark-boring insects. They will even follow the logs of the mill-yards, and persist in their search for this food wherever there is opportunity. By protecting these birds we may therefore derive much benefit from their aid in the destruction of these injurious insects.

CHAPTER XVIII.

PROCESSES FOR INCREASING THE DURABILITY OF TIMBER OR FOR IMPROVING ITS QUALITY.

740. In vegetable, as in animal organizations, life itself is generally sufficient to maintain the elements against decay while it lasts, although in both it inevitably tends to dissolution, with age, if not prematurely destroyed. In most kinds of wood the inner portion, or heart-wood, is more solid and durable than the newer and softer sap wood near the outside. It is generally thought that this mature wood is no longer a living part of the tree, but simply the old fibers

thickened and hardened, by deposit of material peculiar to the species. It is dryer, heavier, and contains less potash than the newer wood. Still, an iron tube driven deeply into the heart of a maple tree will yield sap, showing that there is circulation to some extent still present. In many trees the heart wood may decay without apparently lessening the vigor of growth.

741. Many processes have been devised to increase the durability, not only of the sap wood, but of the whole tree, either by rendering it impervious to moisture, after thorough seasoning, or by neutralizing the tendencies to decay, or by injecting substances in solution that become unalterable and permanent, either by directly uniting with the tissues of the wood or by forming new combinations between different substances injected into it.

742. When the pores of wood are filled with other substances of an oily or resinous nature, they show less tendency to warp or split, simply because they do not absorb and give out moisture with the changes of atmosphere.

743. In some of these processes the attempt is made to render wood harder, stronger, less combustible, more dense, more flexible, or of richer color, or in other ways more valuable, as well as more durable.

744. Of the two hundred or more antiseptic processes that have been recommended for preventing the decay of wood, we can only notice the more important.[1] They consist generally in torrefication of the outside, or in the injection or absorption of metallic or non-metallic salts, of acids and their bases, of essential oils, or of resinous or oily substances. The chemical action appears to be different, according to the process used, the albumen being coagulated in some, while insoluble and durable mineral and organic combinations are formed in others. Wherever metallic salts are applied in the preservation of wood, they should be neutral, as an excess of acid would act upon the vegetable fiber and destroy it. From the latest results of scientific inquiry, it appears that the real cause of decay is probably due to the action of organized ferments, *fungi* or *bacteria*,

[1] About 120 American patents are on record and in force at the time of writing. We can not undertake to enumerate them here; some are not worth notice, and the few that we mention are placed in their alphabetical order, not because they are better than others, but because they are perhaps better known.

which these antiseptic processes tend to destroy, and that those methods are most certain that accomplish this result most uniformly and effectually throughout the wood.

745. *Charring.*—We have elsewhere noticed the extreme durability of charcoal. By slowly scorching the outside of a post or stake before setting it in the ground, its durability is much increased. This is sometimes done with the railway ties in Europe, and two methods are employed.

746. By one of them, the stick is laid upon an iron frame, that admits of an easy sliding motion in all directions, and a tongue of flame, either from a gas-jet or from air blown through flame, is passed over every part. By this means the degree of torrefication may be regulated at will. The process may be applied to all kinds of woodwork, and it may be so managed as not to destroy the sharpness of any work upon the surface.

747. By another process, a long iron tube is filled with flame, and railway ties or other wood may be passed slowly through it on a broad iron chain. Piles charred before using will last for a long period. It was the practice employed at Venice for the piles on which that city was built. In whatever manner the scorching is done, the timber must be first thoroughly seasoned; if not, it will only hasten its decay.

748. There is an advantage in plunging the wood newly charred into coal-tar or melted pitch, or by painting it thoroughly with three or four coats of these substances. The charring process is in favor upon the Belgian railways. It has the advantage of preventing injuries from gnawing animals or white ants, and hence its value in India and other countries where these insects are destructive, as also in the wood work of basements, where there is much humidity, without proper ventilation. It is a most effectual remedy against the *dry rot.*

749. It was formerly customary to slightly char the outside of ship timber after it was prepared for framing, but before it was put together. The "Royal William," one of the most long-lived ships in the British navy, was thus prepared. The fires used in this process were made of shavings or straw, and accidents would sometimes happen.

750. In some timbers used for railway ties, such as oak, it is not easy to inject with mineral salts or other antiseptic substances, and

charring is the best method of preserving them. After they have been used several years, they may be taken up, rasped off, burnt over a second time, and again used. The same may be done with beech and other woods, where they have not been thoroughly impregnated.

751. By a process invented by M. de Lapparent (1862) a blowpipe was devised for carbonizing the outside of railroad ties, under a flame of common burning gas and air, supplied from separate reservoirs, with pipes that unite just as they issue. This process has been largely employed at Cherbourg in preparing wood to resist decay in the French fleet, and a list of twenty-four vessels is given in which this method was used. It has also been employed in Dantzic and Pola.

752. By an apparatus of more powerful construction, patented by a French engineer, Hugon, in 1864, the flame is supplied from coal-oil. This has been used by the Orleans Railway Company, and from four sets of apparatus 288 ties could be prepared in a day, at a very low rate, and it is claimed with excellent result. It is also used in preparing telegraph poles. It has been thought that the preservative qualities obtained by partial charring are at least partly due to the formation of creosote in the pores of the wood—a substance known to be one of the best of antiseptic agents.

753. By painting well seasoned wood with boiled linseed oil thickened with pulverized charcoal, it will last much longer in the ground than without this application. The paint should be allowed to dry before the posts are set.

754. A coat of hot coal tar and sand may be applied to posts to great advantage before setting them in the ground. The end of the wood should especially be well coated, and the covering should extend a foot above the ground. It is claimed that this is particularly valuable when applied to chestnut stakes and posts.

754. Glauber, in 1657, recommended charring the surface of wood, then covering with tar, and immersing in pyroligneous acid. He is said to have been the first to recommend the use of tar, which in one form or another has since been employed in very many of these methods for the preservation of timber.

755. It is said that green Lombardy poplar absorbs boiling coal tar very readily, and acquires thereby very durable properties. It might be tried upon cottonwood and willow, and for some uses it

might prove very effectual. It is even recommended for stakes and posts, which without preparation would speedily decay. The wood should be peeled before boiling.

756. *Immersion in Water, or placing in Soils permanently Wet.* It is well known that piles driven into the soil, or timbers laid in the water, or under a wall where it is always damp, and where access to the air is wholly prevented, will last for an immense period. Wrecks of vessels will thus remain for centuries, and sometimes vessels are sunk to preserve them from decay, as was done with the fleet captured by Commodore Perry on Lake Erie, in 1814. It remained under water in the harbor at Erie, Pa., for many years. Timber is sometimes thus preserved till wanted, or it is immersed at certain seasons to protect it from insects that infest ship-yards.

757. Wood that has been long buried or immersed, finally becomes black and dense, but it retains its texture. Foundations laid upon piles or timbers should of course never be drained, nor should air be ever admitted to them from sewers or otherwise. Washing and immersion in sea-water have been recommended.

758. *Penetration of Liquids, and of Solid Substances in Solution.* This may be secured in a variety of ways, as from simple capillarity by immersion in a cold liquid, or by boiling, or by compression at one end of a piece of timber still covered with its bark, or by first exhausting the air from the pores, and afterwards admitting liquid substances under pressure, or by exposure to antiseptic agents in the form of vapor, generally under pressure, or by absorption in the living trees, by placing liquid substances where they may be taken up as the sap is taken up in the vital process of vegetation.

759. As penetration under pressure after exhaustion of the air, first proposed by Bréant, is employed in many processes, the method may be briefly described, as nearly alike in all. A strong and large iron cylinder is constructed, one end of which may be fully opened, or strongly closed, at will. The wood usually first wrought into shape for use, is placed upon a frame, usually running upon wheels, so that it may be easily run into the cylinder and withdrawn without displacing the wood piled or fastened upon it. The pressure is generally supplied by steam, but sometimes by pumps, and its amount is shown by a gauge. The exhaustion is sometimes obtained

by pumping, and at other times by the condensation of steam, as in low-pressure steam-engines.

760. It may be remarked of all methods of injection, that woods with an open, porous grain, receive better than those that are solid, and that the sap wood is more easily injected than the heart wood. The coniferous species, especially the sap wood, if not already full of resin, generally afford good results, while the oaks and other solid woods can scarcely be injected in their heart wood. It is further found that in wood that has begun to decay the tissues appear to be disorganized, so that solutions will not penetrate, even under great pressure. Without attempting to classify the various processes employed for increasing the durability of timber, we will briefly describe some of the more common methods.

761. *Impregnation with Oils.* This is an ancient process. The essential oils were used in wooden structures in Rome. Perhaps the best is linseed oil, or other vegetable fixed oils, in preference to animal oils, which cause the wood to become brittle. In India, cocoa-nut oil, beaten up with shell-lime, is used as a varnish to plank. Our common paints derive their well-known preservative effect largely from the oils that they contain, but they should never be applied except to wood thoroughly seasoned. Trenails are sometimes boiled in oil before using.

762. *Crude Petroleum* is found to be an excellent preserving agent, and has been employed in ship and house-building with great success.

763. *Common Salt* is sometimes put into ships, while building, and has the effect of rendering the wood durable. It is liable to be dissolved away, and to cause a corrosion of iron fastenings. It also renders vessels damp and unwholesome, and if in excess, it swells the tissues by the crystals that form in drying. The method of salting is required by lake underwriters in new first-class vessels, and it is recommended by the American Lloyds.[1]

[1] "The mode of salting is to fix stops of boards between the timbers of the frames about the height of the load-line, and when the ceiling and planking are worked and the plank-shear ready to go into place, the spaces between the timbers are filled with salt. Near the end of the vessel the salt is sometimes put between the frames, quite down to the dead wood. A vessel of 500 tons will take 100 barrels of salt applied in the usual manner." (*W. W. Bates*, Ag. Rep. 1866.)

764. *Incombustible Wood.* Experiments have been made by order of the English Admiralty, to test a process of Dr. Jones for rendering wood incombustible, by the use of the tungstate of soda, a salt obtained by the action of muriatic acid and common salt upon the tungstate of lime (scheelite). Soft woods are said to be rendered solid and durable.[1]

765. *Alum* tends to render wood incombustible, and claims have been asserted in favor of its antiseptic properties, while others have found that it tends to hasten decay. The soluble nature of alum would render it improper for use where exposed to the rains, but its well-established properties for resisting ignition may render it worthy of notice for inside work.

766. *Borax.* It has been proposed to saturate wood with borax, by immersing and gradually heating to a boiling point, and leaving for half a day. The wood is then piled, and after a time again boiled for less time in a weaker solution. It is claimed that this renders wood less combustible, and the process does not discolor it.

767. *Lime* appears to render wood durable, as we see in the boards used for mortar-beds. M. Lostal, a French contractor, has proposed to place wood in a large basin or receiver, and cover it with a layer of fresh-buried lime, which is watered by degrees till it slacks. Water is then let in till the wood is covered, and it is allowed to stand for some time. It gives a hardness, and it is claimed a durability worthy of notice. It also tends to render wood less liable to ignition.

768. *Sulphate of Iron.* It is well known that copperas or green vitriol will tend to increase the durability in woods, and the lasting qualities of vessels engaged in the coal trade of England are attributed to the pyrites which all English coals contain, and which form this salt by exposure to the air and to moisture. The pieces forming parts of carriage-wheels and other wooden structures, when fitted for putting together, are sometimes boiled three or four hours in a solution of this salt, and then placed for some days in a warm place to dry. It is not corrosive to iron, and nails driven into it *will last as long as the wood itself.*[2]

[1] *Revue des Eaux et Forêts*, 1874, p. 302; 1875, p. 143.

[2] Prof. F. W. Clarke in noticing the disagreement in statements concerning this substance remarks: "At all events, it has had less thoroughly than some other more fashionable preservatives, the test of long experience. It

769. *The Bethell Process* was patented by Mr. John Bethell, in England, July 11, 1838. It consists in subjecting seasoned timber, under pressure, to creosote or oil of tar and other bituminous substances that contain it, and also to pyrolignite of iron, which holds more creosote in solution than any other watery menstruum. While it unquestionably renders wood much more durable, and also proof against the attack of worms in sea-water, it has the disadvantage of rendering it more combustible, and of offensive odor. We have known a bridge frame set on fire and consumed while under construction, by a workman attempting to burn out a hole through two pieces in contact, so as to allow a bolt to fit.

770. Creosote coagulates the albumen, fills the pores of timber with a bituminous substance, prevents the absorption of water, and is obnoxious to animal life. By a patent of 1853, Bethell proposed to first inject timbers with metallic salts, and after thorough drying, inject creosote. He used about 10 pounds of creosote to a cubic foot. It is sometimes carried to twice this amount. It has been most used on pines, and for railway ties, and enormous quantities of the latter have been sent to India and other hot climates. It is also largely used for piles, docks, and bridge timbers.

771. The pressure employed varies from 150 to 200 pounds to the inch, and the liquid is heated to 120° (Fahr.), and admitted after the air has been exhausted. The cost varies widely, but averages perhaps 7 to 8 cents a cubic foot. Railway ties that are half-round last longer when thus prepared than those that are sawn square, and a fine open sand is best for ballast. It is found that ties that have been creosoted are stronger and better able to resist a crushing weight than before, but sometimes in India they have suffered from the white ants.

772. *The Boucherie Process.* In December, 1837, Dr. Auguste Boucherie, of Bordeaux, France, proposed the injection of antiseptic fluids through the natural circulation of the living tree. He succeeded in the use of the sulphates and the acetates of copper, of iron, and of zinc, the bi-chloride of mercury, arsenious acid, and the arseniate of potash, and in some cases of several of these in succession. Of odorous substances, he procured the absorption of

was recommended by Strutzlei in 1834, Earle in 1843, and Apelt in 1853. Bohl . . . has employed it simultaneously with creosote."

camphor, the essential oils of lemon, bergamot, orange, lavender, and rosemary; and of coloring materials a neutral sulphate prepared from indigo, and an aqueous solution of the coloring principle of yellow-wood. Of resinous substances, he procured a considerable absorption of spirits of turpentine, both pure and crude. By introducing the chlorides of lime and magnesia, he proposed to give an unnatural elasticity and flexibility to wood: by using the deliquescent salts, he sought to render it incombustible; and finally, by using various solutions that give precipitates the base of which is silica, he attempted to secure a kind of petrification.

773. He at first gave preference to the pyrolignite of iron, obtained by exposing scraps of iron to the action of the crude acetic acid obtained from wood by distillation. He afterwards abandoned this for the solution of sulphate of copper, and instead of absorption by the living tree, he injected the wood as follows:

774. The logs still full of sap and with the bark still on, were placed upon skids, and a collar fitted closely to one end. The solution was then forced through the pores, either by pumps or by hydrostatic pressure, the wood being still fresh and full of sap. It is found that solid woods, like the cherry, oak, etc., will not receive the solution in the heart-wood, and that the process affords but partial benefit; while in other kinds the success is very great, the woods thus prepared lasting two, three, and even five times longer as railway ties, and for other like exposures, than that which has not been treated. This process has been largely used in France, and its inventor, unlike many discoverers, realized its benefits in his lifetime. He died in 1871, leaving quite a fortune acquired from his patents.

775. This process has been also much employed in Belgium Germany, and Switzerland, in preparing fir timbers for telegraph poles, and many other uses. After injection, the wood should be seasoned before using, which it does very readily, becoming quite light and portable. It is claimed that the sulphate of copper becomes fixed in the wood, somewhat like the mordant in dyes, so as not to dissolve out in fresh water, although in sea water it appears to gradually lose its antiseptic qualities by prolonged exposure. The amount of this salt absorbed is found to be notably diminished by the presence of iron, or of certain saline solutions, or of carbonic

acid. It is less adapted to dry wood than to that newly cut, if, indeed, it is not limited to the latter.[1]

776. It is found that the sulphate of copper penetrates with great difficulty into oak, the ends only absorbing to some extent along the spongy layers of the spring growth, while the hard layers of wood formed later in the season do not absorb the least. Elm will absorb very well, excepting in the close firm knots. Beech will admit of very complete penetration in every part. Pine will absorb only in the sap wood. Locust wholly resists penetration. Ash is in about the same class with oak, and so is the chestnut. Birch, when seasoned, may be prepared very well, and poplar the most completely of all.

777. *The Burnett Process.* This was first brought to notice between the years 1838 and 1840 by Sir William Burnett, formerly Director General of the Medical Department of the British Navy. It consists in an injection of the *chloride of zinc*, at the rate of 1 pound to 9 or 10 gallons of water, under a pressure of 150 pounds to the inch. This salt, although soluble, does not easily come out when exposed to the weather or buried in the ground. It is claimed to render wood uninflammable. The cost is about 6 to 8 cents a cubic foot. Extensive works have been constructed for the preparation of wood by this process, and very favorable testimonials have been offered in its favor. A concentrated solution is sold at 5s. per gallon in London, to be diluted with 40 gallons of water for use by this process, with instructions and license to use.

778. *By Carey's Process* (1829), a mixture of salt powdered charcoal and animal or vegetable oil is introduced into timber by holes in various parts, and the holes are then closed. Various patents have been granted for inserting preservative substances in the wood, such as coal tar and pulverized mineral substances, more or less soluble and antiseptic in their nature.

779. *The Hatzfeld Process.* From the fact that oak timbers buried in contact with ochres and the salts of iron acquire great durability, apparently from the reaction between the tannin of the wood and iron, Mr. H. proposes to inject various woods with tannic acid, and then with the pyrolignite of iron, thus assimilating the wood to the

[1] Baist, in Dingler's Polytechnic Journal, 1861, Vol. 162, p. 397. See *ib.*, 1851, Vol. 120, p. 140; 123, p. 223.

condition of oak long buried. It is claimed to be particularly serviceable for mining timbers and the like, much exposed to moisture, and therefore liable to decay. It is understood that this process is being largely adopted by the Eastern Railway in France and by the telegraph service, under the co-operation and authority of the Ministry of the Interior.

780. *The Houtin and Boutigny Process*, aims to hermetically close the ends of the wood, so as to neutralize the property of absorbing moisture. This might be done, either by covering with some hydrocarbon, as, for example, coal oil, or by charring the end, and then plunging it, while hot, in a melted mixture of pitch, tar, and gum-lac, or by covering the whole piece with tar in the usual manner.

781. *The Kyanizing Process.* On the 31st of March, 1832, Mr. John H. Kyan took out an English patent for a process for preventing timber from decay, by penetrating the tissues with a solution of the *bi-chloride of mercury*, or "corrosive sublimate."[1] This was done by placing the timber in large tanks, so that it could not float, and then submerging it with the solution for about a week. It was afterwards found necessary to apply pressure, equal to about 100 pounds to the inch. The strength of the solution was finally fixed at about 1 pound to 15 gallons of water, although as strong as 1 pound to 2 gallons had been used.

782. There appear to be still conflicting facts for and against this method, and although formerly much practiced, it is now seldom used. The value of corrosive sublimate as a wash to kill dry-rot, and to prevent insect injuries in wood, had been long known, and it is still employed by botanists for preserving dried specimens from insects. Its agency as an antiseptic was ascribed to the coagulation of albumen in the tissues of the wood, and perhaps the differences in effect were due to the greater or less abundance of this material in the wood, or in permeability of the pores by which it could be reached. The principal objections against this process were its expense and the exceedingly poisonous nature of the material used, which rendered it dangerous to the health of the workmen employed.

783. *The Margary Process*, patented in England in 1838, consists in immersing in a solution of acetate or sulphate of copper.

[1] This material had been proposed by Knowles and Davy in 1821, but not practically applied. In 1837, Letellier proposed to use it with gelatine.

784. *The Payne Process*, patented in England in 1841. This consists in using two solutions, one after the other, and both soluble, but forming an insoluble substance within the wood. The earthy or metallic solution is first introduced under pressure; after which the decomposing fluid is forced in. The sulphate of iron and carbonate of soda are said to form the insoluble compound in the pores of the wood. He tried a mixture of the sulphate of barium or of calcium with the sulphate of iron, and various other compounds. The process was costly and imperfect, and is now abandoned.[1]

785. *By Prechtl's Process* (1822) the wood is first exposed to the vapor of water alone, and then to that of a mixture of tar and water.

786. *The Robbins's Process*[2] consists in first removing the surface moisture of the wood by heat, and then thoroughly impregnating and saturating the pores and fibers by oleaginous vapors, as of coal-tar, resin, or other substances, the temperature being from 212° to 250° (F.) for the former, and about 300° or more for the latter part of the process.

787. *The Tait Process* consists in saturating the pores of the wood with a concentrated solution of bi-sulphate of lime or baryta, the same being rendered soluble by an excess of sulphuric acid gas under pressure, or by refrigeration, and being made insoluble as a neutral sulphate, when the pressure or excess of gas is removed.

788. *The Thilmany Process*[3] consists in saturating the wood first with a solution of the sulphate of copper, followed by one of the muriate of barytes, the intention being to form an insoluble sulphate of barytes within the wood.

789. The following application has been recommended as valuable in a German journal: "Melt 12 pounds of resin, and add 12 pints of whale oil and 3 pounds of sulphur; mix an ochre of the color desired, mix very thoroughly in oil, and add. Apply at first a light coat white hot, and in two or three days, when well dried, a second and a third one." This is intended for fences and other wood-work much exposed.

[1] Boston City Docs. No. 100, 1873; in a Prize Essay by Prof. F. W. Clarke, p. 15.

[2] Patents were taken out by Louis S. Robbins, April 4, 1865; April 27, 1869; July 20, 1875, and Dec. 21, 1880.

[3] Patented by W. Thilmany, May 23, 1876.

790. The following recipe is from Dingler's Polytechnic Journal, and is intended for piles and posts: "Take 50 parts of rosin, 40 of finely powdered chalk, 300 (more or less) of fine white sharp sand, 4 of linseed oil, 1 of native red oxyde of copper, and 1 of sulphuric acid. First heat the resin, chalk, sand, and oil, then add the oxyde and with care the acid; stir carefully, and apply as a paint while still hot. If not liquid enough, add oil." This coating when cold and dry is very hard, and it is claimed to be very durable.

CHAPTER XIX.

RESINOUS AND OTHER PRODUCTS OF CONIFERS.

Naval Stores.

791. This term, as used in commerce, includes the several resinous products of pine forests, and particularly the *oil* or *spirits of turpentine*, distilled from crude turpentine; *rosin*, or the solid residuum of this distillation; *tar*, obtained by the combustion of resinous woods or refuse materials, containing resin, in smothered fires, or their exposure to heat externally applied, and *pitch*, which differs chiefly from tar in being solid when cold.

792. Formerly, crude turpentine was an article of commerce, and its distillation was carried on in large establishments near the centers of trade; but in recent years local distilleries have been erected near the forests where the raw material is collected, and the products are sent to market prepared for use.

The Production of Turpentine and other Resinous Materials.

793. When we cut through the bark into the outer wood of a pine, a fir, or a spruce tree,[1] in the spring or early summer, there slowly exudes from the wound a viscid and at first colorless and transparent substance, known in the pine as "turpentine." Upon exposure to the air, it absorbs oxygen and becomes whitish, opaque, and solid. When distilled with a little water, the volatile portion passes off with the vapor, and when condensed, it separates and becomes a limpid, volatile, and strongly scented liquid, known as the *spirits of turpentine*. The portion not volatile, and remaining in the still,

[1] The *Taxus* does not have resiniferous canals in its wood. They are found in the genera *Cedrus*, *Abies*, *Pinus*, *Larix*, *Picca*, *Pseudolarix*, *Thuja*, *Pinus*, *Cupressus*, *Biotia*, *Araucaria*, etc., both in the root and stem.

hardens on cooling, and becomes a more or less translucent and sometimes almost transparent solid, of various shades of yellow and brown, known in commerce as "rosin."

794. Both of these products are of important use in the arts, the former being much used in the preparation of varnishes, india-rubber goods, patent leather, etc., and in painting. It is an ingredient in "camphine" and other burning fluids, and is employed in medicine. Rosin is largely used in the manufacture of soap, candles, paper, sealing-wax, and a vast variety of other articles, and when it can be cheaply procured, it makes an excellent illuminating gas. Before the late war, many villages and cities were lighted by gas made wholly from rosin, but the high prices that this event occasioned made it necessary to substitute the cannel-coals.

795. In former times, turpentine was produced to a limited extent from the yellow or Norway pine (*Pinus resinosa*), and the pitch pine (*P. rigida*), in the Middle and Eastern States; but the chief source of supply within the United States is now almost wholly derived from the long-leaved or yellow pine (*P. australis*) of the Southern States.

796. The "Pine Belt" extends from a little south of the Roanoke river, in North Carolina, through that State, South Carolina, Georgia, Alabama, Mississippi, and Louisiana, into the edge of Texas. It is also found extensively in Florida. This belt is generally from 50 to 150 miles from the coast, and of variable width, the borders being often not sharply defined, and the whole blended more or less with other trees. Sometimes it occurs in detached masses of considerable extent. The differences that occur in its distribution within these limits will probably be found due to geological causes.

797. The "Pine Belt," where it begins on the north, is about fifty miles wide, but as it extends further south and west it widens in some places to twice this width. This species thrives best on moderately hilly, dry, and sandy soils. In level regions with a retentive sub-soil it does not succeed as well as other species.

798. The mode of procuring turpentine, as heretofore and at present practiced, is wasteful and destructive, as compared with processes we will presently describe, and is generally as follows:

799. In winter the trees are "boxed," by cutting a hole in the side, about three inches wide, six inches deep, and twelve inches long, near the foot of the tree, forming a cavity that will hold about

three pints. The turpentine begins to flow early in the spring, and continues till towards the end of summer. The incisions are enlarged and extended higher up, about once in a week or ten days, and sometimes two or three "boxes" are cut in the same tree. The crude turpentine is dipped out of the boxes, and scraped off from the trees from time to time, and now the greater part is distilled near the forests, and the refined products sent from thence to the markets.

800. In North Carolina, the turpentine is collected about once a month, and 10,000 trees will in a good season yield 50 barrels of spirits of turpentine, and 200 barrels of rosin. In other regions, the trees are cut from twenty to thirty times in a season, and yield from eight to ten dippings. A man will "chip" from 10,000 to 12,000 boxes in a week, as a task. From 1,000 boxes they dip from three to five barrels, of 280 pounds each.

801. The yield per box in soft turpentine is from ten to twelve pounds, or twenty to twenty-five to the tree of usual size. A barrel of crude turpentine will yield five gallons of spirits of turpentine, and from sixty-two to sixty-five per cent of its bulk in rosin. The product of the first year yields a fine light resin, and it grows darker from year to year. A still of forty barrels capacity, will distill the crude product of about 350,000 boxes.

802. Turpentine is produced to advantage only in a warm climate, and in a given place, to better advantage in hot and humid seasons than in those that are cold and dry.

803. Trees exposed to the air and the sun yield better than those that are crowded and shaded, and those with a well-developed top and well-set with branches much better than those with thin and light foliage.

804. By the improved methods now in use in Europe, and especially in the south-western part of France, the production of crude turpentine (there obtained from the *Pinus pinaster*, or "maritime pine") is continued many years without killing the trees, and by the following method:

805. In winter the rough bark is smoothed off with a drawing-knife, and as spring approaches, a light incision is made, four or five inches wide and about fifteen inches long, through the bark and a little into the outer wood. This is done with a sharp instrument having a convex edge. At the bottom a lip of zinc is driven in,

and under this a small earthern jar, glazed on the inside and shaped like a flower-pot, is placed.

806. About once a week the cutting is renewed, by taking off a thin slice of wood a little deeper and an inch or two higher up, and this is renewed through the warm season, and from year to year. There are two or more of these incisions on each tree, but never wider than at first begun. They are carried up till they are twelve or fifteen feet high, but there is always left a strip of bark, at least as wide, between them. Gradually the wood growing only under this bark, will close over the incisions, generally leaving a deep crevice to show its place. This wood is again cut into long, narrow bands as before, and so for a long period.

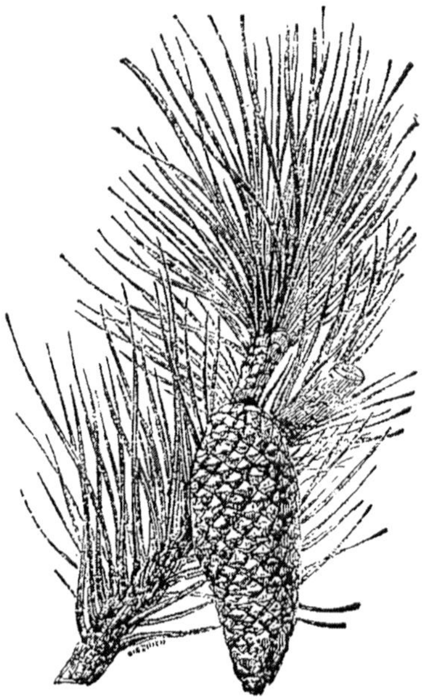

118. The Maritime Pine (*Pinus pinaster*).

807. The general growth of the tree is checked, but the quality of the wood improved by this process. It appears to hasten its maturity, and it no doubt shortens its life; but such trees are kept in production from the age of twenty years till they are fifty or sixty years old. It is, however, generally more profitable to cut them when of good size for timber, to make room for those that are coming up from self-seeding, and that will be more productive.

808. As the incisions extend up, the earthern jars are hung higher up, and they are emptied from time to time. The whitish opaque incrustation is scraped off in the fall, and the jars are left bottom upwards at the foot of the tree till spring. The work of "*resinage*" is commonly done upon shares, and a division is made between the proprietor and the "*resineur*," after the sales are made. Up to a certain price, the division is equal, but at high rates the proprietor receives the greater share of the profits.

Tar-manufacture.

809. In making charcoal from highly resinous woods, *tar* is produced, in notable quantities; and for collecting this a circular floor of masonry is prepared, sloping to a central point, from whence it flows out through a pipe into a reservoir on one side from which it may be dipped.

119. *Foundation of a Tar-kiln,* in which *a, d,* is a sloping brick or stone hearth, with a grating at *d,* through which the tar passes, and is conducted by the pipe, *b,* to the reservoir, *c.*

810. By a more slovenly and wasteful process, the tar is allowed to ooze out into gutters in the soil, and is led from these into barrels sunk in the ground.

811. In the more refined methods of tar-making, the knots, resinous wood, or refuse products of the turpentine works are put into large iron receivers set in masonry, so that heat may be applied externally by fire in an arch. A pipe leads from the bottom of these receivers for carrying off the tar. Another pipe, near the top, conducts away the volatile portions, which are condensed, as in common distillation.

812. *Pitch* is simply tar boiled down till it will become solid when cold. Its principal use is in ship-building, for rendering the seams under water and the rigging exposed to the weather impervious to water. It is also used in roofing and elsewhere for similar purposes.

813. *Lamp-black* is the smoke of resinous woods, or of the refuse strainings of rosin. When these are burned, the smoke is passed into the chambers lined with coarse cloths, which allow the gases to escape, but intercept the carbonaceous portion, which is collected from time to time.

814. *Canada Balsam* is obtained from the blisters that form in the bark of the *Abies balsamea,* or balsam-fir, found growing in the swamps of the Northern States and in Canada. It is used medicinally, and is an officinal article in the pharmacopœias. Among other

officinal resinous products of conifers may be mentioned Burgundy pitch, from *Abies excelsa*, or Norway spruce; Canada pitch, from the *Tsuga Canadensis*, or hemlock; Venice turpentine, from the *Larix Europea*, or larch; gum sandarac, from the *Callitris quadrivalvis;* frankincense, from the *Pinus tedia*, etc.

815. Various essential oils are distilled from the leaves of the hemlock, cedar, savin, juniper, spruce, and other evergreens, and are used medicinally. It is probable that amber is a resinous product of a coniferous tree, although found only in a fossil form. Kauri is the resin of the *Dammara australis*, but gathered only from the soil formerly covered by forests of the kauri pine of New Zealand.

Perfume from Pine Sap.

816. A perfume resembling that from the vanilla bean, and applicable to the same uses, has in recent years been obtained from the sap of the pine and other conifers. The substance has been called *coniferin*, and is collected and prepared as follows:

817. As the trees are cut down in the summer months (about June 1 to August 15), the bark is taken off, and the sap or cambium is scraped off from the trunk with some sharp instrument, wiped off upon a sponge and squeezed into a tin pail. A tree of vigorous growth and medium size will yield from four to five litres of sap (about as many quarts), and where the soil is damp and fertile nearly twice as much. It is greater when gathered in warm damp weather than when it is cold and dry.

818. The sap, when first collected, is milky and clouded, and more or less mixed with impurities, and it contains a kind of glucose, albumen, and coniferin. It would soon ferment and spoil, and must be strained, after boiling ten or fifteen minutes, to coagulate the albumen. It is then evaporated down to one-fifth of its volume, when it is clear and of a yellowish color. It is then set aside over night in a cool place, when little white crystals of coniferin will deposit. These are separated by straining and pressing out the liquid through cloths.

819. A person will collect about three to four pints in a day. The price of the dry crystalline substance, as prepared in the forest, is about $18.60 to the pound avoirdupois. The forest of Murat, in France, furnishes from twenty-five to forty pounds a year. The coniferin is taken to Paris, and there, in chemical laboratories, it is

converted into the material so highly prized for flavoring and perfume.

CHAPTER XX.

USE OF WOOD IN THE MANUFACTURE OF PAPER.

820. In recent years, the employment of wood for paper has come into extensive use, both in Europe and America. For this purpose it must first be reduced to pulp, and mixed with a certain proportion of rags. The chief kinds used in this country are the poplar and the spruce, and in Europe, besides these, various pines and the white birch. The wood should be worked up fresh, and in preparing it the bark and defective or rotten parts must be first taken off. There are two principal methods of reducing wood to pulp—the mechanical and the chemical; and each of these is subdivided into several distinct processes.

821. By the more common of the former, known as the "Völter Process," from Henry Völter, of Wurtemburg, who first brought it into successful use,[1] the wood is ground into pulp upon the edge of broad and large grindstones running vertically in water, the wood being pressed firmly down sideways of the grain, by automatic screws, at four or five places. The feed is about an inch in five minutes, and the speed about 200 revolutions in a minute.

822. Of course the power required to run such machines is very great. The wood is sometimes boiled or steamed before grinding, and the pulp is screened through fine wire cloth, and the coarser parts ground with water between mill-stone like those for grinding grain. This process began to be successfully used about 1846, and is largely used, both in Europe and the United States.

823. By the "Hartmann Process" the wood is ground between two smaller vertical stones, the approach being secured by a weight. By the "Siebrecht Process" the grinding is done upon a great horizontal stone, and the wood is held down by hydraulic pressure. There are other processes by which the wood is sawn into short lengths, and then crushed under heavy rollers, or the fibers are torn

[1] The inventor of this process was F. G. Keller, who took out a patent in Germany, in 1844, for a wood-pulp grinding machine, but not having the capital sold out his interest. He afterwards fell into indigence and was aided by a subscription among the German paper-makers.

obliquely off by saws, and in both of these the wood is ground in a mill before being used.

824. By the chemical process, which is more recent and more costly, but which produces a better result, the wood is first cut into short chips by heavy revolving planes, and then macerated in large and strong boilers, with caustic soda, and under a pressure of 10 or 12 atmospheres. By the "Sinclair Process" this is done in upright boilers. By the "Lee Process" it is done in larger boilers, that are horizontal. By the "Fry Process" water alone is used, under a pressure of 5 or 6 atmospheres, and saw-dust is thus made available as a material. The product is a brown pulp, and used for wrapping paper only.

825. Wood-pulp is chiefly used for making wrapping and newspaper, wall-papers, and the like. It is sometimes used for envelopes, but as at present made it is scarcely proper for writing-paper, nor for the grades required in finer book-work. But the consumption for these is enormous, and constantly increasing, and these industries are here noticed chiefly as affording a profitable business in forest culture.

826. We have elsewhere (p. 90) noticed the strong tendency of poplars to come up as second growth where pines have been cut away, and where the soil has been injured by forest fires, so as to be unprofitable for the cultivation of common field crops. When protected, such poplar groves properly thinned out grow rapidly, and in from ten to fifteen years will be fit to cut for paper-pulp. They will readily reproduce themselves from sprouts, and the cuttings should be so arranged, if possible, that the trees be kept at the same age, and be cut off down to the limit of smallest available size in the same year.

827. Saw-dust of red-cedar is used in the coarse thick paper placed under carpets, upon the theory that it will prevent injuries from moths.

CHAPTER XXI.

TANNING MATERIALS.

828. Supplies of material for tanning leather are derived from the forests, chiefly in the form of bark, or their extracts; but occasionally other materials are used, such as valonia, or the acorn-cups of an oak (*Quercus ægilops*), growing in Greece and Asia-Minor,

nut-galls from the Levant, the leaves of the sumac, and extracts prepared from various herbaceous plants. The tanning principle is not often found in the wood, nor in plants having poisonous qualities or milky juices, and as a general rule it is greater in the bark of young oak trees than of old ones, and more in a deep rich soil than in trees grown upon sterile land.

829. The principal supply of oak-bark used in Europe for tanning purposes is from the *Quercus pedunculata* and *Q. sessilifolia*, the common English oaks. The relative value of different barks used in England for tanning is about as follows: Oak-coppice, 300; chestnut, 243; birch, 162; mountain ash, 125; larch, 131. The spruce also furnishes some tanning material, and is used with oak. By peeling, oak-coppice wood looses about one-eight part of its volume.

830. In the Northern States, the principal bark used comes from the hemlock (*Tsuga Canadensis*), and immense quantities of timber have been wasted by being left after peeling to rot on the ground. This wasteful practice is still continued in some places. In the southern part of Pennsylvania, in Maryland, and southward, as also in many parts of the Western States, and to less extent in New England and New York, the red or black oaks have furnished most of the barks used for tanning.

831. Tanning-extract is prepared by grinding the bark, leeching out the tannin with hot water, and evaporating in vacuum-pans down to the consistence of syrup. In this state it is sent to market in barrels and sold by the pound.

832. When oak is grown in coppices in Europe, for the production of tan-bark, the coppices may be cut on damp soils (where the bark tends to become covered with mosses, and to become rough), at the age of fifteen years. As a general rule, however, it is allowed to grow about twenty years. In older trees the rough corky bark is of but little value. The best comes from trees in a healthy growing condition, with a thick juicy liber, and that are cut in the spring before the leaves have expanded.

833. In peeling oak-coppice, the workmen endeavor to take it as far as they can from the standing tree. If young trees are left a short time after felling, the bark becomes adherent, and the process difficult. The work of peeling is most easily carried on in warm humid weather, and is interrupted by cold, dry winds. The upper part and branches peel easier than the main trunk, and they save

the bark of all that can be obtained. It is first exposed to the sun, with the inside up, for a short time, and is then piled with the outer side up until dry. It is estimated that the trees yield about five per cent of their weight in bark, and that the latter looses about one-third of its weight in drying.

834. Oak bark is much injured by rains, and even when carefully dried and housed it deteriorates by keeping. Quercitron (the bark of *Q. coccinea*) used for dyeing yellow, and for tanning, is usually ground and sold in sacks. Oak wood, when peeled, is used for various manufacturing purposes, and for firewood and charcoal.

The Peeling of Oak Bark by the aid of Heat.

835. The inconvenience of crowding the work of peeling into a busy season of the year, has led to the introduction of a process in Europe, by the aid of which this work can be done at all seasons of the year. It is known from the inventor as the "*Nomaison Process.*" The apparatus consists of several large iron receivers of thin plate iron, strong enough to bear a moderate strain, and air-tight. The wood is placed in these, and steam at about 170° centigrade (338° Fahr.) is admitted from a boiler so placed as to serve several of these receivers. They hold about half a cord each, and the time required varies from an hour and a half to two hours and a half, according to the season when the wood is cut. It is then taken out and peeled. If the heat is continued too long, the bark again becomes adherent.

836. One great advantage to be gained by this process in the working of coppice-wood is, that it is not necessary to cut the wood at the season when the greatest injury is done to the stumps that are to send up a new growth. Careful experiments have been made by order of the French and Prussian governments upon the quality of the bark thus peeled, with favorable results. It is mentioned in this connection as of interest with respect to the future supplies of bark for tanning, as our native woodlands that furnish this material become scarce.

Sumac.

837. The leaves of the sumac contain a tanning material much used in dyeing, and in tanning light leather, and from six to ten thousand tons are imported into the United States annually from

Europe—chiefly from Sicily—for these uses, at a cost of from half to three-quarters of a million of dollars per annum.

838. The Sicilian sumac (*Rhus coriaria*) thrives only in a warm climate, where the orange, the carob, and the pistacia grow in the open air, and the ash produces manna. It will bear an occasional light frost in midwinter. It is particularly liable to injury from a white frost in spring. It is propagated from sprouts that come up around the mature shrubs. They are taken off in December and January, and set in rows, which are ridged up, and well cultivated at intervals through the first year, but it does not begin to produce till the third year.

839. The leaves are harvested by trimming the shoots that spring up around the main stem, a process that is done by men with a pruning-hook, or by picking the leaves by hand, which is done by women and children, during the summer. The leaves and trimmings are then dried, and the leaves are beaten off from the latter by threshing with flails, or treading of animals, preference being given to the hottest hours of the day, as the leaves then separate most easily. The best qualities are baled with the leaves entire, and without their stems. The next grade has the leaves bruised, with the stems adhering; the next, is the leaf crop of one-year old plants, while the lowest and poorest grade is from the tops of branches gathered in the beginning of autumn.

840. In any attempt to cultivate this species in the United States, success could only be expected from fresh cuttings, planted in the southern border of the Gulf States and in Southern California. Of native species we have three that are used to some extent for tanning purposes. They are, in order of preference, the *Rhus glabra*, or smooth sumac, the *R. copallina*, the wing-ribbed or mountain sumac, and the *R. typhina*, or stag-horn sumac.

841. The principal American sumac that is prepared for market comes from Virginia. The leaves are picked by country people, without much regard to the season, from the shrubs found growing wild, and are dried and sold by weight to the owners of mills for grinding. The leaves should be taken when full of sap, and before they turn red or begin to wither, and especially before frost. After being wilted in the sun, they should be spread upon shelves or racks to dry in a shaded but airy place, and should be allowed to remain at least a month, and in damp weather longer, before going to mar-

ket. Its value is judged by the color of the leaves, which should be of a bright green, and the price ranges about 75 cents per 100 pounds. The quantity gathered is about 7,000 to 8,000 tons. It is ground in close compartments, under revolving stone or wooden rollers, and is sent to market in sacks.

842. The difference in quality between Sicilian and American sumacs is about 6 to 8 per cent of tannic acid in favor of the former, while its price is about $50 more per ton. The native sumacs grow readily from seeds and sprouts, and when once started might be propagated with facility. It has not yet been determined as to the differences that may result from climate, but judging from the experience of Europe, a warm climate, and a southern slope, would be more favorable than others, and as it is found growing wild in the most rugged and rocky grounds, it may doubtless be cultivated in such places with profit.

843. A considerable amount of sumac was formerly gathered in Connecticut, and there are still persons who make it an exclusive business to gather, dry, and thresh the leaves for market. It sells in New York and Boston at from $40 to $50 per ton. It is gathered entirely from the wild shrubs, no attempt being made at cultivation.

CHAPTER XXII.

DESCRIPTIONS OF PARTICULAR SPECIES.

844. It is not our purpose to follow a systematic classification in the following pages, nor to introduce botanical descriptions. We shall present some facts concerning the number and distribution of species; more particularly those that appear worthy of attention in forest-culture, without attempting to notice those that are of chief interest for ornamental planting, or that are merely woody shrubs.

The Oaks and their related Species.

845. Of the natural order *Cupuliferæ* to which the oaks, beech, chestnut, etc., belong, there are about four hundred species. They are divided into three tribes, viz: *Betulæ*, including the birches and alders; *Coryllеæ*, including the hornbeam, ironwood, hazel, etc., and the *Quercinæ*, including the oaks, chestnuts, and beeches.

846. The OAKS are, by general consent, ranked by English writers upon sylviculture as of first importance, on account of the great

size to which the more important species grow, the vast age that they attain, and the hardness and durability of the timber. Since the introduction of iron as a building material, the oak has lost much of its importance in ship-building and for structures requiring great solidity and strength, such as bridges and large buildings for business purposes or public use in cities; but the better kinds of oak will always be valued among the most desirable for forest planting, and under favorable conditions as the most profitable that can be grown.

847. The oaks are chiefly natives of the north temperate zone, but some occur upon mountains within the tropics, in the Malay archipelago, and in South America. None are found in Australia; one genus only of the family is found in the south temperate zone, and a few are found within the Arctic circle.

848. About 250 species of the *Quercus*, or oak genus, are known to botanists. They are arranged by De Candole[1] into six sections, four of which are found only in South-eastern Asia. About forty species occur native within the United States. They may be conveniently arranged into two classes, viz., the "white" and the "black" oaks.

849. The *white oaks*, are so called from the grayish or ash-colored tint of the bark, which often tends to separate into scales. The wood is tough, dense, and excellent for cooperage, wagon-making, and other uses requiring closeness of grain, strength, and durability. The trees are slower in growth than the other divisions to be mentioned, but owing to the superior quality of the timber, they may prove more profitable for planting, although longer in coming to full maturity. They are excellent for fuel and charcoal, and most of them are desirable for ornamental planting.

850. The *black oaks*, have a bark which is dark, rough, and deeply cracked. The wood is brittle, porous, and a poor fuel. It is so porous that it can not be used for casks for holding liquids. The peduncles or fruit stems are short or wanting, and the acorns generally ripen the second year, but to this there are some exceptions. Their growth, as compared with the white oaks, is very rapid, generally as two to one, and even more. There is generally less distinction between the heart-wood and the sap-wood, and they occur

[1] *Prodromus*, Vol. XVI.

principally in the Atlantic States. They far excel the white oaks in the tanning qualities of the bark.

851. Michaux described twenty-eight species of the oak in his "Sylva Americana," including three introduced European species; and used as the first basis of subdivision the character of the leaves. In the first division, he placed the species with beardless leaves, and in the second, those in which the lobes are terminated by a bristle. The interval betweeu blossoming and the ripening of the fruit was admitted as a secondary character, which, in the first of his divisions, is generally annual, and in the second biennial.

852. The species that he described were as follows:

FIRST DIVISION: Fructification annual; leaves beardless.

First Section: Leaves lobed.

1. White oak, *Quercus alba.*
2. { Common European oak, *Q. robur.* / European white oak, *Q. robur pedenculata.* }
3. Mossy-cup oak, *Q. olivæformis.*
4. Over-cup white oak, *Q. macrocarpa.*
5. Post oak, *Q. obtusitoba.*
6. Over-cup oak, *Q. lyrata.*

Second Section: Leaves toothed.

7. Swamp white oak, *Q. prinus discolor.*
8. Chestnut white oak, *Q. prinus palustris.*
9. Rock chestnut oak, *Q. prinus monticola.*
10. Yellow oak, *Q. prinus acuminata.*
11. Small chestnut oak, *Q. prinus chinquapin.*

SECOND DIVISION: Fructification biennial; leaves mucronated.[1]

First Section: Leaves obtuse or entire.

12. Live oak, *Q. virens.*
13. Cork oak, *Q. suber.*
14. Willow oak, *Q. phellos.*
15. Laurel oak, *Q. imbricaria.*
16. Upland willow oak, *Q. cinerea.*
17. Running oak, *Q. pumila.*

[1] Except in thirteenth species.

Second Section: Leaves lobed.

18. Bartram oak, *Q. heterophylla.*
19. Water oak, *Q. aquatica.*
20. Black-jack oak, *Q. ferruginea.*
21. Bear oak, *Q. Bannisteri.*

Third Section: Leaves multifid or many-cleft.

22. Barren scrub oak, *Q. Catesbaei.*
23. Spanish oak, *Q. falcata.*
24. Black oak, *Q. tinctoria.*
25. Scarlet oak, *Q. coccinea.*
26. Gray oak, *Q. ambigua.*
27. Pin oak, *Q. palustris.*
28. Red oak, *Q. rubra.*

853. The oaks have been made a subject of careful study by Dr. Geo. Engelmann, of St. Louis, who arranges the native American species according to their natural affinities, as follows: [1]

A. LEUCOBALANUS (White Oaks.)

1. *Seeds maturing annually:*

(*a.*) Leaves deciduous.

Quercus alba, White oak.
" *lobata*, California white oak.
" *Brewerii*, Brewer's oak.
" *Garrayana*, Oregon white oak.
" *stellata*, Post oak.
" *macrocarpa*, Burr oak; overcup oak.
" *lyrata*, Southern overcup oak.
" *bicolor* (*Michauxii*), Swamp white oak.
" *prinus*, Rock-chestnut oak.
" *Muhlenbergii* (*prinoides*), Small chestnut oak.
" *Douglasii*, California white oak.
" *undulata*, Rocky Mountain white oak.
" *pungens*, Arizona white oak.

(*b.*) Leaves persistent.

Quercus oblongifolia, Oblong-leaved oak.
" *dumosa*, Dwarf California oak.
" *reticulata.*
" *virens*, Live oak.

[1] *Transactions of St. Louis Academy of Sciences*, Vol. III., No. 4, p. 388. The common names that we have added, are somewhat uncertain in their use. It will be seen that some have two, some more, and others are applied to more than one species.

2. *Seeds maturing the second year:*

Quercus chrysolepis (*vacciniifolia*), Canon live oak.
" *Palmerii*, Palmer's dwarf oak.
" *tomentella.*

B. Melanobalanus (Black Oaks.)

1. *Seeds maturing annually; leaves persistent:*

Quercus Emoryi, Emory's oak.
" *agrifolia*, Field oak.
" *pumila*, Dwarf oak.
" *hypoleuca.*

2. *Seeds maturing the second year:*

(*a.*) Leaves deciduous.

Quercus rubra, Black oak; Red-oak.
" *coccinea*[1] (*tinctoria*), Scarlet-oak.
" *Kelloggii*, California black-oak.
" *falcata*, Spanish-oak.
" *Catesbaei*, Catesby's oak.
" *ilicifolia*, Black scrub-oak.
" *palustris*, Pin-oak.
" *Georgiana.*
" *aquatica*, Water-oak.
" *laurifolia*, Water-oak.
" *nigra*, Black-jack.
" *cinerea*, Upland willow-oak.
" *imbricaria*, Shingle-oak.
" *phellos*, Willow-oak.

(*b.*) Leaves persistent.

Quercus Wislizeni, California live-oak.
" *myrtifolia.*

One other, the California chestnut oak (*Q. densiflora*), can be classed with neither.

854. Hybrids are occasionally noticed in the oaks, from the cross-fertilization of species, but not outside of the group to which the species belong. The differences between white oaks and black oaks are too great to admit of this crossing, and they have been more frequently noticed in the black oaks. The following black oaks,

[1] The *Q. coccinea* and *Q. tinctoria* are, by some botanists, made separate species.

heretofore described as species, are regarded by Dr. Engelmann as hybrids:

Quercus sinuata, probably from *Q. Catesbaei* and *Q. laurifolia*. (South Carolina.)

" *tridentata*, from *Q. imbricaria* and *Q. nigra*. (Illinois.)

" *Leana*, from *Q. imbricaria* and *Q. coccinea*. (Ohio to Missouri, and near Washington.)

" *heterophylla*, from *Q. phellos* and *Q. coccinea*. (In New Jersey and Delaware.)

855. Oaks succeed best on a deep loomy soil, and on low lands rather than upon hills. They are especially liable to injury from late spring frosts, both in the blossoms and leaves, and having a long tap-root, they are somewhat difficult to transplant, without careful preparation, tending to the suppression of this root, and to the formation of abundant fibers. They may be planted in the fall or early in the spring, in the places where they are to remain, and should be cultivated till they shade the grounds. When started in nurseries, they should be transplanted two or three times before final planting, and the tap-roots should be cut off with a sharp knife, to induce the formation of lateral roots and more abundant radicles.

120. *Quercus pedunculata:* The English Oak—Leaves, Flowers, and Fruit.

856. There is a great advantage in planting them with other species, such as the beech, pines, and spruces, with the view of compelling the trees to form a long straight body; but in this case, reasonable care should be taken to remove those other kinds from time to time, as the growth becomes dense.

857. Where the oak is cultivated in Europe for its bark and wood, it is recommended to cut close to the ground, and in a dry time to cover the stumps with a handful of leaves, or any rubbish that may be convenient, to keep them from becoming too dry. If cut very close, the sprouts will be fewer in number, but stronger, and better rooted. Where this practice is carefully followed, they will reproduce a great number of times.

121. Oak from Provence, France. Very hard, and of rapid growth.

122. Oak from Bourgogne, France. Very hard, but of slow growth.

858. The quality of oak timber is much influenced by the conditions in which it has grown. In a rich and moderately humid soil, and in a warm climate, the fibers acquire their highest qualities of strength and durability. Such wood the French call "*maigre*" (lean), or "*dur*" (hard). The grain is hard and close: it scarcely absorbs water. The wood splits easily without running out on one side, and when planed the shavings form strong tough strips. When such wood is broken, the fracture forms many long sharp splinters. The two specimens on page 217 are also of this class.

859. But when oak is grown in a soil that is submerged for a time in spring, but dry the rest of the year, the spring growth is loose and spongy, while that formed later in the season may be very hard. Such wood can not be either strong or durable, although from the differences in the grain, it may be highly ornamental for inside finishing and for cabinet work.

860. THE AMERICAN WHITE OAK (*Quercus alba*). This tree occurs from Canada southward to the Gulf, and westward to beyond the Missouri, but it comes to greatest perfection in the Middle States, and in the deep, strong, and moderately damp soil. The

land on which it formed a principal part of the timber, generally has proved when brought under cultivation to be well adapted for

123. Italian Oak: Very coarse, but strong when fully ripened.

124. Italian Oak: Coarse, but very strong.

wheat. It derives its name from the whitish color of the bark. The wood has a slightly reddish tinge, and although not as heavy and compact as the common English oak, it is solid, strong, and durable, and is found excellent for heavy timber-work, and for all kinds of structures requiring durability and strength. It is extensively used for staves, agricultural implements, carriage and car-building, cabinet wares, fencing, and various farm purposes, and is a favorite wood in ship-building. Like the European oaks above described, the quality of the wood differs according to the nature of the soil in which it has grown, being relatively more dense, strong, and durable when grown in a warm climate and upon a rich and moderately humid, clayey loam.

861. This timber has been largely exported from the northern borders of the United States, and from Canada by way of the St. Lawrence to England, and in districts where it was once abundant it is now scarce. A considerable amount that leaves the port of Quebec is now brought from Michigan and other states bordering upon the lakes. In floating this timber it is usually made up into rafts with pine, to give it greater bouyancy.

862. THE LIVE OAK (*Quercus virens*), is an evergreen tree found

growing in Georgia, Florida, and along the Gulf Coast, and since an early period in our government it has been an object of protection to some extent on account of its great value in ship-building. Some experiments at cultivation were attempted many years since, but without much success, excepting the clearing away of bushes around young plants found native in the thickets. It could doubtless be grown from acorns with proper care, perhaps by using slight perishable baskets for keeping the soil around the roots in transplanting from seed-beds, as is practiced with bamboo shells in raising the teak and the cinchonas in India. The wood of the live oak is of great strength and hardness, but not of slow growth, the annual layers being often a quarter or a third of an inch in thickness. This tree especially deserves cultivation in regions where it will grow.

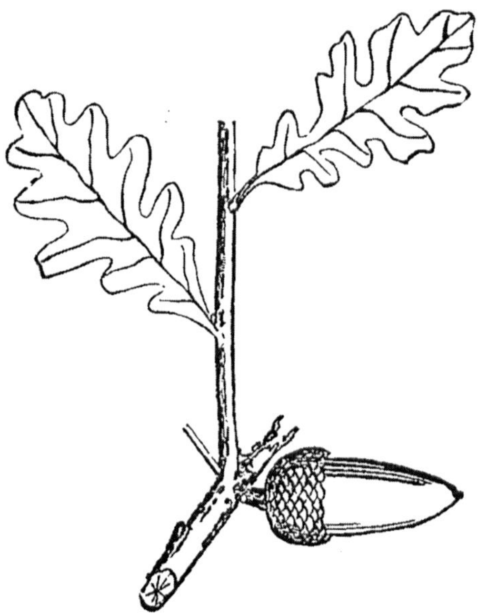

125. *Quercus Hindsii.*—Leaves and Acorn one-half the Natural Size.

863. Among the remaining oaks of the Atlantic States, there are many that have a local value, but none that enter largely into commerce, or that are extensively used in manufactures. Most of them afford excellent fuel and charcoal, and some of them are quite durable when used as railway ties or fence posts. The bark of the "scarlet

oak" (*Quercus coccinea*) furnishes the "quercitron," so highly valued as a yellow dye and a tanning material, and is an article of considerable commercial importance.

864. Upon the Pacific Coast we find a dozen or more species of the oak, some of them fine and ornamental, but none of them of great importance for their timber, which is weak, brittle, and altogether inferior to the general quality of oaks as found in the Atlantic States. They chiefly belong to the "white oak" family. Four or five of them have persistent leaves, the rest being deciduous, and one of them much resembles the chestnut.

865. THE LONG-ACORNED OAK (*Q. Hindsii*) of California, much resembles the white oak of the Eastern States. It is the finest and perhaps most abundant of the oaks of that region, occurring along the foot-hills and the valleys of streams in clumps and belts, branching out low and broad, and sometimes five or six feet in diameter near the ground. The wood is porous and brittle. The acorns are gathered and eaten by the natives, and stored for winter use.

866. THE CALIFORNIA CHESTNUT OAK (*Q. densiflora*) is a small tree with evergreen leaves, found growing on the coast range with the red-woods. It sometimes occurs fifty or sixty feet high, and from one to two feet in diameter. It is often only a shrub. The fruit ripens the second year, and the wood is worthless and brittle. This oak is the only American representative of a group found chiefly in Asia, having strong resemblance to the chestnut, with spines on its cup, somewhat like those on the chestnut-burr. In the Sacramento Valley, it forms a low but handsome tree.

867. THE EVERGREEN OAK of California, often called the "shrub oak" (*Q. agrifolia*, is a low spreading tree, having much the form of an apple-tree, rarely over a foot in diameter, and 30 to 40 feet high. It occurs in the Sacramento Valley, and extends south into Mexico. The wood is hard, brittle, and too small for valuable use.

868. THE CHESTNUT (*Castanea vesca*). This tree is found native from the central part of New England and Central New York southward and westward, extending into the mountains of the Carolinas and Georgia, and occurring abundantly in the eastern part of Kentucky and Tennessee. In Canada it is found only in the peninsula westward from the Niagara river, and is not of sufficient abundance to be of much practical account. It is common in the states north of the Ohio river, where the soil is favorable. Our

American chestnut is a variety of the same species that is cultivated in Europe.

(126. *Quercus agrifolia.*—Leaves and Fruit one-half Natural Size. [See page 219.]

869. The chestnut in Massachusetts forms one of the largest of the native forest trees, growing sometimes in the southwestern part of the state to the height of ninety or a hundred feet. It extends into the southern edge of Maine, but scarcely beyond the 44th degree of latitude, nor does it generally thrive near the sea.

870. The chestnut is early to feel the warmth of spring, and sometimes suffers from late spring frosts. For this reason, it is least apt to suffer on a northern or north-eastern slope. It requires a light, silecious soil, if deep and substantial, and especially prefers that formed by the decomposition of granite, gneiss, mica-slate, or sandstone. Upon granitic gravel and volcanic scoriae it gives the most abundant products. It is useless to plant it upon calcareous soils, nor does it prosper upon clays, or in marshy and undrained situations. It prefers hills and mountains of moderate height, and succeeds much better there than upon plains.

871. For cultivation as a timber-tree, it should be planted upon gravelly hills, and generally where it is to remain. The young plants are robust from the first, and do not prosper in the shade. They are more apt to suffer from frost than the oak. The roots are generally abundant, and strike deep into the soil, but not as deep as the oak. The growth is rapid, and sustained till sixty or seventy

years of age, but it continues to live and grow to more than twice this period, and under favorable circumstances it sometimes lives to an immense age.[1]

872. Of our native forest trees, there are few that show a greater tendency to grow from the sprouts than the chestnut, and on rocky and broken grounds, where this tree will flourish best, there is no crop that under favorable circumstances and proper protection will pay so good a profit upon the land.

873. It is remarked by the highest authorities upon forestry, that "chestnut stumps have a remarkable durability, and that the sprouts they send up afford a growth both vigorous and rapid. It is especially in vine countries that coppices of this wood are found most profitable, from the hoops they furnish for casks and props for the vines."[2] It is not advisable to reserve trees for large growth in a chestnut coppice, as is done with great advantage in the oak, because the shade would do more harm to the young growth than the air and light would benefit the reserves.

874. The trees, when ten or fifteen years old, will begin to bear fruit, and thus assist in re-stocking. It would be advisable to reserve a few trees around the borders of the tract to secure some timber of larger growth, and increase the chestnut harvest.

875. Chestnut "sprout lands" must of course be kept inclosed against sheep, horses, and cattle at all seasons, for although they may be cut off at one time, there will still be sprouts of small size, and these will be needed for re-stocking the ground. The same objection would not exist against the admission of swine, which in fruitful seasons would thrive and fatten without injury to the trees.

876. Where a chestnut grove is to be started in Europe, it is recommended to set the young trees from nurseries, when about three years old, at distances of two or three yards apart, cultivating the ground between as long as it can be conveniently done with potatoes or grain. When the trees have grown to two or three inches in diameter, they carefully cut them off close to the ground,

[1] A chestnut tree (or perhaps a group of trees) formerly stood upon Mt. Etna, more than fifty yards in circumference. It was hollow, and must have been some 2,000 years old. It was called "castagno di cento cavalli." It appears from an account published in 1865, that this remarkable tree no longer exists." (*Revue des Deux Mondes*, July, 1, 1865.)

[2] Lorentz and Parade—*Culture des Bois.*

and the next spring the stump is covered with numerous strong sprouts.

877. In six or eight years, when the shoots have become thick and strong, the smaller rods are cut out, leaving only two or three, which when thus relieved take a vigorous start, and at the end of six or seven years more are from four to six inches in diameter. It is again thinned out, and at 20 to 25 years from the time of planting, the trees that are left have made a truly wonderful growth. The thinnings from beginning have value, first, for coarse basket and wicker-work; and then for hoops and poles, suitable for many uses.

878. Generally a coppice of chestnut is cut off when twelve or fifteen years old, and in Alsace and Eastern France, the profits from such a cutting are twice as great as from the white oak of that region at twice its age, a hectare at fifteen years being worth 3,000 francs.[1] It is there recommended to cultivate the ground with potatoes and rye two or three years after each cutting, the yield of these harvests being more than double the cost of cultivation and seed. Chestnut coppices thus managed will last in Alsace for a hundred years. This cultivation is thought to stimulate the growth of sprouts, by bringing the ends of the roots to the air, besides ridding the ground of bushes and brambles.

879. The European chestnut is an important article of food, especially in Italy, France, and Spain. The fruit is much larger than the American variety, and runs into differences in quality that have been introduced by cultivation, and that are propagated by grafting. In bearing years, the yield of a single tree is often very large, amounting in some cases to a ton or more of the fresh fruit in a single year. This shrinks about one-third in weight upon drying. When used as food it is boiled or roasted. The dried fruit reduced to a meal is made into a kind of bread called in Italy *polenta*. It furnishes a principal article of food to the poor inhabitants of the mountain regions through the greater part of the year.

880. The chestnut product of Italy is about 6,400 tons a year for the markets, and the trees are under cultivation for the fruit upon a million and a quarter of acres.

881. Chestnut wood is heavier and closer grained when grown in

[1] Brolliard's "*Traitement des Bois en France*," p. 108. A hectare is 2.47 acres. The rate here mentioned is a little over $240 per acre for 15 years or $16 per acre annually.

warm climates, and in Italy it is thought equal to the oak for staves. In colder countries it is too porous for coopers' use excepting for dry wares. It is highly prized for carpentry, bears exposure very well, and is very durable for fencing. It is sometimes made into shingles, but although durable, it is very apt to warp. Its lumber is much used for furniture and inside finishing, and shows to fine advantage when oiled or varnished.

882. Throughout France and the south of Europe, young chestnut rods are extensively used for hoops, and from their durability in moist places they will long resist the dampness of cellars. Chestnut coppices are considered valuable property for this use, and are cut off about once in seven years, the smaller rods being saved for hoops, and the larger ones for vine-props. The American chestnut is not found well adapted for this use, as the wood is more brittle, and more liable to split off at the ends.

883. As a fuel, the chestnut ranks with the light woods. Its pores being full of air, it snaps as it burns, and its charcoal is light, but still useful in forges, although not as valuable as the hard-woods in the reduction of metallic ores.

884. The *extract of chestnut* is prepared in France, by cutting the green wood into chips, with revolving planes, that slice across the grain. The chips are then put into great covered boilers, and allowed to mascerate for some time, when steam is admitted, and the process is continued till the tannin in the wood is exhausted. The liquor is then strained out and evaporated to the desired consistence. This acid product is used in preparing silks, and is employed in tanning the lighter kinds of leather. In the neighborhood of Lyons, France, they get 25 per cent of weight of the wood in the form of extract, worth about 18 francs per 100 kilograms, equal to about 500 pounds to the ton, worth $32.72.

885. Chestnut wood has been used to a small extent in the United States for tanning purposes. It appears to require a warm climate, to develop these properties so as to be of much value.

886. *Dying off of the Chestnut.* Throughout the Piedmont region in North Carolina and in the northern part of Georgia and Alabama, the chestnut trees have been dying off in many cases to a large extent, and from causes that have not been ascertained. The mortality is noticed in trees of all ages, and now there is but little of this timber found in a growing condition in North Carolina east of

the Blue Ridge, until we get high up on its peaks and spurs. Westward of this ridge, the trees do not bear fruit now as they did twenty years ago, so that hog-raising, formerly an important business, has almost ceased. Occasionally there is still a good chestnut crop, but it is rare and uncertain.

887. In Europe, a similar fatality has been noticed in some parts of Italy and Spain, and there has been found in connection with the roots a fungus, composed of blackish brown filaments, forming a net-work that penetrates the cellular tissues of the bark and wood, feeding upon the juices of the living tree, and upon the decomposing remains of the dead. No remedy has been proposed there short of grubbing up and destroying by fire the roots of infected trees, and all the debris; but of course in our country such a measure would be wholly impracticable, unless possibly in isolated cases, should this treatment be found effectual, and its necessity urgent.[1]

888. THE CHINQUAPIN (*Castanea pumila*) is usually a shrub or small tree, growing in swamps, in the Middle and Southern States, rarely attaining a height of thirty or forty feet, and generally being too small for use. In Arkansas, however, it grows to a large size—sometimes three and even four feet in diameter, but not to a great height. The fruit is small and sweet, and sometimes finds its way into market. A dwarf variety grows upon poor soils, and bears fruit when not more than a foot in height. It has been recommended for cultivation as a covering for land too poor for other growth, and as affording food for swine.

889. THE WESTERN CHINQUAPIN (*Castanopsis chrysophylla*) is generally a low and unimportant evergreen shrub, growing in California and Oregon; but in the Cascade Mountains, it sometimes grows to thirty feet in height, or even much larger. The leaves have a dark green color above, but are covered with a yellow powder beneath. The nut is small, with a harder shell than the eastern chinquapin, which it otherwise much resembles.

[1] A writer in Carrol Co., Ga., mentions this disease of the chestnut, which appeared about fifteen years ago, and had made a clean sweep—even the bushes having nearly all died; no worms or insects had been found upon them before death, and even now the dead chestnut trees were the most valuable rail-timber they had, it being soft but very durable, lasting longer in the open weather than any other kind. After being dead over ten years, the trees were sound, and without signs of decay.

THE BEECH (Genus *Fagus*).

890. About twenty-five species of the Fagus are described by botanists, being widely diffused in the temperate zones both north and south.

891. In Europe the beech (*Fagus sylvatica*) is very extensively cultivated in France, Germany, and Denmark, constituting a very important timber-tree, preferring a cool to a mild climate, and in warm regions growing only at considerable elevations. It thrives in great variety of soils, but prefers those that are calcareous and gravelly, but not sandy, and where the climate favors, it grows both upon mountains and the plains. It is often cultivated alone, forming great forests by itself; but it grows very well with the oak, fir, maple, Scotch pine, etc., and as its roots spread near the surface, while those of the oak penetrate deep into the sub-soil, these trees appear to thrive very well together.

892. The wood of the beech splits remarkably well when green, but it is very liable to shrink, and should not be used until well seasoned. It is largely used for cabinet work, and for a wide diversity of uses in the industries, but does not bear exposure to the weather nor changes from wet to dry. When injected with the sulphate of copper, it has been much used as railroad ties, but it is not as lasting as unimpregnated oak. It is very highly esteemed for fuel and charcoal, and the oil from its nuts has the same uses as that from the olive.

893. Its growth is rather slow at first, but a little more rapid than that of the oak. It is noticed that under a deep shade the beech will sprout from the seed and grow to a yard or so in height, when it will stop growing, and remain almost indefinitely; but start vigorously again, as soon as the light is admitted.[1] The slight difference in quality between the sap-wood and the heart-wood, allows of the whole being used without the waste of any part.

894. The beech comes to maturity sooner than the oak, and does not grow to so large a size. As there is not much gain in quality when grown to greatest size, it is generally cut when from 24 to 30 inches in diameter. In some forests it is grown as coppice-wood by sprouts from the roots and stump, but in many places this is found an uncertain process, and it is planted from nurseries, or started by natural seeding.

[1] G. Bagneris' "*Manuel de Sylviculture*," 2d. Ed., p. 65.

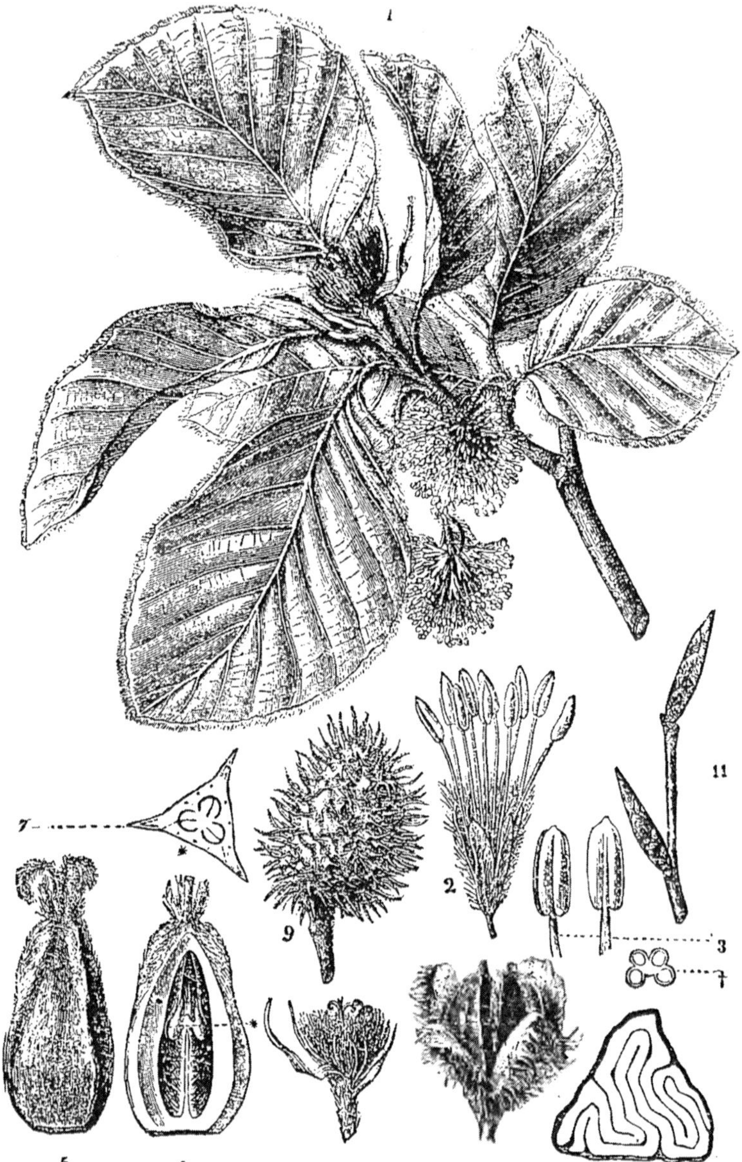

127. *Fagus sylvatica.*—The European Beach. 1. Upper side of a twig in May, with male and female blossoms. 2. A separate male blossom. 3. Anthers, front and rear views, and sections. 4. Female blossoms of natural size. 5. The same, separated and enlarged. 6. Section of the same, showing the germs of seeds, enlarged. 7. Transverse section of the latter, at the point marked by a star. 8. The ripe fruit in its burr. 9. The same, before opening. 10. Cross-section of a nut. 11. Twig with two leaf-buds. Excepting 1, 4, 8, 9, and 11, these figures are more or less enlarged.

895. A very simple method is employed for preserving the nuts for planting. They are gathered, spread in an airy place, turned daily to allow of moderate drying, and then left on a floor under a covering of straw to keep from frost. With the greatest care it is sometimes difficult to keep them alive from fall to spring.

896. In order to succeed in planting the beech, it is necessary to provide shelter for the young plant, which may be found by raking in the nuts upon bare places in the woods, or by planting in east and west rows, some other kinds of trees a year or two before we plant the beech. These nurses may be birch, elm, pine, or whatever else best suits the soil, as they are to be removed when no longer needed.

897. The nuts should be planted like corn, and when up, they should be carefully hoed, *taking care to cover the seminal leaves*, leaving only the leaves proper above the ground. If planted in fall, as is preferable, the seed will sprout in the spring following. Owing to the difficulty in getting plants started from the seed, it is common to seek the young plants where they have been self-sown in the woods, set them in nursery rows, and transplant when of sufficient size. These seed-plants are best taken up with a trowel, and a cool cloudy time should be chosen for the operation.

898. Our native species (*Fagus feruginea*) occurs widely scattered throughout the New England, Middle, and Northwestern States, as far west as Wisconsin, and in Canada, as far north as a line running from a little beyond Lake Huron eastward to the Bay of Chaleurs. It extends southward into the Southern States, growing sparingly upon the low-lands, but to large size in the mountains. It attains its greatest development in Michigan and Wisconsin, and in the heavy forests south of Lake Superior its growth is truly magnificent.

899. In Northern Pennsylvania and in some portions of New England and New York, the beech grows as almost the only tree upon dry rocky ridges, and in fruit-seasons these beech ridges have attracted enormous flocks of wild-pigeons for nesting.

900. Various exceptional forms and tints of foliage have been produced in the beech under cultivation, and are perpetuated by grafting or layers, such as cut-leaved, purple or copper-leaved, golden-stripe leaved, etc. Some of these produce a highly ornamental effect upon the lawn, and in parks and avenues.

901. The beech is termed "red" or "white" by woodmen, from

the difference in color of the heart-wood; but they appear to be simply varieties of the same species, from differences in the soil or exposure. The red beech is much more durable, and under water it appears almost indestructible. It has also been found durable in plank-roads, and in ship-building where permanently under water, and for this reason it is sometimes used for the keels of vessels.

902. The beech of Victoria and Tasmania (*Fagus Cunninghami*) is a magnificent evergreen of colossal size, and living only in cool, damp, rich forest valleys where it not unfrequently grows to the height of two hundred feet. The wood, much used by carpenters and others, is known to the trade as "myrtle."

903. Other evergreen beeches of fine size and much value, (*F. Menziesii*), known as the "red birch;" *F. fusca*, the "black birch;" *F. Solandri*, the "white birch," of colonists) are found in New Zealand. It is not improbable that some of these might succeed under similar conditions, especially in Southern California, where so many Australian species have been found to thrive.

THE BIRCH (Genus *Betula*).

904. About twenty-five species of the birch are known in Europe, Asia, and North America, and they are divided into some sixty subspecies or characteristic varieties. They prefer a cool, humid climate, some growing upon mountains of considerable elevation, and others preferring swampy grounds and river banks.

905. The birch extends about as far into the Arctic zone as woody plants of any kind will grow. In the remote part of the Highlands of Scotland, it forms coppices on rocky elevations where no other ligneous plant is found, and throughout Northern Europe it forms an important article for fuel.

906. It shows a tendency to succeed the pines where they have been cut off, and is readily propagated from seed, but does best on new ground, and can hardly be made to grow where nursery trees have previously been raised. The seeds scarcely admit of any covering, and if simply pressed into the ground with the feet they will grow. A bushel of seed will stock thirty linear yards of a seed-bed four feet wide. When a year old, they may be transplanted to nursery rows, and when two or three feet high may be set for permanence.

907. Cut-leaved, weeping, and other varieties have been introduced for ornamental planting, and are perpetuated by grafting.

Sometimes the wood has knots and curls in the grain that take a fine polish when used as veneers. It is a favorite wood for shoe-pegs, spools, bobbins, and other small articles. It is peeled into brooms, and strips of its wood are braided into baskets and fishing-traps. The smoke of its wood imparts a fine flavor to hams, and

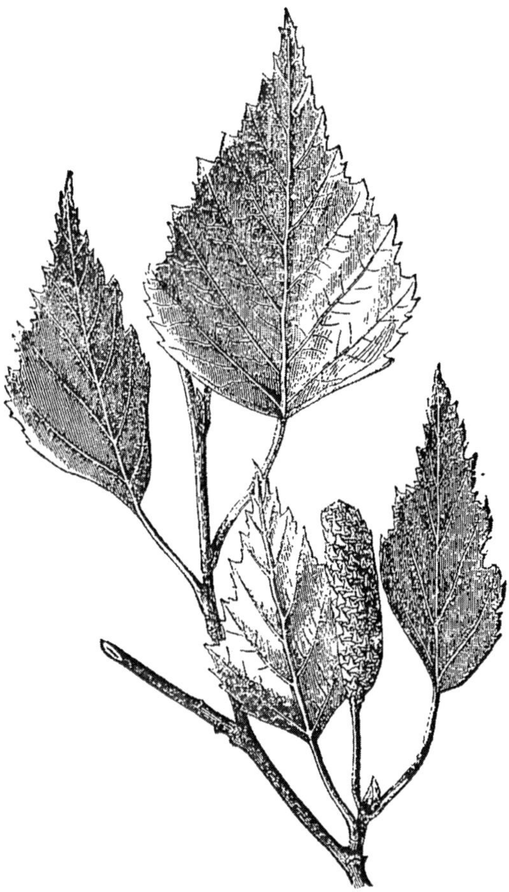

128. *Betula alba.*—White Birch.

its bark is used for tanning leather. An oil prepared from the birch imparts the peculiar odor to Russia leather much used in substantial book-binding. Birch-wine is made from the sap of this tree by fermentation.

908. The seeds of the birch and the alder scatter very soon after

they ripen, and it is difficult to keep them. They should be gathered by hand just as the burrs begin to turn brown, and if possible, they should be sown the same year. An expeditious way to obtain the seed is to cut off the branches that bear the burrs at the time when they are just ripening, and hang them in a dry place till the seed falls out. As they should be covered but very slightly, they are best raked in, upon soil previously prepared, and if sown in autumn, they will start the next spring.

909. The birch can not reproduce with much advantage from the stumps, but it readily springs up from the seed in vacant spots in the woods.

910. THE YELLOW BIRCH (*Betula excelsa*) is a northern species, growing to a greater size than any other of the birches, and when large, the grain is often twisted in a spiral manner. Its wood is solid, fine-grained, and easily worked, and is much used for cabinet wares. The bark possesses tanning properties, yet is but seldom used.

911. THE CANOE BIRCH (*Betula papyracea*) is also a northern species, occurring along the northern border of the United States, and far northward into Canada. The bark is used for making canoes, baskets, and other uses, and its wood, which is white, is largely used for making shoe-pegs, spools, lasts, and cabinet wares. It turns smoothly, and takes a fine finish.

912. THE RED BIRCH (*Betula nigra*) grows in the Atlantic States, from New Englaud to the Carolinas. It is also common in the Western and South-western States, always preferring river banks, and sometimes growing to one or two feet in diameter, but usually much less. It derives its name from the reddish tinge of the bark, which hangs in loose shreds upon the trunk and branches, giving it a peculiarly ragged appearance.

913. THE SWEET BIRCH (*Betula lenta*) sometimes called "Cherry Birch," or "Black Birch," from the dark color of its bark, is a tree of small size; is chiefly a northern species, extending from Canada southward along the mountains as far as North Carolina. The *Betula glandulosa*, a far-northern species, and some others of less account, are also found within our territory, occurring as a low bush upon our northwestern coast.

914. THE WESTERN BIRCH (*Betula occidentalis*) is a shrub, growing 10 to 20 feet high, with a close, dark-colored bark, which becomes light brown, copiously sprinkled with resinous warts. It

occurs in the eastern cañons of the Sierra Nevada, at an elevation of 4,500 to 10,000 feet above tide, where it is said to be common. It is found northward in Washington Territory and in British America, and among the Rocky Mountains to New Mexico. Well-grown trees are found in the northern part of the Frazer basin, and in the Pearl river country, in British Columbia.

THE ALDER (Genus *Alnus*).

915. Of these there are about fifteen species, found in middle and northern Europe, North America, and upon the Andes in South America. About half the number occur in North America.

916. The European alder most commonly cultivated is the *A. glutinosa.* It is indigenous throughout Europe, and when growing wild, seldom attains more than thirty or forty feet in height; but in Great Britain it has, under cultivation, grown to eighty feet with a trunk three to four feet in diameter. It matures at fifty or sixty years. Its timber, when always submerged, is very durable, but not where exposed to alternations of wet and dry. Its brush is used in filling marshy lands, and its wood as staves for fish barrels, and for lasts, turned goods, cabinet wares, etc. To prevent insects from attacking it, the finer pieces are sometimes, in Scotland, immersed for some months in water in a peat bog. If some lime is thrown in, the effect is improved. Such wood has some resemblance to mahogany, and is used for tables, etc. Charcoal from this wood is used in making gunpowder, and the bark for tanning.

917. The alder prefers a rich, damp soil, such as alluvial bottom-lands and the borders of streams. It will, however, grow to a large size on dryer land, and from its rapid growth and great tenacity of life, it is esteemed as a nurse for the more tender kinds in bleak and exposed situations. It is, like the willow, useful for consolidating banks, and to keep it in best condition for this, it is cut as coppice-wood once in eight or ten years. It sprouts readily from the stumps. As a screen for osier fields and the like, it is very valuable.

918. The alder is propagated with facility from the seed, which should be spread in their cones on a dry floor, and stirred from time to time till they are dry. They may be sown at once, or in March or April following, on rich, moist land, previously prepared. They should be thinly covered and rolled, and the next spring transplanted from the seed-beds, and after another year in the nursery,

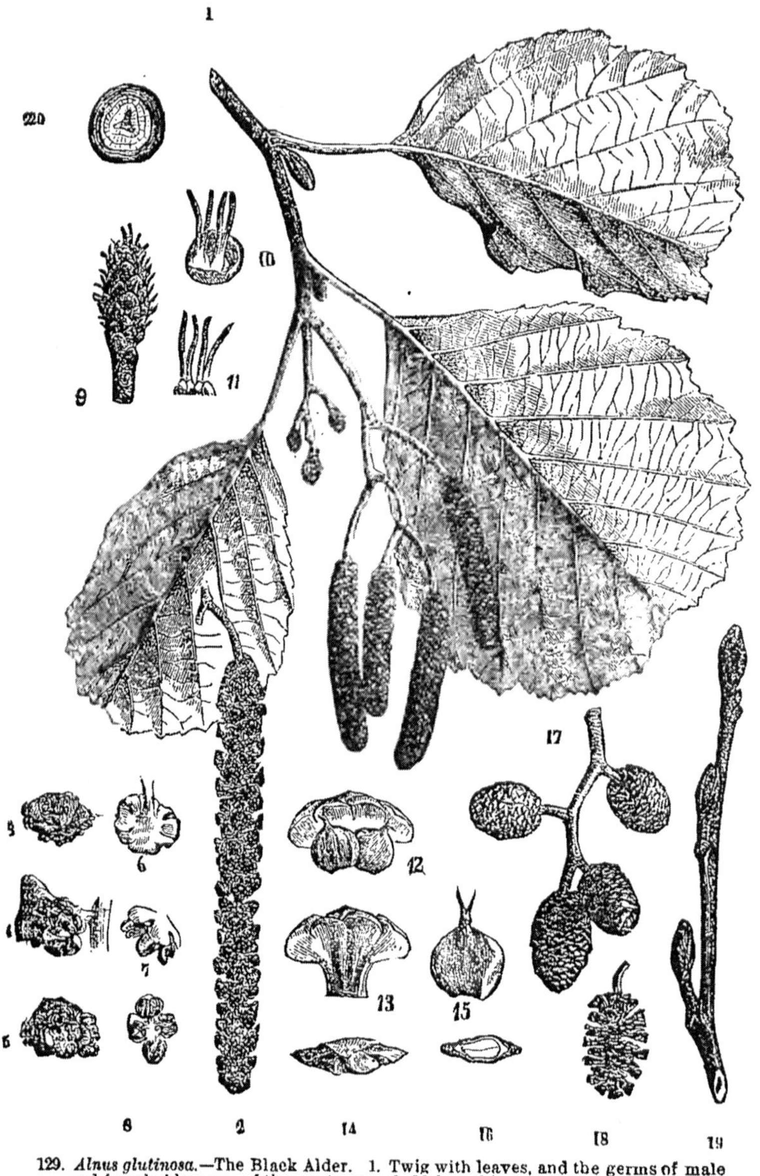

129. *Alnus glutinosa.*—The Black Alder. 1. Twig with leaves, and the germs of male and female blossoms of the next year. 2. Male catkin in full bloom. 3, 4, 5, 6. A full-blossomed capsule, from different points of view. 7, 8. A four-lobed single blossom, side and upper points of view. 9. Female catkin, enlarged. 10, 11, 12, 13, 14, 15, 16. Enlarged view of female blossom, with appendages, and the fruit. 17. The ripe fruit-capsule. 18. The same, opened. 19. A twig, with leaf-buds. 20. Cross-section of a twig. Of the above figures, only 1, 2, 17, 18, 19, and 20 are of the natural size, the remainder being enlarged.

they may be finally transplanted. The alder is rated as a soft wood, and sold at a low price. For general cultivation it is not profitable, but for special uses it has great advantages.

919. THE AMERICAN ALDER (*Alnus incana*), the most widely distributed of our native species, occurs from New England northward far into British America, and westward to Oregon. It is found in New Mèxico, Nevada, and Utah, and in the Sierra Nevada mountains to an elevation of 6,000 to 7,000 feet. It most commonly occurs in dense thickets along the border of streams, seldom growing to a size for any use but firewood.

920. THE RED ALDER (*A. rubra*) occurs along the Pacific from Alaska southward, sometimes growing 30 to 40 feet high. It grows to a small tree on Vancouver and Queen Charlotte Islands and the coast of the mainland, and its wood is sometimes used for charcoal.

921. THE WHITE ALDER (*A. rhombifolia*) occurs from Oregon to Southern California as a tree 20 to 50 feet high and 2 to 3 feet in diameter. It has a light, ash-gray bark, slender branches.

922. The *Alnus oblongifolia* occurs in Southern California and New Mexico as a tree 20 to 30 feet in height.

923. THE OREGON ALDER (*A. Oregona*) is a tree growing to 50 or 60 feet in height, and sometimes two feet in diameter, near the ground. Like the other alders, it prefers the banks of streams. The wood is brittle, and not employed for useful purposes.

HORNBEAM (Genus *Carpinus*).

924. Of the genus *Carpinus*, about nine species are found in the North Temperate Zone of the Old and New World, and but one (*C. Americana*) is found native in the United States. It is known by various common names, such as the "hop-hornbeam," from the clusters of fruit somewhat resembling hops, "blue-beech," "water or swamp beech," etc. It has the general habit of the beech, and its bark is smooth like that tree. The stem is generally somewhat fluted or angular, and it is of smaller size. The foliage becomes crimson, scarlet, and orange in autumn.

925. The hornbeam occurs widely distributed throughout the Atlantic States and Canada; never in dense groves, but scattered through forests of other deciduous kinds. The wood is close, white, hard, and fine-grained, remarkably tough and strong, and well adapted to places where it is required to resist great pressure or friction. When of sufficient size, the wood is useful in the mechanic

arts, and is suitable for the making of levers, tool-handles, and other articles requiring great strength. It forms an excellent fire-wood and material for charcoal used for cooking, or in forges, or for making gunpowder.

926. THE EUROPEAN HORNBEAM (*Carpinus betulus*) is often cultivated for screens and hedges in Europe, and it was thought by Michaux that it might be introduced with profit into the United States. Among its merits are the following: It bears pruning well, is not liable to disease, grows for a long time in a confined form, and does not injure the adjacent crops, probably because its roots draw their support from a greater depth; it grows very close and twiggy, and retains its leaves late; it endures a rough and windy situation, and grows well in a great variety of soils.

927. It seeds abundantly, and when sown immediately, a few spring up the first year, but most of them not till the second year. The usual mode of cultivation is to sow in spring, at the rate of a bushel of clean seed to fifty yards of a bed four feet wide; and as the seeds do not grow the first year, the ground may be occupied by some other light crop, such as onions, lettuce, raddish, or cabbage. They may be thinned out when one-year old by transplanting to nursery rows, but the young plants do best if not taken up till they are two years old. In two years more, they will be suitable for setting in single hedge rows. Under cultivation, the hornbeam has produced cut-leaved and variegated forms that are propagated by layers for ornamental planting.

THE MAPLES (Genus *Acer*).

928. The maples occur widely distributed in the Northern Temperate Zone upon both continents, and upon the eastern rather than upon the western sides. There are about fifty species described, of which nine or ten occur within the United States. They generally grow to trees of considerable size, take when planted alone, a rounded, symmetrical form, and are highly prized for ornamental planting in village streets and by the wayside.

929. The wood of the maples is generally light colored or with a reddish tinge, works smoothly, is not liable to warp or check, and is much valued for cabinet work. In some cases, the grain is curled or contorted in such a manner as to give it, when finished, a highly ornamental effect.

930. The maple leaves in autumn take bright crimson and orange

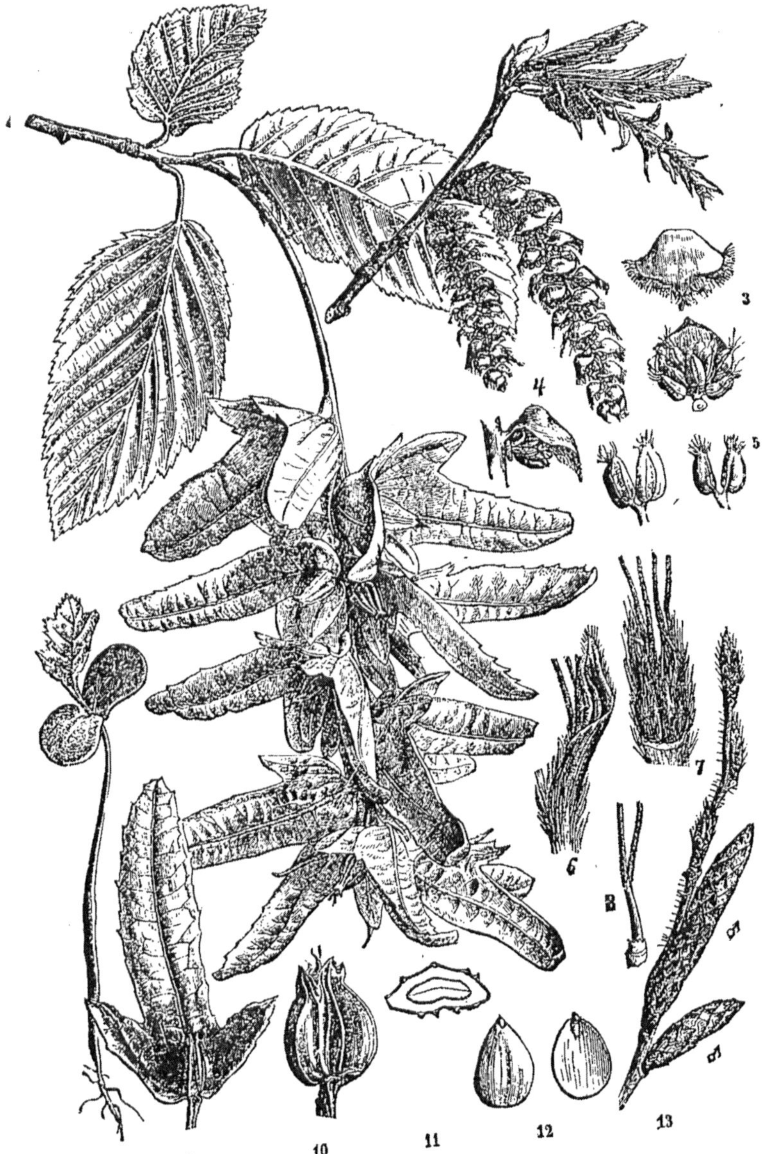

130. *Carpinus betulus.*—The European Hornbeam. 1. Twig, with two male and one female blossoms. 2. A fruitful stem, with leaves. 3, 4. Male blossoms, from upper, lower, and side points of view. 5. A single seed-capsule, with section. 6. Leaf-cover, with the inclosed female blossoms. 7. A pair of female blossoms, with the envelope removed. 8. A single pistil. 9. A ripe seed, with its three-lobed seed-leaf. 10. The seed-capsule, separated and enlarged. 11. Transverse section of the same. 12. The germs, separated. 13. Twig, with three leaf-buds above, and two male flower-buds. 14. Germ, as it first appears upon sprouting.

colored tints, that give a characteristic splendor to the woodlands during the few days that they remain after they are fairly ripe.

931. THE SUGAR MAPLE (*Acer saccharinum*). This tree, which is altogether the most valuable of the maples, is a native of Canada and the Northern States, extending southward along the mountains into the Carolinas, and westward to the Mississippi river. It is abundant in Western North Carolina, but it thrives best in a rather cool climate, and in a calcareous and loamy, rather than a sandy soil. In Canada it extends northward to a line running from the northeastern shore of Lake Superior to a short distance below Quebec, and thence northeastward to the Gulf of St. Lawrence. The "Maple Leaf" is a national emblem with the Canadians, and the gorgeous splendor of the autumnal forests in the north is largely due to the colors assumed by the foliage of this tree at this season.

932. The sugar maple grows to a height of sixty to eighty feet, and to a diameter of two feet and over. When planted alone, it assumes a rounded, symmetrical form, and it deservedly enjoys a high reputation as an ornamental tree in village and roadside planting, but it does not endure the dust and smoke of cities. When grown in woodlands, it assumes a tall, regular form, and it is often found in forests by itself, or mingled with beech, birch, hemlock, and other trees.

933. Upon the prairies of Illinois this tree grows slow when young, but at length takes a more vigorous start, and becomes a fine tree. It will not grow with entire success beyond the Mississippi, and fails altogether in Kansas and Nebraska.

934. In the Northern States and in Canada, when tapped upon the approach of spring, and for a period of thirty or forty days, ending as the buds begin to swell, this tree yields a sweetish sap, which by evaporation may be reduced to syrup and to sugar of superior quality. Several million of pounds of this sugar are made every year, and upon some farms in Vermont and Northern New York more profit is realized from a maple woodland, than could possibly be gained upon an equal area by any agricultural crop. The yield is usually two or three pounds to the tree in the season, but in exceptional cases it may be more.

935. From the limited experiments that have been made, it appears that the sap of the maple contains more sugar in the early part of the season than toward its close, and that different trees vary in the amount of sugar, some giving much sweeter sap than others. As the buds begin to swell, the sap becomes "ropy," and

gives off an offensive odor in boiling. It crystalizes with difficulty, and it is customary to use the last run, partly concentrated by boiling, for making vinegar, by exposing it to fermentation.

936. The flow of sap is much influenced by meteorological conditions, and is best with freezing nights and thawing days, and in a damp atmosphere. It will sometimes flow by night, and a run may last two or three days, and then be suspended, from causes unknown, until another freezing night. The sap flows in drops, at the rate of from thirty to a hundred in a minute, and from three to four gallons will make a pound of sugar.

937. The holes bored in a maple tree will close up in two or three years, and do not appear to injure the growth of the trees. They may be tapped annually from the time when they are ten or twelve inches in diameter till they are seventy or eighty years old, and a maple grove kept inclosed against cattle may be used perpetually for sugar-making, the young trees coming on to replace those that are cut at full maturity.

938. The wood of the sugar maple is highly valued as a fuel and for cabinet work, and varieties known as "birds-eye" are highly valued for the making of veneers, affording some of the most beautiful of the woods used in ornamental work.

939. The Black Maple (*Acer nigrum*) is commonly regarded as only a variety of the *A. saccharium*, and is equally valuable for the making of sugar, and its timber for all the uses to which the sugar-maple is applied.

940. The Silver-leaf or River Maple (*Acer dasycarpum*). This and the next following species are often called "soft maples," or " white maples," from the texture and color of the wood. They bear fruit early in the season, and their seeds must be planted the same year, and while still fresh.

941. This species is planted extensively as a shade tree in the Middle and Western States, and grows very rapidly, but the wood being brittle, the trees are liable to injury by the winds. In rich alluvial soils it grows to a large size; but the tree is not long-lived, and its wood, although used for inside finishing and cabinet work, soon perishes when exposed to the weather.

942. The silver maple is less common in the South than the red maple. In North Carolina it grows sometimes thirty or forty feet high, and the sap is sometimes made into sugar, which has a su-

perior flavor and light color, but is not more than half as productive from a given measure of sap as the sugar maple of that region.

943. Red Maple (*Acer rubrum*). This tree derives its name from the color of its bright red blossoms, that appear early in the spring, and before the leaves. It is sometimes called "white maple," from the color of its wood, and "swamp maple," from its favorite place of growth. It does not generally grow to so large a size, nor live to so great an age as the sugar maple. Its wood is lighter and softer, but is often used in cabinet work. It is not durable when exposed to the weather. When the grain is wavy it has, when finished up, a beautiful glossy luster, affording the variety of fine woods known as the "curl maple."

944. The red maple is found from Canada to Florida and Louisirna, and through the Western States to Nebraska. It does not, in the regions further west, succeed under cultivation so well as the "silver-leaf maple." The sap of the red maple is not so sweet as that of the sugar maple, and is seldom used in making sugar. The young bark affords, with copperas as a mordant, a purplish-black dye, occasionally used in coloring wool and cotton.

945. In North Carolina this tree is found from the coast to the mountains, sometimes seventy feet high and three to four feet in diameter.

946. Striped Maple (*Acer Pennsylvanicum*). This is generally a small slender tree, seldom growing in groves, but scattered here and there among other woods, and never growing to a large size, or living to so great an age as some other maples. The wood is white and soft, and the bark smooth, greenish, and marked with stripes. It is sometimes called "moosewood," "dogwood," or "dogmackie." It may be cultivated for ornament, but is not generally successful unless partly shaded by other trees. In North Carolina this tree is found on the mountains as a shrub, rarely ten feet high.

947. The Mountain Maple (*Acer spicatum*). This is a shrub, generally growing in clumps from a common root, along rocky ravines in the Northern and Eastern States. It is too small for use, but will bear cultivation with other shrubs, in a rocky soil.

948. The Oregon or Large-leaved Maple (*Acer macrophyllum*). This tree grows from fifty to ninety feet in height, and from two to three feet in diameter, and is distinguished by the size of its leaves, which are occasionally a foot across, and usually from 6 to 10

inches. It seldom grows alone in much abundance, but is scattered through the evergreen forests, and seldom growing to as large a size as the sugar maple.

949. It occurs in mountain ravines from Santa Barbara northward to British Columbia, where it is found on Vancouver and adjacent islands, and on the immediate coast of the mainland, never inland, and scarcely beyond 55° north latitude. It there forms a small tree, sometimes a foot in diameter. In California it chiefly occurs on the Coast Range. The young branches present green stripes, not unlike those characteristic of the striped maple of the Atlantic States.

950. The wood is close-grained, hard, takes a beautiful polish, and the grain is sometimes twisted and curled, giving it a highly ornamental appearance.

951. THE VINE MAPLE (*Acer circinatum*). This is also peculiar to the Pacific Coast, growing in pine forests from Northern California to Oregon, and always near the coast. It is a shrub, growing sometimes 30 to 40 feet in height, and rarely a foot in diameter, and usually in several slender trunks springing from one root, as in the mountain maple of the Atlantic States. These do not grow upright, but, arching down, touch the ground, and there taking root, present a tangled thicket most difficult to penetrate. It prefers moist deep soils. Its leaves much resemble those of the sugar maple, and its wood is very tough and strong, heavy, white, close-grained, and sometimes twisted in its grain. It is used in making axe-helves and tool-handles, but is generally too small for cabinet work, although otherwise well adapted to this use.

952. THE SMOOTH MAPLE (*Acer glabrum*). This is an unimportant shrub, found from Colorado and New Mexico eastward to California, and from Yosemite northward. It is too small for useful purposes, and grows chiefly in damp mountain ravines.

953. THE BOX-ELDER, OR ASH-LEAVED MAPLE (*Negundo aceroides*). There are four species of the Negundo, of which the Atlantic States, the Pacific Coast, Mexico and Japan, have each one. It is so nearly allied to the maples that it has, by some botanists, been classed with them as the *Acer negundo.*

954. The box-elder, in the Atlantic States, is somewhat southern in its habits. In North Carolina it is found most common in the middle portion of the state, along the borders of the streams, grow-

ing from 15 to 25 feet in height. It is rare in the lower district. Further north it takes a larger growth, and it is found northward as far as Southern New York.

955. In the Western States, along the Mississippi and beyond, it grows well, and it occurs out on the plains, in the timber belts that fringe the rivers and streams, about as far west as any tree can be found.

956. Under its best conditions this tree grows to the height of 70 feet, but it is usually much less. It grows very rapidly, and comes to maturity in from twenty to thirty years. It is among the best of trees to cultivate for avenues and along public roads, and under cultivation it has produced some varieties having bleached and yellowish foliage, that gives it a fine appearance in ornamental planting.

957. Although it prefers low rich grounds, it bears a drouth very well, and in the more westerly states, on the borders of the Great Plains, it deserves much attention as easily propagated, and likely to succeed where many other kinds would fail.

958. In the Western and Northwestern States, the sap of this tree is made into sugar and syrup of excellent quality and flavor, but less in amount than that from the sugar maple.

959. As the staminate and pistilate flowers of the box elder grow upon different trees, the seeds must be gathered in groves where both kinds occur. The former are easily distinguished when in blossom by the stamens hanging in groups springing from common points, by slender hairy stems, with four or five anthers at the end, while the fertile blossoms show the rudiments of the future wings of the seed, and have two pistils coming out between them.

960. THE CALIFORNIA BOX ELDER (*Negundo Californiensis*). This is commonly a small tree, but rarely it grows to the height of 70 feet. It occurs along streams, following the coast range in California, from San Luis Obispo northward, but not into British Columbia. Its leaves are smaller and narrower than those of the other species, and they are more coarsely toothed; otherwise there is much resemblance between them.

THE LINDEN OR BASSWOOD FAMILY (*Tiliaceæ*).

961. About thirty genera belong to this family, chiefly occurring in the torrid and south temperate zones. They are mostly trees, often of great size, with handsome flowers and foliage, a mucilagin-

ous juice, and tough, stringy inner bark. Some of them yield a succulent and edible fruit. The wood is soft, light, and in some species very elastic. The jute of commerce, a much esteemed fibrous plant of annual growth, belongs to this natural order.

962. Europe has several native species of the *Tilia*, of which the *T. parvifolia* is supposed to be the only one native of Britain, although the *T. Europea*, *T. grandifolia*, and other species, have been long under cultivation, and trees occur several hundred years old. The tree is there chiefly propagated by layers, when raised for ornamental planting, and by this means various ragged-leaved, silver-leaved, and other curious varieties are continued.

963. The linden is a great favorite for ornamental planting in Holland and elsewhere in Europe. The large leaved species grows to the largest size, and reaches the greatest age. In Russia, the inner bark of the basswood is made into textile fabrics, cordage, and the like. The wood is sometimes ground into pulp for paper.

964. Our common basswood, linden, or lime-tree of the Atlantic States and Canada (*Tilia Americana*), is by far the most widely distributed of the four species found native in the United States. It grows to a large size, but when old is very apt to become hollow. The wood is very white, light, uniform in texture, not liable to crack or split, is quite tough, and when sawn into thin boards, may be readily bent into curves. It is much prized for cabinet wares and the panels of carriages, and its lumber is much used for carving and for finishing the inside work of houses, but it does not bear exposure to the weather well, unless painted. When thoroughly seasoned and painted, it makes an excellent material for outside work, as it receives and holds the paint well.

965. The basswood, when standing alone, takes a finely rounded form, and it is one of the best of trees for avenues. The blossoms abound in honey, and in bee-keeping this tree affords a most excellent source of supply.

966. The White Linns (*Tilia heterophylla* and *T. alba*) and the Southern Linn (*T. pubescens*) are much less widely distributed, being southern and western, and the latter a tree of large size.

967. The basswood loves a deep, rich, and humid soil, and under favorable conditions it grows quite rapidly. It is generally considered an indication of a good soil. It seldom occurs in groves by itself, but is scattered among other deciduous trees, often in clumps,

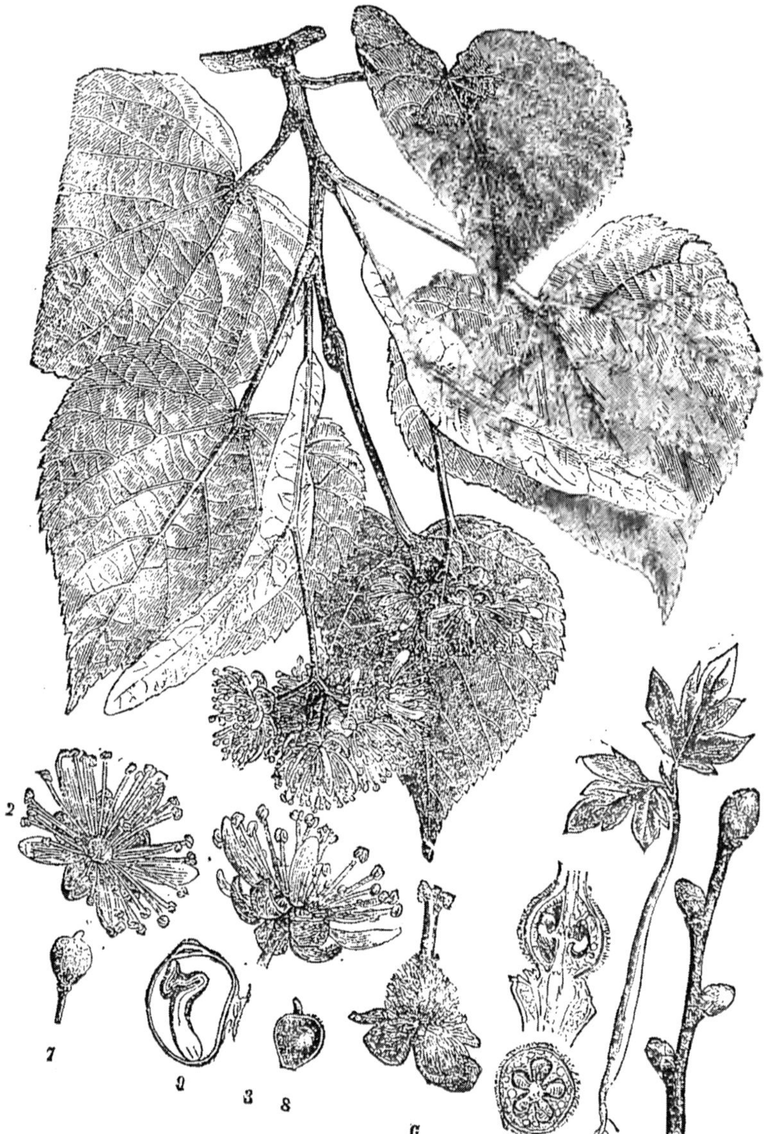

131. *Tilia parvifolia:* The Small-leaved Basswood. 1. A sprig, with blossoms and leaves. 2, 3. The blossoms from upper and under points of view. 4. 5. Transverse and longitudinal sections of a fruit-bud. 6. Pistil. 7. The fruit. 8. Section of the same. 9. Section of the seed. 10. Twig, with buds. 11. Young sprout.

as if from sprouts that have come up around a tree that has decayed. It is easily cultivated from the seed, which should generally be planted in the autumn of the same year that they ripen. For ornamental planting, they should be started in seed-beds, and then transplanted into nursery rows.

THE ELMS (Genus *Ulmus*).

968. About sixteen species and numerous varieties of the elm are known to botanists, chiefly in the north temperate zone of both continents, or upon mountains within the tropics. They are for the most part trees of rapid growth, and attaining a large size, and the wood is strong, tough, fibrous, difficult to split, and useful for a great variety of purposes. It is generally very durable under water, and its quality is much influenced by the conditions of soil, humidity, and temperature under which it has grown. The seeds ripen early in summer, and should be sown the same year.

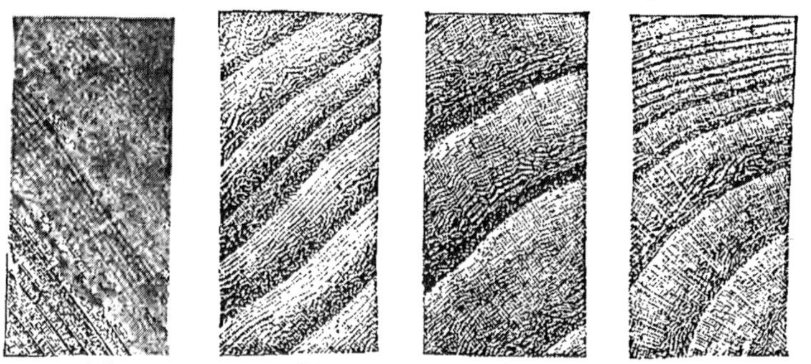

(*a.*) (*b.*) (*c.*) (*d.*)

132. *Differences in the Growth of Elms.*—Sections of the Elm: (*a.*) From Canada—The layers of growth so thin that they can scarcely be distinguished. (*b.*) From Dunkirk, France—Wood very strong, and grown in deep humid soil. (*c.*) From the battle-field of Toulon—Grown on a sub-soil that is very damp, but owing to the heat of the climate the wood is strong. (*d.*) From Provence, France—Grown on soil that is less humid.

969. THE WHITE ELM (*Ulmus Americana*). This tree is justly valued as one of the best for ornamental plantations, and one of the most graceful in form. The branches generally divide at ten or fifteen feet above the ground, and gradually diverging as they rise, spread out on every side and then descend, giving the tree an urn-shaped form, that at once distinguishes it at a great distance from all other forest trees. Some of the New England towns and villages, especially along the Connecticut river, present magnificent avenues of this tree.

970. The quality of the wood is generally excellent, as it is very

tough, strong, and flexible. It is much used for hoops, carriage and wagon making, cheese boxes, and bent-work generally, and is an excellent timber in carpentry, but very apt to shrink and warp when sawn into boards.

971. The "Rock Elm," as a variety of this species is called, is particularly prized for wagon hubs, and although this tree occurs from the Carolinas to Canada, and westward to the Mississippi, the best qualities for this use are found in New England and New York. A fine quality is also found in some parts of Pennsylvania, Ohio, and Indiana. In the rock elm, about five feet of the butt is all that can be used for hubs, and the best qualities are found in trees grown in an open space and freely exposed to the sun and air. For this use the trees should be cut in December or January. The inner bark should be left on, and the sticks should not be left long on the ground. After remaining in cross-piles for two months, they should be cut into blocks for further curing, and the ends dipped in melted lard and rosin, to prevent them from checking. In this condition they should be left under shelter till dry.

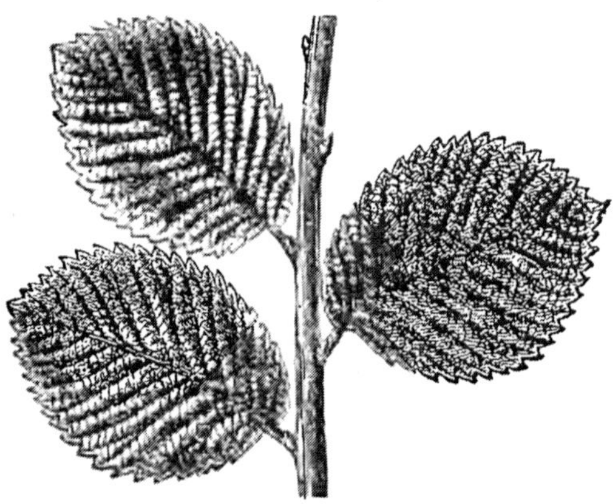

133. Leaves of the Red Elm.

972. The Slippery or Red Elm (*Ulmus fulva*). This tree, is scattered over most of the Northern and Western States. It grows to a large size, but has not the graceful form of the common American elm. The wood is very durable, when not in contact with the ground, and is of a reddish tinge, that gives it the common name. The leaves are coarser and more corrugated than the kind above mentioned, and the inner bark is highly mucilaginous when

steeped in water, giving it valuable medicinal properties, as a demulcent drink, and for emollient poultices. This material, when thoroughly dried, cut small, and ground in a mill, is an article of commerce, and is kept by most druggists.

973. A writer in Iowa, in speaking of the cultivation of the red elm remarks, that this tree has not received the attention that it merits, and sums up its good qualities as follows:

1. It is hardy, even in the most exposed position on the prairies.
2. It grows on rich soil with great rapidity.
3. The seeds are easily gathered, and require no great skill in handling and planting.
4. It is unusually free from disease and injury from insects.
5. It has a large proportion of heart-wood, even when young.
6. When grown thickly in groves, it runs up straight and tall, and when the poles are large enough to split for two rails, it may be divided as easily as the chestnut. When laid as rails, or nailed to posts, they are very durable.
7. When large enough for vine-stakes, if cut in summer, peeled, and dried before setting, they will last well.

974. The Cork Elm (*Ulmus racemosa*). This derives its name from the corky excrescences on the bark of the young twigs and small branches, although this character is far from being constant, nor is it limited to this species. This tree occurs in New England, New York, and westward, and often grows to a large size. Its foliage is of a darker green, and its wood harder, stronger, and more durable than that of the preceding species.

975. The Small-leaved Elm (*Ulmus alata*), sometimes called the "wahoo," is a southern species, and grows to a smaller size than the white or red elm, but it has a very compact wood, which is much used for the naves of wheels, and is even preferred to the black-gum for this purpose. From the inner bark a rope is sometimes made, which has been used in bagging cotton.

976. The English Elm (*Ulmus campestris*). This is a favorite tree for ornamental planting in Great Britain, and has been introduced in many parts of the United States. Some of the finest elms in Boston are of this species. As to its merits for city planting Mr. Emerson remarks: "I have been unable to compare satisfactorily the rapidity of its growth with that of the American elm, but probably in its best condition the latter is of far more rapid growth, although in

the ordinary situations where the elm is planted, and where it generally suffers from insufficiency of root moisture, the European elm is immeasurably its superior in rapidity of growth, length of life, and general thriftiness. The fact that the European is fully a

134. *Ulmus campestris*—English Elm.

month longer in leaf than the American elm, that its tougher leaves would seem to offer a less appetizing food to the canker-worm, the greatest enemy to the American elm in New England, and its adaptability to all situations are strong arguments in favor of giving the preference to the former for general cultivation. Its thriftiness in smoky situations makes the European elm the most valuable tree our climate will allow for city, street, and square planting, and as a shade tree by road-sides no American tree is its equal."[1]

977. The quality of the timber of this species is acknowledged to be superior to that of our native species, and it well deserves attention for cultivation as a timber-tree. All of the elms afford in their ashes a large amount of potash, and hence a top dressing of wood ashes is of great advantage in their cultivation.

978. THE WYCH ELM (*Ulmus montana*). This is also a European species, often planted in parks. It grows to a large size, and more resembles the red than the white elm.

THE PLANERA (*Planera aquatica*).

979. This is a southern tree, found growing in river swamps from North Carolina southward. It has the general habit of the elms, but is of no special importance in forest-culture.

THE OSAGE ORANGE (*Maclura aurantiaca*).

980. This tree, sometimes called *bois-d'arc* (bow-wood), is found native in the South-western States, in Texas, Arkansas, and Indian Territory, sometimes growing to the height of fifty to seventy feet, and to a diameter of three or four feet. The wood is there found to be extremely durable for stakes and posts, and is much prized for wagon-making, on account of its hardness and slight tendency to shrink. In its native region it grows best on a strong alluvial soil, but grows well in other situations, excepting where the soil is damp, and without drainage. It begins to bear fruit when about eight years old, and the ripe "apples" are readily eaten by cattle.

981. It can be cultivated for timber in the South-western States very successfully in strong bottom lands, by preparing the land, planting and cultivating for the first year or two, in the same way as for corn. They must be thinned out to 12 or 16 feet apart, and be trimmed up, in order to secure a straight body and a fine growth, but not more than is necessary to prevent the branches from interlocking or crowding too close. When standing alone, it makes a low spreading tree, with but little trunk. It therefore requires side-shading or trimming to make it grow high. As grown in the

[1] *Agriculture of Mass.*, 1875–6, p. 272.

south-west, it makes a fire-wood of the best quality, nearly or quite equal to hickory.

982. The sap-wood is perishable, but the heart-wood is *very* durable. If cut in winter or spring, it is liable to the attack of borers, but generally not when cut in August or early in autumn. The wood is very easily split, and is therefore unfit for hubs, although very suitable for spokes. From its great durability when exposed to the weather, it is very well adapted for agricultural implements. The wood has a very rich orange color, becoming darker with age, and rendering it valuable for ornamental cabinet work.

983. The osage orange is not a tree of rapid growth. It will require from twelve to fifteen years for it to become large enough for fence-posts, and some twenty-five or thirty years for railroad ties. From its hardness and tendency to split, it is necessary to bore holes before driving spikes. When planted at four feet apart, it will need cultivation for four or five years, and it will need to be thinned out in from eight to twelve years, according to the stage of its growth and the fertility of the soil. As the staminate and pistilate flowers of the osage orange grow in different trees, the seeds must be gathered in its native region, where both sexes of the tree are found growing. But one species is known to botanists.

The Mulberry (Genus *Morus*).

984. Some writers describe from ten to twelve species of this genus, while others reduce them to five. They are found in the north temperate zone, and within the tropics of both the old and new world, and are of great economical interest from the fact that their leaves form the principal food of the silk-worm.

985. We have within the United States a native species, the Red Mulberry (*Morus rubra*), that is widely diffused, being found in most of the Atlantic States, and sometimes growing to the height of sixty to seventy feet, with a diameter of two feet. The wood is strong, solid, and durable, and much valued as fence-posts, and for ship-building. From experiments that have been made in the feeding of silk worms upon the leaves of the red mulberry, it appears that the quantity of silk produced is less, and that the worms are more liable to disease.

986. The White Mulbery (*Morus alba*) has been introduced in many places, under the name of "*Morus multicaulis*," for the feeding of silk worms, and a mania of speculation led to attempts at its cul-

tivation in many regions where a little reason would have shown that it was utterly hopeless. The white mulberry is made to grow without difficulty in most parts of the Middle, Southern, and Western States, and, under intelligent direction, the silk industry may doubtless in many places be carried on with profit. It is propagated

135. The Mulberry Leaves and Fruit.

by cutting and layers, and requires a warm, dry soil, and will succeed in almost any place that will bear a good corn crop. There are many varieties under cultivation, and many special publications have been issued, giving directions for their management.

987. THE RUSSIAN MULBERRY. This tree, which seems to be closely allied to the *Morus nigra*, or black mulberry, and the *M. Tartarica*, a native of Russia, has in recent years been introduced by Mennonite emigrants, and is found to thrive very well in the Western States. Trees six years old are found eight inches in diameter and sixteen feet high. The berries may be eaten fresh, or made into jellies, wine, and preserves. Most of them are black, but some of a reddish white, with an aromatic odor and sub-acid, sweetish taste.

988. The Mennonites set this as a hedge plant, and its leaves are said to be valuable for feeding silk worms. It is easily transplanted, and the timber is excellent for fence posts. For hedges, the plants should be set a foot apart, and they should be kept cut back to

make them thicken up and spread at the bottom. It may be cultivated alone or with other timber in groves, and it makes, when set alone, a handsome street or lawn tree. The Russian mulberry is thought by some to be more valuable than the gray willow or the cottonwood, it being useful from its shelter, its fruit, and its wood. It is grown from cuttings.

THE HACKBERRY (Genus *Celtis*).

989. Over seventy species of this genus are found in the Torrid and North Temperate Zones of both hemispheres. The *C. orientalis*, most cultivated in Europe, much resembles the beech in appearance and in the color of the bark. Its wood is very hard, but is not much cultivated as a forest tree. It is sometimes called the "nettle-tree."

990. The American hackberry (*C. occidentalis*) is somewhat southern in its native locality, but is found scattered here and there throughout the Northern, Middle, and Western States. When planted, it starts very slowly at first, but when it has passed a certain stage of delay, it will start and grow vigorously. It extends from New England and Canada to Oregon, and southward to Florida, Texas, and New Mexico. In the Wahsatch mountains, it grows to an elevation of from 4,200 to 6,500 feet above tide. It is one of the species that deserves attention in planting upon the western plains.

THE TULIP-TREE (*Liriodendron tulipifera*).

991. This tree belongs to the magnolia family, and is known by various popular names, as the "white-wood," the "yellow poplar," and the "tulip-poplar." It is the only species belonging to the genus. It grows to a magnificent size, with a cylindrical trunk, an open, rounded head, a dark, ash-colored bark, somewhat square, truncated, deciduous leaves, and large, greenish-yellow, but not fragrant flowers. The bark of the root and branches is bitter and aromatic, acting as as a diaphoretic and tonic, and is sometimes used in the treatment of intermittent fever and chronic rheumatism. These properties are extracted by alcohol, or it may be used as a powder.

992. It affords a lumber of great excellence for floors, ceiling, and cabinet work, and for inside finishing, but it does not, unless protected by paint, endure well in the open air. Being soft and easily worked, it takes the place of pine for inside work of houses, and paper has been made from the bark.

993. In speaking of the uses of this wood, Mr. Emerson remarks:[1] "In New England, it is preferred to all other kinds of wood, in all uses which require great flexibility, as about stairs, for the wash-board, in circular rooms, and for the panels of carriages; also for the bottom of drawers, and for panels in common wardrobes, and other small articles."

994. The tulip-tree grows to magnificent size, preferring a moist, rich soil, and in good situations it grows to 100 and even 150 feet in height, and from six to nine and even ten feet in diameter.

995. The nature of the soil has an effect on the color and quality of the wood, and in West Virginia, where it grows to great perfection, mechanics class the wood as white, blue, or yellow, but these can not be determined by external signs. The white variety prefers a dry, elevated, and gravelly ground; it has a branching head, with a small amount of heart-wood, and has a coarser and harder grain and a less durability than the other varieties. The blue has nearly the same characters. The yellow is by far the finest, and is extensively used for lumber and shingles. It affords a good foundation for veneers, and is much used in cabinet work.

996. The tulip-tree is readily propagated from seed, and should be sown in a fine, soft mold, in a cool and shady place. If sown in the same autumn of its growth, it will germinate the next spring; but if sown in spring, it may not sprout till the next year.

997. This tree is rather difficult to transplant, and the end of the root should be cut off with a sharp knife when it is taken from the seed-bed and set in a new place. The development of lateral fibers may be encouraged in the same manner as we elsewhere describe for the oak. The tulip-tree occurred native in Canada, west of the Niagara river, but much of it has been cut away.

THE PLANE-TREE, BUTTONWOOD, OR SYCAMORE (Genus *Platanus*).

998. This is the only genus of the natural order *Plataneæ*, and it embraces five or six species, natives of the Northern Hemisphere, in the Old World and the New. They are of rapid growth, and, for the most part, thrive only along river banks and in deep, rich, alluvial soil.

999. The COMMON BUTTONWOOD of the Atlantic States (*Platanus occidentalis*) has a wide range in the Atlantic States, and grows to a

[1] "*Trees of Massachusetts*," 2d ed., p. 606.

large size in rich and humid soils along the rivers and in low grounds, reaching its greatest development in the Western and South-western States. In Canada, it is chiefly limited to the peninsula west of Niagara river. When found of a very large size, it is very often quite hollow, but this does not prevent it from growing to a great age.

1000. This tree is distinguished by the smoothness and whiteness of its bark in the middle and upper part of its trunk and branches. The outer bark falls off in large, irregular scales, leaving a surface which, in winter, is very white, but gradually becomes darker colored. This striking feature in winter enables one to observe the course of a stream for a great distance by the line of sycamores along its banks.

1001. The seeds of this tree form a compact, spherical ball, which remains on till spring, when it falls off and the seeds scatter, just as the leaves are about to open. This tree is very easily cultivated, and bears the smoke and dust of cities better than many other kinds, perhaps from the shedding of its outer bark from time to time.

1002. Our native plane-tree is perfectly naturalized in Europe, and grows rapidly and to a great size. It is chiefly planted along public roads and canals, and in parks and pleasure grounds, growing best on deep, humid soils, and in sheltered localities. The wood is much esteemed for cabinet wares, and for this use is reputed as durable as the oak, but it does not bear exposure to the weather well. The sycamore is easily propagated from the seed, or from cuttings or layers. The seedlings need protection at first, but they grow rapidly, and will bear transplanting early.

1003. The Mexican Sycamore (*P. racemosa*) is found extending into Southern California, and grows to a majestic tree, sometimes six feet in diameter and a hundred feet high. Like the species in the Atlantic States, it thrives along rivers, its bark exfoliates in large flakes, and its general habit is much the same. The leaves are, however, more deeply cut, polished, and of darker green, and the bark remarkably white. The fruit grows in racimes of from three to six, instead of being solitary, as in the common species. The wood is very brittle.

1004. The Oriental Plane-Tree (*P. orientalis*), in its native climate, grows to magnificent size, but as cultivated in Europe it does not equal our common American species. It is said to have been introduced into England about the middle of the sixteenth century, and is often found in parks, but is not valued as a timber-tree.

136. Cross-section of the Wood of the *Platanus orientalis.*

137. *Platanus racemosa.* (Leaf and Fruit, one-half the Natural Size.)

The Horse-Chestnuts, Buckeyes, etc. (Genus *Æsculus*).

1005. The genus Æsculus embraces about fifteen species, half of which occur in North America, and the rest in Asia. Their bark is bitter and astringent, and has been used in some species for tanning. The seeds contain a bitter principle that renders them unpalatable, but it is said that starch has been made from them that was equal to that from wheat.

1006. THE HORSE-CHESTNUT (*Æsculus hippocastanum*). This is a native of Asia, but is found perfectly well adapted to the Northern and Middle States, and is noted for the beauty of its flowers and its stately and rapid growth. It is better suited for lawns than for avenues, and is not of much value as a timber-tree. There are a considerable number of varieties distinguished by the color of the foliage and blossoms, and the habit of growth.

138. The Horse-chestnut Tree.

1007. THE OHIO BUCKEYE (*Æsculus glabra*). This tree grows from Western Pennsylvania and Virginia westward to beyond the Mississippi, and is most abundant in Ohio, Indiana, and Kentucky. It is a small tree, with a rough bark, which has an unpleasant odor. Its fruit is less than half the size of that of the horse-chestnut.

1008. THE SWEET OR BIG BUCKEYE (*Æsculus flava*). This occurs in the Western States and on the mountains in the Southern States, as a tree from 60 to 80 feet in height, and 3 to 4 feet in diameter. Upon the lowlands in the south it is a shrub from 3 to 6 feet high. It prefers the banks of rivers, and is an indication of a rich soil. The seeds are larger than those of the common horse-chestnut.

1009. THE SMALL BUCKEYE (*Æsculus pavia*). This is a shrub from 3 to 10 feet high, found growing in fertile valleys from Virginia southward to Georgia, and westward to Arkansas. It sometimes grows to a small tree. The root is used as a substitute for soap.

1010. The *Æsculus parviflora* is a small shrub found in South Carolina and Georgia, from 2 to 4 feet high, with a fruit said to be edible.

1011. THE CAIFORNIA BUCKEYE (*Æsculus Californica*). This is a shrub seldom growing more than twenty feet high, or more than a foot in diameter. It puts forth flowers in successive crops during most of the spring and summer, and for this reason may be desirable for ornamental planting, although of no account as a timber-tree, as its wood is soft and brittle. It occurs from San Luis Obispo to Mendocino Co. and Mt. Shasta, and on the foot-hills of the Sierra Nevada Mountains.

1012. THE TEXAS BUCKEYE (*Ungnadia speciosa*). This occurs in Texas, where it forms a small shrub or tree, with brittle wood, alternate and unequally pinnate leaves, and showy rose-colored blossoms. The seeds are sweet-tasted like the walnuts, but are said to possess emetic properties. It somewhat resembles the hickories in its leaves, but more the horse-chestnut in its fruit.

1013. THE SOAPBERRY (*Sapindus saponaria*). This is a small tree, growing upon the coast of South Carolina and Georgia, from 20 to 50 feet in height. It derives its name from the soap-like properties of the fruit, which, when pounded up, forms a lather with soft water, and may be used instead of soap. When bruised and thrown into water, the fruit will intoxicate fish. This tree belongs to the same family as the buckeyes. There are one or two other species in the southwest. There are about forty species of the Sapindus known, chiefly found in the tropical and sub-tropical climates, in which alone it can be cultivated with success.

THE LOCUST.

1014. THE COMMON LOCUST (*Robinia pseudacacia*). This is sometimes called the "black locust," the "yellow locust," or the "false acacia," and occurs native west of the Alleghenies from Pennsylvania to Arkansas. In the Carolinas, it is found native only in the

139. Leaves and Flower of the *Æsculus Californica*, of one-half the Natural Size. (See page 255.)

lower mountain ridges, but it is thought that it once grew wild at some distance east of the Blue Ridge, where it is not now found in its native state.

1015. It is widely diffused by cultivation in all the Atlantic States and in Europe. The rapidity of its growth, the beauty of its blossoms, the solidity and durability of its wood, have heretofore led to high expectations of great profit in its planting; and in the early settlement of the prairie region of Illinois and elsewhere, it was for many years a great favorite.

1016. These hopes were in many regions so effectually disappointed by the "borers" that the trees not wholly destroyed by them were to a great extent cut down, and the planting discontinued. The most destructive of these borers are the larvæ of the *Cyllene picta*,[1] already noticed [§ 721], although there are two or three other species that commit great injuries. One of these is a little reddish caterpillar, that bores into the pith of the twigs, which become spongy and brittle. Another is a large grub of an insect, which in its perfect state is a moth. These bore upwards and downwards, in oblique directions, in the solid wood, the holes increasing in size as they grow, and finally coming through the bark to the outside of the trunk.

1017. The locust does not generally succeed well when grown in company with other trees. It is, however, thought by some that when planted alternately with the box-elder, it is less liable to the attack of borers.[2] The age at which a locust coppice should be cut depends much on the uses to which it is to be applied. At ten or fifteen years it yields excellent poles for fencing and other use, but the timber is of greatest value when kept properly thinned out, at forty or fifty years. Upon the banks of streams, and in light shifting sands, it takes a remarkable growth, as it also does upon sheltered slopes in a hilly region, where it gets a good exposure to the air and light. It is more profitable to plant it in clumps or groups in these favorite spots than over great areas. Its strong tendency to sprout renders it inconvenient on the borders of cultivated grounds.

1018. The locust, under cultivation, produces many varieties, some with upright and others with pendant or twisted and deformed branches. It is in some varieties thornless, and in others the leaves

[1] Known as the *Cossus Robinae*, as named by Professor Peck, by whom it was supposed that it remained three years in the caterpillar state The same insect, or some one very nearly like it, perforates the trunks of the red oak.

[2] *Iowa Forestry Annual*, 1881, p. 15.

are crisped or otherwise deformed, and the flowers assume various yellow and pink colors, and different sizes and forms of growth. From its tracing roots it sends up sprouts in great abundance, and it may be propagated from these with great facility.

1019. The wood of the locust is fine grained, yellowish, hard, and very durable. For this reason, it is much used for trenails of vessels. It is also very durable as posts and for studding of wainscots in damp situations.

1020. THE CLAMMY LOCUST (*Robinia viscosa*). This is a small tree, native in the mountains from Southern North Carolina to Georgia, where it grows to the height of forty-feet. It derives its name from a glandular-viscid secretion upon the pods, leaf-stems, and twigs.

1021. THE ROSE-LOCUST (*Robinia hispida*). This is a small and hispid species, found upon the mountains of the Carolinas and Georgia and in pine barrens. It is sometimes cultivated for ornament, the blossoms being twice the size of the common locust and of a rose-red tinge.

1022. KENTUCKY COFFEE-TREE (*Gymnocladus Canadensis*). This tree, one of the leguminous family, grows native in the Western States, and to great perfection in Kentucky and the southern parts of Ohio, Indiana, and Illinois. It occurs in Western New York and west of the Niagara river in Cañada, and extends westward to Nebraska. Under the most favorable conditions, it grows from sixty to eighty feet in height. The bark is rough, the branches stout and abruptly terminated, appearing in winter like a dead tree. It has doubly pinnate leaves, a dense fine-grained wood, suitable for cabinet work. It is readily propagated from the seeds, but these must be scalded and left soaking in warm water for some hours before planting.

1023. THE HONEY-LOCUST (*Gleditschia tricanthos*). This tree is found widely diffused, but grows to greatest size in the Southern States. It is nowhere abundant, but often cultivated for ornament, and affords an excellent tree for hedges. In favorable circumstances, it grows to the height of fifty feet or more, with a diameter of two to three feet. The wood is hard, close-grained, and suitable for many uses in manufactures, and is said to be very durable when used as posts. It extends westward into Iowa and Nebraska, and southward to Mississippi.

1024. This species offers many inducements for planting. It is not troublesome from sprouting, as is the common locust; it is far less liable to insect injuries, and after the first year it is hardy. It bears transplanting much more easily than most other trees.

1025. THE WATER-LOCUST (*Gleditschia monosperma*). This is a small tree, growing in swamps along the Gulf States and as far northward as Southern Illinois. It is of but small size, and the wood of little value.

1026. RED-BUD OR JUDAS-TREE (*Cercis Canadensis*). This is a small but highly ornamental tree, which is covered in spring with bright red blossoms. One of its common names was given by Gerard, an old English gardener (1596), who says that "this is the tree whereon Judas did hange himselfe, and not upon ye elder, as it is said." The common European species is the *C. siliquastrum.*

1027. The red-bud is found native on river banks from New Jersey southward to Florida, and in the Western States. It grows to the height of from 15 to 30 feet, and is often cultivated for ornament. The small, deep, rose-colored flowers appear before the leaves, in clumps of 4 to 8, in March and April. The fruit has an acid taste.

THE ACACIAS.

1028. The genus *Acacia* numbers about 400 species, chiefly found in warm climates, and most abundant in Australia and Africa. We have about a dozen native species, chiefly herbaceous, on the southern borders of the United States, and one (*A. Greggii*) in California. Several species of the WATTLE (*Acacia pycnantha*—the "broad leaf," "golden," and "green" wattle; *A. decurrens*, the "black" wattle; and *A. dealbata*, or "silver" wattle) are extensively used in Australia, and exported from thence as a tanning material. The wattles grow readily on loose, sandy soil, and might be cultivated in the milder regions of the United States, and especially on the Pacific coast.

1029. The wood is tough, hard, and durable, and is used for staves, spokes of wheels, tool handles, and many other purposes. The acacias exude a gum that has commercial value, and furnish excellent firewood. The quality of the bark for tanning depends much upon the soil, and it is of much less value when grown upon a limestone formation. The tree is not long lived, and it is at its prime when about ten years old, at which age the wood is nine or ten inches in diameter. In extreme cases, it becomes two feet thick. The yield of tanning extract varies from thirty to forty-five per cent.

1030. THE VICTORIA MYALL (*Acacia homalophylla*). This has a dark-brown wood, and is much used for turner's work, and is valued on account of its solidity and fragrance. It is also much used for the manufacture of tobacco pipes.

1031. THE BLACKWOOD (*A. melanoxylon*) grows on river flats and in moist, fertile valleys. In irrigated valleys and a deep soil, it will attain a height of eighty feet, and several feet in diameter. The wood is prized for furniture, railway carriages, boat building, billiard tables, the sounding-boards of pianos, etc., and for veneers. It takes a fine polish, and is fully equal to the best of walnut. It bends very well when steamed.

1032. YELLOW-WOOD (*Cladrastis tinctoria*). This species, described by Michaux as the "*Virgilia latea*," and often known among nurserymen as the "virgilia,"[1] occurs native in deep, fertile soil in Western Tennessee and in Kentucky, growing, as a tree, from twenty to forty feet high, and sometimes a foot in diameter. It has a smooth, greenish bark, and a yellow heart-wood, which imparts its color to water, and is used as a domestic dye. It bears large, white flowers, and is cultivated successfully for ornament in the middle latitudes, and as far north as Central New York.

THE PEARS AND APPLES (Genus *Pirus*).

1033. This numbers about forty species, natives of the North Temperate Zone, and widely cultivated for their fruit. In some cases, they are valuable for their wood, which is solid, fine-grained, and of uniform texture; well adapted for turning, and for certain kinds of wood-engraving, although much inferior to the boxwood. It makes an excellent fuel, and in some regions it may be cultivated profitably for this use.

1034. In the open country east of the Cascade mountains in Washington Territory, it appears to be particularly well adapted for

[1] The *Virgilia* is a distinct genus, not represented in the native flora of the United States. The *V. capensis* is a tree growing in South Africa. There is but one other species of the *Cladrastis*, and that grows in Mantchoura, in Asia.

this use, and the Surveyor-General of that Territory, in a report made in 1881, says that a grove of apple or pear trees, if set out at twelve feet apart, will attain a wonderful height in a few years. The fruit will be worthless, but the timber will grow straight and tall, if the bodies are thus kept shaded; and adds: "I doubt if more valuable timber could be grown, for either fuel or manufacturing purposes, all things considered. Such trees would grow wherever planted with but little care or expense."

1035. THE MOUNTAIN ASH (*Pirus Americana*). This species grows in high northern latitudes, from Greenland and Labrador to the Pacific coast, and in the New England and Northern States. It is generally found upon mountains, and grows to a small tree. The fruit, which is red, remains on during the winter, and it is often cultivated for ornament. It much resembles the European mountain ash (*P. aucuparia*), but does not grow to so large a size. The latter grows freely throughout the Northern States under cultivation, and is highly ornamental when in fruit.

140. Leaves, Flowers, and Fruit of the Mountain Ash.

1036. THE SWEET-SCENTED CRAB TREE (*Pirus coronaria*). This tree grows in Western New York, and as far west as Iowa, and southward to Georgia and Louisiana. It forms a tree from ten to twenty feet high, and is sometimes cultivated. The fruit, when ripe, is an inch to an inch and a half in diameter, greenish-yellow, somewhat translucent, and extremely acid.

1037. THE OREGON CRAB-APPLE (*Pirus rivularis*). This occurs as a shrub, usually forming dense thickets, but sometimes growing as a tree from 15 to 25 feet in height, and a foot in diameter, from Alaska southward along the islands and the mainland as far as Sonoma county, California. It has a very hard wood, susceptible of a fine polish, and useful in mill work, where there is great wear. Its fruit is prized by the Indian for food.

1038. THE WESTERN MOUNTAIN ASH (*Pirus sambucifolia*). This is a small shrub, growing at great elevations upon the Sierras, and sparingly in various parts of the interior of British America. It is usually a shrub from 4 to 8 feet in height.

THE PLUMS AND CHERRIES (Genus *Prunus*).

1039. This numbers about eighty species, widely scattered over the North Temperate Zone, and of these some twenty are found in North America, and fourteen in the Atlantic States. Upon the Pacific coast, half a dozen species occur, all of them shrubs, and of but slight account either for their wood or their fruit. These species are often planted at great distances from the parent tree, their seeds being dropped undigested by birds.

141. *Wild Black Cherry.*—Leaves, Flowers, and Fruit.

1040. THE BLACK CHERRY (*Prunus serotina*). This tree, in a rich soil, grows very rapidly, and forms one of the most valued of our native woods for cabinet work. It is almost equal to mahogany, which it in some degree resembles when darkened by age. It grows readily from the seed, which may be planted in the fall or early in the spring, and they generally do best if started in the place where the tree is to remain. The bark, especially that of the roots, possess valuable tonic and sedative qualities, and afford the basis of various remedies sold in market. The leaves are also sometimes used in domestic medicine.

1041. This tree is found to be well adapted to prairie planting in Illinois, Iowa, and other Western States. In a deep, rich soil, it sometimes attains a great size. It is noticed that the fruit improves in quality and size under cultivation, and it begins to bear at an early age.

1042. Bird Cherry (*Prunus Pennsylvanica*). This tree grows to a small tree, but is short-lived, and its wood is too small and perishable to be much value for any purpose but fuel. It is very apt to spring up on land that has been burnt over; often intermingled with poplars, and gradually giving place to larger and more hardy kinds. The fruit grows in small clusters like the garden cherry. The cherries are small, acid, and a favorite food of birds, through whose agency the growth of this tree on a burnt district may be probably ascribed.

1043. The Choke-Cherry (*Prunus Virginiana*). This derives its name from the astringent property of its fruit, which grows in racimes like grapes or currents. This species grows in dense thickets, and not of sufficient size to be of value for its wood.

1044. The Carolina Plum (*Prunus Caroliniana*). This is a highly ornamental southern species, with evergreen foliage, and growing to a height of from thirty to fifty feet. It has a very regular oval head, and smooth branches. Its leaves are said to be very poisonous to cattle. It occurs on the coast and islands of the Carolinas and Georgia, and is well adapted for ornamental planting.

1045. The Chicasaw Plum (*Prunus Chicasa*). This is a native of the South-western States, but is extensively naturalized in the South, and is sometimes cultivated in the North. The fruit is small, and rather astringent, but runs into varieties, some of which are much prized. It has been sometimes cultivated as a hedge-plant, and is worthy of notice in tree-planting in the Western States.

Several other species of this genus grow in the United States, but none of them of much importance in forestry.

THE THORN-TREE (Genus *Cratægus*).

1046. Between sixty and seventy species occur in Europe, in Eastern Asia, and Japan, and in North America. About fifteen species are found in Canada, the United States, and Mexico. The quality of their wood is about the same as that of the apple-tree. They are of slow growth, and unimportant as timber-trees, but they are in some regions remarkably well adapted for hedges, being thorny, and very scraggly in their growth, presenting a thicket that is quite impenetrable by man or beast.

1047. Two species are found in California, viz., *C. rivalaris* and *C. Douglasii.* They are shrubs or small trees, the former growing to 10 or 15 feet, and the latter from 18 to 25 feet, with stout spines and black or dark purple fruit.

1048. THE SCARLET-FRUITED THORN (*Cratægus coccinea*). This thorn, when grown as a hedge-plant, should be trained to grow thin and tall, which can be done best by weaving in the branches in one direction, and trimming them in the other.

1049. DOTTED-FRUIT THORN (*Cratægus punctata*). This is a common species in the Atlantic States, growing naturally along the borders of rivers, and is easily transplanted. When properly trimmed and managed, it makes a superior hedge-plant. The fruit is dull red, or yellowish, and dotted, and the leaves are wedge-shaped, tapering below into a slender leaf-stem.

THE SERVICE-BERRY (Genus *Amelanchier*).

1050. Some four or five species of this genus are found in Southern Europe, Asia-Minor, Japan, and North America. Of these the *A. Canadensis*, variously known as the "shad-bush," "june-berry," etc., is common in the Atlantic States, and the *A. alnifolia* upon the Pacific coast. They are shrubs of small size, of no great interest to the forester. The wood of the western species is very hard, and is used by the Indians for various purposes. The berries are dried and stored away by them in large quautities for winter use.

THE EUCALYPTUS.

1051. Of the genus *Eucalyptus* (of the natural orders *Myrtaceæ*), about 150 species are described, chiefly natives of Australia and the Indian Archipelago, and of these the best known is the *E. globulus*. This was first discovered by Labillardière, in Tasmania, in 1792, but was not much noticed in Europe until 1861. M. Prosper Ramel, who had seen it growing in a botanical garden in Melbourne, was so impressed with its probable value for cultivation in Europe, that he sent the seeds to Paris in 1860, and attempts in planting were made the next year. It grew remarkably well, but was killed down in winter, and it is now well known that it can not survive the frost, at least not till the wood is several years old. It thrives, however, very well in Southern France, and is found peculiarly well adapted to cultivation in Algeria.

1052. It has been tried in many parts of the United States, but not with much success, excepting in California, where, within the influence of the coast climate, but not in the interior valleys, it thrives with great luxuriance, provided that the temperature never goes down below about 28° (F.). The influence of the sea-air appears to give it some immunity against frost.

1053. Under favorable conditions, the growth is truly wonderful. A section was shown at the Centennial Exhibition, in 1878, but eleven years old, that came from a tree sixty feet high and thirteen and a half inches in diameter at five feet from the ground.

1054. About twenty species of the eucalyptus have been tried in that state, of which half a dozen have been planted to some extent, and probably three-fifths of them are the "blue-gums" (*E. globulus*), the rest being chiefly the *E. viminalis*, *F. marginata*, and *E. rostrata*. Of these the first has attracted the most attention, on account of its rapid growth, although its timber is less valuable than some other hard-wooded species. It is estimated that six millions of this tree had been planted in the ten years preceding 1882, mostly in streets and yards, in cities, villages, and around dwellings.

1055. The *E. cornuta* and *E. gigantea* have shown a susceptibility to the frost quite equal to that of the *E. globulus*, although the *E. rostrata* and *E. viminalis* are more hardy. Of 120,000 trees planted at Tipton, and well-cared for, nearly all of the *E. globulus*, *E. cornuta*, and *E. gigantea* died within two years, and the *E. rostrata* thrived, but grew slowly.

1056. The texture of the wood thus rapidly grown is soft and sappy, as compared with that hardened by age, but it is highly probable that it would all the more readily admit of the injection of creosote, or the mineral salts in solution, that would render it hard, strong, and durable.

1057. The mature wood is rather pale, and not so ornamental as many others of the genus, but it takes a good polish, is hard, durable, and nearly equal to English oak as a building timber, but it will not bear contact with the soil or water as well as the red-gum, iron-bark, and box-eucalypts. It varies in solidity according to the conditions of its growth, and is sometimes too heavy to float. It is used in ship-building, carriage-making, and the manufacture of agricultural implements, and for telegraph poles and railway ties. In its native country it is a favorite material for fencing, and various farm uses.

1058. As to profit in the cultivation of the *Eucalyptus globulus* in California, we have returns of twenty acres cleared, when eleven years old, to make room for an orchard, in which after charging every item of cost, and a yearly rental of $5 per acre, the net profits were $3,866.04, or about $17.57 per acre annually. When used as fuel, the wood should be split immediately after felling, or otherwise it becomes soggy and worthless.

1059. In a paper presented at the American Forestry Congress at Cincinnati, in April, 1882, by Prof. R. E. C. Stearns, of the California State University, after presenting the leading facts in reference to tree-planting in that state with evident fairness, he adds: "If one-half of the trees planted, as represented by the preceding figures, are still living and growing, *the past has been really a very great success.* If new plantations are being made at the rate of say only 50,000 or 75,000 per annum, the present is full of promise, and the future full of hope."

1060. The seeds of the *E. globulus* are small (about 10,000 to an ounce), and will keep their vitality about four years. The lower leaves are broad and heart-shaped, but the upper ones turn edgewise, so as to present both sides to the light, and are long-pointed and curved flatwise. For this reason this tree does not shade the ground so much as most forest trees.

1061. The leaves, when rubbed, emit a strong aromatic odor, and afford by distillation an essential oil that is found to possess valuable medicinal qualities. About the year 1870, the exportation of this oil from Australia by a single manufacturer amounted to over 12,000 pounds. It is used also for scenting soaps, for diluting the oil of roses, and for other perfumes. The alcoholic extract of the leaves is found to be efficacious in intermittent fever, and the balsamic odors emitted while growing are believed to be salutary in certain diseases. From the rapidity of its growth, this tree evaporates a large amount of water that is taken up by the roots, and has a tendency by this means to promote the drainage of pestilential swamps.[1]

1062. In its native country the blue-gum grows to the enormous size of 400 to 500 feet in height, and over 80 feet in circumference. It even rivals the giant trees of California in height, but not in symmetry of proportion and in solid contents. Among the other species of this genus there are many that grow to colossal size, and some that excel in beauty and durability of the wood.

1063. THE EUGENIA belongs also to the allspice family (*Myrtaceæ*), and four or five species occur as small trees or shrubs in Southern Florida. The wood closely resembles that of boxwood, and is found to be equally suitable for wood-engraving. It is, however, of small size, and has not hitherto been brought into use for this purpose. An immense number of species of this genus have been described, of which about five hundred are deemed well characterized, and some two hundred others as less certain. They are chiefly natives of tropical and sub-tropical regions in Asia and America, and a few are found in Australia and Africa.

THE CORNEL FAMILY (*Cornaceæ*).

1064. This embraces about a dozen genera, and less than a hundred species, and is widely distributed throughout the north temperate zone. They are mostly unimportant shrubs, but some of

[1] In the autumn of 1881, the author visited the Abbey of Trois-Fontaines, near the city of Rome, and saw the operations of planting this tree that were going on, about 150 convicts being employed in the labor. The seeds are sown in boxes filled with rich soil, and the plants were taken out without disturbing the roots, and set in places first prepared, and well-watered. They need watering the first season, but afterwards will take care of themselves. The soil is excessively hard and dry. This region was so unhealthy that the abbey had been wholly abandoned. The planting began about 1868, and the place is now inhabited by a great number of persons, and in 1881, for the first time, the convicts were lodged upon the premises instead of being taken back to the city every night as formerly.

them grow to a useful size as trees. Their bark is bitter and tonic, and their wood generally very hard and fine-grained.

1065. Of the genus *Cornus*, we find in the United States about a dozen species. Of these in the Atlantic States the FLOWERING DOGWOOD (*C. florida*) is perhaps the most important, as well for cultivation as an ornamental tree, as for the solidity and excellence of its wood.

1066. The *C. Nuttallii* grows in California, and northward to British Columbia, to the size of 50 to 70 feet, and bears a showy blossom. Its wood is close-grained and hard, and it is well worthy of cultivation. There are about half a dozen other species of this genus in California.

THE SOUR-GUM (Genus *Nyssa*).

1067. This genus, also belonging to the *Cornaceæ*, of which five or six species are found in the north temperate zone, in North America, the Himalaya region, and Malay archipelago. The sandal-wood of commerce belongs to this family.

1068. THE PEPPERIDGE (*N. multiflora*) occurs in the Atlantic States from New England southward to the gulf coast. It is variously named the "tupelo," "hornbeam," "snag-tree," etc., and grows chiefly in swamps, and often to a large size. Its wood is exceedingly fibrous and difficult to split, and this quality renders it a valuable material for wagon-hubs, the best being found in the swamps of Maryland and the sea-coast of New Jersey, where it is found in perfection.

1069. When used for hubs, it should be cut in the early part of winter, and from five to ten feet from each tree, near the butt, may be taken. It should be at once deprived of the bark, and be cross-piled in dry open sheds for three years or more, until thoroughly dried. The best qualities are fined-grained, heavy, and the fibers of the wood are so woven together that it can scarcely be split by any force that can be applied.

1070. The wood is also, for this reason, much used for making packing-boxes that require great strength, and at Syracuse, N. Y., it is used in making pipes for distributing the brine at the salt works in that vicinity. Four other species of the *Nyssa*, occur in the Middle and Southern States.

THE ELDERS (Genus *Sambucus*).

1071. The two principal species of the elder found native in the United States are unimportant shrubs. One of them, the red-berried elder, (*S. pubens*) has sometimes an arborescent form, and is occasionally, but rarely, found 15 to 18 feet high. The *S. glauca* of California and Oregon is sometimes of this height, and from six inches to a foot in diameter. The Europeon elder (*S. racemosa* and *S. nigra*) grows to a tree of considerable size at the base, but not high in proportion, and the young branches are straight, and with a relatively large pith, as in the common elder (*S. Canadensis*) of the Atlantic States. Its berries are sometimes used in making pies, and their juice in making wine. Of the elders, about ten or twelve species are known, chiefly natives of temperate regions, except one or two found in South Africa and some upon mountains within the tropics. This genus and the following belong to the natural order *Caprifoliaceæ:*

HAW: SLOE: ARROW-WOOD (Genus *Viburnum*).

1072. Of this genus about eighty species are described, and about a dozen are native in the United States. They are, for the most part, unimportant shrubs, growing in swamps, or damp woods, but some of them preferring a dry situation, and occasionally they become small trees.

1073. The black haw (*V. prunifolium*) grows to the height of 20 feet, and the *V. lentago* to an equal size. Both have a wide range towards the north and west, and varieties of the former endure a dry climate quite well, and may help to make up some diversity in the forest culture of the western regions.

1074. The *Viburnum opulus* is the "high cranberry," sometimes cultivated for its fruit, or as an ornamental hedge-plant. A garden variety of this species, introduced from Europe, has large showy white flowers, all sterile, and is known as the "snow-ball bush." It is easily propagated by sprouts from the root, and by layers, and has a hard fine-grained wood.

1075. THE BUTTON-BUSH (*Cephalanthus occidentalis*), of the natural order *Rubiaceæ*, is an unimportant shrub, growing throughout the Northern and Western States and on the Pacific coast. It prefers the margins of swamps and a rich soil, and sometimes grows to a small tree, but is too small sized for any useful purpose. The fruit closely resembles in form that of the plane-tree, but is smaller. It is sometimes called the "pond dogwood."

THE SNOW-DROP, OR SILVER-BELL TREE (Genus *Halesia*).

1076. The family to which this tree belongs, (*Styraceæ*) contains but two genera within the United States, and this genus but five species, of which two are found in North America, one in China, and two or three in Japan. Our species are small trees, found in the Southern Atlantic States, and bear showy white flowers. They are often cultivated for ornament. The *H. diptera* is found in rich woods along the Gulf States: the *H. tetraptera* occurs in woods and along streams in West Virginia, and from Illinois to Florida, mostly upon or near mountains, and the *H. parviflora* is a southern species.

THE ASH (Genus *Fraxinus*).

142. Leaves, Flowers, and Fruit of the Ash.

1077. This belongs to the olive family (*Oleaceæ*), which includes, besides, the European olive, so valued for its fruit and oil, the Forsythias, lilacs, privets, and fringe-tree, that have been introduced for ornamental planting.

1078. The European ash (*Fraxinus excelsior*) is generally found growing with other kinds, and seldom alone. It thrives best in a warm climate, and is found, not only upon plains, but on slopes and plateaus of considerable size. It succeeds best, however, in the former, but not upon clay nor sand. It generally bears seeds early and abundantly every year. Its leaves are often gathered as forage. The wood is used to advantage in places always wet or always dry, but it does not bear alternate exposures. The timber is especially valued in carriage-making, and for various manufactures.

1079. The genus *Fraxinus* includes about a dozen species within the United States, the principal of which are the following:

1080. White Ash (*Fraxinus Americana*). This tree prefers a deep and somewhat damp soil, and grows in congenial situations rapidly and to a large size. The wood of second-growth white ash has, perhaps, no equal for lightness, elasticity, and strength, and is largely used for the handles of forks, rakes, etc., scythe snaths, agricultural implements, carriage-making, cooperage, and other manufactures, and when sawn into thin boards it furnishes a highly ornamental wood for joinery and carpenter work.

1081. The large "burls" that form on its trunk are especially valued for the making of veneers. The wood splits with great ease and regularity, and is much used for hoops, basket work, and the bottoming of chairs.

1082. The white ash ranks among our best timbers, where grown upon dry ground and under favorable conditions. The wood is light, strong, elastic, and durable. As grown in open ground, it gains rapidly in size, and the wood is of superior quality for scythe snaths, fork-handles, and in wagon-making. In a dry climate it does not grow as well as the green-ash, but the latter does not grow to so large a size.

1083. The ash is best raised from the seeds, which may be gathered in the fall, and kept in a cool damp place till spring. They may be planted like corn, but not over an inch in depth. They may be transplanted from nurseries with facility, but do not get so early a start as when planted where they are to remain. If planted in rows, about three feet apart and two feet between trees, in a cool and damp, but not wet soil, the alternate trees will, at the end of ten years, afford the best of hoop-poles, and afterwards, at intervals of ten or fifteen years, other thinnings of much greater value. As an ornamental tree, it thrives finely in full exposure, but the shade is not dense.

1084. The white ash grows in moist woods, from Canada to Florida and Louisiana. A variety (*microcarpa*), with remarkably small fruit, is found in Alabama, and another variety (*Texensis*, perhaps a distinct species), is found in Texas, near the Rio Grande.

1085. Black Ash (*Fraxinus sambucifolia*). This ash grows chiefly in swamps, and is distinguished by the greater number of its leaflets and the blunt appearance of its branches, as compared with those of the preceding species.

1086. This tree grows very commonly in the Eastern, Northern, and North-western States. The wood is not so valuable as that of the white ash, but is used for hoops, and the large knots upon the trunk are turned into bowls. It should never be planted upon dry land, but on the borders of swamps and in humid soils. It may be planted closely, for the thinnings have value from a small size, being suitable for hoop-poles, poles, etc., up to sizes suitable for fence-rails, rafters, and sills.

1087. The Green Ash (*Fraxinus viridis*) is a small or middle-sized tree, having much the same range as the white ash, and found well adapted to cultivation in the prairie region.

1088. The Blue Ash (*Fraxinus quadrangulata*) is a large timber-tree found growing in dry woods in the Western States, from Michigan to Tennessee. It derives its name from the bluish tinge which its inner bark gives to water when macerated in it.

1089. The Water Ash (*Fraxinus platycarpa*) is a middle-sized tree growing in swamps from Virginia to Louisiana.

1090. The Red Ash (*Fraxinus pubescens*), a middle or large-sized tree growing from Canada to Dakota, and south to Florida.

1091. The Oregon Ash (*Fraxinus Oregona*) is a low-spreading tree, common along the Columbia river and the upper part of the Sacramento Valley. It seldom grows more than a foot in diameter by thirty to forty feet in height.

1092. The following may be mentioned only by their botanical names, as of less importance, viz.:

Fraxinus anomala, a shrub or low tree in Southern Utah.

F. cuspidata, a shrub five to eight feet high in New Mexico.

F. dipetala, a small tree in Western California.

F. Greggii, a shrub five to eight feet high found on limestone soil in South-western Texas and the adjacent parts of Mexico.

F. pistaciæfolia, a small tree found in South-western Texas, and westward to Arizona.

THE OLIVE. (Genus *Olea*).

1093. This embraces about thirty-five species, found in tropical Asia and the region bordering upon the Mediterranean. The common European olive (*O. Europea*) has been long under cultivation in California, but not to considerable extent.

1094. THE WILD OLIVE of the Southern States (*Osmanthus Americana*) has about the same range as the live-oak, and is worthy of cultivation as affording some variety, but it does not grow to a large size.

THE LILAC. (Genus *Syringa*).

1095. Of this there are about half a dozen species, natives of Eastern Europe and Asia. They form desirable shrubs for cultivation, on account of the beauty and fragrance of their blossoms, but are of too small size to be important in forest culture.

THE WALNUT FAMILY. (*Juglandeæ*).

1096. This embraces five genera, and some thirty-two species, widely scattered over the northern hemisphere of both continents, and upon mountains within the tropics. The two genera of especial interest are the *Carya* and *Juglans*, or the hickories and the walnuts, both of which are of the greatest importance as timber-trees, and several of them of great value for their fruit.

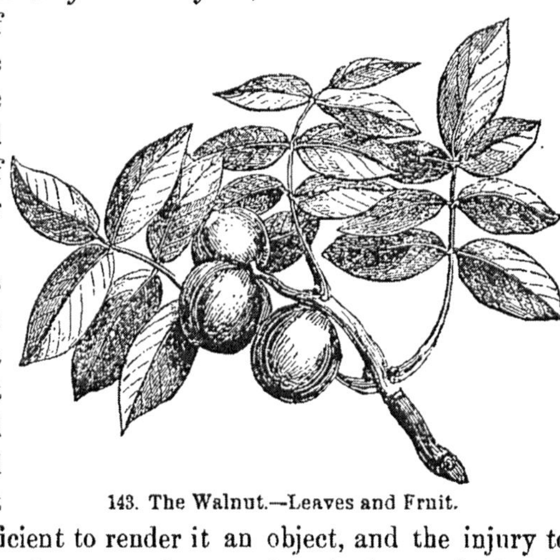

143. The Walnut.—Leaves and Fruit.

1097. All of this family yield, when tapped in spring, a sweetish sap, that may be evaporated down to syrup and sugar. The amount is not, however, sufficient to render it an object, and the injury to the trees would be much greater than any benefit that could be derived from this practice.

THE HICKORIES. (Genus *Carya*).

1098. These occur native only in North America, although fossil species are found in Europe. About ten living species are known in the United States and Mexico. The wood of the hickories is generally heavy, hard, close-grained, and remarkably strong and elastic. As a fuel they rank higher than any other of our native woods.

144. The Walnut.—Young Leaves Blossoms, and Nut.

1099. THE PECAN-NUT (*Carya olivæformis*). This is found growing to the height of sixty to seventy feet along the country bordering the Mississippi and the lower Ohio, from Iowa southward to Louisiana, and westward in Indian Territory. The wood is coarse-grained, hard, strong, and durable, but not so valuable as that of some other species. The fruit of the pecan is considered as one of the best of the hickories, and occasionally a tree is found upon which it is exceptionally fine. There can be no doubt but that these could be greatly improved by cultivation, and that the finer varieties could be grafted upon other species, and grown with much profit.

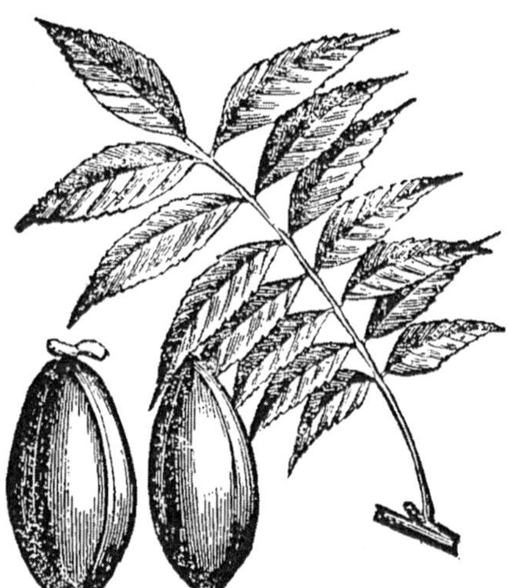

145. *Carya olivæformis*—The Pecan-nut.

1100. THE BITTER HICKORY (*Carya amara*). This species occurs from New England and New York, and southward into the Carolinas, where it is occasionally found from the coast to the mountains. It grows best in a cool rich soil, but the timber is not equal to that of some other species. It comes to greatest perfection in the Western States, and is found as far west as Nebraska. It is sometimes called the "swamp hickory."

1101. The Shell-Bark Hickory (*Carya alba*). This is one of the most widely distributed and most valuable of the hickories. It is found from Massachusetts to Nebraska, and is particularly well developed in deep fertile soil in the Western States. In West Virginia it is sometimes found eighty to a hundred feet in height, and from two and a half to three feet in diameter. Its timber is highly prized in carriage-making, but is not durable in the weather. It is found somewhat sparingly in North Carolina, and is most common in the Southern States, upon the uplands of the interior.

1102. The White-Heart Hickory or Mocker-Nut (*Carya tomentosa*). This species is found from New England southward to the Carolinas, and westward to Iowa and Nebraska. In North Carolina it grows to sixty feet or more in height, and from twenty inches to two feet in diameter. It extends from the coast to the mountains, and is the only hickory that grows on the "barrens." Its timber is much used in carriage-making.

1103. The Thick Shell-Bark Hickory (*Carya sulcata*). This is chiefly a western species, and grows in rich soils to eighty and a hundred feet in height and three feet in diameter.

1104. The Broom-Hickory or Pig-Nut (*Carya porcina*). This is the most common species in the Eastern and Middle States, and is found westward to Nebraska. Its fibers are very tough, and it is sometimes made into brooms. Under favorable conditions it grows to four feet in diameter.

1105. The Pig-Nut Hickory (*Carya glabra*). This species is somewhat widely distributed, and is found disseminated among other hickories in North Carolina and southward. It is found westward to Iowa.

1106. The Water Bitter-Nut Hickory (*Carya aquatica*). This is found in swamps in North Carolina. Its timber is of poorer quality than that of any other of the hickories.

The Black Walnut, Butternut, etc. (Genus *Juglans*).

1107. Of this genus, seven or eight species are known in temperate and sub-tropical regions, of which one is found in Europe and Central Asia, two in Eastern Asia and Japan, and four or five in

Canada, the United States, Mexico, and the West Indies. The fruit is oily and richly flavored, and is sold in the markets for eating, and when young and before the shell hardens, it is often used as pickles. The outer husk of the fruit, and sometimes the bark, are used in dyeing.

1108. THE BLACK WALNUT (*Juglans nigra*). This tree derives its name from the color of the heart-wood, which is of a dark tinge, and it has long been a favorite material for cabinet-wares. When exposed to the weather, it is durable, and in the first settlement of regions where it was common it was much used for posts and rails.

1109. When the wood of this tree has a waved or curly grain, it is highly prized for veneers. Such pieces are best obtained from a crotch of large limbs, or from the stump and large roots, or, better still, from the large burls or excrescences that are sometimes found on the trunk. Enormous prices have been paid for single trees having an exceptionally fine grain.

1110. This may be justly regarded as among the most valuable of our native species, and in a rich and rather humid soil is among the most profitable to plant. It will grow very well, but not so rapidly, upon lands that are dry, and in a climate approaching the arid, and it is found well adapted for cultivation upon the prairies and the eastern borders of the great plains. As it sends down a strong tap-root, and is very liable to suffer in transplanting, it should always be planted where it is to remain. This may be done in autumn or early in the spring, and if the latter, from nuts that have been exposed to freezing, as elsewhere described.

1111. There is another fact to be noticed, in reference to this tree, that deserves attention. In the more westerly States, where the blue-grass thrives, it is very apt to get into a black walnut grove, and unless carefully kept out by cultivation, it will injure its growth. This happens from the fact that the grass starts very early, and even matures its seed before the foliage of the trees is fully opened.

1112. It is therefore best to plant it alternately with other trees that put forth their leaves earlier, although they may not be worth as much for their wood, such as soft maples, box-elder, or cottonwood. The latter have the further advantage of compelling the black walnut trees to run up straight and high, and they serve to shelter and protect it from the hot sun and from drying winds.

1113. These nursing-trees may be taken out when the growth becomes too dense, and they will be then of use as fuel and for various farm purposes. An acre of land requires for planting about seven bushels of black walnuts with the shucks on. They must be planted early, and in a dry prairie soil they require to be covered more deeply than in a humid soil.

1114. In Canada, the black walnut once abounded in the country drained by the tributaries of the St. Clair river, but it has now become scarce, and from present prospects it will soon disappear as a native timber tree.

1115. BUTTERNUT (*Juglans cinerea*). This tree, when grown alone, is noted for its broad-spreading habit, but in woods, among other trees, it grows to forty or sixty feet in height. Its lumber is brownish-white, and in texture much like that of the black walnut. It works smoothly, takes a good finish, and is much used for inside finishings.

1116. This tree is widely distributed throughout the Northern and Middle States, is easily raised from the nuts, and, like the black walnut, it is difficult to transplant. It prefers a rich, calcareous soil, and under favorable circumstances its growth is quite rapid. It must, however, be crowded laterally, if we wish to have it form a tall straight trunk.

1117. The bark of the butternut has medicinal properties that give it the specific name—*Cathartica*, as applied by Micaux. It is also sometimes used for dyeing, and it possesses some tanning properties.

1118. *Juglans Californica*. This is a large shrub or small tree, but sometimes found forty to sixty feet in height and from two to four feet in diameter. It occurs in California, from San Francisco southward.

1119. *Juglans rupestris*. This is a shrub found in Texas, New Mexico, and Arizona, and grows to from six to twenty feet in height.

THE WILLOWS AND POPLARS. (Natural Order *Salicineæ*).

1120. This natural order embraces only the willows and the poplars, concerning which botanists differ greatly in the classification. They are scattered over the north temperate and borders of the Arctic zone; some occur within the tropics, and a few in the southern hemisphere, but none in Australia or on the islands of the Southern Pacific.

The Willows. (Genus *Salix*).

1121. The willows form a great number of species,[1] and run into hybrids and varieties that render their study botanically a matter of unusual difficulty.[2] They occur in a great variety of soil, but generally prefer humid localities, and many kinds occur chiefly along the borders of streams. Their roots in such places present the most efficient means for preventing erosions, and they may be planted for this purpose with great success.

1122. Willows produce seeds much like those of the poplars, and these ripen in the spring. They are, however, best propagated from cuttings from the robust young wood or in sections from the roots.

1123. These cuttings may be made late in the fall or in winter, but always after the fall of the leaf, and before the sap starts in the spring. They should be selected from sound and thrifty young wood, of the previous year's growth, tied in bundles and set in a damp cellar, their lower ends set in sand or wet moss, and their tops prevented from drying; or, instead of this, they may be set in trenches not liable to standing water, and covered from the frost. They should be set early in spring, in ground previously prepared, and will need cultivation till they are above the reach of weeds.

1124. There are several of the willows that grow to large trees and produce valuable timber. Their rapidity of growth, under favorable conditions, is remarkable. The wood is light, tough, and easily worked, and in some kinds it is used for hoops, tool handles, and turned wares. The bark contains tanning and medicinal qualities, and the charcoal from its wood is used for making gunpowder.

[1] About 160 in number, of which about 60 occur in North America.

[2] It is remarked by Grigor that "there is no genus of plants in general cultivation whose species are more confused than that of the willow. This is accounted for partly from the more prominent kinds having been hybridized, and yielded intermediate varieties without number, and partly from each species, containing male and female plants, and the same species differing to some extent in appearance at certain seasons of the year. Add to this the circumstance of old trees assuming a very different appearance from young ones, and that no tree is more apt to change its appearance from a change of soil and climate, and it will not be surprising that some confusion should exist in the genus, and that the more prominent species only should be readily recognized." (*Arboriculture*, page 310.)

The ashes of the willow are rich in potash, and the leaves in some countries are gathered for feeding sheep in winter.

1125. Among the willows of large growth, the WHITE WILLOW (*S. alba*) is by far the most important. It is sometimes called the gray or Huntingdon willow, and is already widely introduced in the prairie region of the northwest, where it is valued above all others as a wind-break.

1126. The white willow is found to thrive exceedingly well in Northern Iowa and in Minnesota, as a hedge and screen. It grows with great rapidity, and its wood is useful as a fuel, and, when peeled and seasoned, as poles for all kinds of farm uses. When split and nailed to posts, it makes a very good fence.

1127. This willow is readily propagated from cuttings, as already described, and they should be set rather deep in soil liable to drouth, and so thick that they will shade the ground early, but care should be taken to thin them out as soon as they become crowded.

1128. THE ROUND-LEAVED OR GOAT-WILLOW (*S. caprea*). This is one of the kinds of willow that grow to a large size, with a tough elastic wood, of about the same market value as the birch. The bark is used for tanning leather. This willow, in England, is much prized for coppice-growth, where there is a demand for hoops, poles, rods for crates, sheep-fences, or similar uses, and no tree cut once in three or four years will yield in a short period a greater bulk of faggot wood. On congenial soil, the growth of one season is from eight to twelve feet long, and an inch in diameter at a yard from the ground. It grows forty or fifty feet high, and from one and a half to two feet in diameter. It stands exposure to the sea winds better than most trees.

1129. THE BEDFORD WILLOW (*S. Russelliana*) is of rapid growth, and the wood equal to that of the white willow, if not superior. The RED-WOOD WILLOW (*S. fragilis*). This has a light, tough, and durable wood, but when old it is very liable to die at the top. The specific name is given from the facility with which the twigs used for basket-work, break from the tree, although the twigs themselves are tough and pliable.

1130. Willow, when sawn into boards, is extremely light, but tough, and is not apt to splinter or receive damage from the fall or friction of hard materials. It is for this reason much prized as a lining for cart-bodies and barrows. In England it is highly prized for railroad-brakes, as it is not readily set on fire by friction. In the works constructed for preventing the erosion of mountain torrents, bundles of willow are often fastened down in the beds of streams, where they sometimes take root and grow. In the jettys constructed by Captain Eades, for improving the mouth of the Mississippi for navigation in recent years, the willow was the principal brush-wood employed.

Cultivation of the Osier or Basket-Willow.

1131. Although this is scarcely a branch of forestry in its ordinary sense, it is often noticed in connection with it, and as it involves some principles in cultivation in common with tree-planting, we will concisely state the principal rules concerning it. It deserves favor on account of the small capital that it employs, the large amount of hand-labor that it affords at remunerative prices, and the considerable amount of money that would be saved to the country were the supplies that we use, wholly produced upon our own soil.[1] It is further to be noticed, that willows may be cultivated upon soil too marshy for most kinds of farm-crops, and that the labor they furnish may be carried on through the year.

1132. The soils best adapted for the willow are rich alluvions, and reclaimed swamps, and the land should be sufficiently drained. It would be better if means were provided for irrigation in dry seasons. If liable to overflow in spring floods, it should have ditches at proper intervals for sooner carrying off the water.

1133. In preparing au osier field for planting, it should be cleared of all vegetation, and the soil should be mellowed by plowing or spading late in the fall before planting.

1134. The kinds of willow preferred in Europe are chiefly the following:

1. Red-willow (*Salix purpurea*).
2. Ural willow (*S. purpurea* var. *Uralensis*).
3. White osier (*S. viminalis*).
4. Narrow-leaved willow (*S. rubra* or *S. viminalis-purpurea*).
5. Soft-leaved willow (*S. mollissima*).
6. Caspian willow (*S. acutifolia* or *S. pruinosa*).

1135. These, under cultivation, run into varieties, so that their

[1] During the ten years ending in 1879, the annual importation of prepared willow averaged $33,000, and that of willow-work $170,000.

distinctive characters are lost. They differ greatly in habit of growth, hardiness, and qualities suitable for various uses. The kinds suited to a given location can not be known before trial, and those who may engage in this planting will do well to experiment with several kinds before planting largely with any. In starting an osier plantation, it is recommended to obtain the cuttings in the latter part of February or the first of March, and carefully kept from drying until ready for use.

1136. The finest stems should be selected, from the wood grown the year before. The ground is marked out by cords, and some prefer to run the lines east and west. For the kinds that are to be cut every year, they may be set in rows 18 to 20 inches apart, and for those to be cut every second year, they should be wider. For the white osier and the Caspian willow the space is sometimes 30 inches between the lines, and the intervals between are planted with some crop. They should be at about one-third of these distances between in the rows. It is important that the ground should be well shaded, and the plants always grow more uniform when somewhat crowded than when wider apart. In more open spaces, the sprouts branch, but the wood is more solid and durable.

1137. The number of cuttings required for an acre will range from 18,000 to 75,000, and may be calculated by the aid of a table elsewhere given in this book. They must be cut smoothly into lengths of ten or twelve inches, and pressed into the soil, the butt-end first, so as to leave about an inch out of the ground. Care must be taken not to peel back the bark in setting, and a hole may be made with an old bayonet, or something of the kind, if the ground is a little hard. They should slope at an angle of 45° towards the north.

1138. It is sometimes preferable to set in trenches, and in poor soils to fertilize with leaf-mold, stable-manure, or bone-dust. The manure should not be put in contact with the cuttings, but near them, and it is highly advantageous to irrigate with the soakings of manure during the summer.

1139. The ground should be kept mellow and free of weeds, and the first cutting, if delayed till the second year, will give a stronger growth to the roots. After the first the cutting may be made annually, or on alternate years according to the sizes desired. It should be done with a very sharp knife, bent flatwise to a right angle, with the cutting edge on the inside.

1140. The time of cutting should be always late in fall, or in winter, *but never in leaf-time, nor when in sap.* The rods should be be sorted into sizes, tied in bundles, dried in the sun, and stored in a dry place till ready for peeling. The rain discolors and injures them. When peeled, the rods are first set in the water, and where assisted by a constant and genial temperature this may be done at any time in the winter. When peeled, they should be dried for a day or so in the sun, and if properly cared for the wood will be white and brilliant. If not, they will have a dull yellow tint, which may be somewhat whitened by sulphur-fumes.

1141. The bark stripped from osiers may be used for tieing bundles, or spread as litter in stables, and to some extent be cut up with straw and fed to stock. It is used in tanning leather for gloves, and for the preparation of *salicine* for medicinal use. In common practice, from 18 to 20 per cent of willows were damaged, either from branching, injury to bark, crooked form, or dead tops. They sell at a discount of sixty to seventy per cent, and are used for inferior work.

1142. When carefully managed, an osier field may last 25 to 30 years, but a single year of neglect will greatly shorten this period. Something may be done to restore vigor, by letting the shoots remain over a year, and by manuring, but as soon as the yield begins to fail it is best to begin anew. If on the same grounds the roots should all be taken out, and fresh soil from below be brought to the surface by spading.

1143. An osier plantation costs about $20 to $30 a year for cultivation, per acre, and will yield from $100 to $125. The cultivation has its perils, as well as its profits. It may be injured by early or late frosts, but only to kill the wood that has not ripened. The willow is sometimes attacked by the saw-fly, the *Nematus ventralis*, or nearly allied species, similar to those that attack the currant and gooseberry, by eating off the foliage. The best remedy is the dust of white hellebore freely sprinkled upon the leaves just after the eggs are hatched. This insect produces two broods a year, one in May and another in September.

1144. Among the other enemies of the willow are a kind of fly (*Cecidomya salicina*), which stings and lays eggs in the tender sprouts, causing a spongy excrescence and a scrubby growth. These insects in turn are attacked by the ichneumon insects, and the balance of nature badly disturbed by the former, has been restored in a single season by the latter. Another insect (*Tipula saliciperda*) and several small beetles have at times proved injurious.

1145. Among mammals the sheep, goat, rabbit, and mouse are often destructive, the former by eating the leaves and the latter by gnawing the bark. The red willow, from the bitterness of its bark, is less liable to injury than other cultivated kinds. In Europe, willows sometimes suffer from hail, and insurance against this damage may be obtained as in other crops.

1146. If exposed to cold and dry winds, the osiery should be protected by wind-breaks of high trees, and the oaks, ashes, and firs are recommended for this use. In the cultivation between the rows when wide apart the first year beets, carrots, cabbages, or potatoes are employed. The weeding or cultivation should not be done when the shoots are forming. When done in fall, after the leaves have fallen, they should be gathered and buried. The bind-weed (*Convolvulus*, several sp.) and the dodder (*Cuscata*) sometimes infest a willow plantation, and must be carefully extirpated.

1147. THE DUTCH OSIER (*Salix lanceolata*) is much used for hoops and basket-work, and is best set in spring, in trenches about four feet apart, and from 30 to 40 inches between, in the rows. They should be fertilized with stable-manure as above described. Upon dryer ground the plants may be set a little closer together. The watering with manure-water is of first importance if the soil is poor.

1148. When used to turn the course of rivers from encroaching upon land, the willow should be cut between October and April, and should be formed into frames, by interweaving the smaller spray with larger timber, securing in place by piles, and covering with sand, gravel, or soil. It is well to load them down also with heavy stones. In a slight current this will often prove sufficient to form an artificial cape, and the mud settling above and below this obstruction will gradually extend out the shore. The willows will push out fibrous roots into the soil and sand, creating a surface vegetation; and may be kept in this condition by being cut back from year to year. If such sloping barriers can form an angle up-stream, the effect is better.

1149. The male plants of the purple, black, yellow, and some other willows, form very ornamental small trees, presenting a gay and rich profusion of early blossoms—the harbingers of summer, and the first food of the bee.

The Poplars and Cottonwoods (Genus *Populus*).

1150. Of these there are about twenty species in the north temperate zone of the old world and the new. They occur in North America from the Arctic zone to Mexico, and throughout the whole breadth of the country from the Atlantic to the Pacific.

1151. The American Aspen (*Populus tremuloides*). This tree is extremely wide in its range. It abounds over the whole of the interior of British Columbia, and towards the north and east, characterizing some of the most fertile lands. In the southern part of the Province it is found usually along the borders of streams, and on the higher plateaux. In the Peace river country it comes up after fires, and often grows to a diameter of two feet.

1152. The aspen is common throughout the region west of the Cascade Mountains and the Sierra Nevada, upon the Pacific coast, upon the slopes of mountains that border the sage plains, along the courses of what in winter are running streams.

1153. In the mountain regions of the interior it is commonly called the "quaking asp," and grows in the upper valleys often in dense groves, where it shows a tendency to succeed the coniferous woods when they have been destroyed. Its wood is sometimes burned into charcoal for smelting ores, and it has sometimes been used for telegraph-poles and railway ties, but it is too soft and perishable for any thing more than temporary employment in these uses.

1154. The aspen is used to a considerable extent for the manufacture of paper. The wood makes a very white pulp, but not as strong as that from spruce.

1155. The White Poplar (*Populus alba*). This is a naturalized foreign species, sometimes called the "abele," "downy poplar," "silver poplar," or "Dutch beech." It is said to be a native of Palestine, and the timber is by some writers supposed to be the "shittim-wood" of Scripture, but more probably that was an *Acacia.*

1156. This is a tree of remarkably rapid growth, and generally it shows a strong tendency to send up shoots from the roots. This renders it troublesome in cultivated ground, but is a valuable quality in woodlands. When grown in dense groves it runs up in slender form, aud in a short time it becomes large enough for poles good for fencing, corn-cribs, and other farm uses. If cut early in summer it peels very easily, and it is then light but durable and strong, if not placed in contact with the ground. Michaux recommended it for extensive cultivation as a substitute for the tulip-tree, and Bryant regards it as superior to any of the native poplars.

1157. It may be propagated by cuttings of the young wood or the roots, and from layers and grafts, and grows with great certainty in

146. *Populus alba.*—White Poplar.

a moderately damp soil. The durability of the wood is increased by painting with coal-tar, which is best applied hot. The stronger contrasts between the upper and lower sides of the leaf are found in the tender varieties, while the kind with leaves lobed like the maple are found to be more hardy.

1158. The Lombardy Poplar (*Populus dilatata*). This tree, from its tall columnar growth, furnishes an admirable wind-break, and it is still in France a favorite tree for planting along the roadside. The fashion in our New England and Northern States was formerly quite prevalent, but the tree is short-lived, and most of these monotonous lines of trees have disappeared. When planted here and there, so as to be seen rising behind and among round-headed and coniferous trees, it has a pleasing effect. The wood is soft, brittle, and of little value except for summer fuel.

1159. This tree bears no pistilate flowers in our country, and it can only be propagated from cuttings and sprouts from the roots. Its chief value is for screens and wind-breaks, and in rich humid soils it grows with great rapidity.

1160. THE LARGE-TOOTHED POPLAR (*Populus grandidentata*). This tree grows to a large size, and its wood is valuable for framing and lumber for inside work. It works smoothly, takes a good polish, and is not liable to shrink. When cut and peeled in summer it is durable in the open air, if not in contact with the ground. This tree is very well suited for inside planting in groves. It can be readily propagated from seeds and cuttings.

1161. For cultivation in the great open country east of the Cascade Mountains, in Washington Territory, the poplars become especially important timber trees, both as fuel and for fencing. The common aspen, as grown there, when peeled and seasoned, may be used for almost any purpose, if kept from the ground. A tree 24 years old, has been known to measure two feet across the stump, and to yield two cords of wood.

THE COTTONWOODS.

1162. Various species of the genus *Populus* are comprised under this name, the principal one being the *P. monilifera*. The common name is derived from the cotton-like tuft attached to the seeds, by which they are borne to great distances by the winds, and the specific name "monilifera" signifies "necklace-bearing," from the seeds being formed in a series of little balls, like a string of beads. This species occcurs native throughout the Atlantic States from New England to Nebraska and Dakota, and southward to Louisiana. It is not seen in Utah, is less frequent in Nevada, but occurs in California and Oregon.

147. Tuft and Seed of the Poplar.

1163. It is extremely easy to cultivate in soils that are not to arid, and may be propagated from the seed, from cuttings, layers, or grafts. The most convenient way is perhaps from cuttings, but the best is from the young plants that spring up along the sand-bars of rivers. These natural nurseries are annually renewed by the seeds floated down by the streams, and furnish, practically, an inexhaustible supply. In pulling out the young cottonwoods from the sand-bars in autumn, by selecting a place but little above the level of the water, they will come out very easily, and more than a thousand may be pulled up in half an hour, with the fibers of the roots entire.

1164. When these are heeled in during the winter, and plowed in early in the spring, they take a vigorous growth, and are scarcely checked by the operation. In setting these young seedlings, they will be sure to take an upward growth, at any angle they may happen to be placed. They generally begin with a new bud near the base of the stock, and the part above soon perishes.

1165. A principal reason for collecting the seedlings of cottonwoods from river sand-bars in autumn is, that the bottom-lands are usually flowed in spring at the time when the young trees are needed. An easy method of securing an abundant supply of plants, is to plow in the branches covered with the seed, or by gathering the fertile catkins when ripe, rubbing them apart, and sowing on mellow, moist soil, lightly covering the seeds with earth.

1166. The Iowa Forestry Annual of 1879 recommends for cottonwood cuttings, pieces two or three feet long and from one to two inches in diameter, sawn into uniform lengths, and the lower end cut in a slope on one side with a very sharp axe. It advises that poplars and willows should be set deeply and firmly in the fall, and as soon as may be after they are cut.

1167. As many as 3,000 cottonwoods may be planted in a day, by two men, a boy, and a team. The ground may be cultivated as for corn, for two or three years, or until the ground is well-shaded, when they will need no further care beyond protection from cattle and from fires.

1168. In deep, rich soils the cottonwood may sometimes do better at eight feet apart than when set at half this distance at first. This subject not only in this species, but in all others, should be an object of careful observation by the planter, and the conditions best suited to the locality can never be fully determined excepting by trial.

1169. A variety known in the Missouri Valley as "yellow cottonwood," appears to belong to this species, and the superior qualities claimed for it appear to be due to the soil and to the density of its growth. Isolated trees are generally more thrifty, and therefore have more sap-wood, and are more difficult to split. When grown in the interior of a grove they are often less tough, and the quality of the wood is generally more dense and durable.

1170. COTTONWOOD OF THE PACIFIC COAST (*Populus trichocarpa*). This tree grows to the height of 30 to 50 feet from San Diego northward. In Washington Territory it is found from 60 to 100 feet high, and from 2 to 6 feet in diameter. In British Columbia it is found chiefly in the valleys of streams and on the banks of rivers throughout the whole Province, and north-eastward in the Peace river district. It is used by the Indians of the interior in making their canoes.

1171. A variety (*P. augustifolia*) is found in the Rocky Mountains, and the *P. balsamifera* and *P. monilifera*, with several varieties somewhat uncertain as to their classification are also found, all bearing the name of "cottonwood." The *Populus Fremontii* grows to a large tree.

1172. ANGULAR-STEMMED COTTONWOOD (*Populus angulata*). This is one of the cottonwoods of the Mississippi river and its tributaries, and is distinguished by its angular stems, and the absence of resinous and aromatic buds. The wood is soft, but of rapid growth. It does not extend up the Mississippi river beyond Lake Pepin.

1173. BALM OF GILEAD POPLAR (*Populus candicans*). This is a tree of very rapid growth, easily cultivated, and well adapted for planting as a shade tree. Its leaves give out a slight balsamic odor, and it has been recommended to plant groves of this tree along the borders of marshes, to intercept the malaria arising from such localities. A narrow-leaved variety, commonly called "cottonwood" or "willow-leaved poplar," occurs from Colorado and New Mexico to Washington Territory and Oregon, being the prevalent species in Nevada and Utah.

THE AILANTHUS.

1174. The *Ailanthus glandulosa*, or "tree of heaven," is a native of China, but has a wide range of adaptation to soils and climates, enduring heat and drouth very well, and thriving upon soils where many other kinds of wood fail. It grows rapidly, and is very apt to send out tracing roots that sprout at a considerable distance from the tree.

1175. The male flowers have a nauseating odor, that render this tree undesirable for cultivation near dwellings. It grows very well in the shade of other trees, and the spreading character of its roots render it useful in consolidating railroad embankments, and for reboisement of mountains. It is grown from the seed, but is most easily propagated by planting sections of its roots, one end being exposed to the air.

The Arbutus, or Madrona, of the Pacific Coast (*Arbutus Menziesii*).

1176. This occurs upon Vancouver and the neighboring islands, but always near the coast. It is a handsome evergreen, yielding a closely-grained and heavy wood, much like the box, and grows to from eighteen inches to two feet in diameter, and to the height of fifty feet. It extends southward to Mexico and Texas, and, under favorable conditions, grows to eighty and a hundred feet in height, and to a diameter of from one to three feet.

The Manzanita.

1177. This is the *Arctostaphylos glauca* of Lindley, and the *Xerobotrys glauca* of Nuttall. It belongs to the heather family (*Ericaceæ*), and is a large evergreen spreading shrub, with a red exfoliating bark and pinkish white flowers in a terminal racime. It abounds in California and Oregon—has great powers of endurance in drouth, and it is worthy of cultivation for variety in parks and pleasure grounds. The wood is very dense, reddish, and hard, but too small for much use. There are over a dozen species of the *Arctostaphylos*, mostly humble shrubs. The *A. glabra* grows to from 8 to 24 feet, and the *A. pungens* to from 3 to 20 feet in height.

The Pawpaw (*Asimina triloba*).

1178. Some seven or eight species of the Asimina are found in North America, mostly in the Southern and Southwestern States and in Mexico, and, excepting the one above named, unimportant shrubs. The pawpaw grows to some fifteen or twenty feet in height, generally in thickets, and it is chiefly important for its fruit, which in form and flavor somewhat resembles a bannana.

SOUTHERN CATALPA (*Catalpa bignonoides*).[1]

1179. This tree is found native in Georgia and other Southern States, but has been widely cultivated for ornament in the Middle States and in Europe, where the climate is not too cold. It is found susceptible to frost, and sometimes, after several years of apparent success, it will suffer great injury, or be wholly killed by a hard winter following a season that favored a late growth.

1180. Under favorable conditions, it grows with great rapidity, and to a large size, being fifty feet or more in height, and from eighteen to twenty inches in diameter. It has large showy blossoms, broad leaves, a silver-gray bark, which is but slightly furrowed, and a wide spreading top. The branches are relatively few in number, and the capsules long, cylindrical, and pendant. The wood is grayish-white, of fine texture, and brilliant when polished, much resembling that of the butternut, but of less reddish hue and of greater durability.

1181. HARDY CATALPA (*Catalpa speciosa*). For many years there has been cultivated in Ohio, Indiana, and other Northern and Western States a form of catalpa that was long considered a hardy variety of the *C. bignonoides*. It was found to be not only hardy, but very durable. Its habit was more erect, growing in dense groves, with stems 50 feet in height; the bark was more closely adherent and furrowed vertically, much like that of the white ash. The flowers are larger, nearly pure white, and about three weeks earlier than the other species.

1182. It is described by Dr. Engelmann (omitting the technical description of the flowers) as follows:[2] "A middle-sized tree, with grayish-brown, much cracked or furrowed, at last slightly flaky bark, and light-yellowish gray wood; leaves large, truncated, or more or less cordate at base, slender, acuminate, soft, downy on the under side, inodorous. . . . Common in the low, rich, sometimes overflowed woodlands near the mouth of the Ohio, along the lower course of that river and its confluence, and in the adjoining lowlands of the Mississippi, in the States of Illinois, Indiana, Ken-

[1] Thus named by Walther. It is named *C. cordifolia* by Elliott; *C. syringaefolia* by Sims, and *Bignonia catalpa* by Michaux.

[2] *Botanical Gazette*, V. No. 1, January, 1880.

tucky, Tennessee, Missouri, and Arkansas. According to Michaux, abounding near the borders of all the rivers which empty into the Mississippi further south. Whether the localities cited by him in West Florida produce this or the eastern species is unknown. Flowers in May."

1183. The specific name above adopted was given by Dr. John A. Warder, through whose writings, and those of the late E. E. Barney, of Dayton, Ohio, and others, the excellence of the tree for prairie-planting and profitable timber-growth have been chiefly made known.

1184. The wood of this catalpa is light, yet strong enough for most purposes of construction. It has been used to advantage in bridge-timbers, where exposed to the weather; it is a favorite material for fences, is easily worked, and durable as shingles, and is found serviceable as railroad ties.

1185. This tree prefers low rich bottom lands, but is found to thrive upon a great variety of soils. It has been planted with much success upon the bluff-formation of Missouri, Iowa, Kansas, and Nebraska. It is readily propagated from cuttings and layers, but to best advantage from the seed. These should be started in seed-beds, and be transplanted either in the fall or in the spring of the following year. In sowing, the seed should be covered a quarter or a half of an inch deep with fine soil, and they should be well cultivated and kept clear of weeds until they shade the ground. The practice has been adopted, to some extent, of cutting back the growth of the first year or two, so as to secure a strong, vigorous sprout from the roots after they have become well established.

MOUNTAIN MAHOGANY (Genus *Cercocarpus ledifolius*).

1186. This is a shrub or small tree, seldom growing more than thirty feet high and a foot in diameter, with an excessively hard close-grained wood. It grows in the most arid and rocky places, not usually in groves of considerable size, and from its great weight and hardness, it is most expensive to procure and to work. Its growth is exceedingly slow, and cultivation is quite out of the question, with any view of profit. There are about four other species in the United States and Mexico. They generally occur at from 6,000 to 10,000 feet above tide.

PERSIMMON (*Diospyros Virginiana*).

1187. This tree, sometimes called the "date plum," belongs to the Ebony family, and is the only American representative of the *Ebenaceæ*. Several species of this genus furnish the ebony of commerce. They grow chiefly in the torrid zone, and are distinguished for the hardness of their wood, which is intensely black.

1188. The persimmon grows to a tree sixty or seventy feet in height, from the southern part of New England, westward to Iowa, and southward to Florida and Louisiana. Its fruit is intensely astringent when green, but becomes palatable when frozen. Some Asiatic species bear a large edible fruit, and have been introduced in California, with fair prospect of success.

1189. THE MEXICAN PERSIMMON (*D. Texana*) is a shrub from 10 to 30 feet in height, and occurs in Southern and Western Texas, and in the adjacent parts of Mexico.

THE BURNING-BRUSH (Genus *Euonymus*).

1190. Of this shrub there are three species native to the United States. They are sometimes trailing, or climbing by rootlets, and are very ornamental in autumn when their bright red fruit is ripe. The SPINDLE TREE (*E. atropurpureus*) grows in dark, shady woods, the Atlantic States, from Canada to Florida, and has dark purple flowers, and a crimson fruit. The STRAWBERRY TREE (*E. Americana*) has about the same range of latitude, and extends west to Iowa and Nebraska. The remaining species (*E. augustifolius*) is found in Georgia.

THE HOLLY FAMILY (Natural Order *Ilicineæ*).

1191. This includes but three genera, of which the *Ilex* is the only one that claims our notice. It embraces about 145 species, mostly South American and tropical; some of them are, however, widely scattered through the temperate zones. They are rare in Africa and Australia, and a dozen or so are natives of the United States.

1192. THE COMMON HOLLY (*Ilex opaca*) is an evergreen tree, found growing in the Atlantic States, from Eastern Massachusetts southward, reaching its greatest development in the Southern States. In West Virginia it is found along mountain streams and gravelly and stony soil, fifteen feet in height. In North Carolina it grows to thirty and forty feet, with a diameter of twelve to fifteen inches.

1193. It is finely adapted for planting in avenues, and the wood is remarkably white and fine-grained, and is much used for inlaying, turning, and the finer grades of cabinet-work. Bird-lime is prepared from the middle-bark of the holly, and its leaves and bark are reputed to possess medicinal properties. It much resembles the European holly (*Ilex aquifolium*),

1194. THE DAHOON (*Ilex Dahoon*) is a small southern tree, found growing on the borders of pine-barren ponds and swamps in the coast region of North Carolina and further southward. It sometimes grows to twenty-five feet in height.

1195. THE YAUPON (*Ilex Cassine*), or "emetic holly," is a shrub growing in the coast-region of the Southern States, sometimes reaching twenty feet or more in height, but generally less. Its leaves act as a diuretic, and are used medicinally. The Indians used a cold infusion, that they called "black-drink," at their councils, and it is said to enliven them in the place of opium. According to some accounts, however, this drink was a compound one, prepared from various roots.[1]

1196. Other species of the (*Ilex* (formerly described under the genus *Prinos*) occur as deciduous shrubs in swamps throughout the Atlantic States, but they present no interest for forest-culture, or practical use.

1197. The "Maté" or Paraguay tea of South America, is made from a holly closely related to the *I. Cassine*, and it is not improbable that some advantage may be derived from its cultivation in the Southern States.

LAUREL (Genus *Kalmia*).

1198. There are abont half a dozen species of this genus, chiefly growing in swamps, or upon rocky hill-side, with thick evergreen leaves and showy red blossoms. Only one of them (*K. latifolia*) grows to much size, but this is sometimes found 30 feet high. The wood is very hard, close-grained, and often twisted into irregular forms, rendering it available for rustic furniture, for which it is chiefly employed.

1199. Another species (*K. augustifolia*), which grows further

[1] Procher's *Resources of the Southern Fields and Forests*, p. 431.

northward, is found in swamps, and is reputed to be poisonous to sheep, when its leaves are eaten. The honey gathered by bees from the laurels is also said to be poisonous. A drab-colored dye is got from the leaves, using copperas as a mordant. The *K. glauca* of California is an humble shrub.

THE SWEET-GUM (Genus *Liquidambar*).

1200. Of this there are two species; one American, the other a native of Asia-Minor. The former of these (*L. styraciflua*) occurs widely distributed from New England to Mexico, and from the states bordering upon the Great Lakes to Louisiana and Florida. It prefers a deep, fertile soil, exposed to temporary inundations, and attains a large size in the Southern States. A tree is mentioned by Michaux as found growing in a swamp near Augusta, Ga., that was fifteen feet and seven inches in circumference at five feet from the ground.

1201. In very warm climates a balsamic secretion is obtained from this tree. It comes from Mexico under the name of "copalm resin." It has some use in medicine, and is used as a perfume. The wood is compact, fine-grained, and susceptible of a bright polish. The heart-wood is reddish, and marked transversely with blackish belts. It is used to some extent for cabinet-wares and inside finishing, but does not bear exposure to the open air. It is cultivated in Europe, but does not there bear seeds.

THE MAGNOLIAS (Genus *Magnolia*).

1202. There are fourteen species of the magnolia, of which six occur in Japan, and eight are natives of the United States and Mexico. Our native magnolias chiefly occur eastward of the Alleghenies, and prefer a mild climate and a moist and fertile soil.

1203. THE "CUCUMBER TREE" (*Magnolia acuminata*). This occurs in the states north of the Ohio river in great perfection, and grows to a large size. It is also found in the western parts of New York and Pennsylvania, in West Virginia, and the South-western States. Its leaves are deciduous, and under cultivation they fall into varieties differing in shades of color, forms of leaf, and tints of flowers.

1204. It prefers a deep, rather damp and argillaceous soil, and a climate rather moist and not too cold. The seeds do best when sown in fall, with a covering of straw or litter in the winter, and in the second or third year they may be re-set in the nursery. It is hard to transplant this tree when it gets of much size. It should be done in spring, and without cutting back the head. As it tends to put out lateral branches when young, it should be somewhat crowded until it gets to sufficient height. If trimmed, it should not be done in sap-season, and the wounds should be covered with some substance that will exclude the air.

1205. The "SWAMP LAUREL," or "BEAVER TREE" (*Magnolia glauca*), has large oval leaves, that remain on in winter, and large fragrant and showy white blossoms. It is not of much account for its wood, but is valued as an ornamental shrub. It occurs native in swamps as far northward as Cape Ann, in Massachusetts, but thrives best in Southern New Jersey and further south along the Atlantic Coast.

1206. The "LARGE-FLOWERED MAGNOLIA" of the Southern States (*Magnolia grandiflora*) is a magnificent evergreen tree, with oval lanceolate leaves, rusty on the under side. It grows in the low country of the Southern States, and when in blossom it is unquestionably the most showy of American trees. The flowers are very fragrant.

1207. As cultivated in Europe, this tree forms many varieties, differing in the form and size of the leaves, the earlier or later appearance of its blossoms, their size, and other peculiarities. The most esteemed in France are *la Maillardière* and *la Galissonière.* When propagated from seed, they should be sown as soon as ripe, in a light moist soil, and the young plants require careful nursing when young. The varieties are multiplied by grafting by approach.

1208. The UMBRELLA TREE (*Magnolia umbrella*) grows in the interior, as far north as Pennsylvania, chiefly in moist and wooded valleys, along and near the mountains.

1209. The HEART-LEAVED MAGNOLIA (*Magnolia cordata*) has deciduos leaves, which are bread, heart-shaped, and slightly downy beneath, and flowers that are yellowish and faintly streaked with red. It occurs sparingly in the interior and mountainous portions of the Southern States.

1210. The LARGE-LEAVED MAGNOLIA (*Magnolia macrophylla*) has a smooth stem, with little branches, whitish bark, large deciduous leaves, one to three feet long and six to eight inches wide, and large white fragrant flowers tinged with purple.

1211. The AURICLE-LEAVED MAGNOLIA (*Magnolia auriculata*) has also large broad leaves, eight to twelve inches long, with an ear-shaped appendage at their base, deciduous and smooth upon both sides. It grows to a height of 30 to 40 feet in the mountains of the Southern States, and bears large fragrant white flowers.

1212. The magnolias do not bear transplanting well, and can be best started in pots, carefully removing all the soil with the roots when it is placed in the ground.

1213. THE PRIDE-OF-INDIA (*Melia Azedarach*). This is a deciduous tree, introduced from Asia, but now common as a shade tree from cultivation in the Southern States. It grows to forty or fifty feet in height and often three feet in diameter.

1214. THE IRON-WOOD (Genus *Ostrya*.) Of this genus there are but two species, and these are scarcely distinct. One is found in the Old World and one in the New. Our iron-wood (*O. Virginica*) does not grow to a large size, nor does it occur in groves by itself, but scattered here and there among other hard woods. Its bark is thin, brown, and rough, and its wood unusually solid and strong. It is not often cultivated for ornament, but grows very well when a little sheltered by other trees.

1215. The iron-wood of the Western Territory is of a different genus (*Olneya tesota*), and is of considerable value for its wood.

1216. THE SORREL-TREE OR SOURWOOD (*Oxydendrum arboreum*). This is a tree growing in fertile woods in Western Pennsylvania, in Ohio, and along the Allegheny range southward into the Southern States. It grows to a hight of 15 to 40 feet, and derives its name from its acid foliage.

1217. MESQUIT (*Prosopis glandulosa*). This is one of the leguminous family that thrives in the southern portion of the territories, in the hot dry valleys, and on the Mesas. It grows to a foot in diameter, and to thirty feet or more in height. The wood is hard and durable, and the fruit, a kind of bean, is eaten by animals. In Western Texas, a gum is collected from this tree much resembling gum-arabic.

1218. THE SCREW-POD MESQUIT (*Prosopis pubescens*). This is smaller and less common than the preceding, but of similar qualities.

1219. THE BUCKTHORN (*Rhamnus catharticus*). This is a European shrub that is sometimes cultivated as a hedge-plant, and when alone growing to a small sized tree. About sixty species of the Rhamnus are described by botanists, occurring as natives of Europe, Asia, and America. They prefer the warmer parts of the temperate zone, are rare in the tropics, and do not occur in Australia or the Pacific islands. About a dozen species occur within the United States, mostly thorny shrubs, some of them with evergreen leaves, but not of much account for cultivation, unless, perhaps, as hedge plants.

THE SUMACS (Genus *Rhus.*)

1220. Of these there are some 120 species, chiefly found in South Africa, and the warmer parts of extra-tropical countries in both hemispheres, a few being found within the tropics. About 14 species occur within the United States.

1221. THE STAG-HORN SUMAC (*Rhus typhina*). This is a small tree or more frequently a shrub, growing from Canada southward to South Carolina and Louisiana, and westward to Iowa. It sometimes is found 25 feet high and one foot in diameter. The wood when freshly cut has a rich, glossy, golden and brown color, but this fades when exposed to the sun. The leaves are used for tanning and dyeing.

1222. THE SMOOTH SUMAC (*Rhus glabra*). This occurs in about the same range as the preceding, but is smaller. The leaves contain more tannin than the last named, and afford most of the sumac that comes to market from Virginia, as a tanning material.

1223. *Rhus lauriana.* A large evergreen and leafy shrub, with an aromatic odor, found in California from Santa Barbara to San Diego. The pulp of the dry fruit is waxy, and the seeds are said to contain a pungent oil.

1224. *Rhus integrifolia.* This is a stout-branching evergreen shrub, 5 to 10 feet high, occurring along cliffs near the sea, from Santa Barbara to San Diego, and also in the interior. The bark exudes an astringent gum resin.

1225. Several of the sumacs (*Rhus toxicodendron*, *R. venenata*, *R. pumila*, *R. diversiloba*) are poisonous to some persons, when handled, causing a painful eruption and swelling that may continue several days.

THE SASSAFRAS (*Sassafras officinale*).

1226. This belongs to the laurel family, and is widely distributed from New England to Iowa, and throughout the Middle and Southern States. In Massachusetts it is found thirty feet in height and a foot in diameter. In West Virginia it is sometimes seventy or eighty feet high and three feet in diameter, and in West Tennessee a specimen has been measured five feet across the stump within the bark. In Canada it is only found westward of the Niagara river. The wood is soft, brittle, close-grained, and sometimes used in cabinet-work, when stripped of its bark, and seasoned, it is durable as fence-posts.

1227. An essential, oil having valuable medicinal qualities, is distilled from the bark of the roots, and the pith from the young twigs is mucilaginous and medicinal, being worth from $3 to $4 a pound. The roots also yield a drab-colored dye, with copperas as a mordant, and the leaves when steeped in water afford an agreeable and healthy mucilaginous drink. The roots of sassafras are very tenacious of life, and will sprout and grow with a remarkable persistency until wholly eradicated.

1228. THE BUFFALO BERRY (*Shepherdia argentea*) is a spiny shrub, growing 5 to 18 feet high, and occurs east of the Sierras and from New Mexico far into the northern regions of British America. It has been mentioned as available on account of its fruit, and as a hedge plant in the west.

1229. THE MAHOGANY (*Swietenia mahoganii*). This highly prized wood for fine cabinet-work, chiefly comes from the West Indies, Mexico, and Central America, but is found adapted to cultivation in Florida, and has been considered a native of that state. Although an exogenous tree, the lines of growth, as in many other tropical species, are seldom sharply defined, as where the growth has been distinctly interrupted by a cold winter.

147. Cross-section of Mohogany.

1230. ARROW-WOOD (*Tessaria borealis*). This is a branching willow-like shrub several feet high, growing on the sand-banks of rivers from New Mexico to California. The Indians are said to use the wood for arrows.

1231. THE CALIFORNIA LAUREL (*Umbellularia Californica*).[1] This

[1] By some botanists called "*Oreodaphne Californica.*"

tree, sometimes called the "mountain laurel" or "spire-tree," grows to the height ef seventy feet, in favorable locations, but ordinarily not more than from 10 to 30 feet. It gets its finest development in Oregon, but extends southward into Mexico. The wood is well adapted for cabinet-work, and is sometimes highly ornamental.

148. Leaves, Flowers, and Fruit of the *Umbrellularia Californica*, of one-half the Natural Size.

CHAPTER XXIII.

THE CONIFERS.

1232. The *Coniferæ* may be undoubtedly regarded as the most important timber trees known in commerce, and of the greatest utility to man. They are, for the most part, evergreen, and are widely scattered in both temperate zones and upon mountains within the tropics, being the last every-where to disappear at the timber-line. [§§ 107, 108.] In Northern Europe, in Siberia, and upon the western coast of North America, they form the principal and often the only trees over wide areas.

1233. Their wood, under the microscope, shows an abundance of bordered pits [§ 256], by which the smallest fragment may be identified, even in the fossil form. The sexes of the blossoms are separate, on the same or on different trees; they have no floral envelopes, and their pollen is provided with an arrangement that renders it buoyant, so as to be carried unusual distances in the winds. The ovules or young seeds have no pericarps, and are fertilized by direct contact of the pollen, without either stigma or style, and for this reason they are called *gymnosperms.*[1] The seeds contain several cotyledons [§ 132], instead of one, as in endogenous plants, or a pair, as in most of the species noticed in the preceding pages, and from this they are also called *polycotyledonous.* The number is usually from six to ten, and hence the germinating seed presents leaves of corresponding numbers.

1234. The seeds of this order are usually placed between hard, woody scales, arranged spirally and regularly around an axis, forming, until ripe, a solid conical or ovoid mass, and they are in many species provided with a wing that enables them to be wafted by the winds, when they are liberated by the opening of the scales. The structure of the blossoms and seeds of one of the most important of the genera in this order may be seen in the annexed engraving.

1235. In some cases, the cones that bear the seed can scarcely be recognized. The scales become pulpy and the fruit berry-like; in many species there is no trace of a wing to the seed, and the fruit may be solid and nut-like. Sometimes the seeds are large and edible. In the structure of the cone, and otherwise, the coniferæ present analogies to the higher lycopods or club-mosses, and to the vegetation that prevailed in the carboniferous period, the remains of which form the bulk of our mineral coal.

1236. In most of the conifers we find resiniferous cells in the wood of the trunk, branches, and roots, the bark, and sometimes, as in the pines, in the leaves. [§ 793.] The leaves in transverse sections present a cellular structure, very uniform in the different species, and affording characters upon which a classification has been based. We see an example of this in Fig. 20 of the accompanying engraving.

[1]A term from the Greek, signifying "naked seeds."

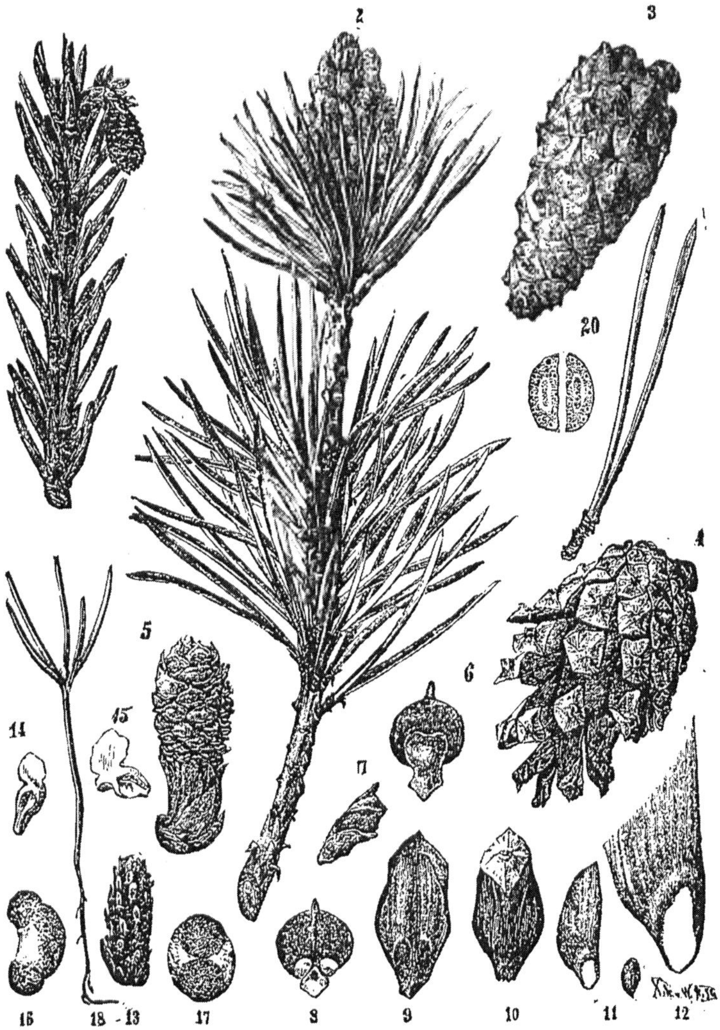

149. *Pinus sylvestris:* Scotch Pine.—1. A twig with a defected pistilate flower. 2. An older twig, bearing a cluster of oval staminate flowers. 3. The former enlarged, as it approaches the period of maturity. 4. The same after the scales have opened to allow the seeds to escape. 5. The pistilate blossom, somewhat enlarged. 6, 7, 8. Scales. 9. The inside of a scale, with the seeds in place. 10. Back view of a thickened scale. 11, 12. The seed, with its wing, natural size, and enlarged. 13. Staminate flowers, somewhat enlarged. 14, 15. Stamens. 16, 17. Pollen-grains inflated. 18. A seedling, showing five seed-leaves. 19. Leaves in pairs. 20. Transverse section of a leaf, showing the structure of cells, some of them being resiniferous canals.

1237. Although the conifers thrive in a great variety of soils and situations, it may be said that no soil which is compact, clayey, and underlaid by an impervious sub-soil, preventing it from drainage, is suited to them. But a few will grow in the mud, but with these exceptions almost every other kind of soil agrees with one or another, and especially those where the calcareous or the silecious element predominates.

1238. When young, nearly every species delights in a sandy loam, although when more advanced they may sometimes require a more substantial kind. The seeds should be sown early, and be covered thin. A mixture of about one-third sand and two-thirds mold is generally suitable for the seed-bed. Many kinds do very well in a dry soil, but they need more humidity in the early years, which is secured in the natural forests under the shelter of the parent trees. It is more effectual, if accompanied by a high temperature. All of these conditions are best managed in seed-beds and nurseries, and hence the advantages generally of starting conifers in nurseries first and of transplanting them while small. Of all trees the conifers suffer most and soonest from the exposure of their roots to the air, and the greatest possible care should be taken to prevent them from drying.

1239. Among the conifers there are many ornamental species and varieties that can be multiplied and perpetuated by grafting and by cuttings. These are delicate operations, and require special skill and convenient arrangements, found only among professional nurserymen. We can only here state some of the principal points concerning them.[1] Cuttings may be taken from the trees in spring, before vegetation has started, or in fall, after the growth of the year has formed. They are set in little pots, filled with light sandy soil, or in little beds, under glass, in a multiplying bed, where the temperature is regulated, and they are properly sprinkled.

1240. For grafting, the terminal shoot is taken as a scion, and if the hardened wood is used, the best time for grafting is in autumn. By a delicate, but generally certain process, the shoots, while still herbaceous, may be grafted in the growing season, in the month of May. In grafting conifers, care must be taken that the stock be as

[1]A detailed description of these methods is given in *Forestry Report*, Vol. II., p. 75 to 80.

nearly related to the scion as may be; as, for example, pines should both be two-leaved, three-leaved, or five-leaved, and some, like the white pine, are very difficult to graft at all. We can not take different genera of conifers, nor those of the same genus and subdivision, unless of equally vigorous growth.

1241. For reasons already stated [§ 299], we can not cultivate the conifers of the Pacific Coast in the Atlantic States with success. Those from the mountains can be removed with much better chances of their living, but to do this with certainty the greatest care must be taken to keep the roots from the air, and to bring an abundance of the soil with them.

1242. After excavating around the tree, so as to include as many of the small roots as possible, and without disturbing them, a sheet of coarse canvas should be passed under the roots and bound firmly arouud them. The trees should not be more than three or four feet high; they should be selected from open places, and the more undisturbed soil that is taken with them the greater will be the chances of their living.

1243. In planting conifers in the prairie regions west of the Mississippi, the greatest difficulty has been met with, on account of the dryness of the climate, aud the great and sudden changes of temperature that occur. Indeed, very many have failed altogether; perhaps after giving some promise of success for a few years, until overcome by a dry season or other adverse conditions.

1244. The kind of all others most likely to succeed iu Iowa and Southwestern Minnesota, is the native *red cedar*. According to the opinion of careful observers those that next after this should have order of preference would be: 1. Scotch pine; 2. White pine; 3. Austrian pine; and, 4. Red pine.

1245. The conifers embrace about 300 species, which are arranged by Bentham and Hooker[1] into six families, based upon common resemblances, as follows:

I. The Cypress Family (*Cupressinæ*), including seven genera, of which the California white cedar (*Libocedrus*), arbor-vitæ or common white cedar (*Thuja*), cypress (*Cupressus*), and junipers (*Juniperus*), are native in the United States. The remaining three occur in Asia,

[1]*Genera Plantarum*, iii., Part I., p. 420 (1880).

Africa, Australia, and South America, but may be cultivated to advantage in some parts of the United States.

II. THE BALD-CYPRESS AND ALLIED FAMILY (*Taxodieæ*), including the Japanese cedar (*Cryptomeria*), bald cypress (*Taxodium*), redwood and giant tree (*Sequoia*), and two other Australian and Eastern Asiatic genera.

III. THE YEW FAMILY (*Taxeæ*), including the yew (*Taxus*), California nutmeg (*Torrega*), ginkgo (*Salisburia*), and three other Australian and South American genera.

IV. The *Podocarpeæ*, of which three genera occur in Asia, Africa, Australia, and South America.

V. NORFOLK-ISLAND PINE FAMILY (*Araucarieæ*), three species of which are found in Eastern Asia, China, Australia, South Pacific Islands, and South America.

VI. THE PINE AND FIR FAMILY (*Abietineæ*), embracing the pines (*Pinus*), cedar of Lebanon (*Cedrus*), spruce (*Picea*), Hemlock (*Tsuga*), Douglas fir (*Pseudotsuga*), fir (*Abies*), and larch (*Larix*).

1246. In the cypress family we have 14 species of the *Callitris* or Atlas cedar, the stump and roots of which afford the costly "thuja" of cabinet-makers, and one of the finest of woods. The gum-senegal of commerce comes from trees of this genus. None of them are found in North America, but are natives of Africa, Madagascar, Australia, and New Caledonia. Two other genera, *Actinostrobus* and *Fitzroya*, are also exotic.

1247. THE CALIFORNIA WHITE CEDAR (*Libocedrus decurrens*). This is sometimes called "incense cedar," and occurs widely distributed in California and Oregon, chiefly upon the mountains of the interior, where it sometimes grows to six or seven feet in diameter, at a yard from the ground, and to a height of 100 to 150 feet. There are about 8 species known, but this is the only one within our limits. In general habit and quality of wood, it much resembles the common white cedar of the Atlantic States (*Thuja occidentalis*), and it thrives very well in the east, where it forms a fine ornamental evergreen.

THE ARBOR-VITÆS OR WHITE CEDARS (Genus *Thuja*).

1248. These as now arranged by the authors above cited, embrace under this genus a dozen species, of which five occur within the United States. The cones consist of scales, from eight to twelve in number, which have a pair of ovules at the base of each. The seeds ripen the first year, and when ripe the scales become strongly reflexed. In the Atlantic States and Canada, we find two species, viz.:

1249. THE ARBOR-VITÆ (*Thuja occidentalis*) is found in swamps, and upon rocky bluffs, throughout the inland portions of the Northern and Northwestern States, extending far northward in British America, but not into the Southern States. The wood is soft and easily split, has an agreeable balsamic odor, and is very durable. It is made into shingles, pails, churns, buckets, and other hollow-ware, is durable, and much prized for fence-posts, and is largely used for telegraph-poles, and in late years for railroad ties. It grows well under cultivation, and makes one of the most excellent of screens and wind-breaks. Nothing would prove more effectual than this for preventing drifting snows, in exposed places along the public roads.

1250. It is best propagated from seeds in nurseries, and then transplanted in spring. It should have some shelter on the south side, as every one must have noticed, who has attempted to plant on both sides of a board fence running east and west. It would be well to provide a row of some other trees for this use, two or three years before the cedar is set, and take it away when no longer needed. This tree when cut back will thicken up very well at the bottom. When set it should be well watered, and if followed by a dry summer, the watering should be repeated till the plants get well rooted.

1251. This cedar will endure burying in the sand to a remarkable degree. In one instance on the shore of Lake Michigan, one of these trees had been gradually buried to a great depth, and afterwards left bare by the drifting away of the sands. It was found that roots had been successfully put out from the trunk, to the height of more than thirty feet. This quality renders it valuable in fixing drifting sands, wherever it can be made to grow.

1252. THE "WHITE CEDAR" (*Thuja sphaerœdalis*—formerly known as "*Cypressus thyoides*," or later "*Chamaecyparis thyoides*") is the common white cedar of the Atlantic Coast. It also occurs, but less frequently, in swamps along rivers in the interior. It extends from Massachusetts to Texas, and occurs abundantly in New Jersey, growing in dense masses in swampy ground. In some places along the southern coast it is called the "juniper." It prefers the lowlands along rivers and the forest swamps of the low pine barrens, and grows sometimes to 70 or 80 feet in height, with a diameter of two feet.

1253. This is one of the most valuable timber trees of the country, the wood being fine-grained, soft, light, and easily worked, with a strong aromatic odor. It is used for frames of buildings, shingles, and coopers' wares, and its charcoal for gunpowder. Lamp-black of the best quality is made from its smoke.

1254. "Enormous quantities of this wood are found buried in salt marshes in Southern New Jersey, where no timber now grows. In searching for it, the marshes are probed with iron rods, and when a tree is found, its size, direction, and quality are ascertained. By tearing off a piece of wood, it may be known by the odor, whether it fell from age, or was blown down by the winds. If the latter, it is more valuable, and after cutting away the turf at the top, the wood is sawn off in two places, when it will rise and float, always *bottom upwards*, because the lower side is soundest, and the upper side may have been long exposed to the weather. The wood has all the buoyancy of fresh cedar, not being in the least water-logged, and the under bark is still fresh.

1255. "Occasionally a log will be got out that is thirty feet long. It is generally shorter, and is worked up into shingles of the very best quality. Tree after tree, from 200 to 1,000 years old, may be found lying across one another, some partly decayed, as if they had stood a long period after they were dead. The larger logs are sometimes sawn into boards.

1256. "From $9,000 to $10,000 worth of shingles, valued at $15 per M., have been made in a single year from this buried cedar in the vicinity of Dennisville. The occurrence of this cedar on a level now below that of the sea, is deemed conclusive evidence of the subsidence of this coast; but this timber must have grown many thousand of years ago, and must have been growing for a long period to accumulate so great a quantity."[1]

1257. THE GIANT ARBOR-VITÆ (*Thuja gigantea*) is by far the finest of the cedars, and grows to a size scarcely inferior to that of the Douglas fir and the sugar-pine. The branches are drooping and the tree more symmetrical than the common white cedar, and the wood is white and easily worked. It grows to great perfection

[1] *Forestry Report*, 1877, p. 459, and authorities there cited.

in Oregon, Washington Territory, and northward to Alaska, being especially well developed upon the Coast and Cascade Ranges, where it grows from 100 to 250 feet high, and from 3 to 12 feet in diameter. When free to develop itself, it takes a narrow pyramidal form, with somewhat drooping branches and a light green foliage. It is not common in California, but is found as far south as San Diego.

1258. In British Columbia, this is called the "yellow cypress" or "yellow cedar," and is limited to the coast and islands. It often exceeds six feet in diameter, and the wood is strong, free, and of fine grain, with a pale golden yellow tint, and a slight peculiar resinous smell. It is very durable, and has been used to some extent for boat-building and for various ornamental uses. The giant-cedar is an important timber tree in British America, and on the coast it often exceeds fifteen feet in diameter, with a height of 100 to 150 feet, but such trees are invariably hollow. The Indians use this tree for making their large and elegant canoes, and from the fiber of the inner bark they make ropes.

1259. THE NOOTKA CEDAR (*Thuja excelsa*), heretofore known as the "*Curpessus Nutkanus*," is found from Alaska southward to the Columbia river, and grows to the height of 80 to 100 feet, with a soft white and valuable wood. It is sometimes known as the "Oregon cedar," the "white cedar," the "ginger pine," etc.

1260. LAWSON'S CEDAR (*Thuja Lawsoniana*) is a handsome tree, growing in the Shasta mountains and northward, in the Cascade range. This species is often cultivated for ornament, and it runs into varieties, which are often very beautiful.

THE CYPRESSES PROPER. (Genus *Cupressus.*)

1261. These differ from *Thuja*, in being of stiffer and stronger growth, having larger cones, with thick scales, and ripening the second year. About a dozen species are known, of which four are found in the United States, chiefly upon the Pacific Coast.

1262. THE MONTEREY CYPRESS (*Cupressus macrocarpa*) grows in a very limited region, near Monterey, and is a tree 40 to 50 feet high, with a diameter of two to four feet. It is quite ornamental. Three other species, the *C. Goveniana*, *C. Macnabiana*, and *C. Arizonica*, have been described, but are of slight importance as timber trees. The first grows to the height of seventy feet, and is said to be a beautiful tree.

The Junipers. (Genus *Juniperus.*)

1263. Of these there are about twenty-five species, widely distributed over the northern hemisphere, in temperate and cold climates, but in the tropics only on high mountains. They are mostly small trees, thick at the base, as compared with their height, and a few of them growing to a large size. The bark is generally thin and fibrous, and the wood fine and compact (but not hard), durable, and exceedingly slow of growth. The outer layer of wood and the inner bark are resinous. The fruit ripens the second year, and is commonly called a berry, which, in the common juniper, is employed medicinally. There are some eight other species of the juniper in North America, and most of them occur within the United States. The principal of these are as follows:

1264. The Red Cedar (*Juniperus Virginiana*). This is the largest and most widely spread of the junipers, extending from about latitude 45° in Canada, to the Gulf States, and from the Atlantic to the mountains that border the Pacific States. Between the Sierras and the Wahsatch Mountains it occurs at an elevation of 5,000 to 7,000 feet above tide, and is there a small tree, usually not over a dozen feet high, and of low, compact form, scattered over the dry slopes, but nowhere in groves of much density.

1265. In Tennessee, this tree occurs native to greatest perfection along the out-crop of the "glady limestone" forming an irregular belt, somewhat circular in outline, extending quite across the central part of the State. It has there been found three feet in diameter, near the ground, and sixty feet to the branches. It is being rapidly worked up, and in many counties, where once abundant, it is now exhausted.

1266. The red cedar occurs along rocky ravines, in the region bordering upon the Great Plains, where it is the principal conifer found native, and the one most capable of cultivation for ornamental and useful purposes.

1267. It is propagated from the seeds, and for planting, the berries should be bruised and mixed with an equal or greater bulk of wet wood ashes. In three weeks the alkali will have cut the resinous gum, when the seeds can be washed clean from the pulp. This should be done in March. In preparing the ground for seed-beds, it should be spaded to a foot or more in depth, and three or four inches at the surface should be covered with a mixture of well rotted leaf-mold (or wood soil) and sharp sand.

1268. The beds should be shaded, as is common with evergreens, and should be watered occasionally in the evening in case of drouth. They may be transplanted to nursery rows the second spring, and three years after, the alternate rows should be taken out. Screens of this evergreen are generally to be preferred to all others for orchards and buildings in the Northwestern and Western States.

1269. The Western Juniper (*Juniperus occidentalis*). This species in Oregon grows to a tree sometimes three feet in diameter and forty feet high, but is more commonly a much smaller tree, and often bushy. It much resembles the red cedar, but it has larger berries, more glandular and resinous leaves, a loose reddish bark, and a white wood. It grows east of the Sierra Nevada and Cascade Mountains in Oregon and Washington Territory, and varieties often with excentric layers of wood and scraggy growth occur in Nevada, Utah, Colorado, and New Mexico. In Western Texas it forms an important timber-tree, but not so large or useful as the red cedar.

1270. The California Juniper (*Juniperus Californica*) is a stout shrub or small tree, rarely 30 feet high, fouud growing from San Francisco southward, chiefly along the Coast Range and the islands. A variety of smaller size extends over the southern parts of Utah into Arizona and Nevada, forming a small tree 20 feet high, that furnishes fire-wood to some extent in these regions.

1271. Another juniper (the *J. pachyphlœa*) occurs as a middle-sized tree, with a spreading rounded top, thick aud much cracked bark, and pale reddish wood, is fouud in the interior of Arizona and New Mexico. It is probable that some of the junipers now regarded as Mexican species may be found across our border, but they are of limited and altogether local importance.

1272. The Savin (*J. Sabina*) is a prostrate shrub found in high northern latitudes, in both Europe and America, and occurs in the northern border of the United States, and upon mountains from the Atlantic coast to the great lakes, and in British Columbia on the Pacific coast. It spreads in dense masses over the rocks and sand,

and it has a red heart-wood like the red cedar, but is too small for any use.

THE BALD-CYPRESS, RED-WOOD, AND ALLIED FAMILY.

1273. These are included in the tribe *Taxodieæ*, and are distinguished by the arrangement of the scales of the aments, which are thickened, woody, close, and spirally placed. The ovules, instead of being in twos, are from two to six on each scale. The leaves are two-ranked or imbricated and alternate.

1274. THE JAPANESE CEDAR (*Cryptomeria Japonica*) deserves notice in this connection as an easily-cultivated ornamental tree, a native of China and Japan, and suited to the climate of the Middle and Southern States.

1275. THE BALD-CYPRESS (*Taxodicum distichum*). This conifer is deciduous, and a native of the Middle and Southern Atlantic

150. Leaves and Cones of the *Taxodium distichum*.

coast. It also occurs in Southern Ohio, Indiana, and Illinois, and in the States southward, preferring a rich swampy soil, but growing very well on dryer land. The trunk of the tree widens out towards the roots, and excrescences called "cypress-knees" are thrown up from the root where the growth is luxuriant and the soil damp. These do not bear leaves, and often resemble bottles. The larger ones are conical and hollow, and are used for bee-hives, tar-buckets, and other purposes.

1276. The wood of the bald-cypress is reddish, soft, and easily split, but it works smoothly and is very durable. It is largely used for shingles, and is a valuable material for building, where great solidity is not required. In the swamps along the southern coast this timber is found buried, but still of excellent quality after thus lying for an unknown period.

1277. This tree, when young, has a regular pyramidal form, but when older, a broad spreading top. It is easily cultivated, and much esteemed on account of its delicate and elegantly pinnate leaves, its slender spray, and bright green foliage, which becomes red in autumn. In the Bartram garden, near Philadelphia, there is a tree, planted by its founder, that is 130 feet high and beautifully proportioned.

1278. There are three grades of lumber from this tree known in the timber trade—the red, black, and white cypress, differing in the color of the heart-wood. The red is most valued, is less liable to split, and grows with a straight trunk, swollen at the base, the top is small, and the wounded bark reddish. The others can scarcely be distinguished from it until cut. There are two other species of this genus, one in Mexico, and besides these others now found only in fossil remains.

1279. The bald-cypress, besides being exported in large quantities as planks and shingles, is much used in the manufacture of doors, window-sashes, and other building purposes. It scarcely has an equal in durability when set as posts.

The Sequoias.[1]

1280. There are but two living species of this genus—the *S. gi-*

[1] Sequoia, known by the English name of George Guess, was a quarter-breed Cherokee Indian, wholly illiterate, and without any knowledge of the English or of the sound of any letter in written language. Having heard of writing, he applied himself to the construction of a syllabic alphabet, which, when once construed, became in a short time in common use among his people, and so simple that it could be learned in a day. It consisted of 86 characters, each representing one syllable. Sequoia was forced to emi-

gantea, or giant-tree of California, and the *S. sempervirens*, or red-wood. The former grow in limited quantities, in groves known as those of Calaveras, Tuolumne, Merced, and Mariposa. In Fresno county, Cal., there have been found others in recent years, in one place scattered over a region forty miles in length by six or eight in width, and the tree is now raised from seed in various parts of the world. It has been tried many times in the Atlantic States, but from differences of climate it has almost uniformly failed, perhaps after a few years of apparent success. In England, it has been found to do best in a heavy clay soil, a damp climate, a moist sub-soil, but prefers high lands to low, and is likely to be injured by severe frosts and by east winds.

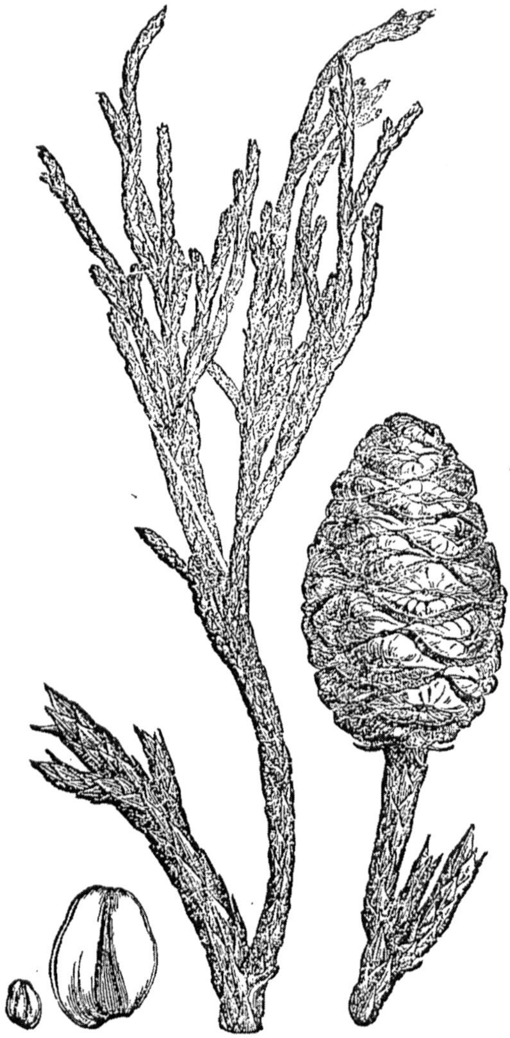

151. Leaves, Cone, and Seeds of the *Sequoia gigantea*.

grate with his tribe to beyond the Mississippi, and died in New Mexico in 1845. One of his grandfathers was a white man, but in appearance and habits he was wholly Indian. The name was applied by Endlicher, and has preference over "*Wellingtonia*," as used by some English botanists.

1281. In its native region, it is considerably elevated above the sea level, and in summer it is warm and dry, with scarcely any rain. In winter the snows fall six feet or more in depth, and remain on till May.

1282. The "big trees" range from 250 to 360 feet in height, and from 40 to 64 feet in circumference. The bark is reddish-brown, and about two feet thick, and the wood soft, and much like that of the common white cedar in quality.

152. *Sequoia sempervirens:* Leaves, Cone, and Male Flowers of the natural size. Both forms of the leaves are shown in this engraving.

1283. The *red-wood,* although second in size, is first in value, because more abundant and of exceedingly fine quality for joinery and all other uses for which the pine is commonly employed. The wood is not strong, but is durable, and has a reddish tint like red cedar;

but this fades when exposed to light. It grows to ten and fifteen feet in diameter, and in extreme cases it has been seen over twenty feet in diameter and three hundred feet high. The range of this tree is limited to the western slopes of the Coast Range, and upon the metamorphic sandstones, which seem to be almost as essential to their welfare as the ocean fogs.

1284. The scene presented by a red-wood forest is one of the most impressive kind. "Let one imagine an entire forest, extending as far as the eye can reach, the trees from eight to twelve feet in diameter and from two hundred to three hundred feet in height, thickly grouped, their trunks marvelously straight, not branching till they reach a hundred or a hundred and fifty feet, and then forming a dense canopy that shuts out the view of the sky; the contrast of the bright cinnamon-colored trunks with the somber, deep, yet brilliant green of the boughs; the utter silence of these forests, where often no sound can be heard except the low thunder of the distant ocean,"[1] and one finds a combination of the sublime and the beautiful that woodland scenery nowhere else presents.

1285. This tree never extends far inland, nor beyond the fogs and rains of the Pacific coast, and it scarcely reaches the line of Oregon on the north. The red-wood has the property not common among the conifers, of sprouting from the stump, and its specific name is derived from this tenacity to life that it shows when cut.

THE YEW FAMILY (*Taxaceæ*).

1286. This differs greatly from the other conifers in its fruit, which is reduced to a single ovule, which, when ripe, is a hard seed surrounded by a pulpy covering. The leaves are linear, flat, arranged in two rows, and the blossoms are diœcious, solitary, and axillary. There are but two native genera to be noticed in this family.

1287. THE AMERICAN YEW (*Taxus Canadensis*) is a prostrate spreading shrub, common throughout the Northern States, and often known as "ground hemlock." It is of no account for its wood, but might be made ornamental in covering rock in parks and other places.

1288. THE WESTERN YEW (*Taxus brevifolia*). This is an upright

[1] *Whitney's Yosemite Book*, p. 106.

tree, growing to the height of from 50 to 80 feet, with a thin and rather light yellowish green foliage, much resembling the common yew of the Atlantic States in its blossom and fruit, but with shorter leaves, and an upright habit. This tree occurs on Vancouver's Island and the main shore opposite, in British Columbia, sometimes reaching a diameter of two feet. It is found southward across the whole Pacific coast, to or near the Mexican line. The wood of this tree is very tough, hard, and of beautiful rose color, and is used for various ornamental purposes. It was formerly used by the Indians in making bows, spear-handles, fish-hooks, etc.

1289. THE EUROPEAN YEW (*Taxus baccata*). This is readily cultivated for ornament, and there are many varieties. The "Irish juniper," one or these, has a tall, narrow growth. Other varieties form excellent screens in ornamental planting.

THE CALIFORNIA NUTMEG TREE (*Torreya Californica*).

1290. This is a rare tree, growing along the Coast Range and the Sierras, to the height of from 50 to 75 feet, and closely resembling the yew in its foliage and general appearance. It derives its name from the fruit, which has the texture and apeparauce of a nutmeg, but is strongly charged with turpentine, and of no available use.

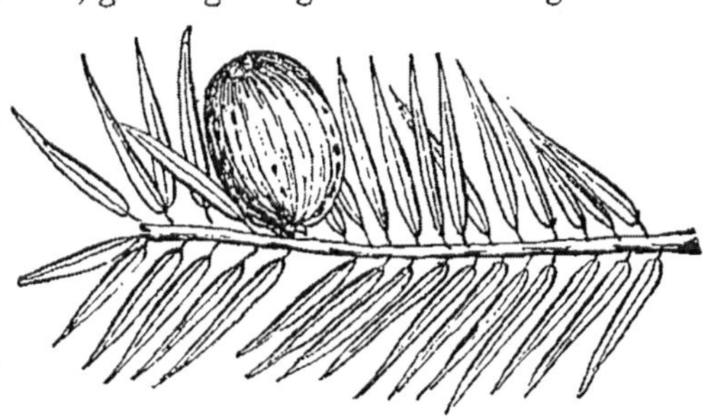

153. The Fruit and Leaf of the *Torreya Californica.*

1291. Another species, the "stinking yew" (*T. taxifolia*), occurs within a narrow range in North-western Florida, where it is a small tree of from twenty to forty feet in height. It derives its name from the fœtid odor of the leaves when bruised.

THE GINKGO (*Salisburia adiantifolia*).

1292. This remarkable "conifer" is introduced from China and Japan, and is easily cultivated. Although belonging to the conifers, its single seed is imbedded in a pulp; although associated with the evergreens, it sheds its leaves promptly in autumn, and it has no resin in its wood, as most of the "resinous species" have with which it is classed. Its leaves are broad and wedge-shaped, usually two-lobed, and as unlike the usual form of coniferous leaves as can well be imagined. Its wood is soft and spongy, and its bark smooth and ash-colored. It has bôrne fruit in the United States, and in China it grows to enormous size.

1293. It does not thrive in a frosty climate, but will live and bear leaves, without gaining in size, in Northern New York and in corresponding latitudes. Near Philadelphia trees have grown to 60 feet or more in height. This tree shows in its mode of branching some relationship to the spruce, and is most interesting from the exceptional character of its leaves, and its general habit of growth. The remaining genera of the yew family are all exotic, and will not be noticed. The same remark applies to the families *Podocarpeæ* and *Araucarieæ*, which present many interesting species, of great value in their native countries for their timber, aud of interest with us only where they may be used in ornamental planting.

The Pine Family.

1294. The sixth and last family of the conifers—the *Abietineæ*—includes seven genera, viz.: *Pinus*, the pines; *Cedrus*, the cedar of Lebanon; *Picea*, the spruces; *Tsuga*, the hemlocks; *Pseudotsuga*, the Douglas fir; *Abies*, the firs; and *Larix*, the larches. All of these but the second are natives of the United States, and find within our limits their grandest development. Their commercial importance demands a special notice.

The Pines. (Genus *Pinus*.)

1295. Botanists describe about seventy species of the pine, chiefly in the northern hemisphere, and of these about twenty-four belong to the old world. In the United States we have about thirty species, of which a dozen occur in the Atlantic States, and the remainder in the Rocky Mountain region, and upon the Pacific Coast. Some sixteen or seventeen are found in Mexico and the West Indies. They are divided into groups, depending upon the number of leaves in a common bundle, the form of the seed-scales, and other characters.

1296. The pines bear their seeds in pairs, between the scales, of the cones, and usually ripen in the autumn of the next year after they blossom. Occasionally the cones remain closed for several years, and in these cases the seeds retain their vitality a long time. The leaves come out from a sheath, in groups of two, three or five, except in one species, where they are single. They are linear, and from one to sixteen inches in length, and remain on two or three years, or even longer. In transverse section, they show resin-ducts and air-cells that are symmetrical, and, in a given species, very constant in their arrangement. The seeds of the pines are generally winged, and in some species they are large and edible. The number of cotyledons varies from 4 or 5 to 15 or 18, and is nearly constant in a given species.

1297. In some species, as in the sugar-pine, and the heavy yellow pine of the Pacific States, they grow to a size surpassed only by the *Sequoias*, and sometimes they live to a great age. A section of white pine, from Canada, was shown at the Centennial Exhibition at Philadelphia, that was 664 years old, and a plank, without waney edges, was eight feet four inches wide, and nine inches thick. The growth of the pines is most rapid in early years, the annual rings being generally narrower as the trees approach maturity.

1298. The sap-wood does not change to heart-wood until after many years—in some cases 100 or over, and on an average about 20 years. This sap-wood is white, but is generally perishable, especially when exposed to the weather. It is owing to this quality, that second-growth pines have a poor reputation for lumber, and are actually worth but little, except for the coarser uses.

1299. Commercially, the pines afford the most important timber of the American markets, and immense quantities are used every year in building, fencing, and for exportation. Our space will not admit of a detailed description of all the species found native in the country, which could not be done without involving technical descriptions that properly belong to special botanical works.[1]

1300. The pines are divided into two sections, viz.: *Strobus* and *Pinaster*. In the first of these, or the "white pines," the scales of the cones are thin and smooth, and the leaves occur in fives. The

[1] One of the latest revisions of the Pines is given by Dr. George Engelmann, in the Transactions of the Academy of Science of St. Louis, Vol IV., No. 1. (1880).

species in this section are *Pinus strobus*, *P. monticola*, *P. Lambertiana*, *P. flexilis*, and *P. deflexa*.

1301. In the section *Pinaster*, the scales are thickened at the apex, and often bear a point or hook. They embrace by far the greater number of species, which may be enumerated as follows—the number of leaves in a group being prefixed to each:

3 to 5. *Pinus Parryana*—Parry's Pine.
3. " *edulis*—Piñon or Nut Pine.
1 or 2. " *monophylla*—One-leaved Pine.
5. " *Balfouriana*—Balfour's Pine.
" " var. *aristata*—bristled var.
2. " *resinosa*—Red or Norway Pine.
5. " *Torreyana*—Torrey's Pine.
5. " *Arizonica*—Arizona Pine.
3. " *ponderosa*—Western Yellow Pine.
" " var. *Jeffreyi*.
" " var. *scopulorum*.
3. " *Chihuahuana*.
2. " *contorta*—Twisted-branch Pine.
" " var. *Murrayana*.
3. " *Sabiniana*—Hard-nut Pine, or Digger-Pine.
3. " *Coulteri*—Coulter's Pine.
3. " *insignis*—Monterey Pine.
3. " *tuberculata*.
3. " *tæda*—Old-field, or Loblolly Pine.
3. " *rigida*—Pitch Pine.
" " var. *serotina*—Pond Pine.
2. " *inops*—Spruce, or Jersey Pine.
" " var. *clausa*.
2. " *pungens*—Prickly Pine.
2. " *muricata*.
2. " *mitis*—Short-leaved Yellow Pine.
2. " *glabra*—Spruce Pine.
2. " *Banksiana*—Gray, or Scrub Pine.
3 to 5. " *australis*—Long-leaved Pine.
2 to 3. " *Elliottii*—"Old-field," or Elliott's Pine.

1302. The White Pine (*Pinus strobus*). This is the most valuable of all the native pines of the Atlantic States, and the one that has furnished by far the greatest amount of lumber and timber for domestic use and the foreign trade. It is sometimes known in England as the "Weymouth Pine," and by the French as "Pin du Lord," from Lord Weymouth, an English nobleman, whose name is associated with the early settlement of New England.

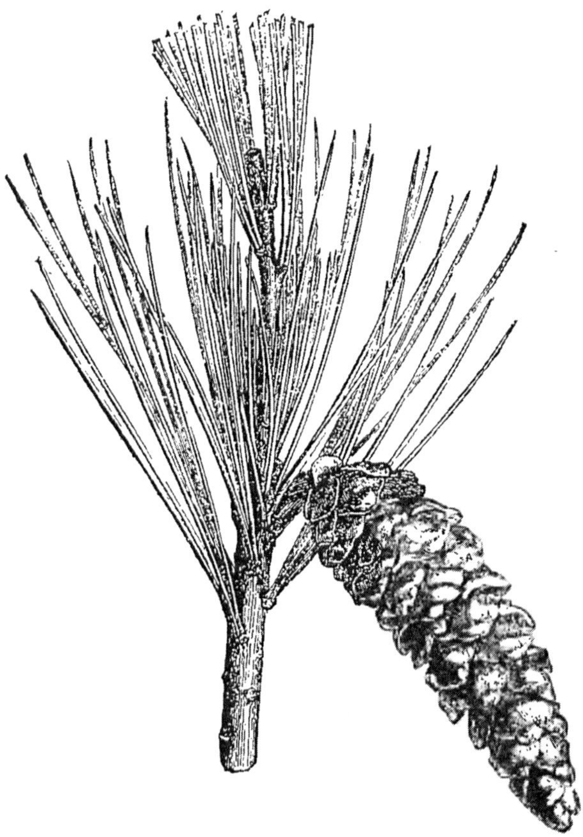

154. *Pinus strobus.* The White Pine: Cone and Leaves.

1303. The great bodies of this timber, when lumbering began, were found around the upper waters of the rivers in Maine, in Northern New Hampshire, in Northern and Southwestern New York, in Central and Northwestern Pennsylvania, in Central Michigan, and along both sides, but not the northern part of the lower peninsula, in the upper peninsula of that State, in Northern Wisconsin and in Eastern Minnesota. This species extends along the mountains into the Southern States, and in Western North Carolina it grows to from 60 to 70 feet in height, but is not accessible to markets, and is only of local use. This, and the red pine, in Canada, do not extend much north of a line running from north shore of the Gulf of St. Lawrence, at first S. W. and then N. W., passing a little north of Lake Nipigon, north of Lake Superior. South of the St. Lawrence the pine has been mostly worked out in Canada, and the supplies now come from the upper waters of the St. Maurice and the rivers flowing southward into the Ottawa.

1304. The white pine thrives best in a light sand, with a clay subsoil, and it prefers plains and broad river valleys to higher lands. It can scarcely be made to grow upon a limestone soil, and has not answered expectations in some places abroad. In the plantation of M. Vilmorin, at Barrès, France, it was found that "the wood is soft, light and worthless, even for firewood. It is of no use but for ornament. Although it grows well with its own kind, it has no chances when planted with other species."

1305. According to Lorentz & Parade,[1] it is found to succeed in France, excepting in the south, and it has a very rapid growth; but time had not yet been allowed for it to ripen, and the best quality of wood had not yet been produced.

1306. Western White Pine (*Pinus monticola*). This pine occurs in Oregon and Washington Territory, growing from 7,000 to 10,000 feet above tide, and to a height of 60 to 70 feet, with a diameter of three feet. It is the western representative of the common white pine of the Atlantic States, which it most resembles in habit of growth and texture of wood, but it is not equal to it in quality. In British Columbia this is known as "white pine," and it is common in the interior of Vancouver Island, and along the Southern Coast Range. The Indians collect the seeds of this tree for food.

1307. The Sugar Pine (*Pinus Lambertiana*). This is the most magnificent of pines in dimension, and among the choicest in the quality of its wood. It occurs between the Rocky Mountains and the Pacific, and from Mexico to near the Columbia River, growing

[1] *Culture des Bois,* 5th ed., p. 158.

to great perfection upon the slopes of the Sierras and the transverse ranges that connect the Cascade and Coast Ranges. It does not generally form separate forests, but towers here and there above other and more common kinds, with a symmetry and vigor that has been admired by all travelers. It grows to 300 feet in height and 20 feet in diameter, although the more common sizes are 200 and 10 feet respectively. The branches appear thin and sparse, as compared with the trunk. The leaves are of a dark blue-green. The cones are from 12 to 18 inches long, and proportioned as in our cut (p. 322). The lumber much resembles the best of white pine. The resinous exudation from partly-burned trees has a sweetish taste, like manna, and from this the tree derives its name.

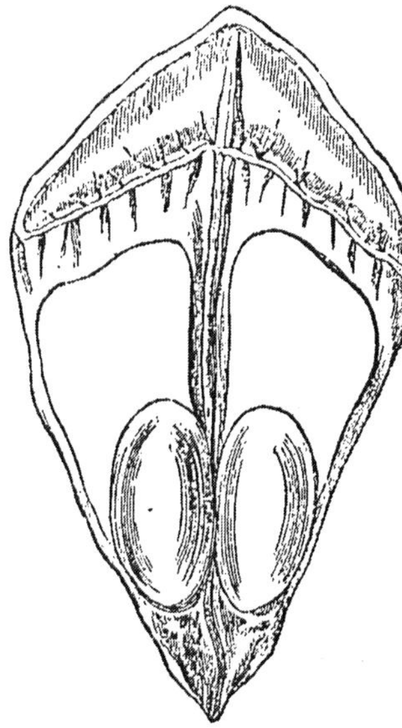

155. Scale and Seeds of the Sugar Pine of the natural size.

1308. The lumber is a favorite material for doors, sash, and blinds, and for finishing-lumber generally. The species is named from Aylmer Bourke Lambert, an English botanist, who died in 1842. He was the author of several works of merit, and among them one on the pines. The last edition of the latter, in three volumes, atlas folio (1828–37), ranks among the most costly and elaborate botanical publications ever issued. His herbarium, which was considered among the best of its kind in Europe, be bequeathed to the British Museum.

1309. The Flexible Pine (*Pinus flexilis*). This is a middle-sized tree, with warty horizontal branches, found growing in the Rocky Mountains and from New Mexico to Washington Territory. It is the prevailing pine east of the Humboldt Mountains, in Nevada, and is frequent in the Wahsatch and Unita Mountains, from 6,500 to 11,000 feet above tide. It grows to a great age, and when from 250 to 500 years old, becomes 2 to 3 feet in diameter, and rarely over 50 feet in height. It is coarse, cross-grained, and too knotty for good lumber. The wood is pliable, and from this quality

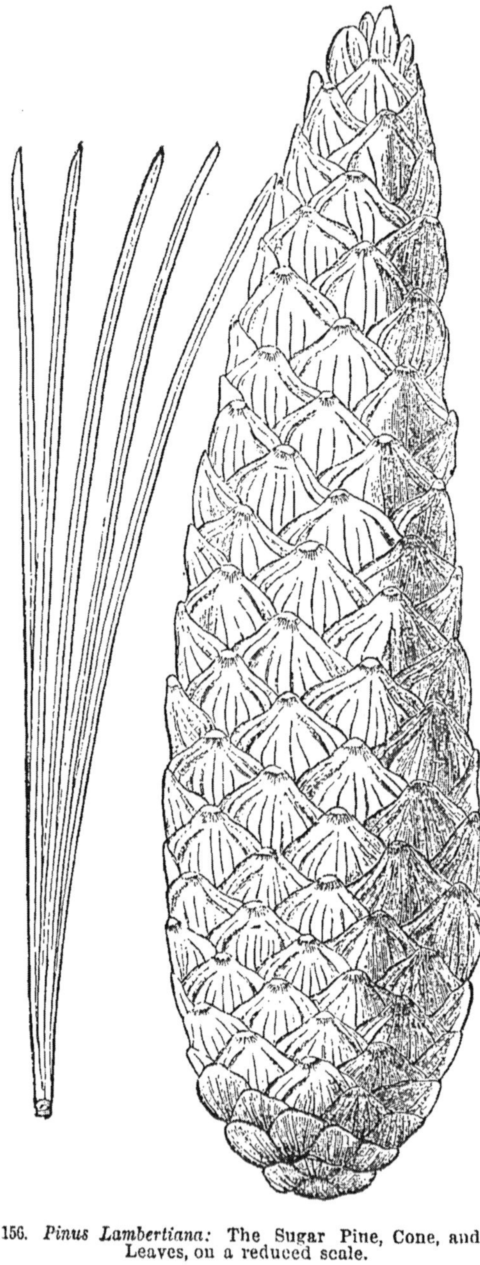

156. *Pinus Lambertiana:* The Sugar Pine, Cone, and Leaves, on a reduced scale.

the common name is given. In British Columbia it is known as the "White Pine," or "White-barked Pine," and the seeds are collected by the Indians for food. A variety, *albicaulis*, (described by Professor Newberry as the *Pinus cembroides*), grows on the Cascade Mountains, up to the timber-line, with a height of fifty feet and a diameter of two feet. The bark is thin, milk-white, and in appearance something like that of white oak. The wood is tough, and the leaves near the ends of the branches.

1310. The *Pinus reflexa* grows on the Mexican border, in Arizona, and is nearly related to the preceding species.

1311. The *Pinus Parryana* is a small tree, growing upon the Mexican border, in California and Arizona, bearing edible seeds. It is closely related to the following species:

1312. THE PINON PINE (*Pinus edulis*). This abounds in the mountains of Arizoua and New Mexico, occupying the lower ridges and the swells of land on the "divides" between the headwaters of these regions. The seeds are sweetish and edible, when roasted, and are kept for sale in the markets. The tree itself is of a crabbed shrubby growth, spreading out like an old neglected apple tree, and usually does not grow more than 25 to 30 feet high. The wood is excellent for fuel; but too small and poor for lumber or other uses.

1313. ONE-LEAVED PINE (*Pinus monophylla*). This occurs as a low tree, from 20 to 25 feet high, with an open rigid habit, and branches spreading or sub-deflexed. It grows from the eastern slope of the Sierras, and from thence eastward, in Nevada, Arizona, and Utah. It also occurs in Oregon, at an elevation of from 4,500 to 5,000 feet above tide. It has large edible seeds, and is nearly allied to the piñon piue of Southern Colorado and New Mexico. From the Sierras to the Wahsatch, this pine occurs scattered over the dry slopes, and seldom more than 15 feet in height.

1314. *Pinus Balfouriana.* This is a middle-sized tree, growing in Northern California and on the summits of the mountains east of the Humboldt range, in Nevada.

1315. THE NORWAY OR RED PINE (*Pinus resinosa*). This is a northern species, growing in Canada and New Brunswick, and along the northern border of the United States, from Maine to Minnesota. It does not generally form large bodies of timber, but occurs in detached clumps. The wood is coarser than that of the white pine, but is stronger, and much used for bridges and other timbers, where strength and elasticity are required. It grows to the height of sixty to seventy feet.

1316. The *Pinus Torreyana* is a small tree on the southern coast of California, bearing large, thick, heavy cones with edible seeds.

1317. The *Pinus Arizonica* grows on the Santa Rita Mountains in Arizona, and is nearly related to the following species:

1318. THE HEAVY OR WESTERN YELLOW PINE (*Pinus ponderosa*). This species is widely scattered throughout the Rocky Mountain region, in the Western Territories, and the Pacific States. It

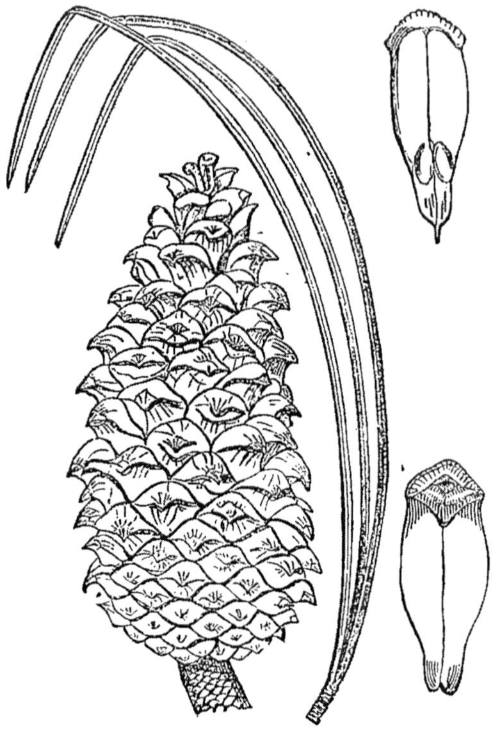

157. Cone, Scales, and Leaves of the *Pinus ponderosa*, of two-thirds the Natural Size.

covers large areas as the only tree, and it is mixed in places with the sugar and other pines. It grows to magnificent dimensions, and thrives upon arid mountain slopes, and to an elevation of 11,000 feet, or quite up to the "timber-line." It is found from 5 to 8 feet, and even 12 feet in diameter, and from 200 to 250 feet high, in favored localities. The leaves of this species are of a dark yellowish green, differing in this from the deep blue-green of the sugar pine, and the light blue-green of Sabine's pine, with which it is often associated. The bark is of a light red, but yellowish brown within, and divided into large plates, four, six, or eight inches in breadth, and flat and smooth, affording a characteristic appearance to the trunk of the tree at a considerable distance.

1319. The timber of the yellow pine is heavy and highly resinous, but is not as strong as in some other conifers. In recent years it has been used in immense quantities for railroad ties, and it is also much used for mining timbers. The grain is often twisted, and sometimes into the closest spiral.

1320. In general habit it most resembles the pitch pine (*P. rigida*) of the Atlantic States, but it grows immensely larger, the bark is smoother, and the wood less resinous. The latter quality appears to depend upon the soil and exposure, and differs considerably in different places.

1321. This pine is known in British Columbia as the "Yellow Pine," "Red Pine," and "Pitch Pine," and in that Province it is found only in the central dry region, between the Coast Ranges and Selkirk and Gold Ranges, northward, from 49° to 51°, and sparingly on the east side of the Rocky Mountains. It is there sawn into lumber, but is rather brittle, and not durable where exposed to the weather. In that Province it does not generally exceed four feet in diameter, and at 3,000 feet above tide, it is replaced by the Douglas fir and twisted-branch pine.

1322. THE TWISTED-BRANCH PINE (*Pinus contorta*). This tree is found in the region of the Rocky Mountains, and in the Pacific States, growing to a moderate sized tree, from 50 to 60 feet in height, and a foot in diameter at a yard from the ground. It derives its name from the curving downward and inward of the dead branches in the lower part, as the foliage drops off. This peculiarity is noticed to less extent in other pines. The cones remain on for several years, which gives the tree a peculiar appearance. In the Cascade Mountains it forms large forests in the lower valleys, and it thrives best in moist valleys and plains, although found at 6,000 feet above tide. It much resembles the *Pinus inops*, or spruce-pine of New Jersey and Maryland, but is more slender, and grows to a larger size. It is sometimes locally known as the "Red Pine."

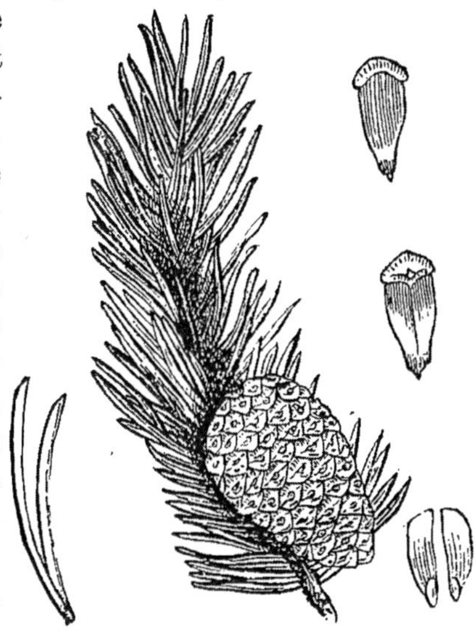

158. Cone, Leaves, Scales, and Seed of the *Pinus contorta*, of two-thirds the Natural Size.

1323. The "Western Scrub-Pine," "Bull-Pine," or "Black-Pine," as this is variously called in British America, extends from the coast to the Rocky Mountains, forming a characteristic tree over the northern part of the interior plateau, and densely covering large areas. On the coast it grows small and gnarled, upon the dunes and exposed rocky coast. In the interior it is found from 60 to 100 feet in height, but usually not more than two feet in diameter. In Alaska it extends as far as the Yokun river, ond over large areas into the Peace-river region. The wood is seldom used for timber, owing to its small size, but is white and fairly durable. The cambium layer contains much sugar, is eaten by the Indians in the spring, and in some instances large quantities of it are collected and dried for winter use.[1]

1324. THE HARD-NUT PINE OR DIGGER-PINE (*Pinus Sabiniana*). This pine so notable on account of the great size and solidity of its cones, does not form dense forests, but is widely disseminated in California and Oregon, being generally scattered sparsely over the most rocky surfaces not occupied by other trees. The seeds afford subsistence to the Indians in many places.

1325. Dr. Douglas describes this tree as of Alpine habit, but Prof. Newberry's observations disprove this.[2] The tree spreads out more like an oak or a maple than a conifer as it usually grows; its foliage is a pale bluish-green, and thin, and the whole aspect of the tree is light and airy. The author last quoted describes the cones as solitary, ovid, sometimes as large as one's head, and very ponderous, being covered with spurs or strong curved spires an inch or more long, of which the broad bases cover all the exposed portion of the scales. The seeds are as large as beans, and very palatable, having, however, a slight terebinthine taste. The leaves are in threes, from eight to ten inches long. The timber is of little value, on account of its irregular and spreading form.

1326. The *Pinus Coulteri* much resembles the above, and has a very thick, rough, blackish bark. The leaves are in threes, six to ten inches long, stiff, erect, and crowded at the ends of the branches. Its cones are as large, but the seeds are smaller. They are both found on the Coast Range, where we also find two unimportant species, the *P. tuberculata* and *P. muricata.*

1327. THE MONTEREY PINE (*Pinus insignis*), grows upon a very restricted area, to the height of 80 to 100 feet, in the vicinity of Monterey. Its cones are one-sided and in clusters, of rather large size; but it is too limited in amount to be of interest as a timber tree.

1328. LOBLOLLY, OR OLD-FIELD PINE (*Pinus tæda*). This pine

[1] *G. M. Dawson's "Trees of British Columbia,"* p. 8.

[2] *Pacific Railway Explorations*, Vol. VI., Part iii., p. 40.

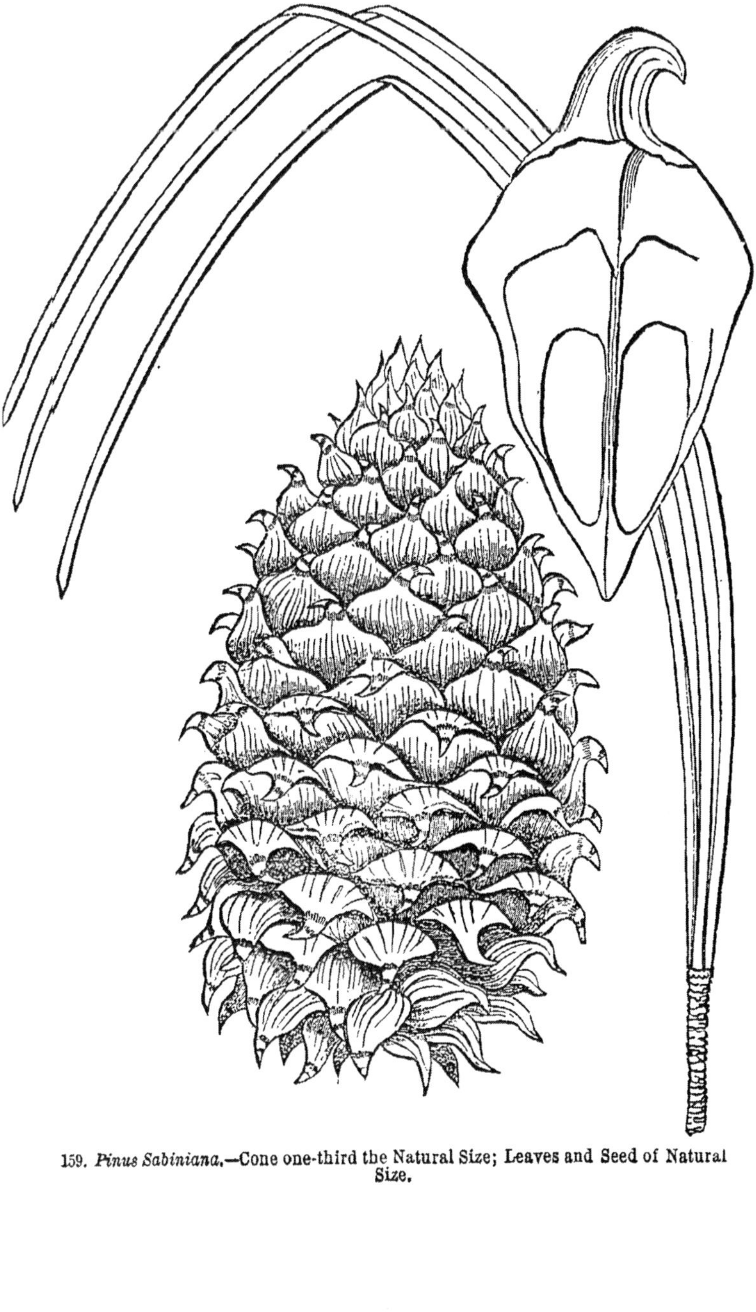

159. *Pinus Sabiniana.*—Cone one-third the Natural Size; Leaves and Seed of Natural Size.

derives its common name from coming up spontaneously in abandoned fields. It grows from 50 to 70 feet in height, with a diameer of two to three feet, and a spreading top. The wood is sappy and coarse, liable to warp and shrink, and is not durable on exposure. It is sometimes tapped for turpentine, but yields less than the long-leaved pine.

1329. Varieties are known in North Carolina as "Swamp Pine," "Slash Pine," and about Wilmington as the "Rosemary Pine." In the West-Roanoke Swamps, it has been found 5 feet in diameter, and 150 to 170 feet in height.

1330. PITCH PINE (*Pinus rigida*). This pine grows to great advantage upon sandy soils in New England and New York, and extends into the Western and Southern States. It has been seen in Maine and Massachusetts, four to five feet in diameter and 100 feet high, but its usual size is from 40 to 50 feet and its diameter from one to two feet. It grows very rapidly in early life, and on account of its deeply penetrating roots it is difficult to plant, and is usually sown in the place where it is to grow. It has been found peculiarly well adapted to the sandy soil upon Cape Cod, and in other light soils near the sea coast.

1331. The custom of planting there is as follows: In the latter part of October the cones are gathered, put up in boxes or barrels, and kept in a cool place. Before spring they will have mostly opened, and the seeds will readily come out. Sometimes they are heated a little, but this is liable to injure the vitality of the seed. From a half to three-fourths of a pound will plant an acre of land, and the seed is worth from $1.25 to $1.50 per pound. A bushel of cones will produce about a pound of seed.

1332. They may be planted at any time of the year, but best in early spring, as soon as the frost is out of the ground. The custom generally is, to run a series of furrows 5 or 6 feet apart over the land, but some plant in rows only 4 feet apart, while others allow a space of 8 to 10 feet. The seeds are dropped in by hand, three or four in a place, and about three feet apart, and are very slightly covered with a hoe. Sometimes a seed-planter is used, and at much less cost of labor, with good success. A boy should follow to cover up the seeds not covered.

1333. The cost of planting varies from $3 to $5 per acre. Generally no further care is taken, the trees coming up of themselves.

They bear fruit early and show a tendency to self seeding. Upon Nantucket, we have noticed that they spread most toward the east or southeast under the effects of prevailing winds, and this will generally be found the case elsewhere. These plantations are liable to suffer from fire, and occasionally from insect ravages.

1334. In Virginia this species is sometimes called the "Black Pine." It grows from 30 to 50 feet in height. The wood of the pitch pine, is coarse, resinous, and heavy, and generally very knotty. It is sometimes used in making tar, but is not of value in commerce, although from its resinous properties it makes an excellent firewood.

1335. The variety *serotina*, known as "Pond Pine," is a southern species, growing in swamps to a height of 40 to 50 feet. It has sometimes been used for the masts of small vessels.

1336. Spruce, or Jersey-Pine (*Pinus inops*). This pine, in New Jersey, Maryland, and southward to Florida, shows a tendency to spread and occupy vacant lands. It is variously known as "Cedar-Pine," "River-Pine," and "Scrub-Pine," and grows to from 20 to 40 feet in height and from 12 to 18 inches in diameter. It is chiefly valuable for firewood.

1337. Prickly Pine (*Pinus pungens*). This is sometimes called the "Table-Mountain Pine." It grows from Pennsylvania southward, but to best advantage in North Carolina. It is common on the eastern spurs of the Blue Ridge, but not further west. It grows from 30 to 50 feet in height, and from 12 to 20 inches in diameter.

1338. Short-Leaved Yellow Pine (*Pinus mitis*). This pine is widely diffused, but grows to best size and quality in the Southwestern and Southern States, where it is used for lumber. It usually grows from 40 to 60 feet in height, and from 15 inches to 2 feet in diameter. The heart-wood is fine grained, but moderately resinous, but the sap-wood is perishable.

1339. The Spruce-Pine (*Pinus glabra*) is a southern species, found in South Carolina, Georgia, and Florida.

1340. Gray or Scrub-Pine: Bank's Pine (*Pinus Banksiana*). This is a northern species, occurring from Maine westward to Northern Wisconsin and the upper peninsula of Michigan. It is found in Canada and far northward in British America, growing from fifteen to thirty feet in height, but nowhere of size to make it suitable for lumber. Its leaves are in pairs, short and rigid, and its cones are slightly curved and with pointless scales. They sometimes remain on for many years.

1341. THE LONG-LEAVED OR SOUTHERN YELLOW PINE (*Pinus australis*). This is by far the most important of the southern pines, and extends from Virginia around into Texas. It usually grows to the height of 60 to 70 feet, with a diameter of 15 to 20 inches, but in favorable conditions to a larger size. In richer soils it is less resinous, and from a reddish tinge to the wood is called "Red Pine." A tree with a small top is said to indicate the best heart-wood. This species furnishes most of the resinous products of the Southern States, as already described. [§ 795.]

1342. As a timber, it is scarcely rivaled by any of the pines for durability and strength, and large quantities are exported annually to foreign markets and to the Northern States. Trees that have been worked for turpentine are less valued as timber, and such are sometimes excluded in contracts for supplies.

1343. The long-leaved pine was noticed by Michaux as a poor seeder, and in unfruitful years a cone can not be found within hundreds of miles. A correspondent remarks: "According to my observation, these unfruitful years are far more common than the fruitful ones. In its struggle for existence in our days, the odds of a survival of its kind among the arborescent vegetation that disputes its ground are greatly against it. Taken from the flat moist lands, it is replaced almost exclusively by the Pond and Old-field Pine; the hilly, broken, dry upland, denuded of the grand old pine forest, is with surprising rapidity covered by a dense and shrubby growth of black-jack, turkey-oak, scarlet and upland oak, above which seldom a young pine raises its head, crowned with its large white-fringed terminal bud.

1344. "Full of resinous juices through all stages of its life, the young trees are not as able to withstand the raging fires that annually devastate the woods as the less resinous species and the deciduous-leaved trees; besides that, being of much slower growth, this noble tree is doomed to extinction, if not protected by man. On tracts sheltered from the invasion of fire, groves of young trees from 15 to 25 feet can be observed around Mobile, testifying that its existence for the future can in some measure be secured, if protected from these destructive influences, unnecessarily caused by man."[1]

1345. Elliott's Pine (*Pinus Elliottii*). This is a southern-coast pine, growing in light damp sandy soils, along marshes, and near the mouths of rivers, never far inland, and showing a tendency to form a second growth where other timber has been cut away. It generally bears fruit every year, while the long-leaved and other pines in that region generally are fertile on alternate years. It blossoms early, and has a dense heavy head, dark foliage, and larger and heavier branches than most other southern pines. The leaves are generally in threes. The timber is heavy, very tough, and more resinous than that of the long-leaved pine. It grows rapidly while young, and from the facility with which it may be propagated, it may become an important tree in forest-culture in the future.

1346. This has formerly been considered a variety of the Old-field Pine (*P. taeda*), but it appears to present distinct specific characters, that have led Dr. Engelmann to recently describe it as a separate species.

1347. Scotch Pine (*Pinus sylvestris*). This foreign species is here mentioned, because it has been introduced for cultivation, and has been found exceedingly well adapted to certain light sandy soils, where it grows with great luxuriance. It is the principal pine of Central and Northern Europe, and is spread over all North-

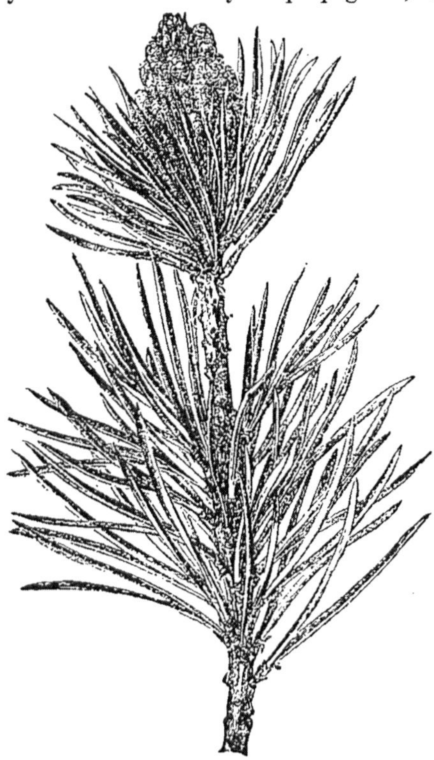

160. *Pinus sylvestris:* Scotch Pine—Leaves and Blossoms.

[1] *Dr. Charles Mohr. Forestry Report*, ii., 36.

ern Asia, wherever pines grow. It has been found to grow very well in Iowa, and has been planted with good success upon Cape Cod, in Massachusetts. Between these regions it can be planted almost anywhere, if the soil is sandy and somewhat fertile.

1348. The Scotch pine comes to maturity and greatest value in Northern Europe in 60 to 80 years; after which its growth in cubic contents is slow. At Balmoral, Scotland, a crop, under favorable conditions, at 60 years, averaged 60 cubic feet to a tree, and at 200 years 25 cubic feet, and 90 to 100 trees to the acre. The choicest portions of the forest yielded 30 to 35 feet to the tree, and 120 to 130 trees to the acre. The height ranged from 70 to 80 feet. On moor-pan soil, at 60 years, they yielded but 8 cubic feet each, and at 100 years but 10 cubic feet. In Prussia this tree constitutes over half of the public forests. In Europe it is known under a great variety of names, as "Riga Pine," "Haguenau Pine," etc., and it differs very greatly under cultivation, as well in the form and habit of its growth as in the quality of its wood, as variously modified by climate, soil, and other influences.

THE SPRUCES. (Genus *Picea.*)

1349. Of this genus there are about a dozen species, of which two are found in Europe, five in Asia, and five in North America. Of the latter, two are found on the eastern and three on the western side. The spruces have pendulous cones, with the bracts shorter than the scales, and both persistent. The cones ripen in the fall of the same year that they form, but do not open to disperse their seeds till the spring following. The engraving (page 333) represents a twig of the common European spruce, now widely introduced as an ornamental tree, and when young quite a beautiful object, the branches coming out symmetrically from the ground upward, and the whole taking a dense and compact pyramidal form. It does not grow with us to as great a size or age as in Northern Europe, nor is it an object inviting to notice for forest culture, but exceedingly well adapted to the formation of screens and wind-breaks.

1350. The two eastern species in the United States are the *Picea alba*, or WHITE SPRUCE, and the *P. nigra*, or BLACK SPRUCE. They are found most common along the northern border of the United States, from Maine to Northern Minnesota. The former extends further northward, being found as an important timber tree only in the northern part of Maine aud further north in Canada. The latter forms extensive forests in Northern New England and New York, and both extend along the mountains southward to North Carolina, but do not occur as important timber trees in that region.

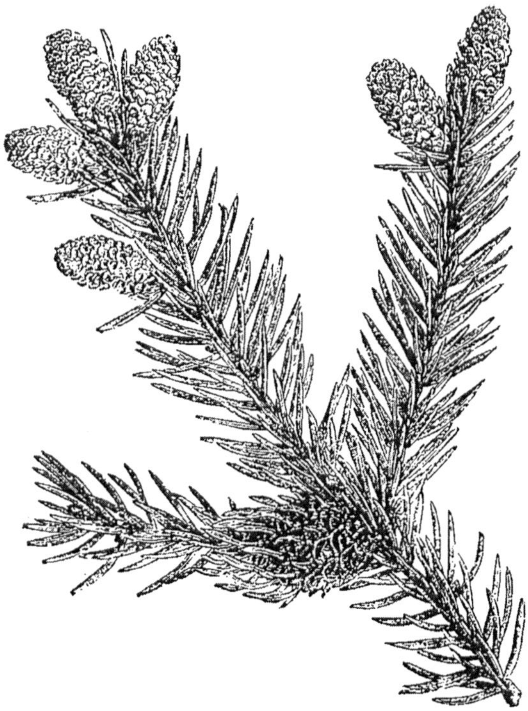

161. *Picea excelsa:* Common European or Norway Spruce, Leaves, Blossoms, and a False Cone formed from Insect Injurics.

1351. The wood of both the white aud the black spruce is white, strong, and elastic, but rather coarse-grained. It is much prized for flooring, and for building-timber, but is not durable when exposed to the weather, excepting when laid with the grain of the wood vertical. Shingles made of spruce are sometimes very good, but are inferior to those of white pine, cypress, cedar, red-wood, and many other kinds.

1352. From its lightness and strength, this wood is valued for yard-arms and small masts in vessels. The roots and base of the trunk are used for knees for canal-boats, barges, etc. The spruce best adapted for working, and the strongest, most elastic, and most durable, comes from elevated regions, a dry soil, and a southern exposure. It is from such localities that the best material for sounding-boards of pianos is derived, and it would be useless to seek this wood of best quality for this use in trees grown upon low swampy grounds. When sawn for this purpose, the logs are first quartered, and then sawn as near as may be vertically to the lines of growth.

1353. The black spruce, when grown in dense masses, makes a tall and slender tree, very strong and elastic, and well suited for poles for scaffolding, flag-staffs, and the like, and for rafters and sleepers in buildings. In dry situations, as hewn timber, it is strong and durable, but light, and for this reason easier to place than most of the hard-woods, while it surpasses the most of them in strength.

1354. The growth of the spruce is remarkably rapid, and under careful management it is much less liable to be run out by other trees than most other species. A spruce forest carefully protected against fires, and the cutting limited to trees that are large enough for sawing into boards, may be cut over at intervals of ten or fifteen years to great profit. The young shoots of the spruce are used in making beēr; an essential oil is distilled from the leaves, and a gum having a market value exudes from the trunk.

1355. Engelmann's Spruce (*Picea Engelmannii*). This much resembles the black spruce of the Northern States and Canada, but grows to greater size. It is found upon the interior plateau from British Columbia southward to California, and in Montana and New Mexico. Its northern and north-eastern limits are not definitely ascertained. It has been found on Peace river in British America. It forms a superior timber, and is very durable.

1356. This is a tall pyramidal tree, with a thin scaly bark of a reddish or purplish brown color, and white soft wood. East of the Humboldt Mountains, in Nevada, and on the Wahsatch and Unita Mountains, it grows to an elevation of 8,000 to 10,000 feet. In these regions it is known as the "White Pine."

1357. The Blue Rocky-Mountain Spruce (*Picea pungens*). This is a Rocky Mountain species, extending from New Mexico through Colorado and Utah to Idaho and Oregon. It grows to a large size, and at elevations of 7,000 to 10,000 feet above tide. This is found to be well adapted to the Northern and New England States, being hardy, of rapid growth and of remarkable beauty of foliage, the color being a bluish green. It has long been known under the name of the *Abies*, or *Picea Menziesii*, but the "Menzies Spruce" of the coast belongs to the following species, and is now known under the name by which it was described at an earlier period:

1358. The Menzies Spruce (*Picca Sitchensis*) is found from Mendocino Co., California, to Alaska, and is strictly a coast species. It seldom grows at an elevation of more than 500 feet, but in Oregon, Washington Territory, and British Columbia, it attains a large size, being sometimes 150 to 200 feet in height, with a diameter of six to nine feet. It is exported as a timber, and is coarse but strong. It grows to best advantage on a damp sandy soil. The common name is given in honor of Dr. Archibald Menzies, who was surgeon and botanist in Vancouver's exploring expedition, about the end of the last century, and died in 1842.

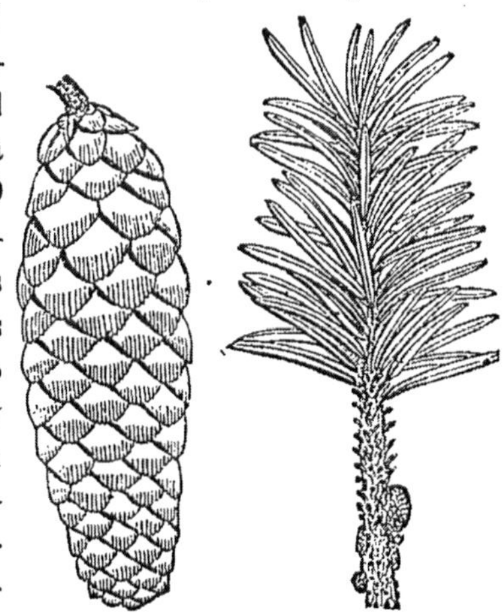

162. Leaves and Cone of the Menzies Spruce, of two-thirds the Natural Size.

The Hemlocks. (Genus *Tsuga.*)

1359. There have usually been described under the genus *Abies*, but are now classified separately. The cones are usually small and pendant at the ends of the twigs, the bracts shorter than the scales, and both remain adherent to the axis. The leaves are flat or angled, in two rows, and with a very short petiole. There are five species, of which one is found in Asia, and four in North America. Of the latter, two are found on the eastern and two on the western side.

1360. The Hemlock (*Tsuga Canadensis*). This is one of the most widely diffused and most useful of the conifers in the Northern States, extending from Maine to Wisconsin, and along the Alleghenies southward to North Carolina. It is abundant in New Brunswick, and in Ontario and Quebec. In North Carolina, where it occurs on the borders of mountain ravines and in cold swamps, it is known as "Spruce-Pine." It is sometimes called the "Hemlock-Spruce," and by the French of Canada "Peruche."

1361. In the Northern States, and especially in New York and Pennsylvania, its bark is used to an immense extent for the tanning of sole-leather, and in some regions where the trees have been cut and peeled for their bark, the lumber is still allowed to rot upon the ground.

1362. It sometimes occurs of immense size, and in considerable bodies by itself, but is very often intermixed with deciduous kinds. The wood of the hemlock is coarse, but strong, and is largely used in the form of planks and scantling for building purposes, bridges, and the like, or as boards for fences, roof-boards, the siding of barns and other coarse purposes. When the grain is placed vertical, it endures exposure to the weather for a long period. The young wood is much used for railway ties, but is not as durable as many other kinds.

1363. This is one of the most beautiful of our native species, when planted in parks among deciduous kinds, or singly, and is less liable to injury from insects than the spruces and the pines.

1364. The *Tsuga Caroliniana* is a southern species, occurring on the mountains of Western North Carolina, and much resembling the one above described.

1365. The *Tsuga Pattoniana* grows in the upper timber-region of the Sierras, from 8,000 to 10,000 feet above tide, but at this elevation it is only a shrub. In lower localities it is found from 100 to 150 feet high, and from 2 to 4 feet in diameter. It is a large, graceful, and slender tree, with bright green foliage, and purple cones, from an inch and a half to two inches in length. It has formerly been known as the "*Abies Williamsoniana.*"

163. View of the Side and Base of an old cone of Williamson's Spruce, with Scale, Seeds, and Leaf, of two-thirds the Natural Size.

1366. THE OREGON HEMLOCK (*Tsuga Mertensiana*). This is a tree found native upon the Pacific Coast from California to Alaska, being often found from 100 to 200 feet high, and 6 to 8 feet in diameter. The wood is finer than our common hemlock, and the bark is more red, and is used for tanning purposes. It does not extend beyond the region of abundant rainfall.

THE DOUGLAS FIR. (*Pseudotsuga Douglasii.*)[1]

1367. This is incomparably the finest of the firs, surpassing them all in size, and equaling the best in value as a timber tree. It extends from Mexico, New Mexico, and Colorado, through the mountain regions of the Pacific Coast, occurring in Oregon to the enormous size of 200 to 300 feet in height, and from 15 to 20 feet in diameter. It is more commonly about 150 feet high, and from 4 to 8 feet in diameter.

164. Cone and Leaves of the Douglas Fir, of two-thirds the Natural Size.

1368. This tree has a tall pyramidal growth, with horizontal and drooping branches. The bark is rather thin, of an ash or reddish color, and the wood is coarse-grained, but tough and hard. It extends northward into Alaska, and is largely developed in British Columbia. Professor Newberry in describing this tree as it grows in Oregon, says:

1369. "The trees stand relatively as near each other, and the trunks are as tall and slender, as the canes in a canebrake. In this case, the foliage is confined to the tuft at the top of the tree, the trunk forming a cylindrical column as straight as an arrow, and almost without branches for two hundred feet. The amount of timber on an acre of this forest very much exceeds that on a similar area in the tropics or in any part of the world I have visited."

1370. The Douglas fir, in British Columbia, forms the principal lumber yet exported from that Province. It forms dark and dense forests of considerable extent, the wood being, for the most part, of excellent quality for ship-building, but varying considerably in strength and texture, according to the conditions under which it

[1] Commonly described as the "*Abies Douglasii*," and known by a great variety of common names, such as "Red" or "Black" Fir, "Red" or "Black" Spruce, "Hemlock," "Oregon Pine," "Western Pitch Pine," etc. In the Uinto Mountains, it is known as the "Bear River Pine," or "Swamp Pine."

has grown. It is shipped for masts and spars to Great Britain, South America, Australia, India, China, and the Sandwich Islands.

1371. This tree is very accommodating as to soil, but prefers that which is deep and damp, with a stiff subsoil, provided that it is well drained. It has been introduced into Scotland with much success, and is there a favorite tree for planting, both for ornament and for timber. It is found to withstand the drouth better than most conifers, while it equals or surpasses most of them in growth. It was first introduced into that country in 1826, and a tree planted the next year is now 100 feet or more in height, and in 1873 had a girth of 9 feet 7 inches at 3 feet from the ground.

1372. It is found, from observation, that in the colony of Victoria, this tree will not flourish in exposed situations or near the sea, but it is admirably adapted to form large bodies of forests in Alpine glens, and in the cooler climate of the mountain regions.

1373. The specific name of this splendid tree was given by Professor Lindley in honor of Dr. David Douglas, who was sent by the Horticultural Society of London, in 1825, to study the flora and collect seeds and specimens upon the Pacific Coast. He returned in 1827, and in a subsequent journey lost his life, by an accident, in the Sandwich Islands, in July, 1834.

THE FIRS. (Genus *Abies.*)

1374. Of these there are about eighteen species, of which eight are found in the United States—two in the Atlantic States, and the remainder among the Rocky Mountains and upon the Pacific Coast. The firs have the bracts of the cones longer than the scales—sometimes conspicuously long, and when ripe they fall to pieces. The cones are erect. The leaves are in two ranks on the twigs, and relatively short and rigid. The details of inflorescence in this genus, as they are found in the silver fir, will be seen upon a subsequent page.

1375. THE BALSAM FIR OF NORTH CAROLINA (*Abies Fraserii*), much resembles the silver fir of Europe, but seldom grows more than 40 feet high and 12 to 15 inches in diameter. It is found on the western mountains over 4,000 feet above tide, sometimes forming forests of itself, and giving name, from its dark foliage, to the "Black Mountains."

1376. THE BALSAM FIR (*Abies balsamea*). This is common in

Canada and in swamps and damp soils in the Northern States, extending southward into Virginia, and westward beyond the Mississippi. It has a very symmetrical growth, and its regular conic form gives a characteristic aspect to the forests where it occurs. It grows to 50 or 60 feet in height, and its wood is coarse and white, but not strong. It is used however for lumber, but should be protected from the weather. This tree grows well under cultivation in a humid soil, and it may be used with success, in wet place, in planting wind-breaks. The "Canada Balsam" of druggists is obtained from blisters in the bark of this tree.

1377. The Balsam Spruce (*Abies subalpina*), much resembling the Northern Balsam Fir, grows in Colorado and northward into British North America, occurring on the highest mountains and quite up to the timber-line. It grows to a tree two feet in diameter and a hundred feet or more in height, in sheltered places, but the wood is soft and poor. This species, in British Columbia, appears to take the place of the *A. grandis* in the region east of the Coast Range. It extends into the Peace River district, and occurs in cold, damp situations in the country between Lesser Slave Lake and the Athabasca River. The tree often exceeds two feet in diameter, but the wood is said to be almost worthless.

1378. *Abies concolor*. This is the "White Balsam," or "White Fir," of South Colorado, Utah, and Arizona, and is found westward in the Sierras and northward to Southern Oregon. It grows at an elevation of 3,000 to 8,000 feet, and to a height of 100 to 150 feet, and a diameter of two to four feet. It derives its common name from the light color of its foliage, both of the under and the upper sides of its leaves.

1379. Red Fir (*Abies magnifica*). This species grows on the high Sierras of California and northward, at an elevation of 7,000 to 10,000 feet, and sometimes to a height of 200 feet and a diameter of eight to ten feet. The wood is of a reddish color, from whence its name, and it is strong and durable. This species bears larger cones than any other of the genus.

1380. The Western Silver Fir (*Abies amabilis*). This tree occurs among the Cascade Mountains. It grows with remarkable symmetry of form, and in favorable situations, to more than a hundred feet in height, forming a slender spire of dark green, and when occurring with other kinds sometimes presenting groups of remarka-

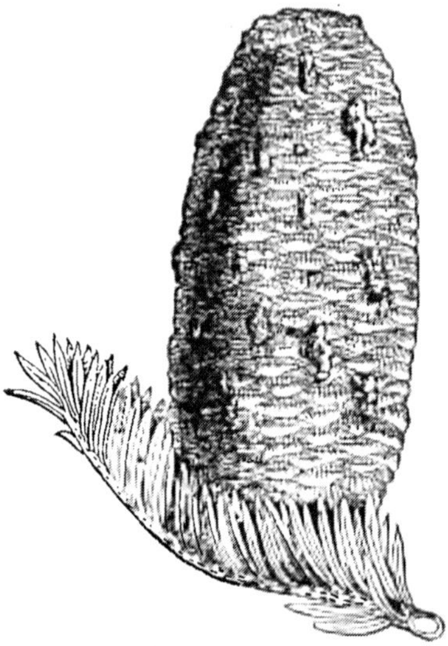

165. Cone and Leaves of the *Abies amabilis*, of one-third the natural length

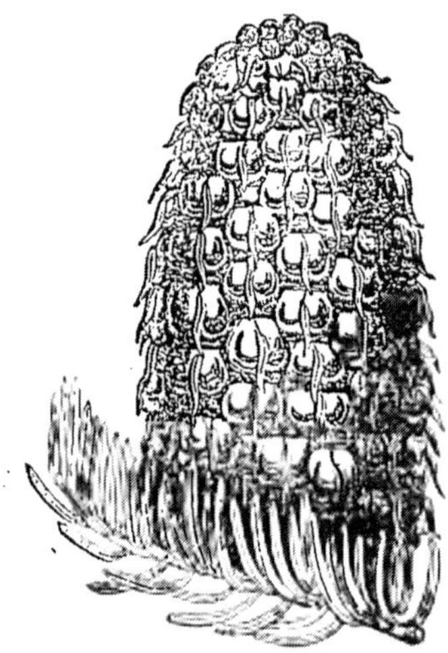

166. Cone and Leaves of the *Abies nobilis*, of two-thirds the natural size.

ble beauty. Its range extends from Washington Territory to Wyoming and New Mexico.

1381. THE NOBLE FIR (*Abies nobilis*). In general aspect, this resembles the Western Silver Fir (*A. amabilis*), but the foliage is of lighter green, and the branches more rigid. It grows to a height of 200 feet, with a diameter of six to ten feet, and it has a thick cinnamon-colored bark, which is red on the inside. This tree is known also as the "Red Fir," and forms forests in Northern California. It is found on Mount Shasta, at from 6,000 to 8,000 feet above tide; on the Cascade Mountains, and on the Columbia River. Its wood is said to be superior to that of any other of the firs.

1382. THE WESTERN BALSAM FIR (*Abies grandis*). This is a large tree, nearly resembling the Western Silver Fir. It occurs in Oregon and California, upon the Sierra Nevada and Cascade Mountains, along with the sugar and the yellow pines, which are at times scarcely superior to it in size. On the Columbia and the Willamette, it is known as the "White Spruce," to distinguish it from the Douglas Spruce. Most of the lumber exported from Oregon is from these two trees. This tree grows to the height of 200 to 300 feet, and a diameter of four to six feet. In British Columbia it is limited to the coast, and its wood is soft, white, brittle, and not durable. The growth of this species is more rapid than that of most of the firs. It prefers a rich and somewhat humid soil, and river flats are particularly favorable to its success. It is not as liable to suffer from late spring frosts, as most other firs.

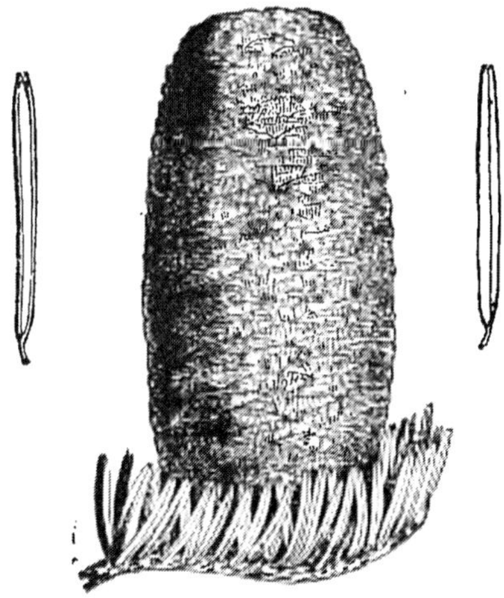

167. Cone and Leaves of the *Abies grandis*, of two-thirds the natural length. [Page 340.]

1383. The *Abies bracteata* is a tall, slender, and strictly pyramidal tree, growing to the height of 100 to 150 feet and a diameter of two feet. It occurs on Santa Lucia Mountains, upon the California coast, along a narrow belt, perhaps a hundred miles in length, and at an elevation of 3,000 feet and upwards above sea level. The long bracts of the cones give them a bristly appearance, and suggest the specific name. These bracts are, in fact, a modified form of leaves, and somewhat resemble them in appearance.

1384. We will conclude our notice of the firs by adding the most important of the European species, it being convenient, in connection therewith, to present an engraving from Rossmassler, illustrating the inflorescence, germination, and foliage of the species.

1385. The European Silver Fir (*Abies pectinata*). This is an important timber tree, and grows to a large size in the Pyrénées, the Cévennes, the Alps, the Jura, and the Vosges, and some fine forests are found in Northern Italy and in Normandy. The timber is softer and less durable than that of the pine and larch, and it is much used for shingles, cabinet-work, boat-building, and constructions generally, and is not liable to warp or shrink. When young, the tree is very tender, and easily injured by frost, which it seldom escapes many years together; but when it gets larger it becomes hardy and thrives at high altitudes. It comes to a size profitable for working in about seventy years, but lives to twice this age. The Strasburg turpentine of druggists is obtained from this tree. The

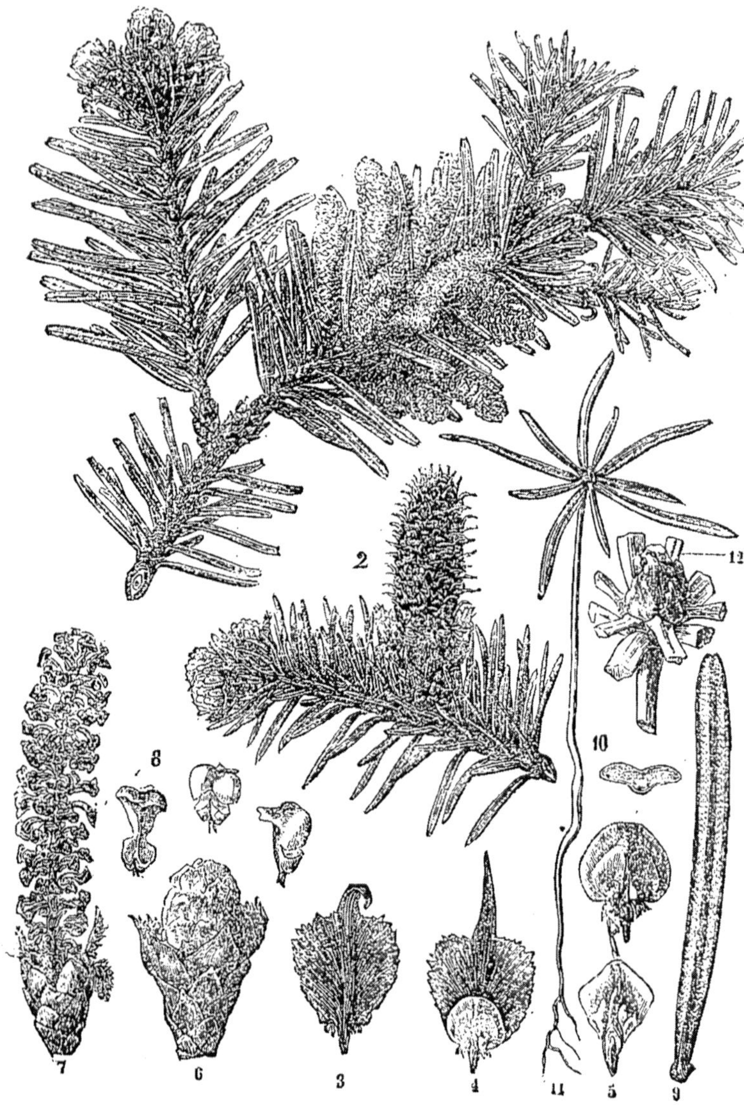

168. *Abies pectinata:* The Silver Fir. 1. A twig, with staminate catkins. 2. The pistilate flowers. 3, 4. Scales of the pistilate flower, with the two seeds still minute on the inner side. 5 (and the figure above). The seed-scale separate the two sides, as shown in the preceding figures. 6, 7. Staminate catkins as a bud, and fully open, and of twice the natural size. 8. Anthers. 9. Leaf of twice the natural size. 10. Transverse section of the leaf, also magnified. 11. Germ of a young plant. 12. Germ-bud of the latter, with the leaves removed, greatly enlarged.

details of its inflorescence, etc., are shown in the accompanying engraving.

THE LARCH. (Genus *Larix.*)

1386. Of this there are 8 species, native of the North Temperate and Arctic Zone of Europe, Asia, and America. We have three native species, of which one grows in Canada and the Atlantic States, and two upon the western coast. The larches have deciduous leaves, that are collected in fascicles of from ten to twenty in a group, and small cones, with the bracts usually shorter than the scales. The foliage takes a bright yellow color in autumn a little before the fall of the leaves.

1387. THE TAMARACK (*Larix Americana*). This is in some regions called "Hackmatack," and in commerce in Maine and New Brunswick it is sometimes known as "Juniper." The tamarac grows in swamps in Canada and the Northern States, from Maine to Wisconsin. It can be cultivated in humid soils, but does not thrive well upon dry grounds. It grows to the height of thirty to forty feet, and comes to largest development in Canada. Extensive swamps are sometimes almost exclusively occupied by this tree.

1388. THE WESTERN LARCH (*Larix occidentalis*). This is a tall slender tree, with short, thick, and small branches, thin, light, and yellowish-green leaves. It grows to a hundred and fifty feet in height, with a diameter of two to three feet. It extends northward in British Columbia, in the valleys of the Selkirk and Gold Ranges, within the limits of abundant rain-fall. It is not found on the coast. The timber is said to be strong and durable, but coarse.

1389. The *Larix Lyallii* is a little known species, found growing at high elevations upon the Cascade Range in Oregon.

1390. THE EUROPEAN LARCH (*Larix Europea*). This tree has been found in Scotland the most profitable that can be grown. Although not adapted to such valuable uses as the oak, it will mature two crops while the oak is bearing one. It comes to maturity there in about 60 years, in which time it has eight or nine thinnings, at from 5 to 10 years. An acre has been known to yield over $2,464 at the end of 60 years, or over $40 a year above the cost of management.

1391. In recent years it has suffered from a disease that has rendered success less certain, and led to the substitution of other species of conifers, and especially the Scotch pine (*Pinus sylvestris*), fir (*Picea excelsa*), and some of the California species, especially the Douglas fir.

1392. Experience in the North-western States has somewhat disappointed expectations with reference to the European larch; not as to the rapidity of its growth, but as to the durability of its timber. As a general rule the solidity, strength, and durability of the wood in any given species, is in inverse proportion to the

169. *Larix Europea.*—European Larch, Blossoms, Leaves, and Fruit.

rapidity of its grown, and it is not until the light and porous sap-wood has had an opportunity to change by time into the mature and more solid heart-wood, that it acquires those qualities that give it greatest value.

1393. It is not improbable that the larch of rapid growth might in time acquire these qualities of excellence, but it is hopeless to expect them at once. These considerations should in no way discourage from plantation, as the young wood, in dry situations, still has great value, and it may be found suited for some of the processes of injection that would give it durability in exposed places.

1394. The larch in France, prospers most on northern or eastern slopes. At greater elevations it was found on southerly and westerly aspects, but not of so good growth.

1395. The larch at high elevations is more solid than on low lands, although the amount of ashes in the latter is greater. It requires more than double the amount of alkali and of phosphoric acid than the pine, and three times as much as the beech.

1396. In planting the European larch, only such trees should be set out as have been once transplanted. Their growth the first year or two is very slow, and in exposed situations they are liable to suffer from the winds. As the leaves appear early, it must be planted as soon as the ground can be prepared, and great care should be taken to protect the roots from the air. They may be dipped to advantage in a mud composed of a rich mellow soil and water of about the thickness of white-wash. The tops should remain dry, and the roots damp, till they are finally set.

1397. Where the larch is cultivated in masses, and kept of one age, it is not injurious to pasture with cattle after a certain time. A woodland of this timber will in some regions pasture one cow to a hectare (about 2½ acres) through the summer. In a genial soil and climate the larch is aggressive, and tends continually to spread over the neighboring fields, especially on the side opposite to that of the prevailing winds. From this tendency to seeding, it is easy to re-stock a forest, by leaving here and there a sufficient number of seed-trees, and by raking the surface here and there so that the seeds can find fresh soil to sprout in.

1398. It is sometimes tried in Europe to get a resinous product from the larch, but it leads to a very thin profit, at a great loss. The bark is in some countries used for tanning leather.

CHAPTER XXIV.

TREE-PLANTING IN KANSAS AND NEBRASKA.

1399. The Kansas State Horticultural Society began, in 1880, the publication of an annual Report upon Forestry, as an extract from its general report for the preceding year. In the second of these there is given a summary of replies to circulars from its correspondents, in which they mention their preference for kinds of trees that have been cultivated with success. They may be condensed as follows, but to save repetition they will be referred to by numbers, corresponding with those in the following list:

1400. *Names of Trees that are successfully cultivated in Kansas.*

	COMMON NAMES.	BOTANICAL NAMES.
1.	Ailanthus.	*Ailanthus glandulosa.*
2.	Ash—	*Fraxinus*—
3.	Blue.	*quadrangulata.*
4.	Green.	*viridis.*
5.	White.	*Americana.*
6.	Box Elder, or Ash-leaved Maple.	*Negundo aceroides.*
7.	Catalpa.	*Catalpa speciosa.*
8.	Cherry, wild.	*Prunus serotina.*
9.	Chestnut.	*Castanea vesca*, var. *Americana.*
10.	Coffee-bean.	*Gymnocladus Canadensis.*
11.	Cottonwood.	*Populus monilifera.*
12.	Elm—	*Ulmus*—
13.	Red (Slippery Elm).	*fulva.*
14.	White.	*Americana.*
15.	Hackberry.	*Celtis occidentalis.*
16.	Hickory.	*Carya* ——.
17.	Honey Locust.	*Gleditschia tricanthos.*
18.	Locust—	*Robinia*—
19.	Black.	*pseudo-acacia.*
20.	Yellow.	var. (?)
21.	Maple—	*Acer*—
22.	Soft (Silver-leaf Maple).	*dasycarpum.*
23.	Sugar.	*saccharinum.*

	COMMON NAMES.	BOTANICAL NAMES.
24.	Mulberry—	*Morus*—
25.	Red.	*rubra.*
26.	Russian.	——.
27.	White.	*alba.*
28.	Oak—	*Quercus*—
29.	Burr.	*macrocarpa.*
30.	Osage Orange (Bois d'arc).	*Maclura aurantiaca.*
31.	Peach.	*Amygdalus persica.*
32.	Pecan.	*Carya olivæformis.*
33.	Pine—	*Pinus*—
34.	Black, or Austrian.	*Austriaca.*
35.	Scotch.	*sylvestris.*
36.	White.	*strobus.*
37.	Poplar—	*Populus*—
38.	Balm of Gilead.	*candicans.*
39.	Lombardy.	*dilatata.*
40.	Silver-leaf.	*alba.*
41.	Red Cedar.	*Juniperus Virginiana.*
42.	Sycamore.	*Platanus occidentalis.*
43.	Walnut—	*Juglans*—
44.	Black.	*nigra.*
45.	Willow—	*Salix*—
46.	Gray or White.	*alba.*

1401. *Trees reported as grown successfully in the several Counties of Kansas, arranged in order of preference.*

[Where two or more series of numbers are given, they show returns from different correspondents.

Allen, 44, 7, 17, 30, 5, 42, 12, 11, 22.
" 44, 2, 7, 12, 22, 6.
Atchison, 22, 11, 44, 39.
Barton, 44, 11, 6, 46
Butler, 11, 39, 30, 44, 6, 41, 2, 12, 45.
Chautauqua, 11, 43, 39, 6, 22, 5.
" 11, 22, 44, 12, 6.
Cherokee, 44, 11, 21, 39, 32.
Cloud, 11, 6.
Cowley, 44, 7, 6, 22.
Crawford, 11, 21, 43, 7, 6, 23.
Davis 44, 6, 45, 22.
" 44, 22, 11, 6.
Dickinson, 6, 14, 13, 44, 4, 15, 11.
Edwards, 11, 6, 44.
Ellis, 11, 6, 17, 30, 12, 44, 8, 2.
" 11, 44, 6, 1, 17, 7, 12, 22, 2, 30.
" 43, 11, 6, 2, 7.
" 11, 44, 6, 15, 2, 30.
Elk, 43, 11, 21, 7, 6, 39.
Franklin, 43, 11, 21, 2, 12, 42.
Harper, 11.
Harvey, 11, 6, 43, 13, 15, 5, 22, 39.

Jackson, 11, 6, 43, 37, 46.
Jefferson, 11, 22, 43, 14.
Jewell, 11, 6, 43, 2, 22.
Johnson, 11, 43, 37, 21, 2, 6, 7.
Kingman, 44, 7, 17, 6, 2, 21.
Labette, 11, 22, 39, 43.
Leavenworth, 11, 22, 43, 42, 23.
Lincoln, 11, 6, 5, 13, 14, 44.
Lyon, 11, 43, 12, 6, 2, 45, 17, 10, 30.
Marshall, 11, 6, 45, 22, 2, 18, 43, 24, 16, 28.
Miami, 11, 22, 14, 44, 7, 23, 5, 6, 41, 36.
Mitchell, 17, 11, 44, 6, 13, 14, 30.
McPherson, 7, 44, 11, 46, 30, 6.
Montgomery, 11, 22, 7, 2, 43.
Morris, 11, 44.
Ness, 11, 6, 12, 2; 43, 10, 1.
Nemeha, 11, 22, 6, 17, 43, 12.
Neosho, 11, 22, 39, 45, 14, 13.
Ottawa, 11, 43, 6, 2, 22.
Pawnee, 1, 17, 6, 11, 44, 12, 46.
Pottawatomie, 11, 22, 6, 44, 17.
Pratt, 11, 6, 44.
Reno, 11, 6, 5, 7, 44, 12, 46.
Rice, 6, 2, 44, for uplands; 11, 44, for lowlands.
" 43, 6, 7, 22, 19, 17, 12, 11, 41, 1.
Rush, 11, 6, 43, for lowlands; 11, for uplands.
Russell, 2, 6, 44, 30, 22, 11, 7.
Saline, 11, 6, 44, 5, 19, 17.
Sedgwick, 11, 19, 46, 6, 7.
Shawnee, 44, 11, 22, 7.
Sumner, 44, 22, 12, 6, 11.
" 11, 6, 43.
Wallace, 11, 6, for lowlands; 5, 43, 22, for uplands.
Wabunsee, 11, 6, 44, 22, 13.
" 11, 44, 6, 13, 14, 41, 17, 2, 7.
Washington, 11, 6, 43.
Woodson, 22, 1, 44, 11.

1402. It appears from the above, that the cottonwood is found successful in 56 reports out of 60; the walnut, or black walnut (probably intended to be the same), in 56; the box-elder in 48; the maples (probably the soft maples only) in 37; the elms in 29; the ash in 25; the catalpa in 18; the honey-locust and willows each in 13; the poplars (besides cottonwoods) in 10; the osage orange in 10; the ailanthus in 5; the red cedar in 4; the hackberry, locust, and sycamore, each in 3; the coffee-bean tree and wild cherry each in 2; and the hickory, pecan, mulberry, oak, and white pine, each in 1.

1403. As *first* on the list, we find the cottonwood in 37 reports; the walnut or black-walnut in 12; the soft maple and the box-elder each in 2, and the ailanthus, ash, catalpa, and honey-locust each in 1.

1404. In 1878, a list of preferences was published by this same society, in which the cottonwood is mentioned by 40 correspondents; black-walnut by 33; box-elder by 30; white-maple by 29; white and red elm by 22; oaks and catalpa by 14; mulberry by 11;

ailanthus by 9, and the Lombardy and abele poplars and hackberry each 7.

1405. Of evergreens, 30 had succeeded with the red cedar; 26 with the black Austrian pine; 22 with Scotch pine; 16 with white pine; 10 with Norway spruce, and 6 with arbor-vitæ.

1406. The "*Forestry Manual*" of this society, published in 1882, reports the black-walnut as cultivated successfully in 57 counties; the catalpa in 45; the osage orange in 39; the honey-locust in 34, and the mulberry in 30.

1407. The experience of planters in Kansas and Nebraska has been hitherto adverse to the cultivation of the beech, birch, chestnut, hard or sugar-maple, and most of the conifers. The white willow, that succeeds admirably further north, in Iowa and Minnesota, and in states further east, does not succeed in many parts of Kansas. It has suffered badly from the locusts.

Propagation from Cuttings and Native Seedlings.

1408. The cottonwoods and other poplars were almost invariably reported as easy to propagate by cuttings. The willows, and less frequently the catalpa, are also mentioned as easy to propagate in this manner.

1409. As to the time of procuring cuttings, opinions varied, the greater number advising that they should be cut late in fall or early in winter, when the wood was not frozen, and that they should be buried below the reach of frost, to be set as soon as possible upon ground previously prepared, in the spring. When thus preserved the lower end would have a callus just ready to put forth roots, and they would get an early start. The last season's growth should be taken, and in pieces ten inches or a foot in length. They were found to do best when set deep (some mentioned a sloping position as best), but so that only a small part—one or two buds—should be above the ground. The earth should be pressed down firmly upon them at the time of setting.

1410. Seedlings, plowed up along the sand-bars of rivers, should be gathered in the fall, tied in bundles, and buried upright in trenches until spring. They are generally more sure to get a start than cuttings. If cut back to near the ground when set they will often take a more vigorous growth. The soil should be firmly pressed down around them at the time of planting, as in the case of cuttings. The lowlands in Kansas and Nebraska are rather more favorable for the growth of timber than the uplands, although the cottonwood, box-elder, soft maple, walnut, catalpa, osage orange, Lombardy poplar, and other trees are cultivated upon the latter with success, when well cared for.

1411. The ailanthus has been found well adapted for resisting the drouth in Kansas as far west as the 100th meridian, and it is readily reproduced from sprouts and cuttings from the roots.

Distance between Trees.

1312. It is almost the universal experience of correspondents, that trees do best when planted close, and generally in rows 4 feet apart and three or four feet between. If at equal distances each way and set upon land marked both ways, they can be cultivated by cross-plowing very conveniently. In planting it is well to put in several seeds, and when cultivating the plants afterwards, pull up all but one, leaving the most thrifty. The plants thus taken out may be lifted with the soil still upon the roots, and set into vacant places.

1413. The frequent stirring of the soil with a cultivator, by preventing the surface from becoming packed or crusted over, is found most beneficial in a dry time, and should not be omitted, whether there are weeds to kill or not.

Effect of Shelter-Belts.

1414. With scarcely an exception, the opinion was expressed by correspondents of the Kansas Society, that trees planted in belts in that state had afforded protection to fields of grain, or orchards, gardens, and stock-yards. As to the width at which they should be planted, opinions varied from four or five to twenty or thirty rods. As a screen around buildings, the red cedar was much recommended, and for success the plants should be started from seeds in seed-beds, and be set when small. It was not fully settled by experience as to whether a shelter-belt should run east and west, or north and south, in order to afford the most protection. This would probably depend somewhat upon the general slope of the surface.

1415. Since trees have been planted in groves in the prairie region, it is noticed that insectivorous birds have become more common. They should be protected by a law supported by strong public sentiment.

The Locust-Tree in Central Kansas.

1416. A correspondent in Central Kansas,[1] reports to the State Horticultural Society unexpected success in planting the black locust. It had escaped the borers, and had lived through severe drouth. Trees planted in 1873 were in eight years large enough for two fence-posts, and produced an abundance of material for vine-stakes and other uses. He estimates that 2,000 trees can be grown on an acre, and that by extreme care and cultivation they would in seven years produce 4,000 posts worth at 20 cents each the sum of $800. Allowing a broad margin for casualties, there would still be a strong motive for planting this tree, should it hereafter be found that it is not there liable to the insect injuries that have proved so disastrous in Illinois, or if more effectual means for preventing these injuries should be hereafter discovered.

Gathering and Preservation of Seeds.

1417. Nuts with a hard shell like the black-walnut must be gathered as soon as ripe, and may generally be planted the same fall. It is commonly preferred, however, to spread them upon the ground, with a light covering of litter and soil, or in a box mixed with earth and moistened from time to time. They should be exposed to frost, and in the spring *should be planted for permanence, as they will not bear transplanting.*

1418. We advise that generally every alternate tree be a walnut, and the remainder a cottonwood, white willow, or box-elder, where it is intended that a fine, high, and regularly formed grove of the walnut is finally desired. The nurses may be taken out as the trees begin to crowd one another. A little mixture of other kinds, such as the ash, oak, catalpa, elm, and perhaps of red cedar might be desirable, and of more profit than all of one kind.

1419. Seeds of the Osage orange, ash, box-elder, sycamore, catalpa, and honey-locust may be put away in a cool, dry place, and kept till spring. They generally do best when planted early. In Kansas they do best as forest trees when planted where they are to grow. The seeds of the honey locust must be scalded before planting.

[1] J. B. Schlichter, of Sterling, Rice Co.

Preparation of the Ground.

1420. This is uniformly necessary in a prairie country, and can best be done by thoroughly plowing and harrowing, after raising one or two crops of grain. For early planting or setting of cuttings or young seedlings pulled up along the sand-bars of rivers, the plowing may best be done the fall before, and the markings when ready to plant or set.

1421. The weeds must be kept down by passing between the rows with a cultivator, and afterward by hoeing, as with corn. This should be done only in the early part of summer, (never later than the middle of July), and should be repeated three or four years, until the ground is well shaded, after which the trees will need only thinning out from time to time, and protection from cattle and from fires. It is not until the trees get so large that their foliage is above the reach of stock, that cattle may be admitted safely to a plantation.

1422. The rubbish from fallen leaves, etc., should always be left to decay on the ground. A bed of leaves tends to hinder evaporation from the soil, and to keep the ground moist longer after a rain.

1423. In setting any of the evergreens, we would decidedly recommend their purchase from nurseries, as they are difficult to get started from the seed without careful management. They will be best likely to succeed where sheltered in the south side by a grove or hedge. They will also need a heavy mulching in dry seasons.

Tree-culture in Places well advanced upon the Plains.

1424. The plantation of cottonwoods for temporary use, ma some-times be practiced in places well advance upon the plains, where in very dry seasons they may sometimes fail when six or eight inches in diameter. Such failures may cause disappointment, but are by no means a total loss. The wood is still available for firewood, and the trees while they lived, proved a shelter to fields and orchards, and perhaps may have protected the slower growing kinds that survived the drouth. This should not discourage from renewed attempts in planting, with the view of securing these temporary benefits, even if the trees grow no larger than poles. In such case, it would be worth while to plant a certain portion of land every year, expecting perhaps only a crop of firewood and poles. They will be worth what they cost, although it might not be expected that they would become larger trees.

1425. In river valleys upon the plains, where the water disappears wholly from the surface in summer, and the channels appear to be utterly arid, the water may still, in many places, be found by digging to a distance not greater than that which may be reached by the roots of trees.

1426. The black walnut appears to be the best adapted to these situations, and although not so rapid in growth as some other trees, it makes a success where the sub-soil is not too firm and moisture is within reach. In such localities, transplanting is impossible, and the nuts previously sprouted must be planted where the trees are to grow.

1427. The general statements in this chapter, drawn chiefly from the experience of Kansas, will apply, with some modification, to Nebraska. The soil is very nearly the same; in both States the surface rises at about the same grade as we go west, and the difference in latitude would scarcely be felt, except in a very few species. The Osage-orange would be found less hardy in Nebraska, and the white willow probably more thrifty.

1428. In both States, we can not too strongly urge the importance of the cottonwoods and other rapidly growing kinds as nurses for the more valuable, which can not be started without shelter when young. It is also found that fall planting has many advantages not formerly realized, and in some situations a decided preference. It is an excellent practice, in new and untried locations, to multiply experiments in the small way, before investing largely in any thing in the way of tree-planting. These experiments may apply to different species—to different times and methods of sowing or planting—different soils, and various modes of management. By these means alone can one depend upon the particular course best adapted to his location, and the manner of obtaining the best results.

RECENT DECISION UNDER THE TIMBER-CULTURE ACT.

Since printing Chapter IX., in this work (pages 91 to 96), the following decisions have been made:

"In timber-culture entry, there is no restriction upon an entryman as to the time when the work must be done, provided it is done within the time required by law. The work can be done by the entryman, his agent, or his vendor.

"If one purchase land which has been in whole or in part broken, planted, or cultivated by another, the spirit of the law is as fully met as if he had personally performed the work."

INDEX.